LEARNING IN HUMANS AND MACHINES: TOWARDS AN INTERDISCIPLINARY LEARNING SCIENCE

Journals of Related Interest

Learning and Instruction

LEARNING IN HUMANS AND MACHINES: TOWARDS AN INTERDISCIPLINARY LEARNING SCIENCE

Edited by

Peter Reimann and Hans Spada
Universitat Freiburg-Psychologisches Institut, Germany

PERGAMON

U.K.	Elsevier Science Ltd, The Boulevard, Langford Lane, Kidlington, Oxford OX5 1GB, U.K.
U.S.A.	Elsevier Science Inc., 660 White Plains Road, Tarrytown, New York 10591-5153, U.S.A.
JAPAN	Elsevier Science Japan, Tsunashima Building Annex, 3-20-12 Yushima, Bunkyo-ku, Tokyo 113, Japan

First edition 1996

Library of Congress Cataloging in Publication Data

Learning in humans and machines: towards an interdisciplinary learning science/ edited by Peter Reimann & Hans Spada.
p. cm.
Includes bibliographical references and index.
1. Learning. 2. Machine learning. 3. Cognitive learning.
4. Transfer of training. I. Reimann, Peter. II. Spada, Hans.
LB1060.L4243 1995
370.15'23 – dc20
95-25493

British Library Cataloguing in Publication Data

A catalogue record for this book is available from the British Library

ISBN 0 08 042569 0

Printed and bound in Great Britain by Biddles Ltd, Guildford and Kings Lynn

Acknowledgement

Producing this book would not have been possible without the support from European Science Foundation, Strasbourg. The European Science Foundation is an association of its 56 member research councils, academies and institutions devoted to basic scientific research in 20 countries. The ESF assists its Member Organisations in two main ways: by bringing scientists together in its Scientific Programmes, Networks and European Research Conferences, to work on topics of common concern; and through the joint study of issues of strategic importance in European science policy. The scientific work sponsored by ESF includes basic research in the natural and technical sciences, the medical and biosciences, the humanities and social sciences. The ESF maintains close relations with other scientific institutions within and outside Europe. By its activities, ESF adds value by cooperation and coordination across national frontiers and endeavours, offers expert scientific advice on strategic issues, and provides the European forum for fundamental science. This book is one of the outcomes of the ESF Scientific Programme on "Learning in Humans and Machines".

Contributors

Michael Baker
CNRS-IRPEACS
Equipe COAST
Ecole Normale Superieure de Lyon
46, alee d' Italie
69364 Lyon Cedex
France
michael.baker@ens.ens-lyon.fr

Agnes Blaye
UFR de Psychologie
Universite de Provence
29, avenue Schumann
13621 Aix en Provence
France
crpde@frmop22.cnusc.fr

Erik De Corte
University of Leuven
Centre for Instructional Psychology and
Technology
Vesaliusstraat 2
B-3000 Leuven
Belgium
Erik.DeCorte@ped.kuleuven.ac.be

Pierre Dillenbourg
Université de Geneve
TECFA/FPSE
9, route de Drize
1227 Carouge
Switzerland
pdillen@divsun.unige.ch

Werner Emde
Gesellschaft für Mathematik u. Datenverar-
beitung - FIT.KI
Schloss Birlinghoven
53754 St. Augustin
werner.emde@gmd.de

Hans Gruber
Universität München
Institut für Empirische Pädagogik und Päda-
gogische Psychologie
Leopoldstr. 13
8000 München 40
Germany
gruber@mip.paed.uni-muenchen.de

Pat Langley
Robotics Laboratory
Computer Science Department
Stanford University
Stanford, CA 94306
USA
langley@flamingo.stanford.edu

Lai Chong Law
Universtät München
Institut für Empirische Pädagogik und Päda-
gogische Psychologie
Leopoldstr. 13
8000 München 40
Germany
law@mip.paed.uni-muenchen.de

Heinz Mandl
Universität München
Institut für Empirische Pädagogik und Päda-
gogische Psychologie
Leopoldstr. 13
8000 München 40
Germany
mandel@mip.paed.uni-muenchen.de

Katharina Morik
Universität Dortmund
Lehrstuhl Informatik VIII
Postfach 50 05 00
4600 Dortmund 50
Germany
morik@kirno.informatik.uni-dortmund.de

Stellan Ohlson
University of Pittsburgh
Learning Research and Development Center
2929 O' Hara Street
Pittsburgh, PA 15260
USA
stellan@lrdc2.lrdc.pitt.edu

Claire O' Malley
University of Nottingham
Dept. of Psychology
University Park
NG7 Nottingham
UK
com@psyc.nott.ac.uk

Peter Reimann
Universität Freiburg
Psychologisches Institut
Niemensstr.10
79085 Freiburg
Germany
reimann@psychologie.uni.freiburg.de

Alexander Renkl
Universität München
Institut für Empirische Pädagogik und Päda-
gogische Psychologie
Leopoldstr. 13
8000 München 40
Germany
renkl@mip.paed.uni-muenchen.de

Roger Säljö
University of Linköping
Departement of Communication Studies
581 83 Linköping
Sweden
rogsa@tema.liu.se

Lorenza Saitta
Università degli Studi di Torino
Dipartimento di Informatica
Corso Svizzera 185
10149 Torino
Italy
saitta@di.unito.it

Maarten van Someren
Universtity of Amsterdam
Dept. of Social Science Informatics
Roeterstraat 15
1018 Amsterdam
Netherlands
maarten@swi.psy.uva.nl

Hans Spada
Universität Freiburg
Psychologisches Institut
Niemensstr. 10
79085 Freiburg
Germany
spada@psychologie.uni-freiburg.de

Stella Vosniadou
National and Capodistrian University of
Athens
Dept. of Psychology
33 Ippokratus Street
10680 Athens
Greece
svosniad@atlas.uoa.ariadne-t.gr

Table of Contents

Towards an Interdisciplinary Learning Science

Peter Reimann and Hans Spada

Whereas learning has for some time been a minor issue in the cognitive sciences, it has now become one of the most active research fields in psychology, the neurosciences, and computer science. The subdiscipline of machine learning in particular engages in the analysis and construction of computational systems that learn. Research in this area proliferates, and it is hard to keep an overview in one discipline, let alone of ongoing research in all these disciplines. This is where this book fills a need: To provide an overview of the state-of-the-art of research in various disciplines that concern themselves with learning, an overview that should help students with some knowledge in one of these fields to get started, but also an overview for the specialist scientist who wants to learn more about alternative approaches and conceptualizations of learning in other disciplines.

The book has as its guiding theme the analysis, comparison and integration of computational approaches to learning and research on human learning. The human learning perspective focuses on psychological research, but includes contributions from other behavioral and social sciences such as sociology and educational science. The computational learning perspective comprises in particular machine learning research, but also contributions from other areas of artificial intelligence such as research on intelligent tutoring systems and multi-agent problem solving. One important current research direction is not considered in this book: neuropsychological approaches to learning and what many consider the adequate framework for capturing learning on that level computationally: connectionist learning methods. The neuropsychological perspective is not considered because it - as of yet - has had little to contribute to the kind of learning phenomena focused on in this book: Those relating to knowledge intensive learning and knowledge communication, such as change of mental theories in learning and development, selection and coordination of representations and learning strategies, sequencing effects, situatedness of transfer, collaborative learning. Representatives of the cognitive and social-cognitive camp as well as from instructional science speak currently more to these topics than do researchers concerned with the analysis of the neuropsychological basis of learning.

Even so scientists in psychology, instructional science and computational science work increasingly often on related problems - examples of which are knowledge communication, multi-agent learning and problem solving ("collaborative learning"), knowledge-intensive learning ("theory change"), consideration of the learning context (learning goals, "situated learning"), and new approaches to computer based instruction and training - it is by no means the rule that they share their methods, insights and questions across disciplinary borders. Whereas learning research is an area where a shared understanding of scientific methods and strategies from other disciplines is often required to do justice to the phenomena, it is not easy to come by. This is one of the reasons why a number of scientists together with the European Science Foundation, Strasbourg, developed an interdisciplinary research program with the objective of promoting cooperation among the different disciplines engaged in studying learning phenomena. The program, which started in 1994, is entitled "Learning in Humans and Machines" (LHM), and its guiding theme is the comparison and integration of research on human learning with computational approaches to learning.

The mission of this book is to provide the basis for this interdisciplinary cooperation; it attempts to sketch out important findings and developments for areas of learning research where interdisciplinary research attempts seem necessary to make progress. Going beyond a description of the state of the art, the chapters try to identify promising research issues for the near future, parts of which at least will be addressed by the LHM program itself.

Interdisciplinary Learning Research: Success Stories

Even though they are not numerous, one can find good examples for learning research that combines computational techniques to psychologically and instructionally relevant learning issues. Since later chapters in this book treat these areas in more detail (see, for instance, the chapters by Vosniadou, by Ohlsson, by Langley, and by Saitta et al.) we shall only mention some prototypical examples. Two areas that have seen particularly fruitful results of this orientation are the study of skill acquisition and of concept acquisition.

Skill Acquisition. The most important theory of skill acquisition in modern cognitive psychology is best known by the name of the computational model that implements the theory's central mechanisms: ACT (Anderson, 1983; 1987). This theory describes how knowledge that is initially represented in declarative form (and, hence, needs to be processed by a general interpreter in order to lead to performance) changes gradually under the influence of practice (problem solving) into a procedural format in which it can then be immediately executed. The ACT theory/model has been extensively tested against data of human learning and its basic mechanisms, in particular the processes behind *proceduralization*, are rather well established. The ACT theory also has important instructional implications, indirectly as it allows for the derivation of a normative theory of learning by doing, as well as directly by its extensive application in the domain of intelligent tutoring system (ITS, see Anderson, Boyle, Corbett, & Lewis, 1990; Anderson, 1993). In applying it to instructional topics, the flow of information has not been unidirectional from the theory to the development of ITS; to the contrary, Anderson used the instructional applications as the main way to test his theory of learning, the rationale being: If the instructional measures derived from the theory do not work, there must be something wrong with the theory.

Another success story in the area of skill acquisition is the SOAR theory and model, developed by Newell and co-workers (Laird, Newell & Rosenbloom, 1987; Newell, 1993). Like ACT, SOAR does not only include proposals for general learning mechanisms, but integrates these in a general cognitive architecture, i.e., it commits itself to specific constraints regarding knowledge representation, memory structures and memory access processes. Since this limits the model's degrees of freedom considerably - the parameters of the system that can be tuned to fit specific observations - it can fairly directly be decided if the model's predictions are met by empirical observations about human learning (for more on the problems of testing computational models of psychological phenomena see VanLehn, Brown & Greeno, 1984; Pylyshyn, 1984). Although SOAR has as of yet not been used as the basis for direct instructional interventions, it can, like ACT, serve as a normative theory of skill acquisition and hence indirectly influence the design of instruction.

One final example of research in this area is SIERRA (VanLehn, 1983; 1990). This model does not propose an encompassing cognitive architecture, even so it contains many of the ingredients required to specify one. Rather, it analyzes in depth how a set of clearly described learning processes in interaction with psychologically motivated representational assumptions can be used to explain the origins of certain mathematical misconceptions (error-prone procedures) in children. This kind of explanation can of course be used to guide instruction; for instance, it allows the derivation of guidelines for the sequencing and layout of math examples in textbooks. SIERRA is not only valuable as a psychological theory (with extensive computational support), but also as a methodological exercise in how to relate computational models with data on human learning.

Concept Acquisition. Turning to a second area where we have seen many examples of fruitfully combining computational modelling with psychological theorizing, we set out by mentioning the work of Medin, Wattenmaker & Michalski (1987). They examined constraints and preferences employed by humans in learning decision rules from preclassified examples. Comparing data from experiments with undergraduates and artificial intelligence inductive learning programs, they found that humans' rule inductions emphasized certain characteristics of categories to a greater extent than did the AI programs. They explained these differences by assuming that humans place severe constraints on the process of inductive inferencing, whereas many machine learning programs employ product-based constraints (such as avoiding disjunctions). As humans are more robust learners and less tempted to produce overgeneralizations, this observation may also lead to improved machine learning algorithms.

Another example where machine learning techniques and psychological data were brought in close connection are studies on scientific discovery (Langley, Simon, Bradshaw & Zytkow, 1987, for an overview). This line of research attempts to understand how humans - both professional scientists as well as the layperson engaged in discovery learning - come to induce scientific concepts and relations (such as Ohm's law) by starting from quantitative and/or quantitative observations (e.g., outcomes of experiments). Computational models have been constructed to account for these discovery processes. For instance, the BACON program (Langley, 1981) induces scientific laws by searching two spaces, one for instances (data, experiments) and one for hypotheses (generalizations, laws), guided by a hill-climbing heuristic for search control. BACON, despite the fact that it employs fairly simple procedures, can account for quite a number of historically reported discovery processes. The dual-search-space theory has also been used to account for observations on laypersons' discovery processes (Klahr & Dunbar, 1988; Reimann, 1989) and to guide the design of instructional discovery environments (De Jong, 1991; Schauble, Glaser, Raghavan & Reiner, 1991).

Our third example also deals with the acquisition of scientific concepts but takes a more general stance as to how scientific concepts and theories are acquired. Discovery is only one - even though a very important - way; of course, one can also acquire knowledge about science by being told and by asking questions. For instance, Vosniadou & Brewer (1994) describe how children acquire naive theories about astronomy, and Morik and Vosniadou (this volume) delineate first attempts to model such processes of theory acquisition and modification with methods from inductive logic programming. This is clearly an extension of former work on concept acquisition and scientific discovery, as concepts are here not acquired in isolation and not based almost exclusively on data, but what is acquired are conceptual structures, clusters of concepts related among each other by explanatory links and often only loosely connected to observations. This indicates a trend from knowledge lean to knowledge-intensive concept acquisition, a trend that is reflected in other recent research as well (cf. Fisher, Pazzani & Langley, 1991).

An issue that pertains to most forms of concept acquisition, and certainly to all those that have psychological relevance, are order effects, or effects of instance presentation sequence. This issue has received much attention in psychology, instructional research and machine learning research and two chapters of this book (by Langley and by Morik & Vosniadou) treat it in more detail.

That learning may at a more than metaphorical level be described as the acquisition and modification of (mental) theories leads us to consider other recent developments in research on human learning and instruction, developments that are not always as well captured by computational models as in the examples we have provided so far.

Before we further delineate the contributions of the individual chapters, let us first provide a short overview of the LHM program.

The Research Program "Learning in Humans and Machines"

The main impetus for setting up this program was the observation that learning issues tackled in psychology and instructional research seem to share increasingly often characteristics with issues tackled in computational studies of learning. This growing similarity results from an increasing interest in both human and computational learning sciences in complex learning phenomena: When and how do learners change representations and conceptualizations of the domain? How do they capitalize on multiple respresentations? How are they dealing with the - at least for human learners inevitable - problems resulting from sequential learning? How do physical and social resources influence learning? How can multiple agents coordinate their learning and problem solving activities? These research questions are considerably more complex than asking how learners acquire knowledge about artificially construed concepts - the kind of learning research that dominated studies both on human and computational learning for many years. They are at the same time more relevant for the study of human learning, as they exhibit many of the complexities addressed in the research questions. Because of this, the study of complex learning phenomena holds the promise of increased relevance for the instructional research community, if not the practitioners in education.

However, in order to be fruitful, interdisciplinary research requires more than just interest in similar phenomena. What is also required are a basic methodological openness and active attempts to bridge the gaps between disciplines that result from different research orientations and methods. In the Seventies, the hope of many was that fruitful cooperation could flourish under the umbrella of "cognitive science" (Gardner, 1985). But even today, some twenty years after the invention of this integrative discipline for the study of intelligence and mind, it is too often the case that different disciplines work in parallel beside each other under this umbrella, sharing some common interests and phenomena, but sharing little in terms of methods, tools and outcomes. There are exceptions, one of them being psycholinguistics. The LHM initiative in comparative and multi-disciplinary research on Learning in Humans and Machines attempts to relate research on human and machine learning more systematically by supporting cooperative research that goes beyond merely sharing results. This could lead to a development similar to the one in psycholinguistics, giving rise to a new learning discipline with roots in psychology, computer science, educational science, and sociology.

Even though it is clear that learning research is an area where a shared understanding of scientific methods and strategies from other disciplines is helpful, this is easier said than done. For instance, computer scientists who develop programs that learn rarely feel the need to study systematically if the algorithms they propose resemble those possibly used by human learners. Scientists working on human learning, on the other hand, are usually not tempted to give an account of their learning theories in terms of computational models and implementations. Obviously, one reason for this missing interaction is that it requires methodological competence which is difficult to achieve in one field, let alone in two or more. Ideally, a scientist would be trained in experimental methods and data analysis methods as well as in computer science techniques to be able to bridge in her research both worlds. This is hardly realistic. A more realistic approach is to couple researchers with different, but incremental competencies and to hope for synergistic effects. It is one of the main objectives of the LHM program to provide an initial infrastructure for such interaction on a European-wide scale. In particular, in order to succeed in the goal of building a repository of information about data on human learning and of relevant computational learning models, international cooperation is required since both data and models are to be found in many different places.

In the course of the program more can be learned about methods for theory formulation and testing. Whereas disciplines from the social sciences attempt to develop empirically based theories of learning, research in Machine Learning takes a more formal-constructive tack in developing theories and models of learning phenomena. The two approaches each have their own strengths. Methods and techniques used in the Machine Learning field have interesting properties especially for the task of theory/model *construction*, whereas the more empirically oriented social science disciplines have developed a rich repertoire for theory *testing*.

It is only under a naive perspective of scientific methodology that these two aspects can be seen as independent. Rather, methods developed for theory testing assert a strong influence on the way theoretical statements are formulated. One way to find out about blind spots in social science theories is by formulating them in a different manner, for example in the language of data structures and algorithms as they are used in computer science. The heuristic and practical value of building computational models of learning phenomena - that is, formulating and refining certain parts of a theory in a manner so that the analyzed phenomenon can be (re)produced, - has yet to be fully appreciated and critically evaluated in the social sciences. Another methodological goal for the program is to reflect more thoroughly on what it means to "empirically evaluate" a computational model of learning, i.e. under which circumstances a learning model can be said to have "psychological plausibility".

Scope and Limitations

The focus of the program is on learning in humans and machines. Since this is too broad a topic to be tackled by a single research program, a more specific orientation was developed. The focus is on such studies of learning phenomena that show a clear potential to contribute to two applied areas: primarily to instructional research, but also to research on knowledge acquisition for knowledge-based systems (formerly known as expert systems). This implies that learning research that can be subsumed under this orientation deals with learning in realistically complex domains, attempts to address if not to empirically demonstrate the psychological relevance of proposed learning theories (possibly indirectly by demonstrating their instructional effectiveness), and treats comprehensibility of learning outcomes as an important issue. This also implies that research on animal learning and very basic human learning processes is not in the focus of the program, also, most developments in cognitive neuropsychology and in neural net modelling are not (yet) of direct importance for this program.

The program described above is unique in that the social science point of view provides a new perspective onto many of the ongoing research activities in machine learning. Social science researchers make an attempt to study learning phenomena by taking into account research from computer science. Learning phenomena are studied for which both social science and computer science contributions exist, but in an as of yet unrelated form. Learning phenomena are considered which are known to be important for humans but have so far received little attention from the Machine Learning community and have until now withstood formal accounts. While interdisciplinary work between different social sciences is something that is realized in existing ESF programs, combining social sciences and computer science to study phenomena of common interest is a rather new approach.

The LHM program concentrates on higher-order learning processes: How do "naive" theories abut the physical world change under the influence of experience and formal instruction? How does the (mental or computational) representation used to describe objects and events change under experience and under the pressure of pragmatic constraints such as efficiency of cognitive functioning? How can transfer of knowledge be accomplished? These are examples for the research questions to be tackled by the program. In short, learning as understood in the program deals with the acquisition of knowledge and belief.

Applications to Instruction and Knowledge-Based Systems

It should be stressed that the LHM program is concentrating on basic research issues; its field is the theory of learning. However, answers to some of these questions will have implications for applied issues in instruction and teaching. Where appropriate, following on these implications will become part of the program's activities. Let us therefore shortly delineate the general form of interaction between the two fields: theory of learning and instructional science.

A deeper understanding of how knowledge is represented and integrated into a body of pre-existing knowledge could supply very useful hints on student modelling and teaching techniques. Research on learning in humans and machines - in particular the computational formalization of models of learning - is especially relevant for computerized instruction. What is needed in order to make software more useful is the capability to adapt it as much as possible to the individual pupil/student. One elegant way to make software adaptive is to enable it to learn about the student, that is, to generate automatically a student model. Theoretical and technical advances from cognitive learner modelling are of direct relevance for these issues.

One has to distinguish between learner models that are used for evaluative purposes (and can be used off-line) from on-line models which guide the presentation of instructional materials for the individual student. Given the current and foreseeable developments in software engineering and AI, constructing on-line learner models will stay as a research issue for quite a while.

From the perspective of authoring, student models that can be used for formative evaluation are especially interesting since such programs will exist in the near future. "Artificial students" (VanLehn, 1991) can be used for the formative evaluation of instructional programs, in particular computer programs. This use of learner models has obvious advantages. For instance, one does not have to waste human resources in order to get a first impression of the quality of the courseware. Furthermore, evaluation can be done with only partially specified courseware so that immediate feedback on design and/or implementation decisions becomes available.

It is widely recognized that the effective development of knowledge-based systems cannot avoid making strong use of automated means for at least partially acquiring the knowledge they need. Furthermore, to provide systems with the ability of self-adapting to environment changes and of automatically evolving toward higher levels of performance would make these systems much more attractive to the potential users. To meet these goals, machine learning research tries to move from a purely syntactic perspective, in which learning was identified with the task of producing some inductive hypothesis for observed data, to a knowledge-intensive process, in which learning does not only mean discovering regularities in the world, but also providing explanations and finding possible causes underlying those regularities. This more "human-like" approach to machine learning calls for a closer cooperation with the cognitive science perspective on learning. This cooperation is a two-way process: results from studies on learning in humans can provide useful hints for the development of effective artificial learning systems, whereas machine learning can provide tools to model human learning.

Research Themes in the LHM Program

The program is divided into five task forces. On the following pages, the themes that guides the work in the Task Forces are described as well as research objectives and an initial research program. The reader will without doubt realize that even though an attempt has been made to treat each Task Force theme from the human and the machine perspectives, the weights are not always equally balanced. Task Force 1 has a more distinguished machine learning orientation, whereas in Task Forces 4 and 5 the view from the social science side dominates. This reflects to some extent the state of the field. It is hoped that research conducted in the LHM program will result in removing some of these imbalances from the research scene.

Task Force 1: Representation Changes in Learning[1]

The theme of Task Force 1 concerns the "Representation Changes in Learning". There is a general agreement that one key to success for the development of an intelligent system is a suitable choice of representation formalisms for all kinds of information relevant to achieving a system's goal. This is especially true in learning activities, both in humans and in artificial systems. On the other hand, it is not always easy, or even possible, to select from the beginning an effective representation for a given type of knowledge. New information coming in and new experiences could affect the original choice, requiring representation updating, ranging from small adjustments to deep restructuring.

The objective of Task Force 1 is to effectively bring together the know-how from the fields of cognitive psychology and machine learning in view of the fulfillment of two main goals. The first one, mostly relevant for cognitive psychology, is to achieve a deeper understanding of the evolution of the models, intended as representations of the world, built up by people, with the help of computational models, clearly formalized and precisely testable. The second one, relevant for machine learning, is to obtain powerful guidelines for a more effective design strategy of learning systems, starting from the very basic issue of what knowledge they should handle and how to represent it.

Choices of representations affect every aspect involved in performing a task. Four main levels have been distinguished:

- Choice of the ontology of the domain: what kinds of objects and phenomena are to be considered as relevant?
- Choice of the internal representations, i.e., mental models of the objects and events.
- Choice of specific representational formalisms.
- Choice of the specific content of the knowledge.

All the preceding choices, when made at the task set up time, may be questioned later on, as experience in performing the task becomes available. It is then a primary concern to understand why, when and how changes in representations, at every level, occur. This involves, among other issues, investigating the nature of the prerequisites for a representation change, extrapolating global effects possibly induced by local changes and establishing links between representation(s) and tasks.

The objectives of this research are hard ones and go far beyond the reach of a small, sectorial group, however qualified. They can be possibly attained only by a synergistic, cooperative effort, bringing together interdisciplinary expertise from cognitive sciences, psychology, computer science and machine learning. Even though a set of research issues can be delimited and autonomously pursued, strong connections can be established with other Task Forces, especially with Task Force 2, which takes the complementary point of view of analyzing representations from a problem-solving perspective, and Task Force 4, because it has to be taken as granted that the context in which a learning act occurs is of outmost importance.

Most machine learning systems currently use a single representation formalism, for instance, logics or semantic nets or conceptual dependency graphs. However, some proposals of using

---

1. Lorenza Saitta is Speaker of this Task Force and has contributed to this section.

knowledge represented in different formalisms, supporting different cooperating reasoning mechanisms, have recently appeared (Saitta, Botta, & Neri, 1993), and the topic attracts an increasing number of researchers. Regarding the changes of representation, learning systems may be able, today, to modify certain aspects of a given formalism, e.g., adding a new predicate in a logic representation scheme (de Raedt & Bruynooghe, 1991), but, at the moment, they seem unable to move from one formalism to another one. Instances of first paradigms are emerging, concerning the representation of the same model or of the same data at various levels of abstraction.

One of the first attempts to use abstractions to guide model learning was described in Mozetic (1990), whereas a general framework for concept acquisition, based on a semantic notion of abstraction has been proposed in Giordana & Saitta (1990) and Giordana, Roverso & Saitta (1991). Recently, automatic construction of an abstract model on top of a detailed one is also attracting attention. The investigation of how human models of the world are built up and changed as new experimental data come from the world, has also been the target of several experimental psychological studies (Tiberghien, 1989; Vosniadou & Brewer, 1994). In particular, the evolution of students' conceptions about every day phenomena have been extensively studied in different domains of Physics, notably in Mechanics, Electricity and Heat. These studies have been conducted in close relationship with teaching.

For complex cognitive activities, as those involved in education and professional activities, there are important differences according to the domain in which those activities take part (e.g., arithmetic, reading, writing, space and geometry) and according to the way these activities are observed and analyzed (in ordinary life situations, at school, in laboratories, etc.). Moreover, the complexity level of the task deeply affects the way in which it is analyzed. Unfortunately, there is no general review available on those different fields.

Research Issues

The research program assumes the following basic scenario: given a target behavior in a chosen domain, all the knowledge required to perform the task has to be selected and represented. Selection and representation are not one-step activities; on the contrary, the current choices can be scrutinized, modified, or extended at any time. In order to make this dynamic adaptation possible, two main challenges, reflected in the two issues in which the program is articulated, have to be faced. A third, complementary one, namely multiple represented knowledge, is treated in Task Force 2.

1. Evaluation and Selection of Representations. In order to trigger possible changes in a representation, we have first to establish the adequacy of it and, then, to select an updating strategy. The first issue concerns the evaluation, i.e., the definition of criteria to assess differences (or similarity) between the target behavior and the behavior obtained using the current representation schemes. The second issue involves a decision: what learning strategy do the comparison results between the target and current behaviors suggest? Several possibilities are open; one, for instance, can be not to learn (i.e., to leave things as they are), another one, to try to make the minimum changes sufficient to account for the new piece of information, whereas still another one can lead to a deep restructuring of the current representation(s). Concerning this last point, we can also notice that new experience may not be the only occasion to make changes: modifications accumulated over a time period may call for a periodical systematization, possibly resulting in a deep reorganization of the way knowledge is represented. Then, the question of whether, when and how to perform a representation restructuring is an important one to be answered.

2. Explicit Relations between Task and Representation. Apparently, humans are good at selecting the correct way of representing knowledge for a given task (behavior). Trying to make explicit the relationships between tasks and representations could lead to substantial improvements in the design of intelligent systems and also in teaching techniques. To approach this problem, two aspects are to be considered: how can a task be represented and, moreover, what are the characteristics of a representation scheme which make it suitable for achieving a target behavior?

Task Force 2: Multiobjective Learning with Multiple Representations[1]

The core issue of the Task Force can be illustrated with the following scenario: Given a person who uses knowledge about a single domain (lets say, some area of medicine) for multiple objectives, e.g., to accomplish diagnostic problem solving tasks quickly and correctly as well as to explain to her students how diagnosis is done in the field. Under such circumstances it is probable that over time she has developed different more or less related representations for the same domain, one that enables her to do expert problem solving diagnosis and one that covers the deep knowledge about the (patho-) physiological relations and explicit strategic knowledge about how diagnosis is done correctly.

The theme of research in this Task Force concentrates therefore on learning processes that are based on the use of multiple representation forms in the context of one or more performance tasks (multiple objectives). This situation occurs frequently in practice since people learn from information that is presented in different forms (e.g. scientific principles, mathematical formulae, worked-out examples, rules of thumb, experience by learning by doing) and needed in different ways. When working on a task they have to use this multiply represented knowledge. In addition, this knowledge may change its form when it is used.

The structure of multirepresentation problem solving is likely also to structure the learning process. Knowledge for various objectives and for representation forms will be learned in different ways. It will be necessary to coordinate these to some degree. Methods for doing so need also to be learned.

Multiple Representation Forms. A learning process usually involves different types of knowledge. The ones we want to focus on comprise the following dimensions:

- *Naive - Scientific.* A naive representation makes use of the concepts that are more or less salient in a domain description, whereas a scientific representation includes inferred, theoretical concepts developed in sciences like physics and medicine. For instance, a novice may refer to a physics problem in terms of blocks and strings, whereas an expert interprets the situation in terms of bodies and forces.

- *Qualitative - Quantitative.* Many relationships and laws in the sciences can be represented in a qualitative fashion ("when x increases, y decreases") or in a more precise quantitative form ("$y = 2.07\ x$"). Between the two, interesting pragmatic relationships hold. For instance, it may be the case that in order to use equations correctly, one may first have to develop an appropriate qualitative representation.

- *Cases - Generalizations.* Reasoning can make use of specific instances or generalizations or combine the two. For instance, one can solve a textbook problem by reasoning analogically to a worked-out example, or by using general laws. Besides pragmatic relationships, the two are related by a developmental process: Generalizations can be developed using repeated case-based problem solving experiences.

---

1. Maarten van Someren is Speaker of this Task Force and has contributed to this section.

- *"Deep"* - *"Compiled"*. Knowledge can be represented in a form that is close to basic (often causal) relationships, or it can be represented in a form optimized for certain performance tasks. For instance, one can diagnose a medical case by reasoning based on one's pathophysiological knowledge, or by "knowing" that symptoms *s* go with disease *d*. Again, the selection between the two depends on pragmatic (task-related) aspects and "genetic" relations hold: compiled knowledge is often acquired by reasoning repeatedly with deep models.

If one has different representation forms for knowledge, then problem solving (or other performance tasks) consists of two types of processes: *transforming* the information contained in one representation into the other and back into the first *,* and *applying* knowledge that is available in the used representation.

Not all types of knowledge are always necessary for problem solving. For example, a problem may be solved only by analogy-based reasoning, without using any "deeper" physics and problem solving knowledge. The work of Task Force 2 concentrates on situations where the use of multiple representations is a common and/or necessary practice to solve a performance task effectively. Multiple representations may be used because of "genetic" reasons: Knowledge is acquired by problem solvers in different forms (e.g., first deep, than compiled; first qualitative, than quantitative). Multiple representations may also be used for reasons of cognitive "economy": people re-represent knowledge in a form that is more suitable for the task at hand (in terms of economic use of resources such as working memory and retrieval from long-term memory). Coordinating different representations should be particularly often required when performing for different objectives, e.g., problem solving *and* explanation.

In situations such as these, a learner/problem solver is occasionally confronted explicitly or implicitly with questions such as: *When* to reason with *which* representation. *How to coordinate* the two representations, for instance, how to translate inference outcomes from the one into the other.

Goal-oriented Learning. The approach taken by this Task Force to this problem is goal-oriented learning. The focus is on goal-oriented activity, directed at completing, tuning or refining knowledge in the context of using it for different purposes. Basic learning mechanisms that are supposed to be part of the architecture of the human problem solver (storing new knowledge in memory, chunking elements into larger units) are assumed to be the machinery that is used by learning processes to acquire the knowledge needed for adequate performance. A basic assumption is that learning is aimed at improving the "cognitive economy" of the system. The economy is monitored at a kind of metalevel and the system searches for opportunities for example to reduce memory load, search during problem solving, etc. Monitoring can pertain to knowledge structures (for instance, the "observation" that a generalization captures too many "cases" and needs therefore to be refined) and/or to processes that make use of knowledge, such as realizing that a class of problems can not be solved without much backtracking. We are particularly interested in two problematic knowledge states:

- Realizing that solving a task with a single representation does not work effectively; the learning goal would be to find an alternative representation and to translate the problem to that one (and back).

- Realizing that while using two representations for one task, the coordination becomes difficult or impossible; the learning goal would be to find ways of improving the coordination.

The notion of goal-oriented learning is chosen as an approach to analyze multiobjective learning with multiple representations for several reasons:

- If information for the learning process is supplied in different forms then learners are likely to have trouble relating these. Such impasses are likely to give rise to learning goals.

- Active learning is likely to be better observable than elementary learning processes such as chunking or tuning of knowledge.

- Active learning is practically important. Observations have shown that "better" learners are goal-oriented and more inclined than others to generate questions when reading a textbook or when solving problems.

Research Issues

Key issues are:

- A preparatory issue concerns the role of these representations in problem solving. How can they be used? When are they used by people engaged in actual problem solving?

- When and how does a learner arrange for having different representations synchronized or even integrated?

- What is the role of basic learning mechanisms (such as chunking, generalization, etc.) in this type of learning?

- How do people detect the need to acquire a new representation form? How do they describe this learning problem? What actions do they take to solve it?

- Can differences in effective learning be predicted from differences in the above processes?

- How does the work on tasks interact? In particular, how does achieving learning goals affect performance on (related) tasks?

The basic method followed is to build simulation models of cognitive processes involving problem solving and learning and to compare these with data from think aloud protocols of these processes. This method can of course be complemented by experiments focussing on a particular aspect of multiobjective learning. In part, data and simulation models of research projects of the Task Force participants are analyzed from the perspective of this sub-theme of the program.

Task Force 3: Learning Strategies to Cope with Sequencing Effects[1]

The issue of sequencing effects in knowledge acquisition is fundamental to our understanding of learning strategies. Currently we find researchers working in machine learning who specify order sensitive algorithms, psychologists who study the sequence of knowledge acquisition in humans and educational technologists who design instructional materials in which the order of study plays an important role. Collaboration among these three communities will have the following three beneficial outcomes. Firstly, it will allow a taxonomy of machine learning algorithms from the point of view of sequencing effects. Secondly, more precise symbolic representations of human learning strategies can be refined. These are also relevant to the third outcome namely, instructional design methods related to supporting the variations in human learning strategies with regard to optimal knowledge acquisition sequences. So the Task Force on Learning Strategies provides a productive research focus for European work on machine learning, human knowledge acquisition, and instructional design.

---

1. Tim O'Shea is Speaker of this Task Force and has contributed to this section.

The sequence in which input is provided to a learning system - be it human or machine - and the sequence in which concepts are formed are of great importance for both the efficiency and the product of learning. This Task Force has as its goal to analyze sequence dependency of learning in detail. For both humans and machine learning programs characteristics of optimal and sub-optimal sequences are analyzed. This research topic allows for interesting comparisons between learning in humans and machines with respect to issues such as the robustness of learning process/outcome against sub-optimal sequences and the ability to recover from wrong generalizations. The Task force considers only those machine learning systems that are able to learn incrementally since they cannot hold arbitrary amounts of information in memory for delayed analysis. Such results are directly relevant for instructional design, in particular in the area of computer-based teaching.

Research Issues

The following items are expected to result from Task Force activities:

- A taxonomy of human and machine learning theories from the point of view of ordering.
- Identification of order-independent, yet incremental learning processes.
- Insight into the robustness of human learning.
- Design of empirical tests and data selection to compare learning in humans and machines with respect to ordering effects.

- How does prior knowledge affect ordering effects?
- Analysis of past work on human and machine learning from the point of view of ordering effects.
- Analysis of experiments comparing the effects of specific input sequences on learning in humans and machines.
- Analysis of extreme cases: order independent vs. very sensitive learning algorithms.

Sequencing effects occur at two levels: on the one level, the order in which examples or observations are experienced by the learner may ease the formation of a particular concept. On the other level, the availability of the concept may be the prerequisite for acquiring another one. For instance, before multiplication can be learned, addition must have been learned. This Task Force analyzes strategies of acquiring a knowledge structure for both, human and machine learning.

Specific research questions are:

1. Analysis of incremental learning processes
- Are there general strategies for determining a most appropriate order of examples/observations?
- Are there order-independent, yet incremental learning processes?
- What makes these processes robust?
2. Analysis of sequencing in a complex concept structure
- In which order does spontaneous human learning develop a concept structure?
- Which order of concept acquisition is the most appropriate one in guided learning?

- What kinds of simple concepts are appropriate as a starting point for further elaboration?

3. Overgeneralization and revision

- What is the function of overgeneralization?
- How does prior knowledge condition overgeneralization?
- When should generalization be revised?

Task Force 4: Situated Learning and Transfer[1]

Classical approaches in psychology and cognitive science assume that learning can be understood in terms of highly general processes located in the learner's head. The particular context or situation in which the learning is occurring might facilitate or inhibit learning, or moderate its expression, but would not affect its fundamental character. Since the structures of learning are highly general in character, spontaneous transfer is to be expected, and explanations are called for where it fails.

By contrast, certain current positions stemming especially from cultural anthropology effectively deny, or exclude from consideration, any individual cognitive processes underlying learning. Learning is understood entirely in terms of the achievement (by largely tacit apprenticeship) of situationally appropriate patterns of behavior. Since the emergence of these patterns is entirely tied to and sustained by the situation, transfer is necessarily limited.

Between these extremes, a considerable number of attempts have been made in recent years to find ways to understand the impact of situation on learning and transfer. In particular, in social and developmental psychology interpretative or hermeneutic approaches have focused upon the processes of social construction of meaning in different situations. From this perspective contexts or situations for learning cannot be understood as having any existence independently of the sociocultural and intersubjective processes which give them meaning.

Such a stance shifts the focus of learning research from the individual, without denying the need to understand how the individual represents the situation. A variety of concepts have been offered to capture the sense in which social practices can enter into and frame individual learning. Pragmatic schemata are envisaged as semi-abstract frameworks grounded in, for example, social regulations such as permissions or obligations. Scripts similarly provide frameworks for learning which are grounded in familiar patterns of everyday activity.

More generally, cognitive scientists have come to recognize that contexts and situations do more than simply moderate the expression of cognitive competencies. The shift from preoccupation with abstract high-level syntactic approaches towards concern with the mental models which subjects create in diverse situations reflects this. So too does the increasing interest in case-based and analogical reasoning, and in strategy choice and the situational factors which affect it. Each of these approaches shows similarities to, and differences from, each of the others. Most have been developed to deal with fairly circumscribed ranges of situations, and their wider utility as models of learning has been little explored.

The literature on 'situated action' (and more generally the sociocultural approach) holds a number of messages for the study of learning. It directs attention towards learning as an aspect of physical and practical activity, shaped by the resources available in a given context. Whereas most research in the field of learning has implied a separation of learning from doing, most learning arguably occurs incidentally to the pursuit of effective action in context. Moreover, contexts are preinvested with meaning in a variety of ways - in learning to act effectively in a given

---

1. Paul Light is Speaker of this Task Force and has contributed to this section.

context people become parts of systems of knowledge already available in society. One way in which this occurs is through the tools (both material and symbolic) which are available to support learning. Information technology provides a particular and distinctive subclass of such tools.

The literature on transfer of learning to new situations shows that such transfer is far from automatic and indeed is often very difficult to achieve. The conditions for effective transfer may be analyzed in terms of characteristics of the learners, of the task and of the learning context, and a considerable body of research exists in relation to each of these. Nonetheless the 'holy grail' of transferable learning has proved elusive. From the perspective of situated action the idea of transferring knowledge or mental representations, acquired in one context to another new and different context is an inappropriate one. Rather, analysis should start from what given situations 'afford' for learning. What a learner acquires in a given situation is mastery of an activity elicited and supported by certain properties of that situation. 'Transfer' can occur (without the necessity of intervening mental representations) when the transformed situation contains the same or similar affordances for the learner as the initial context. Of course this simply recasts the problem, but it does so in a way which draws attention to the adaptive responses educed by different contexts and to the resources in that situation which learners find and use successfully.

Research Issues

The agenda for this Task Force is to further explore, clarify and articulate these attempts to conceptualize situated learning and transfer. Learning in the context of practical activity, in settings in which the achievement of effective action (rather than learning per se) is the goal of the participants. Most everyday situations are of this type, where learning is only implicitly rather than explicitly involved. Moreover, most everyday learning takes place not only in the context of other people, but also in the context of various artifacts, tools and devices designed to support appropriate action in that situation. The Task Force intends to focus particularly upon situations which involve fairly sophisticated technological devices of this kind, for example, computers and software designed to support constructive and communicative activities on the part of the user.

The starting point is to bring the various theoretical (and epistemological) perspectives to bear on a number of cases of this kind. Some examples have already been identified, based on existing projects. Documentary material on the cases will be used to generate a spectrum of accounts in advance of the program workshops, in order to stimulate critical discussion of the basis and utility of these accounts and of the relationships between them. This process will need to be iterative, since different perspectives on what is being learned in these rich situations will inevitably highlight the need for different kinds of data.

The learning phenomena and the way they are conceptualized in this Task Force do not allow for a formulation in terms of machine learning mechanisms which are ready-at-hand. Research in computer science has not looked into learning phenomena from the stance proposed here. However, this is not to say that there are no points of contact. For instance and in particular, current research in AI on analogical and case-based reasoning and learning deals often with similar issues, but phrases them differently. It is one of the goals of the Task Force to identify the relationship between these research lines, and to allow for a substantial transfer.

The research program for Task Force 4 consists of a family of projects funded independently of ESF, through national research funding agencies. These projects focus upon learning in the context of collaborative and situated use of information technology-based tools, with examples drawn from instructional contexts, work and play. Different artifacts afford very different possibilities for activity and joint activity, but they also differ greatly as a function of the context of use.

The first level objective of these studies is essentially descriptive; exploring ways of characterizing complex authentic learning situations. The second level objective raises the question of transfer (or flexible application) of learning. How does learning in one situation affect, modify or facilitate learning in another? Can we test our 'readings' of the affordances of different situations by trying to create situations which extend the range of applicability of what is learned? One element of the longer term agenda thus involves the articulation of design principles for the support of flexible, applicable learning in the context of information technology.

Task Force 5: Collaborative Learning[1]

Research on collaborative learning is inscribed within the larger debate on the individual versus social nature of human cognition. Piaget and Vygotsky are respectively known as the tenants of these positions. For Vygotsky, individual cognitive processes result from internalizing the tools used in social interactions, mainly the language. Inversely, the Piagetian tradition focuses on conflicts between individual's knowledge and restricts the role of the group to social pressure to solve conflicts. Nowadays this distinction between social and individual levels is fading out. Under the influence of the situated cognition approach and due to the contribution of distributed AI, cognition is viewed as being shared by or distributed over individuals. Cognitive processes are perceived as a property of a group in interaction.

Within these theoretical positions, empirical research has attempted to get a better understanding of collaborative learning by comparing cases where collaboration effects positive cognitive change and cases where it does not. Researchers have identified several factors that influence the effects of collaborative learning. Some of these factors concern the composition of the pair: the general development level or the domain specific skills of the pair as a whole, the difference of skills among peer members, the subjective perception of those differences, the gender and so forth. Other factors concern the task being performed collaboratively: whether it can be easily divided among individuals, whether the task constrains peers to coordinate their action, whether the task authorizes peer members to use divergent conceptions, whether the task requires a lot of planning, etc. A third group of factors describes the communication channel between members, for instance by contrasting situations where the subjects work in front of a computer with situations where they collaborate through a network, on remote terminals.

Most of these factors interact with each other in a complex way. To understand how they affect learning, one must decompose the condition-effect causal link into two segments: (1) different conditions of collaboration create different interaction processes and (2) different interaction processes lead to different learning effects. The description of interactions is then perceived as the central point to understanding collaborative learning. Interactions have been described with respect to the quality of explanations, the type of conflicts, the mechanisms of social grounding, and various taxonomies of communicative acts, inspired by linguistic theories. Computational models of dialogue have been used to support human collaboration or implement collaboration in multi-agent systems. The goal of distributed AI is to implement networks of agents able to solve together problems that are beyond their individual abilities. Coordinated multidisciplinary research efforts concerning the analysis of interaction processes would positively impact on the understanding of collaborative learning.

Recent developments in psychological research open a connection with AI researchers, especially with computational models of dialogue. In the field of expert systems, some systems are

---

1. Pierre Dillenbourg is Speaker of this Task Force and has contributed to this section.

able to learn from a user when he provides an interesting solution. However, these apprenticeship systems (Wilkins, 1988) focus on how the explainee integrates the explanation, i.e. they are more interested in instruction than collaboration.

The work on computational modelling of collaboration is very recent. Hutchins (1991) and Dillenbourg (1991) used the same representation (a network) to represent the individual and social levels of cognition. There exists a promising link between computational and psychological investigations of collaborative learning. Distributed AI (DAI) studies show how a network of agents can collaborate in order to solve problems that are beyond their individual abilities (Durfee et al, 1989). The required level of modularity can be obtained with object-oriented programming environments; the issue remains to achieve an efficient coordination of individual contributions.

Research Issues

Objectives:

- To compare theoretical perspectives (reported in the previous section) at a concrete level.
- To compare collaboration processes observed with different paradigms (see below).
- To propose psychologically grounded solutions for distributed systems.
- To specify how software can better support human collaboration (groupware).

A basic objective is to further improve the tools used for describing, understanding and modelling the interaction processes during collaborative learning. These tools include dialogue analysis taxonomies and quantitative interaction variables which co-vary with learning effects. The outcome will be:

- Standard tools for interaction analysis will improve exchange between researchers on different domains.
- These tools will facilitate the exchange of data among researchers in psychology and AI; they may serve as a basis for computational modelling.
- These tools will improve the design of interface used in software that supports collaborative work.

Work is done along two axes: (1) the theoretical axis refers to the theories explaining the cognitive benefits of collaboration, socio-cognitive conflict, scaffolding, internalization, social grounding, and so forth; and (2) the paradigmatic axis distinguishes four paradigms or experimental settings.

1. Human/human collaboration on a computer-based task. This setting aims to observe 'natural' collaboration between two humans. The choice of a computer-based task enables the researcher to control the environment, e.g. to tune some task parameters, to record how learners use the environment, etc.

2. Human/human collaboration through network facilities. By comparison to (1), this setting allows the study of the relation between communication channels and collaborative mechanisms: when learners communicate through a keyboard, non-verbal communication (e.g. facial expressions) is reduced, the cost of interaction is increased, etc. Another advantage of this setting is that it provides simplified dialogue protocols that are likely to be useful for computational modelling.

3. Human/machine collaboration. The study of human-machine collaborative learning enables, for instance, the tuning of the behavior of the artificial learner and the observation of the effects on the human learner. It also allows to explore how computers and humans can contribute optimally to a common task, this knowledge being useful for any interactive system designer.

4. Machine/machine collaboration. Collaboration among artificial agents can be studied per se, for developing powerful systems or for psychological modelling.

It is interesting to build experiments which compare paradigms. For instance, the comparison between the settings (1) and (2) could indicate how restricting communication channels influences collaboration.

Chapter Overview

Recent developments provide interdisciplinary research with some challenges, all of which are addressed in one form or another in the chapters of this book. We shall first summarize these challenges and then provide a sequence-oriented overview of the book's chapters.

One issue that receives increasing attention has to do with the question how *learning goals* arise in the first place. Whereas most machine learning systems (and to some extent pupils in formal school settings) have learning goals pre-specified for them, under a more general perspective it is in many cases up to the learning agent to invent learning goals. Considering how learning goals are constructed by agents is important for at least two reasons: firstly, increasing evidence is produced in psychology showing that learning goals influence both learning activities and learning outcomes (e.g., Ng and Bereiter, 1991); secondly, in the machine learning field it is conceded that goals form an important class of constraints (bias) on learning processes and outcomes. And, obviously, if the research goal is to develop integrated cognitive architectures - i.e., architectures for agents who can solve problems, learn and act - then goal-setting processes become a central issue. The chapter by Van Someren and Reimann has more to say on this issue. Also directly relevant is the chapter by Ohlsson, who discusses learning processes that serve *epistemic* goals such as arguing, critiquing, and explaining. It becomes clear that learning mechanisms invented for skill acquisition (or, more generally, for speed-up learning) are not well suited to support learning for other, for instance epistemic, purposes.

Current research both in psychology and machine learning has begun to again address questions of *representations for learning*. This is a somewhat new topic in the learning field, but has a long-standing tradition in problem solving research (Larkin, 1983; Amarel, 1981). This development goes hand in hand with an increasing interest in *multi-strategy learning systems* (Michalski, 1994; Saitta, Boti and Neri, 1993). If a learning system has several learning methods available, then the effectiveness of employing these will depend (a) on the learning goal, and (b) on representational issues: the quality of learning method outcomes depends on the representation used. Hence, it becomes an issue for learning research how to *select* among different representations, how one representation *changes* into another one, and how multiple representations can be *coordinated* for learning purposes. Topics such as these are addressed in this book in the chapters by Vosniadou, by Saitta et al. and by Van Someren and Reimann.

Even when a learning agent has committed itself to one learning goal, one representation and a single learning method, problems related to ordering effects still present a problem. This is an old problem in psychology, instruction and machine learning, but has so far not been "solved" and hence still constitutes a challenge. Even more so in recent learning studies where the acquisition of concepts and principles has been described in terms of acquiring mental models and theories. Since these are highly interrelated, complex structures, problems resulting from order effects become correspondingly harder to track and control. Order effects are treated in the chapters by Langley and by Morik and Vosniadou.

A final group of challenges to current learning research results from what may be called "doing justice to the *social dimension*". The social dimension of learning receives increasing attention from two directions. One is research on *collaborative learning*. Collaborative learning becomes much more often practiced in and out of school because it prepares for collaborative problem solving (which is the rule rather than the exception in complex working environments) and because it becomes technically feasible thanks to the rapidly developing computer and tele-communication infrastructure. However, it is not well understood how humans learn collaboratively let alone how machines can be made to learn together. The chapter by Dillenbourg, Baker, Blaye and O'Malley reports on current developments, analyzing research that pertains to three forms of collaboration: human-human, human-machine, and machine-machine.

The second impetus for including the social dimension in learning research originates in research on transfer of learning and pins down the major reason for missing transfer in the social setting rather than the mental state of learning agents. This so-called *situated cognition* view insists that in order to understand cognitive phenomena in general and transfer of learning in particular, one must not only focus on the knowledge represented in the mind of single agents, but consider in addition their social and environmental resources. Without such a perspective, transfer could neither be understood nor fostered. In its most radical form, this view does away with representations completely (Clancey, 1992). Even if one does not subscribe to this radical stance, the concepts beginning to develop within the situated cognition approach constitute some interesting challenges to the now classical, purely cognitivistic view of the mind. If this view would indeed solve the transfer problem, then more symbolic-cognitivistic approaches to learning will need to adjust their theoretic underpinnings as well. A number of authors address situativity theory in this book, among them Säljö, and Gruber, Law, Mandl and Renkl.

Let us now turn to delineating the chapter sequence. The first five chapters are devoted to discipline-oriented overviews. The following seven chapters have been written with a Task Force specific perspective, also stressing interdisciplinary research attempts.

Chapter 2, by Stella Vosniadou, provides us with an overview of the main directions research on learning has taken in cognitive psychology in the last ten years. In the first part, she focuses on the advances made in representing learning processes for procedural knowledge (skill) and declarative knowledge that have for instance been described in terms of schemata and models. She proposes to take the view more seriously that learning declarative knowledge may consist in acquiring mental theories and that considering theory change in the sciences can provide researchers with a fruitful metaphor for cognitive research. She supports her argument not only with psychological learning research, but also with observations from developmental psychology. In the second part of her chapter, Vosniadou summarizes and analyzes some of the recent challenges to established cognitive learning theories.

Stellan Ohlsson's chapter is also written from a psychological perspective. It contrasts research on the acquisition of practical (also often called procedural) knowledge with the acquisition of declarative knowledge. As Ohlsson argues, comparatively little is known about how people acquire declarative knowledge (facts and principles) that they use for purposes such as arguing, explaining, persuading. A central problem he identifies is that it is difficult to analyze the medium in which declarative knowledge is displayed: discourse. It is much easier to analyze actions (for instance, problem solving behavior), the medium in which practical knowledge can be assessed. Identifying the principal differences between practical and declarative knowledge as done by Ohlsson is important since it is a necessary step towards identifying appropriate research concepts and methods for the study of declarative knowledge acquisition.

The chapter by Werner Emde gives an overview of some of the central aspects of a machine learning perspective on learning. The chapter presents an overview of goals and research directions in machine learning related to the issue of understanding more about the striking ability of human beings (as individuals as well as communities) to acquire knowledge from experience. Part one and part two describe research directions rooted in different areas of computer science. Emde describes here two well-known machine learning programs that perform a task which is also well analyzed for human learners: the acquisition of concepts. In the third part, he briefly describes some approaches influenced by research in psychology and philosophy and discusses how this research direction is able to complement the other ones. The last part of this paper lists some open scientific questions, which reflect the need for more interdisciplinary research.

Roger Säljö summarizes the current arguments from the perspective of socio-cultural psychology and sociology as to how learning phenomena should be conceptualized. Under this perspective, it makes little sense to study the individual learner in isolation, separated from the physical and social resources he or she would use under normal circumstances. After delineating some of the core differences between the cognitivistic and the socio-cultural view of mental phenomena, he focuses on the use of tools by humans and how tool usage affects thinking and communication. His conviction is that thinking can be adequately described only as pursued in conjunction with tools and other artifacts, and that hence the consequence must be to focus in learning research on the modes in which cognition and practical action are shared between actors and mediational means.

Eric De Corte addresses in his chapter the relationship between learning theory and instructional science. He stresses that the starting point for any theory of learning must be an understanding of competent performance, of expertise. Also, historically seen, the recent surge of interest in learning in the fields of psychology and machine learning is to some extent due to the intensive analysis of expertise. De Corte sets out therefore to analyze in the first part of the chapter the aptitudes involved in skilled learning, thinking and problem solving. Next an overview is given of the major characteristics of effective learning in humans, derived from recent research in instructional psychology. The main part of the chapter in devoted to an analysis of the current research on transfer of knowledge and cognitive skill. Transfer is hard to achieve for human learners and notoriously difficult for machine learners. The chapter concludes by developing implications for the design of instruction.

This concludes the series of chapters that provide an discipline-oriented overview. We enter now a sequence of chapters which focus on issues, motivated by the thematic orientation of the five task forces that make up the LHM research program.

Chapter 7, written by Lorenza Saitta and the members of Task Force 1, gives an overview of work on basic principles and computational models of knowledge representation change, occurring in humans and machines during learning activities. In Machine Learning, selecting a representation amounts to selecting a formal language, such as first-order logic, thereby defining a language bias for the machine learning program. Such biases are necessary for all learning systems - including humans - because they constrain to some degree what can be learned by the system. Change of representation has a less clearly defined meaning in psychological research because it is an open empirical issue how humans represent their environment. The chapter contains an overview of the various ways psychologists have characterized representation changes and ends with the description of two research proposals that will shed more light on the thorny issue of representation change in humans and machines.

Maarten van Someren and Peter Reimann discuss in Chapter 8 various recent developments in Machine Learning research and in psychology concerning the relationship between the goals a learner holds, the learning strategy employed, representational issues and performance. The chapter focuses particularly on those forms of learning that arise in the context of problem solving and serve the goal of improving problem solving competence. It is well known that advanced human problem solvers (experts) utilize and/or develop various representations of a problem, but it is not clear as of yet how this characteristic affects learning. The general theme of this chapter is a concern for cognitive architectures, i.e., for questions that arise when one considers learning capabilities as having to be coordinated and integrated with other cognitive activities like problem solving, acting, and epistemic tasks such as explaining.

The chapter by Pat Langley tackles order (or sequencing) effects, a topic that has received much attention in studies on human learning as well as on machine learning because it concerns any learning system that works incrementally, but which still provides many challenges. After having defined more clearly what incremental learning and order effect mean, Langley discusses order effects on three levels: effects of concept, instance, and feature order. For each level, main results from Machine Learning research and psychological research are reported. Further, an attempt is made to sketch the essential instructional consequences of order effects on the three levels. It becomes obvious that the issue of order effects is a very promising one for interdisciplinary learning research because the Machine Learning community has developed concepts and programs which in some instances resemble very closely those order effects occurring in humans. Direct comparisons seem therefore within reach, the results of which could have immediate effects on instruction.

Chapter 10 by Gruber, Law, Mandl and Renkl, contributes to a better understanding of the transfer of learning problem by reviewing the literature on situated cognition and by analyzing its contribution to learning theory and instruction. After reviewing some of the major experimental findings that capture the problem of missing transfer, the authors describe the position of five of the leading proponents of situated cognition. In doing so, they identify the proposals made by these theorists on how to improve transfer, in particular the transfer from schooling situations into real-world situations. In the second part of this chapter, is it discussed to which extent computer- and multimedia-based learning environments that have been inspired by situativity theory succeed in capturing the essential characteristics of situated instruction. Some of the best known approaches are described. The authors end by raising a skeptical voice concerning the vision of realizing situated learning by relying predominantly on technological developments.

Collaborative learning is the issue of the chapter by Dillenbourg, Baker, Blaye, and O'Malley. It is organized along the historical axis, describing previous and current approaches to study collaborative learning. After introducing the major theoretical orientations - social-constructivist, socio-cultural, and shared-cognition approach - the central methodological problems concerning the empirical investigation of collaborative learning are identified. The authors conclude that factorial research designs cannot be the method of choice, and continue by describing research that focuses on detailed process analysis of collaborative behavior. The chapter concludes with a description of appropriate research tools for three classes of collaborative learning scenarios: human-human, human-computer, and computer-computer.

The final chapter by Morik and Vosniadou is intended to provide a case-study for the kind of interdisciplinary research that is envisioned in the LHM program. Starting from empirical observations on how children in different age groups reason about the phenomena involved in the day/night-cycle, and taking psychological theorizing into account, a computational model has been developed that on some level of abstraction is able to solve the same task children in the empirical study had been confronted with: to answer why-questions about the day-night cycle. Moreover, at least a subset of the answers produced by the computer program are based on the same line of reasoning as has been observed in the answering process of children. Furthermore, the model learns about the domain and hence changes its theory about the domain in a manner that is similar to developmental changes observed in children.

References

Amarel, S. (1981). Problems of representation in heuristic problem solving. Related issues in the development of expert systems. In R. Groner, M. Groner, & M.W. Bischof (Eds.), *Methods of heuristics*. Hillsdale, NJ: Lawrence Erlbaum.

Anderson, J.R. (1983). *The architecture of cognition*. Cambridge, MA: Harvard University Press.

Anderson, J.R. (1987). Skill acquisition: compilation of weak-method problem solutions. *Psychological Review, 94*, 192-210.

Anderson, J.R. (1993). *Rules of the mind*. Hillsdale, NJ.: Erlbaum.

Anderson, J.R., Boyle, C.F., Corbett, A.T., Lewis, M.W. (1990). Cognitive modeling and intelligent tutoring. *Artificial Intelligence, 42*, 7-49.

Brooks, R. (1991). Intelligence without representation. *Artificial Intelligence, 47*, 139-160.

Clancey, W. J. (1992). Representations of knowing: In defense of cognitive apprenticeship. *Journal of Artificial Intelligence, 3*, 139-168.

Jong, T. de (1991). Learning and instruction with computer simulations. *Education and Computing, 6*, 217-229.

De Raedt L., & Bruynooghe M. (1991). CLINT: A multistrategy interactive concept learner and theory revision system. *Proceedings of the First International Workshop on Multistrategy Learning.*

Fisher, D., Pazzani, M., & Langley, P.(Eds.) (1991). *Concept formation: Knowledge and experience in unsupervised learning.* San Mateo, CA: Morgan Kaufmann.

Gardner, H. (1985). *The mind's new science*. New York: Basic Books.

Giordana, A., & Saitta, L. (1990). Abstraction: a general framework for learning. *Working notes of the Workshop on Automated Generation of Approximations and Abstractions.* (Boston, MA).

Giordana, A., Saitta, L., Roverso, D. (1991). Abstracting concepts with inverse resolution, Proceedings of the *8th Int. Machine Learning Workshop*. (Evanston, IL).

Klahr, D., & Dunbar, K. (1988). Dual space search during scientific reasoning. *Cognitive Science, 12*, 1-48.

Laird, J.E., Newell, A., & Rosenbloom, P.S. (1987). Soar: An architecture for general intelligence. *Artificial Intelligence, 33*, 1-64.

Langley, P. (1981). Data-driven discovery of physical laws. *Cognitive Science, 5*, 31-54.

Langley, P.W., Simon, H.A., Bradshaw, G., & Zytkow, J. (1987). *Scientific discovery: Computational explorations of the creative processes.* Cambridge, MA: MIT Press.

Larkin, J.H. (1983). The role of problem representations in physics. In D. Gentner & A. L. Stevens (Eds.), *Mental models*. Hillsdale, NJ: Erlbaum.

Medin, D.L., Wattenmaker, W.D., & Michalski, R.S. (1987). Constraints and preferences in inductive learning: An experimental study of human and machine performance. *Cognitive Science, 11*, 299-339.

Michalski, R.S. (1994). Inferential theory of learning: Developing foundations for multistrategy learning. In R.S. Michalski & G. Tecuci (Eds.), *Machine Learning - A multistrategy approach Vol IV.* San Francisco: Morgan Kaufmann.

Mozetic, I. (1990). Abstractions in model-based diagnosis. *Working notes of the Workshop on Automated Generation of Approximations and Abstractions.* (Boston, MA).

Newell, A. (1990). *Unified theories of cognition*. Cambridge, MA: Harvard University Press.

Ng, E., & Bereiter, C. (1991). Three levels of goal orientation in learning. *Journal of the Learning Sciences, 1*, 243-271.

Pylyshyn, Z.W. (1984). *Computation and cognition: Towards a foundation for cognitive science.* Cambridge, MA: MIT Press.

Reimann, P. (1989). Modeling scientific discovery learning processes with adaptive production systems. In D. Bierman, J. Breuker, J. Sandberb (Eds.), *Artificial intelligence in education.* Amsterdam: IOS.

Saitta, L., Botta, M., & Neri, F. (1993). Multistrategy learning and theory revision. *Machine Learning, 11*, 153-172.

Schauble, L., Glaser, R., Raghavan, K., & Reiner, M. (1991). Causal models and experimentation strategies in scientific reasoning. *Journal of the Learning Sciences, 1*, 201-238.

VanLehn, K. (1991). Two pseudo-students: Applications of machine learning to formative evaluation. In R. Lewis & S. Otsuki (Eds.), *Advanced research on computers in education.* (pp. 17-26). North Holland: Elsevier.

Tiberghien, A. (1989). Learning and teaching at middle school level of concepts and phenomena in physics. The case of temperature. In H. Mandl, E. de Corte, N. Bennett, & H.F. Friedrich (Eds.), *Learning and instruction. European research in an international context, Volume 2.1.* Pergamon Press, Oxford, UK.

VanLehn, K. (1983). *Felicity conditions for human skill acquisition: Validating an AI-based theory.* Tech. Rept. CIS21. Palo Alto, CA: Xerox .

VanLehn, K. (1990). *Mind bugs: The origins of procedural misconceptions.* Cambridge, MA, US: MIT Press.

VanLehn, K., Brown, J.S., & Greeno, J. (1984). Competitive argumentation in computational theories of cognition. In W. Kintsch, J. Miller, & P. Polson (Eds.), *Methods and tactics in cognitive science.* Hillsdale, NJ: Erlbaum.

Vosniadou, S., & Brewer, W.F. (1994). Mental models of the day/night cycle. *Cognitive Science, 18*, 123-182.

A Cognitive Psychological Approach to Learning

Stella Vosniadou

Introduction

A basic tenet of cognitive psychology is that the mind is a system that constructs and manipulates symbols. Cognitive psychologists seek to understand how symbols are represented and processed and how they are related to observable human activity and particularly thoughtful activity. Within the framework of cognitive psychology learning is the study of how symbolic representations and processes change and how these changes affect observable actions[1].

Learning has not been a priority in cognitive psychology, as it did, for example, in the case of behaviorism. Mandler (1985) observes that "until the 50's, learning and motivation were the reigning king and queen of American psychology. It is sometimes difficult to comprehend their demise in the ensuing 30 years, but cognitive psychologists were either preoccupied with the steady state organism or unsure how to handle the problem of cognitive change until they understood what it is that changes during learning" (p. 108). The emphasis on the description of cognitive performance on the outcomes of learning, rather than on learning as it proceeds (Glaser, 1995) seems to have been a necessary first step in the development of a theory of cognition (see also Newell & Simon, 1972). In the 30 years or so since cognitive psychologists opened the black box of the mind to study internal states, they have been struggling with fundamental issues regarding representation and process. Take for example the proliferation of proposals aimed at characterizing the representational level, such as frames, scripts, schemas, theories, mental models, etc. In view of the fact that different specific theories of representation allow different conceptualizations of learning, it is not surprising that the study of learning per se has stayed behind. Despite the relative neglect of issues of learning, cognitive psychology has succeeded in providing detailed descriptions of complex cognitive performance that bring us much closer than ever before to an understanding of mental phenomena and of the mechanisms responsible for problem-solving and the acquisition of expertise.

My purpose in this chapter is to capture some of the changes that have occurred in the treatment of learning within cognitive psychology. To do so I have divided this chapter in two parts. The first part describes some of the advances cognitive psychologists have made in conceptualizing the changes that occur with in the strategies that individuals use to process information and in the way knowledge is organized and represented in long term memory. In the second part, some recent challenges for major assumptions of the information processing paradigm, such as the view that there is a unitary theory of learning, that learning is rule-based and that it involves the manipulation of symbols, are briefly discussed. I argue that more attention needs to be paid to the development of theories of knowledge representation and representational change, which lie at the heart of cognitive psychology, but that this should be done without neglect of the biology of the human brain on the one hand, or of the social, cultural, and historical environment within which our thoughts and behaviors are modeled on the other.

---

1. As will be discussed later, the assumption that the mind is a system that constructs and manipulates symbols is being challenged both by the connectionist movement and by situativity theory.

Learning as Change in the Way Information is Represented and Processed

The dominant framework within which cognitive psychologists have conducted their research is the information processing paradigm. Within this framework it is assumed that the mind is a limited-capacity processing system that interprets information that comes from the outside on the basis of information stored in long term memory and processes it in different ways necessary for the execution of different tasks. In this context, there are two main areas where changes can occur as a result of learning and affect human behavior: (1) in the strategies the cognitive system uses to process information, and (2) in the representations that underlie human cognitive activity.

Strategies for Processing Information

Learning involves the acquisition of new procedures for processing information as well as the revision of existing ones. Learning to do things, such as learning to play tennis or learning to play the piano involves the acquisition of complex motor-skills which become faster, more accurate, and more automatic with the acquisition of expertise. Learning to solve problems requires the acquisition of strategies and algorithms that make it possible to devise and execute a solution plan. Remembering has been described in terms of the acquisition and use of memory strategies, such as rehearsing, self-testing, and the use of visual images, while learning to comprehend requires the development of metacognitive strategies such as planning, comprehension monitoring, questioning, summarizing, predicting, etc.

Initially, cognitive psychologists focused on the analysis of problem solving activity paying particular attention to the description of the way information was processed. The idea was that problem solving involved the acquisition and use of certain general problem solving strategies that require little or no specific knowledge and can be employed in a broad range of tasks. For example, in the influential problem-space theory established by Newell and Simon (1972) problem solving is seen as a process of search through a state space. A number of strategies make it possible for the problem solver to move from the original state to the goal state. One such general strategy with wide applicability is means-ends analysis. Means-ends analysis is a strategy that identifies the differences between the current situation and the goal and selects the best action that will reduce these differences. If needed, means-ends analysis will help the problem solver to select a sub-goal.

In the ensuing years it was realized that general problem solving strategies may be successful in dealing with well-defined problems that require little or no prior knowledge to be solved, like the Tower of Hanoi problem. However, such general strategies are not very useful when it comes to solving problems in subject matter areas where a great deal of prior knowledge is required, such as in the case of physics or medicine. In these areas, expertise involves the acquisition of a rich stock of domain relevant knowledge and the development of specific strategies that are tailored to meet the needs of the problem solver in the domain.

For example, research by Chi and her colleagues (e.g., Chi, Feltovich & Glaser, 1981; Chi, Glaser & Rees, 1983) has shown that expertise in physics is highly dependent on specialized representations of the relevant domain that direct the search for applicable domain-specific strategies. Other research (e.g., Lar, 1983) has shown that experts are more likely to use specific strategies for solving physics problems, working forward from the information contained in the problem to produce a solution, whereas novices´ procedures are weak and general.

A great deal of research in cognitive psychology has been directed towards describing the specific heuristics, strategies and procedures individuals use in the solution of problems in physics, math, geometry, programming, medicine, chess, etc. For example, solving an equation can be described in terms of strategies such as the reduce strategy (i.e., carrying out all the operations indicated by the problem as soon as possible), or the attraction (1), collection (2), and isolation (3) strategies described below (Mayer, 1992).

(1) Attraction: changing 16+2R=3R-24 to 16=3R-2R-24

(2) Collection: changing 16=3R-2R-24 to 16=R-24

(3) Isolation: changing 16=R-24 to 16+24= R

Such descriptions are sometimes accompanied by computational models which often take the form of a production system[1].

In such systems learning was originally described in terms of the deliberate creation of new productions through a build operator. In the continuous development of production system architecture, a number of different learning mechanisms have been described to account for the gradual refinement of goal directed problem solving procedures that occurs with practice (see Anderson, 1983; 1989). Some of the learning mechanisms that have been proposed are the following:

- *Strength accumulation:* Successful procedures accumulate strength through generalization and discrimination mechanisms that try to distinguish the problem features that are predictive of success or failure of a particular procedure. Through this mechanism successful strategies are strengthened and unsuccessful are weakened.

- *Tuning:* Procedures are tuned so that they can apply better to a domain. This learning mechanism attempts to capture the selectivity and rapid success that characterizes expert learning. Tuning is achieved through generalization and discrimination mechanisms that make the application of a rule broader or narrower, depending on its history of success and failure.

- *Composition:* This is a learning mechanism that combines a set of procedures and collapses them into a single one. Composition speeds up the process of learning by creating new operators that embody the sequences of steps used in a particular problem-solving domain.

- *Proceduralization:* The mechanism of proceduralization gradually replaces declarative information with procedures. Anderson (1983) makes a distinction between declarative and procedural components which he thinks is very important because it makes it possible to account for the difference in learning facts versus procedures. According to Anderson facts are easy to learn, but new procedures take much longer to encode in memory. "Proceduralization gradually replaces the interpretive application with productions that perform the behavior indirectly. Thus instead of verbally rehearsing a rule and figuring out how it applies to a problem, students eventually have a production that recognizes the rule immediately" (Anderson, 1983). Once a procedure is formed it can be refined further using the learning mechanisms described earlier.

- *Inspection:* This mechanism achieves learning through an inspection process (Larkin, 1983). New rules can be acquired by inspecting the results of a solution attempt and encoding important regularities.

- *Analogy:* The mechanism of analogical learning makes it possible to transform the solution worked out for one problem into a solution for a similar problem from the same domain or from a different domain. Anderson (1989) describes a mechanism for analogical reasoning in

---

1. A production is a set of condition-action pairs. The condition specifies some data patterns and the action specifies what to do when that patterns occurs in working memory.

problem-solving and skill acquisition situations in the PUPS production system which is the theoretical successor of ACT* theory. Other attempts to deal with analogy in the context of problem solving are described in Vosniadou & Ortony, 1989.

Mechanisms such as the ones mentioned above are meant to describe the kind of learning exhibited by high school or college students when they try to solve problems in mathematics, geometry, physics, etc. In these situations information is usually derived from a textbook and used in problem solving. Some of the learning phenomena that need to be accounted for in these cases are the gradual increase in speed and accuracy in the problem-solving strategies that students use. While a great deal of progress has been made in understanding some of the learning mechanisms that may be responsible for such phenomena, more work is needed in order to understand and model the flexibility that people exhibit in their problem solving behavior, their ability to change goals, to have conscious knowledge of their inductive processes, and their engagement in analogical reasoning. Finally, more attention should be paid to the relationship between strategies for processing information and knowledge representations, and more specifically to the issue of how changes in strategy are related to changes in underlying representations.

Knowledge Representation

In its original formulation, information processing psychology conceptualized the mind as a sequential information processor. Basic perceptual processes occurred first and attentional processes followed. Information was deposited in short term memory and was then transferred to long term memory. However, the assumption that the human mind processes information in a serial manner is inconsistent with a great deal of psychological evidence that shows that cognitive processes are influenced not only by the nature of the perceptual stimuli but also by the nature of individuals expectations, prior knowledge, past experience, etc. By the mid 70's cognitive activity was thought to consist of interactive top-down and bottom-up processes which occur in parallel fashion (Neisser, 1976).

In order to capture more adequately the top-down type of processing that goes on in human cognitive activity, particularly as such activity takes place in the usual fussy and ill-defined situations of everyday thinking, cognitive psychologists started to consider the changes that may occur with learning in the way knowledge is represented in long term memory. The issue of knowledge representation is a thorny one and cognitive psychologists have experimented with a number of different conceptualizations in their effort to find a way to account for the complex variety of phenomena that characterize intelligent human functioning. In this section I describe some of these proposals.

 Concepts and Conceptual Structures

It is generally assumed that people divide the world into concepts that are organized in larger conceptual structures. One of the earlier proposals regarding the nature of concepts, known as the "classical view", describes concepts in terms of a set of necessary and defining attributes which specify which instances belong to a given conceptual category and which not. This view has been challenged both on theoretical and empirical grounds (see Smith & Medin, 1981). More recent attempts consider concepts to be organized around certain prototypical or characteristic attributes, although there appears to be a great deal of variability across individuals or with the same individual across different tasks.

Concepts are thought to be organized in long term memory in hierarchical structures in which some concepts are superordinate and others are subordinate. Cognitive psychologists have described different kinds of changes that can occur in such conceptual structures as a result of learning. The simplest kinds of changes involve the addition or deletion of features or attributes in a concept (Keil, 1989). More complex kinds of changes involve the addition or deletion of relations among concepts or are described in terms of changes in the hierarchical organization of concepts in a conceptual hierarchy. For example, Chi, Feltovich & Glaser (1981) described changes in the knowledge structures of novice and expert physicists in terms of a structural reorganization according to which what is a superordinate category for the novice becomes a basic category for the expert. More recently, some more radical kinds of conceptual changes have been added to the list and these involve movement from one conceptual domain to another (known as "tree branching" and "tree switching", Thagard, 1992), or from one ontological category to another (Chi, Slotta, de Leeuw, 1994). These latter types of changes are usually meant to characterize cases of radical theory revision observed in the history of science or in differences between novices and experts.

   Schemata

Another proposal about the way concepts are organized in memory is schema theory (Schank & Abelson, 1977; Rumelhart & Ortony, 1977). Schemata are meant to encode the generic knowledge that can be applied in many specific situations. There are different kinds of schemata (e.g., scripts, scenes, plans, frames, etc.) but they all have certain characteristics in common, such as that they consist of slots or variables that can take different values. For example, a script is the kind of schema that contains the sequence of actions one goes through when carrying out certain every-day events, such as going to a restaurant. Within a script the relations are the various actions, like walking or sitting. Role slots capture the various parts in a script, like the cashier and the waiter. Slots in the script can contain sub-schemata that specify how related actions or events are related to the script (Schank & Abelson, 1977). In this way it is possible to create structures that characterize peoples' background knowledge about many stereotypical situations.

Schema-like structures are most successful in capturing the top-down processing that goes on when people interpret information that comes from the outside and in explaining the errors that often occur in such situations. Schemata can also explain how people free up the cognitive system from having to analyze all aspects of a visual scene in everyday situations where they have many expectations about what they are going to see. One of the limitations of schema theory is its inflexibility. People can deal quickly with unexpected situations or with situations where no prior schema existed.

It is not clear how schemata are acquired in the first place, but it is assumed that this happens though induction from everyday experience. Analogy is also a mechanism that can account for the creation of a new schema out of an old one (Vosniadou, 1989; Vosniadou & Ortony, 1989). One of the ways schema learning can occur is by having an instantiated schema from working memory be deposited in schema memory. This schema can then serve as a new more specific schema. An object is recognized easier the second time by having its schema match the representation in working memory.

The kind of learning that can occur within a schema framework has been described by Rumelhart and Norman (1977) in terms of accretion, tuning, and restructuring. Accretion refers to the changes that occur in existing schemata through the gradual accumulation of factual information. Tuning describes the kinds of changes that improve a schema's accuracy with continuous use, such as generalizing or constraining the applicability of a schema or determining its default values. Restructuring refers to changes in the structure of a schema or the creation of new schemata to account for new information or to reinterpret old one.

The notion of restructuring has been further elaborated by Vosniadou & Brewer (1987), who distinguish between weak restructuring and radical restructuring. Weak restructuring has been described in terms of changes in the relational structure of a schema or in terms of the creation of abstract relational schemata that did not exist before (Chi, Feltovich, & Glaser, 1981; Chi, Glaser, & Rees, 1982).

The radical restructuring view assumes that knowledge is represented in theory-like structures as opposed to schema structures (Carey, 1985; Murphy & Medin, 1985), and describes radical restructuring as involving a change in theory. In this view the novice does not have an impoverished schema as compared to the expert, but a different theory, different in terms of its structure, its individual concepts, and the domain of phenomena it explains. Some researchers who hold this position point to correspondences between theory changes in the history of science and changes in individuals' theories as they acquire knowledge in a domain (Kuhn, 1977).

 Theories

Most researchers who use the term theory to define knowledge structures do not refer to an explicit and complete scientific account, but rather a commonsense explanatory structure that provides some coherence to a group of concepts about certain phenomena. A theory structure is different from a schema in that it provides a causal explanatory framework within which the phenomena it describes can be understood. Schemata are not explanatory structures, although they may contain implicit theories of entailment between the events that comprise them.

The idea that knowledge structures can be described as theories has its origins in two relatively independent sources. On the one hand it is an attempt by researchers involved in traditional concept acquisition research to account for how individual concepts are organized in more complex categories, since it has been shown that notions such as similarity cannot explain individuals' categorization judgments (e.g., Rips, 1989) or provide a satisfactory account of conceptual coherence (Murphy & Medin, 1985; Medin & Wattenmaker, 1987).

The other source is the work of cognitive developmental psychologists who try to characterize aspects of the developing thought of the child and need to account for phenomena such as children ability to transcend the purely phenomenal (e.g., Keil, 1994; Wellman & Gelman, 1992), their ability to form hypotheses which are resistant to counterevidence, and the appearance of cores of explanatory beliefs that appear early on in life and seem to constrain later learning (e.g., Vosniadou, 1994).

Within a theory framework, learning can be conceptualized in terms of theory enrichment or theory restructuring, as was already discussed earlier. One important question concerns the acquisition of theory-like structures. How do explanatory systems emerge in the first place? Traditionally cognitive developmental theorists have assumed that children start by forming unprincipled conceptual clusters through induction on the basis of phenomenal similarity (e.g., Inhelder & Piaget, 1964; Bruner, Oliver, & Greenfield, 1966; Vygotsky, 1986). The problem with such empiricist approaches lies in providing a satisfactory account of how systems of explanatory beliefs that are "abstract" and principled emerge out of conceptual clusters that are bound by the laws of association and are based on phenomenal similarity alone.

One solution to this problem is to assume that the knowledge base consists of theory-like explanatory structures from the beginning on. This proposal has been expressed in a number of forms. Some cognitive developmental psychologists argue that infants are equipped with biologically predetermined constraints or principles that guide the developmental process (e.g., Spelke, 1991). Others think of biologically based predispositions to construct intuitive theories which then become differentiated and restructured (Carey, 1985; Vosniadou, 1994).

Mental Models

Mental models are analog representations that preserve the structure of that what they represent. As such, they are generative and dynamic, in the sense that they can be used as the basis for constructing explanations of phenomena that were not explicit in the knowledge base. The construct of the mental model has been used in two different ways. Some researchers think of mental models as a form of knowledge structure, a proposal about how knowledge is organized and stored in memory (e.g., Gentner & Stevens, 1983). Other researchers treat mental models as transient representations which are constructed on the spot to deal with particular situations (e.g., Johnson-Laird, 1983; Holland et al, 1989; Vosniadou, 1994; Vosniadou & Brewer, 1992, 1994). According to this view a mental model is a representation constructed on the spot to deal with the implicit demands and expectations that flow from unique situations.

Despite their transient nature, mental models can provide important information about the underlying conceptual structures that constrain them. Vosniadou & Brewer (1992; 1994; see also Morik & Vosniadou, this book) have shown that elementary school students answer questions about the shape of the earth and the day/night cycle that are consistent with a small number of relatively well defined "generic" mental models. A close examination of these "generic" mental models reveals important regularities in the underlying knowledge base. For example, elementary school students' mental models of the earth appear to be constrained by the presuppositions that space is organized in terms of the vertical direction with respect to a flat ground and that unsupported objects fall "downward".

From the point of view of a theory of learning, mental models are important because they are the point where new information is integrated in the knowledge system and therefore represent a major source of cognitive change in existing knowledge structures. Mental models can change in different ways as a result of learning. One kind of change involves changes in the mental model itself and not in the underlying structures that constrain it. Some learning phenomena, such as the creation of misconceptions and contradictions can be explained as attempts to incorporate incoming information into an existing mental model with little or no change in the underlying presuppositions that constrain it (Vosniadou, 1994). More radical changes in mental models require changes in underlying knowledge structures. For example, the creation of a mental model of a spherical earth surrounded by space with people living all around it on the outside, requires that children revise their understanding of gravity from the notion that unsupported objects fall "down", to the notion that unsupported objects fall toward the center of the spherical earth (Vosniadou & Brewer, 1992).

Summary

To conclude, there are a number of proposals that cognitive psychologists have made about knowledge organization and representation and their changes as a result of learning. Some of these proposals are "syntactic" as they are primarily concerned with the organization of conceptual structures, whereas others are more "semantic" in the sense that they attempt to describe the explanations, beliefs, presuppositions, and theories that lie behind concepts. The two approaches are not necessarily contradictory to each other but a great deal more work is required to show how these two levels of description are related and combine them in a unified framework.

An additional issue concerns the notion of transient mental representations. I have argued that there may be a distinct advantage in making a distinction between a flexible, transient representation and more permanent knowledge structures in long term memory. The notion of a mental model constructed on the spot to deal with the demands of unique situations avoids the inflexibility of schemata, can explain how people use relevant prior knowledge to deal with new situations and in general can provide an account of how situational variables affect problem solving behavior (an issue which will be discussed in the section on situativity theory). Last but not least, the notion of mental model may also be found capable of reconciling neurologically inspired associationist accounts regarding knowledge organization (again, an issue which will be discussed in the next section) with the idea that people are capable of constructing explanations of phenomena, if we can find a way to have explanations generated out of an associanistic knowledge base in the form of analog mental models that interpret perceived structure.

Challenging Cognitivism

Cognitive psychology and its dominant paradigm, the information processing paradigm, have their origins in the metaphor of the mind as a computer. The computer has served as the most powerful model for thinking about thinking in the context of cognitive psychology. Computers have played such an important role in the development of cognitive psychology because they legitimized the return to mentalism and provided a solution to the problem of dualism.

Behaviorism's denial of the mind was the most radical reaction to the problem of finding an objective and scientific way to study mental phenomena. By the end of the 1950's it was becoming obvious that behaviorism needed to be replaced with more complex and dynamic theories that did not avoid to deal with mentalistic evidence. The notion that the relationship between mind and body can be conceptualized as analogous to the relationship between a program and a computer removed a great deal of mystery from mental phenomena and made their study legitimate.

From the beginning, the relationship between cognitive psychology and computers has been rather intimate. The results of empirical research in cognitive psychology have been used as the basis on which cognitive scientists have built computational models of human performance, while the computers models that cognitive scientists have proposed have shaped the way many cognitive psychologists think about mental phenomena, including learning.

While the computer metaphor has been extremely fruitful in generating hypotheses about how the human mind operates, a great deal of the evolution of cognitive psychology can be described as the correction of erroneous analogical mappings between these two kinds of systems. Examples of such erroneous analogical mappings of the hypothesis that the mind is a sequential information processor and the emphasis on syntactic rather than on semantic or pragmatic approaches to cognition. Other consequences of using the computer as a model for the mind has been the neglect of affective and motivational factors in human performance, the emphasis on individual, internal representations and processes at the expense of the surrounding environment, the lack of concern for the characteristics of biological systems and the neurobiology of the brain, and the belief that there is a unitary theory of learning. Some of these issues are discussed in this section.

Is a Unitary Theory of Learning Possible?

A basic tenet of the information processing paradigm is that there is a unitary cognitive system that underlies all higher level processing. The notion that there is a unitary cognitive system does not mean to deny the possibility that there may exist special purpose systems for processing information. The claim is that all such possible sub-systems can be explained by a common set of principles that underlie all human cognition and apply equally well to diverse domains such as language, mathematics, music, or visual learning (Anderson, 1983; Newell & Simon, 1972). According to Anderson (1983) "the unitary theory found an important metaphor in the modern general-purpose computer and, perhaps more significantly, in symbolic programming languages, which showed how a single set of principles could span a broad range of computational tasks. It also became clear that the set of computational functions was unlimited, meaning that general processing principles were essential to span broad ranges of tasks. It made no sense to create a special system for each conceivable function." (p. 2).

A challenge to the unitary theory has recently emerged in the what is known as the domain-specificity approach to cognition. Chomsky (1988) has articulated one of the best known accounts of the domain-specificity view. According to this account, the mind consists of separate systems (the visual system, the language system, the number system), each of which has its own unique principles that determine its function. These principles cannot be attributed to the operation of a general learning mechanism. The dominant metaphor employed by the domain-specificity view is, obviously, not the computer metaphor, but the metaphor between cognitive faculties and physical organs. Cognitive faculties such as the number system or the language system can be thought of as "mental organs", likened to physical organs such as the heart and the liver, each one of which functions in its own unique way.

A variant of domain-specificity is the modularity view (Fodor, 1983) which focuses on the specificity of cognitive architecture. According to Fodor, the mind consists of modules (e.g., modules for color perception, recognition of faces, of voices, analysis of shape, and others), which encode and represent information about different aspects of the world in distinct formats.

The domain-specificity and modularity view poses an interesting challenge to cognitive psychology and has already made cognitive psychologists more cautious about making generalizations regarding learning processes that happen across what may seem to be different domains. Nevertheless there are serious theoretical problems that remain to be solved that center around the question of how one defines a domain. Are domains to be thought of as the product of innately guided learning mechanisms with specific patterns of behavior associated with them as a result of the biological evolution of the members of our species? Or, are domains to be specified in terms of certain environmental constraints that define their relationship to the external world? What are the origins and what is the nature of the subject-matter domains in which the sciences have evolved? How can one account for the development of expert knowledge in artificial skill domains such as chess, or knowledge about dinosaurs that cannot be explained in terms of biological constraints?

Learning Without Rules

Triggered by the desire to represent subcognitive processes that are not based on rules (Hofstadter, 1985) connectionist models of human cognition have emerged within the last few years. Connectionist models describe mental processes in terms of activation patterns defined over nodes in a highly interconnected network (Hinton and Anderson, 1981, PDP group, 1986). The nodes themselves are elementary units that do not directly map onto meaningful concepts. Information is conveyed not by particular individual units but by the statistical properties of patterns of activity over collection of units. An individual unit typically will play a role in the representation of multiple pieces of knowledge. The representation of knowledge is thus parallel and distributed over multiple units.

In a connectionist model the role of a unit in mental processing is defined by the strength of its connections to other units. In this sense, "the knowledge is in the connections" as connectionist theorist like to put it, rather than in static and monolithic representations of concepts. Learning viewed within this framework consists of the revision of connection strengths between units. Connectionist systems thus differ from production systems in that they do not learn rules, although they can learn the equivalent of rules. They can do this by establishing new stable patterns of activation over sets of units through revision procedures. What we have in such systems is not explicit rule generation but an implicit generation of new "rules" as the outcome of revising the strengths of a large set of existing connections. The proponents of connectionism believe that this is a much better situation since the rule-like quality of human behavior is an illusion (see Anderson & Hinton, 1981 and Hinton & Anderson, 1981).

For some cognitive psychologists there is no contradiction between rule-based systems and connectionist systems. According to Anderson (1983), for example, production systems and connectionist systems model cognitive activity at different levels of description. "Just as both higher level and lower level computer languages exist (a program in a high level language is compiled in machine code but the fact that the machine code executes the program does not mean that it is not derived from the high level language) so do both cognitive rules and neurons" (p. 35)

Other researchers believe that it is unlikely that the human cognitive system operates without using rules. Holland et al. (1989) think that connectionist systems cannot account for the way humans form sequences because they cannot generate higher order elements that may be crucial in planning and sequential problem solving. In the production system they describe, the capacity to generate new rules creates the possibility that new elements representing higher order features can be added to a system by inductive mechanisms.

It appears likely that models of human cognition will ultimately have to incorporate aspects of both the PDP and the classical "serial-symbolic" models. Lower-level perceptual processes can be accounted for adequately in terms of PDP models but higher level conceptual or linguistic processes will be modelled using a more complex, multilevel representational account. We are already seeing the first attempts to provide such combined systems.

Learning Without Symbols

A basic assumption of cognitive psychology is that the mind is a system that constructs and manipulates symbols in various cognitive processes. This assumption is being challenged by a collection of views that are usually referred to as situativity theory. The basic tenet of this theoretical approach is that behavior, including learning and cognition should be investigated as interactions between social agents and the physical environment in which they live.

In its most radical expression, situativity theory claims that humans and their interactions with the world cannot be understood using symbol system models and methodology, but only by observing them within real world contexts or building nonsymbolic models of them. In its less extreme form, the differences between cognitive psychology and situativity theory concern mostly the role of mental representations and symbols. According to this view, symbols and representations are an important aspect of the situations that people interact with but constitute only some of the phenomena that a theory of cognitive activity should explain and not the central phenomena (Greeno, 1993).

In my opinion, situativity theory deserves praise for bringing to the attention of cognitive psychologists that fact that cognition takes place not only in the head but in the interactions amongst people in a social and physical environment. It is true that in its reaction to behaviorism, cognitive psychology focused too much on individual cognition, paying attention to internal mental processing and ignoring what was outside the head. The bringing back of the physical and social environment into the study of cognition is an important development in the direction of the scientific study of learning and cognition.

However, bringing the social environment into the study of cognition does not mean that we should now exclude from our investigations the study of internal processes or that we should forget the accomplishments of cognitive psychology. As Gardner (1985) argues, one of the most significant accomplishments of cognitive psychology has been the clear demonstration of the validity of positing a level of mental representation. "The triumph of cognitivism has been to place talk of representation on essentially equal footing with these entrenched modes of discourse - with the neuronal level, one the one hand, and with the socio-cultural level, on the other. Whoever wishes to banish the representational level from scientific discourse would be compelled to explain language, problem solving, classification and the like strictly in terms of neurological and cultural analysis. The discoveries of the last thirty years make such an alternative most unpalatable" (p. 283).

Finally, radical situativity theory approaches seem to ignore the fact that a great deal of human interaction with the environment is interaction with human-made symbolic systems. As humans we are not only capable of forming internal representations of our experiences; we can manipulate and change these representations and by doing so change culture itself. According to Vygotsky (1981), the very essence of human behavior and memory lies in the fact that "human beings actively remember with the help of signs. It may be said that the basic characteristic of human behavior in general is that humans personally influence their relations with the environment and through that environment personally change their behavior, subjugating it to their control" (p. 51).

In the way our culture has evolved, learning requires the acquisition and use of complex systems of symbolic expressions used in different symbolic media. Learning to use oral and written language, acquiring the number system, learning arithmetic, algebra and calculus, learning to use computers and to program, understanding graphs, tables, and formalisms in science all require the ability to manipulate, connect and understand the meaning and interrelationships of different kinds of man-made external representations which are central for participation in cultural activity (Glaser, Ferguson & Vosniadou, in press). One of the important areas where cognitive psychology will undeniably need to make progress in the future is in our understanding of how individuals master external symbolic systems and the relationships that exist between external representational systems and internal, qualitative and informal representations

Conclusions

Cognitive psychology has made significant advances in our understanding of cognitive performance and in the ways symbolic representations and processes change as a result of learning. The question of how information is organized in the knowledge base and how knowledge organization and representation change as a result of learning continue to be major questions that need to be answered in the future. It is very possible that we will see models of human cognition that combine aspects of PDP architecture to model lower level perceptual processes with more classical rule-based systems to model higher level functioning. The issue of how the situational and cultural context influences cognitive activity has long been ignored and it is time that more attention is paid to how such factors influence learning. Recent trends seem to point to the development of interactive models of human cognition where individuals interact with a social and physical environment which they change as they are influenced and changed themselves. Last but not least, a cognitive theory of learning must also take into consideration motivational and affective factors. More specifically, what seems to be needed is an account of how motivational beliefs about the self influence learning as well as how the cultural, social and institutional characteristics of a learning environment influence students' motivation and cognition. A number of proposals have started to appear about how it is possible to move in this direction (see Ames, 1992; Deci & Ryan, 1985; Pintrich, 1994).

References

Ames, C. (1992). Classrooms: Goals, structures, and student motivation. *Journal of Educational Psychology, 84,* 261-271.

Anderson, J.R. (1983). *The architecture of cognition.* Harvard: Harvard University Press.

Anderson, J.R., & Thompson, R. (1989). Use of analogy in a production system architecture. In S. Vosniadou & A. Ortony (Eds.), *Similarity and Analogical Reasoning.* New York: Cambridge University Press.

Anderson, J.A. , & Hinton, G.E. (1981). Models of information processing in the brain. In G.E. Hinton & J.A. Anderson (Eds.), *Parallel models of associative memory.* Hillsdale, N.J.: Erlbaum.

Bruner, J.S., Oliver, R.R., & Greenfield, P.M. (1966). *Studies in cognitive growth.* New York: John Wiley.

Carey, S. (1985). *Conceptual change in childhood.* Cambridge, MA: MIT Press.

Chase, W.G., & Simon, H.A. (1973) Perception in chess. *Cognitive Psychology, 4,* 55-81.

Chi, M.T.H., Feltovitch, P.J., & Glaser, R (1981). Categorisation and representation of physics problems by experts and novices. *Cognitive Science, 5,* 121-152.

Chi, M.T.H., Glaser, R. , & Rees, E. (1983). Expertise in problem solving. In R.J. Sternberg (Ed.), *Advances in the psychology of human intelligence, Vol. 2.* Hillsdale, N.J.: Lawrence Erlbaum Associates Inc.

Chi, M.T.H., Slottta, J. D., & de Leeuw, N. (1994) From things to processes: A theory of conceptual change for learning science concepts. *Learning and Instruction, 4.*

Chomsky, N. (1988). *Language and the problems of knowledge.* Cambridge, MA: MIT Press.

Deci, E.L., & Ryan, R. (1985). *Intrinsic motivation and self-determination in human behavior.* New York: Plenum Press.

De Groot, A.D. (1965). *Thought and choice in chess.* The Hague: Mouton.

Fodor, J (1983). *Modularity of mind.* Cambridge, MA: MIT Press.

Inhelder, B., & Piaget, J. (1964). *The early growth of logic in the child.* New York: Norton.

Gardner, H. (1985). *The mind's new science.* New York: Basic Books.

Gentner, D., & Stevens, A.L. (Eds.) (1983). *Mental Models.* Lawrence Erlbaum Associates Inc., Hillsdale, NJ.

Glaser, R. (1995). Application and theory: Learning theory and the design of learning environments. Invited talk, *International Congress of Applied Psychology,* Madrid, Spain.

Glaser, R. , Ferguson, E., & Vosniadou, S. (in press). Cognition and the design of environments for learning: Approaches in this book. In S. Vosniadou, E. De Corte, R. Glaser, &H. Mandl (eds.). *International perspectives on the construction of technology-supported learning environments.* Hillsdale, N.J.: Erlbaum.

Greeno, J.G. , & Moore, J.L. (1993). Situativity and Symbols: Response to Vera and Simon. *Cognitive Science 17,* 49-59.

Hinton, G.E., & Anderson, J.A. (1981). Parallel models of associative memory. In L.A. Hirschfeld & S. Gelman. (1994), *Toward a topography of the mind.* Hillsdale, N.J.: Lawrence Erlbaum Associates Inc.

Hirschfeld, L.A. & Gelman, S. (Eds.). *Mapping the mind: Domain specificity in cognition and culture.* New York, N.Y.: Cambridge University Press.

Hofstader, D.R. (1985). *Metamagical themas.* New York: Basic Books

Holland, J.H., Holyoak, K.J., Nisbett, R.E., & Thagard, P. (1989). *Induction. Processes in inference, learning and discovery.* Cambridge, Mass: M.I.T. Press

Johnson-Laird, P.N. (1983). *Mental models.* Cambridge: Caimbridge University Press.

Karmiloff-Smith, A., & Inhelder, B. (1975). If you want to get ahead, get a theory. *Cognition, 3,* 195-211.

Keil, F. C. (1989). *Concepts, kinds, and cognitive development.* Cambridge, MA: MIT Press.

Keil, F. C. (1995). The birth and nurturance of concepts by domains. The origins of concepts of living things. In L. A. Hirschfeld & S. Gelman (Eds.), *Mapping the mind: Domain specificity in cognition and culture.* New York: Cambridge University Press.

Kuhn, T.S. (1977). *The essential tension.* Chicago: University of Chicago Press.

Larkin, J.H. (1983). The role of problem representation in physics. In D. Gentner & A.L. Stevens (Eds.), *Mental models.* Hillsdale, N.J. : Lawrence Erlbaum Associates Inc.

Mandler, G. (l985). *Cognitive psychology.* Hillsdale, N.J.: Erlbaum

Marr, D. (1982). *Vision: A computational investigation into the human representation and processing of visual information.* San Francisco: W.H. Freeman.

Mayer, R. E. (1992). *Thinking, problem-solving, cognition.* New York: Freeman & Co.

Medin, D.L & Wattenmaker, W.D. (1987). Category cohesiveness, theories, and cognitive archaelogy. In U. Neisser (Ed.), *Concepts and conceptual developemnt: Ecological and intellectual factors in categorization.* New York: Cambridge University Press.

Murphy, G.L., & Medin, D. L. (1985) . The role of theories in conceptual coherence. *Psychological Review, 92,* 289-316.

Neisser, U. (1976). *Cognition and reality: Principles and implications of cognitive psychology.* New York: Freeman.

Newell, A., & Simon, H.A. (1972). *Human problem solving.* Englewood Cliffs, N.J..: Prentice Hall.

Pintrich, P. R. (1994). Motivational beliefs and coceptual change. Paper presented at the *Symposium on Conceptual Change,* Jena, Germany.

Rips, L. J. (1989). Similarity, typicallity and categorization. In S. Vosniadou & A. Ortony (Eds.), *Similarity and analogical reasoning.* New York: Cambridge University Press.

Rumelhart, D.E., & Ortony, A. (1977). The representation of knowlede in memory. In R.C. Anderson, R.J. Spiro, & W. E. Montague (Eds.), *Schooling and the acquisition of knowledge.* Hillsdale, N.J: Erlbaum.

Rumelhart, D.E., & Norman, D.A. (1977). Accretion, tuning and restructuring: Three modes of learning. In J.W. Cotton & R.L. Klatzky (Eds.), *Semantic factors in cognition.* Hillsdale, NJ.: Erlbaum.

Schank, R.C. & Abslson, R.P. (1977). *Scripts, plans, goals, and understanding.* Hillsdale, NJ: Erlbaum.

Spelke, E.S. (1991). Physical knowledge in infancy: Reflections on Piaget's theory. In S. Carey & R. Gelman (Eds.), *Epigenesis of mind: Studies in biology and cognition.* Hillsdale, NJ: Erlbaum.

Thagard, P. (1992). *Conceptual revolutions.* Princeton: Princeton University Press.

Vosniadou, S. (1994) Capturing and modeling the process of conceptual change. *Learning and Instruction, 4,* 45-69.

Vosniadou, S., & Brewer, W.F (1987). Theores of knowledge restructuring with development. *Review of Educational Research, 57,* 51-67.

Vosniadou, S. (1989). Analogy as a mechanism in knowledge acquisition. In S. Vosniadou & A. Ortony (Eds.), *Similarity and analogical reasoning.* New York: Cambridge University Press.

Vosniadou, S., & Brewer, W.F. (1992). Mental models of the earth: A study of conceptual change in childhood. *Cognitive Psychology, 24,* 535-585.

Vosniadou, S., & Brewer, W.F. (1994). Mental models of the day/night cycle. *Cognitive Science, 18,* 123-183.

Vosniadou, S., & Ortony, A. (1989). *Similarity and analogical reasoning.* New York: Cambridge University Press.

Vygotsky, L.S. (1934/1986). *Thought and language.* Cambride, MA: MIT Press.

Vygotsky, L.S. (1978). *Mind in society.* Cambridge, MA: Harvard University Press.

Vygotsky, L.S. (1981). The genesis of higher mental functions. In J.V. Wertsch (Ed.), The concept of activity in Soviet psychology. Armonk, NY: Sharpe.

Vygotsky, L.S. (1986). *Thought and language.* [A. Kozulin, Trans.] Cambridge, MA: The MIT Press.

Wellman, H. M., & Gelman, S. A. (1992). Cognitive development. Foundational theories of core domains. *Annual Review of Psychology, 43,* 337-375.

Learning to Do and Learning to Understand:
A Lesson and a Challenge for Cognitive Modeling

Stellan Ohlsson

Different types of knowledge are acquired through different learning processes. In the past fifteen years, research on the acquisition of practical knowledge (competence, expertise, skill) has culminated in powerful and sophisticated theories. Those theories are possible because they are based on an explicit model of performance. The latter consists of a task analysis, a generic conception of performance, a knowledge representation and a mechanistic control structure. Research on the acquisition of other types of knowledge, particularly abstract declarative knowledge, is not as far advanced. It is suggested that epistemic activities (arguing, describing, explaining, predicting, etc.) are more relevant for such higher-order learning than goal-oriented action and that discourse is the primary medium in which those activities are carried out. There are as yet few analyses of discourse tasks, only vague or obviously insufficient ideas about how people perform them and almost no well-documented empirical phenomena. These difficulties have to be overcome before we can model higher-order learning.

On Routes and Maps

Imagine yourself arriving late at night in an unfamiliar city. Checking into your downtown hotel after a bus ride through darkness, you have no knowledge of the spatial layout of the neighborhood. The following morning, you ask for directions to a nearby bookstore. The concierge responds with a route, i. e., a set of directions: "Turn left outside the front door and walk through the first intersection; at the next traffic light, turn left again just on the other side of the big yellow brick building ..." etc.

The route enables you to reach the desired destination, but it might tell you little about the spatial relation between your hotel and the bookstore. Back in the hotel lobby, you might not be able to point in the direction of the bookstore and your only way to help someone else to find it might be to repeat the route. If the route has many twists and turns, you will probably not be able to draw an accurate map of the area between the hotel and the bookstore.

Instead of drawing your own map, you could buy one. Once you have located your hotel and the bookstore on the map you know the exact spatial relation between them, but it remains to figure out how to get to the store. This involves choosing streets (remember that you cannot walk on freeways), translating relations on the map into directions in reality (if you are facing east, points north are to your left, correct?) and identifying landmarks (the large yellow brick building is neither large nor yellow on the map, but it might be marked "Post Office"). The spatial relation between the hotel and the bookstore does not in and of itself determine the appropriate route.

Routes and maps illustrate two qualitatively different types of knowledge. On the one hand, there is knowledge of how to perform tasks, produce desirable effects or reach goals and destinations. This type of knowledge is variously called competence, expertise, "knowing how" and skill; I will also use the term *practical knowledge*. The term "procedural knowledge" is sometimes used (Ohlsson, 1994b). However, it carries the unfortunate implication of referring to knowledge about explicit procedures, specifically, as opposed to knowledge that underlies action in general. The term "practical knowledge" is thematically congruent with the standard usage of such terms as "practical" (as in referring to a convenient way of accomplishing something), "practical reasoning" and "practice" (as in a professional practice).The individual unit of practical knowledge is a disposition to act in a particular way when pursuing a given goal under certain circumstances, e. g., the disposition to push the relevant button when you want the elevator to come.

On the other hand, there is knowledge of the structure of relations that inhere in a particular situation or state of affairs. This type of knowledge is called *declarative knowledge* or "knowing that" (Ohlsson, 1994b). Concrete *facts*, e. g., the type of knowledge items communicated in news reports, are declarative in nature. However, in this chapter I focus on concepts, ideas and principles. Both scientific theories and spontaneous belief systems provide examples of such *abstract knowledge*[1]. In this way of slicing the knowledge pie, concrete and abstract knowledge are two kinds of declarative knowledge. Table 1 gives an overview of the proposed usage of these terms.

A competent adult possesses vast amounts of both practical and declarative knowledge. For a personal estimate of how much, put your favorite cookbook on the floor and place your automobile instruction book on top of it; continue with manuals and handbooks for every apparatus, device or software system that you know how to use and every skill you have mastered (archery? knitting?). To represent the declarative side of your knowledge, extend the stack with a medium-sized encyclopedia, abstracts of any novel, play and movie that you remember, plus one of those book length summaries of contemporary events that major newspapers issue at the end of each decade. Top it off with the manuscript for your autobiography and the family album to represent your autobiographical knowledge. The content of that stack roughly approximates the content of your knowledge store.

How was it all acquired?

There is no reason to believe that there is a single answer to this question. The existence of two distinct types of knowledge suggests that there are at least two types of learning processes (Ohlsson, 1990). The processes involved in the acquisition of practical knowledge are studied in the field of *skill acquisition*. The processes involved in the acquisition of facts have been studied extensively in the fields of memory and text comprehension, but research on the learning of abstract declarative knowledge has not yet coalesced into a field of its own. For lack of a better term, I call it *higher-order learning*[2].

---

1. The term "conceptual knowledge" has been suggested (Alexander, Schallert & Hare, 1991) but it suggests that the intended referent is knowledge of concepts, specifically. However, higher-order knowledge has many other types of components than concepts, such as ideas, principles, schemas, theories, etc.

2. The term "conceptual change" is frequently used, particularly in the developmental literature. However, it inappropriately suggests that the changes referred to are changes in concepts, specifically, rather than changes in abstract knowledge generally. The term "belief revision" is popular in social psychology but it has the unfortunate feature of presupposing that abstract knowledge consists solely of beliefs.

Table 1: A preliminary taxonomy of knowledge.

A. Practical knowledge
1. Sensori-motor skills
e. g., driving a car, throwing a ball
2. Cognitive skills
e. g., chess, computer programming
B. Declarative knowledge
1. Concrete facts
e. g., "Stockholm is the capital of Sweden"
2. Abstract knowledge
a. Principles
e. g., Newton's' laws of motion
b. Ideas
e. g., the idea of a gravitational field

Skill acquisition and higher-order learning contrast with each other on many dimensions; Table 2 summarizes some of them. The outcome of skill acquisition is competence. The criterion of competence is effective goal attainment. The outcome of higher-order learning, on the other hand, is understanding. A preliminary definition of understanding is isomorphism with the actual structure of its object; maps, including mental maps, have to be accurate to be useful. The starting point for skill acquisition is the set of general methods (analogical reasoning, heuristic search, hill climbing, means-ends analysis), while the starting point for higher-order learning is the stock of abstract concepts, ideas and principles acquired in previous learning. Extended practice causes a skill to become automatized and to fade from consciousness. In higher-order learning, change proceeds in the opposite direction: Reflection causes increased awareness of the content and structure of the relevant domain. The medium for skill practice is action while the medium for reflection is discourse.

Skill acquisition is a highly successful branch of the cognitive sciences that has continued to accumulate empirical results and theoretical insights over a century. As a result, we now have cognitive models of skill acquisition that are both theoretically powerful and empirically grounded. In contrast, the modeling of higher-order learning is still in its infancy.

Powerful models of skill acquisition became possible in the 1970s because researchers had by that time acquired a powerful and precise model of the processes and structures involved in performing skill tasks. In *Human Problem Solving*, Allen Newell and Herbert Simon explained why models of learning had to await models of performance:

> "Learning is a second-order effect. That is, it transforms a system capable of certain performances into a system of additional ones ... . The study of learning, if carried out with theoretical precision, must start with a model of a performing organism, so that one can represent, as learning, the

changes in the model. ... If performance is not well understood, it is somewhat premature to study learning."(Newell & Simon, 1972, pp. 7-8)

Table 2: Some contrasts between two types of learning

Dimension	Skill Acquisition	Higher-order Learning
Outcome	Competence	Understanding
Success criterion	Effective goal attainment	Isomorphism with the world
Starting point	General methods	Prior understanding
Direction of change	Knowledge becomes increasingly	Knowledge becomes increasingly
	- automatic - tacit - simple - domain specific	- conscious - explicit - elaborate - abstract
Process	Practice	Reflection
Medium	Action	Discourse

The point can be stated more generally: A system can only change in a limited number of ways, so the study of change must begin with a description of the system that is changing. After articulating this point *vis-a-vis* skill acquisition, I discuss its implications for the modeling of higher-order learning.

Learning to Do

The problem of explaining the gradual improvement in performance over the course of skill practice was posed for the first time as a fundamental scientific problem by Edward L. Thorndike in the 1890s (Clifford, 1984).[1] Since then, research on skill acquisition has focused on the effects of practice, typically studied in the following type of situation: Present a novice with an unfamiliar task, give him or her repeated opportunities to perform the task, measure performance on the successive attempts (trials) and describe the change in performance from trial to trial. Today, this seems like the obvious way to study how competence is acquired, but this is due to a century of tradition.

Practice remained the focus of attention throughout the behaviorist era, but progress was mainly empirical. In 1979, researchers at Carnegie-Mellon University reformulated the problem of skill acquisition within a cognitive framework (Anzai & Simon, 1979; Anderson, Kline & Beasley, 1979). The result was an unprecedented flowering of theory. More hypotheses about the cognitive mechanisms involved in the acquisition of competence have been proposed in the past fifteen years than in the preceding century (Anderson, 1981; Bolc, 1987; Chipman & Meyrowitz, 1993; Holland, Holyoak, Nisbett & Thagard, 1986; Klahr, Langley & Neches, 1987;

---

1. Significantly, William James, who was Thorndike's thesis supervisor, did not include a chapter on learning in his Principles of Psychology. Material that we today would consider relevant to learning was distributed over the chapters on habit, memory and association (James, 1890). The Principles appeared five years before Thorndike began his thesis work.

Kodratoff & Michalski, 1990; Laird, Rosenbloom, & Newell, 1986; Schank, 1986; Siegler, 1995; Shrager & Langley, 1990).

Today, skill acquisition research proceeds in a manner that is familiar from the natural sciences: Hypotheses are translated into formal models and the latter are evaluated by how well their consequences account for empirical regularities. Research has not yet converged on a single set of principles that has the same intellectual authority as, for example, Newton's laws of motion, but it proceeds within a framework that makes such convergence possible. That framework is a formal model of agency.

A Model of Agency

Agents are systems - animals, computers, organizations, individuals, robots, space aliens - that perform tasks. The existence of agents is somewhat surprising. One would not predict their existence from the principles of physics and chemistry. Agency is an emergent property. The cognitive sciences differ from the natural sciences precisely in that they concern themselves with agents as opposed to causal systems.

How do agents perform tasks? What mechanisms and processes make a system into an agent? The model of agency that underlies modern skill acquisition research is built on four interlocking conceptual advances: (a) a structural analysis of task environments, (b) a generic conception of the process of performing complex tasks, (c) a formal hypothesis about the representation of practical knowledge and (d) a mechanistic model of how such knowledge is applied.

Structure of environment. Complex tasks are typically solved via a *sequence* of actions, where each action requires a decision among *multiple* options. To play chess is to make a sequence of choices as to which piece to move next and how; to diagnose a patient is to make a sequence of decisions as to which diagnostic question to ask next or which test to run; to navigate a car through an urban traffic environment is to make a sequence of decisions with respect to direction and speed; and so on. At each point along the way, many different actions are possible, only some of which are appropriate in the sense that they are on the path to the desired end state or goal. Each action leads to a new situation which, in turn, presents the agent with yet another set of options. A task environment that is characterized by sequentiality and multiplicity can be described as a tree structure with situations as nodes and options as branches; I refer to such descriptions as *situation trees.*[1]

Nature of performance. If a task is a tree of decision points, then performance is *repeated decision making*. More precisely, to perform a task is to traverse the corresponding situation tree from the root node (the initial state) to one of the leaf nodes (a goal state). The traversal process has a cyclic, iterative structure: Perceive the current situation, select an action and perform it; keep doing this until the goal has been reached.

Representation of knowledge. If task performance is repeated decision making, then competence consists in knowing which decisions to make. For example, after having navigated a particular urban traffic environment for many years, a driver knows which turns to make to get where he or she wants to go. In contrast, a newcomer constantly makes wrong turns and has to backtrack

---

1. A situation tree is obviously very similar to a problem space (Newell & Simon, 1972). However, a problem space is a hypothesis about how a task is represented in the mind, while a situation tree is a tool for describing the environment.

and try alternative routes. Practical knowledge is knowledge about how to choose among the options available in each successive situation.

What is the unit of practical knowledge? At a minimum, a decision has to consider what the agent is trying to accomplish, the features of the current situation (as perceived by the agent) and the agent's capabilities. This suggests that competence consists of associations between goals, situations and actions. Such three-way associations can be formalized in *rules*[1] of the general form

$$\text{Goal, Situation} ===> \text{Action,}$$

where the Goal is a description of some desired state of affairs, the Situation is a conjunction of features that describes a type of situation, and the Action specifies a possible response to the Situation. Such a rule encodes the disposition to do the Action when confronted by the Situation during the pursuit of the Goal. For example, experienced drivers have a disposition to look in the rear view mirror (Action) before they change lanes (Goal) while driving on a highway (Situation).

Control structure. The rule is the elementary unit of practical knowledge, a single atom of competence. To perform even a moderately complicated task the agent's mind must be stocked with a large number of rules, many of them relevant for the same Goal or the same Situation. Indeed, some rules might share both Goal and Situation but recommend different Actions. The question then arises how a repertoire of rules produces effective, organized action.

To complete the description of the agent, we need to specify a control structure[2] that carries out the three functions of identifying, selecting and execution rules. The available options are identified by retrieving (activating) rules that match the current situation and the current goal. A decision is made by selecting a rule for execution. Once a rule has been selected, it remains to execute it.[3] Because cognitive models seldom include an interesting analysis of motor action, execution is usually taken as unproblematic.

The characterization of the agent as a decision maker and the control structure are not two separate constructs. The control structure specifies how decisions are made. Its cycle of operation - activate, select, execute - is a theoretical interpretation of the perceive-decide-act cycle of observable behavior.

Discussion. The four ideas reviewed above - task environments are situation trees, performance is repeated decision making, competence is encoded in rules and the core of the cognitive system is the control structure that applies those rules - are the basic components of what is commonly known as the *rule-based model* of agency. According to this model, agents traverse task environments by mapping goals and situations onto appropriate actions. The four ideas are

---

1. For historical reasons, rules of this form were called "production rules" when they were introduced into the cognitive literature (Newell & Simon, 1972). However, the historical origin has become increasingly irrelevant to current research and the shorter form "rule" is now generally adopted.

2. The terms "production system architecture" (Newell, 1990) and "cognitive architecture" (Anderson, 1983) have been proposed. I find the term "control structure" more descriptive, even though its engineering flavor is somewhat alien in a psychological context.

3. Strictly speaking, the phrase "executing a rule" is inaccurate. It is the action recommended by the rule that is executed. However, the phrase "executing a rule" has become accepted shorthand for the longer phrase.

tightly interwoven: Once tasks have been conceptualized as trees of decision points, performance is naturally conceptualized as decision making; competence is then naturally represented in decision rules; and so on.

The rule-based model of agency is complete in the technical sense that specifies a type of system that, once implemented, can perform skill tasks. This is a key feature for cognitive modeling, because models have to produce behavior, otherwise they cannot be empirically validated. Another important feature is generality. A rule-based model can be constructed for any task that is characterized mainly by sequentiality and multiplicity.

The rule-based model does not in and of itself address the question of change. It is dynamic in the sense that it models the process of performing a task, but it models performance as a steady state process. To model *adaptive* agents, a rule-based system must be augmented with change mechanisms. The structure of rule-based systems both constrains and inspires hypotheses about how they might change over time. To clarify this requires an example.

Learning from Errors

To illustrate how the rule-based model influences the analysis of learning, consider the problem of learning from error. Novices make many errors, while experts make only few. Hence, skill acquisition is, at least in part, the elimination of errors. How can agents unlearn their own errors?

Mechanisms for the detection and correction of errors must consider how errors arise. Given the hypothesis that practical knowledge is encoded in Goal-Situation-Action rules, there are only a handful of possibilities. The most obvious source of error is an overly general rule. If the Situation part of a rule is underspecified, the rule will become active in many situations, possibly including situations in which its Action is not appropriate, correct or useful. Because the control structure considers all active rules during decision making, an incorrectly activated rule has some probability of displacing the correct rule and an error results (in some proportion of situations).

If overly general rules cause errors, then errors can be corrected by specializing those rules. Adding conditions to the Situation description restricts a rule so that it becomes active in a smaller set of situations. If that smaller set only includes situations in which the Action is appropriate, correct or useful, then the error has been eliminated. Surprisingly, this analysis pictures skill acquisition as proceeding *from* the general *to* the specific (Anderson, 1987; Langley, 1985). Both common sense and systematic analyses tend to assume that learning proceeds in the opposite direction, from the specific to the general.

How does the learner constrain the overly general rule? For an error to be corrected, it must be attributed to some particular cause or circumstance. For example, a person who discovers that he or she is not driving on the right road has to have some idea about where he or she took a wrong turn in order to correct the error. The error is successfully corrected when the learner has identified the circumstances that constitute counterindications to the particular action he or she did take, and added (the opposite of) those circumstances to the Situation component of the faulty rule.

For example, consider a novice driver who ventures onto a two-lane highway. He or she might have a disposition to turn into the left-hand lane when he or she approaches a slower vehicle. This rule is overly general, because there are many situations in which it is dangerous to switch lanes, e. g., when a faster car is coming up from behind. Recklessly turning into the left lane, the novice is likely to hear loud honkings or screeching tires, feedback that marks the action as an error. To unlearn this error, the novice needs to constrain the overly general rule, "when approaching a slower vehicle, switch to the left lane" to the more constrained rule, "when approaching a slower vehicle *and the left lane is empty*, switch to the left lane". The goal of verifying that the left lane is indeed empty leads, via means-ends analysis, to the action of looking in the rear view mirror and the error is eliminated.

In summary, the structure of a rule-based agent suggests three hypotheses about learning from error: (a) Inappropriate or incorrect actions are caused by overly general rules. (b) Errors are corrected by specializing the overly general rules. (c) The particular specialization chosen is a function of the learner's perception of why the action was inappropriate or incorrect.

This analysis of learning from error has been implemented in a computer model called HS (Ohlsson, 1992b, 1993a, 1994a; Ohlsson, Ernst & Rees, 1992; Ohlsson & Rees, 1991a, 1991b, 1992). The performance component of the model is a standard rule-based system. At the outset of learning, HS is supplied with an initial set of rules that encodes some general method that is applicable (but not effective) to the relevant task, e. g., heuristic search.

In addition, the HS model has a task-specific, declarative knowledge base. The unit of declarative knowledge is a constraint. When overly general rules generate problem states that violate one or more constraints, the model interprets this as negative feedback and tries to revise the responsible rule. It identifies the cause of its error by regressing the violated constraint through the rule; the result is a new condition that is added to the faulty rule. As a result, the rule will no longer be evoked in situations in which those conditions hold and the error is eliminated.

The HS model has been applied to two different number tasks (Ohlsson, 1992b; Ohlsson & Rees, 1991a, 1991b, 1992; Ohlsson, Ernst & Rees, 1992) and to one task in college chemistry (Ohlsson, 1993a). In each domain, the model was given a general method and a set of constraints and it acquired a correct, domain-specific skill by solving practice problems, detecting its own errors and correcting them.

Empirical validation of a model like HS consists of investigating how well it accounts for empirical regularities. The regularity that has occupied researchers most during recent years is the learning curve (Lane, 1987; Newell & Rosenbloom, 1981). If the effort to complete a task is plotted as a function of training trials, the result is a more or less smoothly decreasing, negatively accelerated curve. If such a curve is plotted with logarithmic transformations on both axes, the curve typically appears as a straight line, indicating that it belongs to a particular class of mathematical curves known as power laws (see Figure 1). There is no logical or *a priori* reason why the gradual improvement from trial to trial should follow this type of curve rather than some other type of curve; hence, this fact is something that needs to be explained.

The hypothesis embedded in the HS model, in conjunction with the plausible hypothesis that learners react to positive feedback by increasing the strength of a particular rule, predicts a power law learning curve. Figure 1 shows an example of a simulation run with a computer model that learns both by eliminating wrong actions and by strengthening correct actions. The points plotted are averaged over 20 simulated subjects learning a task that requires 20 steps and that presents 10 options in each step. Further details of how the simulation experiment was conducted are available in Ohlsson and Jewett (1994, 1995). It is quite interesting that a set of hypotheses that were invented to explain learning from error also explains the shape of the learning curve.

For present purposes, the main point is that the analysis of learning from error that is embedded in HS is a direct outgrowth of the underlying performance model. Given the hypothesis that the agent is a rule-based system, there are only a few possible sources for errors and hence only a limited number of possible methods for detecting and correcting them. The structure of the agent both suggests and constrains the space of change mechanisms that can reasonably be considered. This turns out to be true not only of the HS model, but of the field in general.

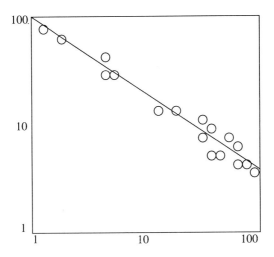

Figure 1: Learning curve for a simulation model that combines error correction with strengthening, plotted in log-log space.

A Broader View

In the past fifteen years, the space of change mechanisms suggested by the rule-based model of agency has been rather thoroughly explored. We can identify four separate classes of hypotheses, corresponding to the different principled ways in which a repertoire of rules can change. Table 3 provides an overview.

First, a set of rules can change by *the addition and deletion of entire rules*. Where do rules come from initially? Three answers suggest themselves:

a) Proceduralization: Declarative knowledge structures, including both task instructions (Anderson, 1983; Hayes-Roth, Klahr & Mostow, 1981) and general background knowledge (Ohlsson, 1987b), are translated into rules.

b) Analogical inference: Rules learned in some other context are used as templates for new rules (Anderson, 1993; Carbonell, 1983; Holland et al., 1986).

c) Procedure induction: Rules are constructed from direct perception of a model or an example problem solution (VanLehn, 1990). The deletion of rules is also a logical possibility, but I know of no cognitive model in which such a process plays a major role.

Table 3: Types of changes in rule-based systems.

Type	Examples
1. Creation of new rules	Proceduralization (Anderson)
	Analogical inference (Carbonell)
	Procedure induction (VanLehn)
2. Modifications of individual rules	Rule generalization (Anderson)
	Rule discrimination (Langley)
	Genetic algorithms (Holland)
3. Optimization of rule sets	Rule composition (Lewis)
	Redundancy elimination (Neches)
	Serial-to-parallel conversion (Schneider)
4. Adjustment of relative priority	Strengthening
	Weakening

Second, a repertoire of rules can change via *modifications of single rules*. In how many different ways can a Goal-Situation-Action rule be modified? The structure of such rules naturally suggests three possible change mechanisms:

d) Rule generalization: The Goal and Situation parts of rules can be generalized by deleting individual features or by replacing them with variables (Anderson, 1983; Ohlsson, 1983, 1987a).

e) Rule discrimination: The Goal and Situation parts of rules can be specialized by adding features or by replacing variables with particular properties (Langley, 1987; Ohlsson, 1983, 1987a).

f) Action replacement: A rule can be revised by replacing its Action part (Anderson, 1983, pp. 247-248; Anderson, Kline & Beasley, 1978, p. 87; Holland et al., 1986, p. 88).

Many important rule modifying mechanisms produce changes that are unrelated to the feedback the system receives from the environment. The changes are justified *a posteriori*, as it were, by the subsequent performance of the system. A variety of such mechanisms have been proposed:

g) Random mutations: New rules are created by making arbitrary changes in existing rules (Siegler, 1984, 1995; Lenat, 1983). Schank (1986) has introduced the useful term "tweaking" for this process.

h) Genetic algorithms: The changes mimic the changes that occur in chromosomes during the formation of new gametes (DeJong, 1990; Holland, 1975, 1986).

Third, a rule set can be changed by *optimizing* it:

i) Rule composition: Two or more rules can be replaced by a single rule that has the same effect (Anderson, 1983; Lewis, 1987). More complex versions of this mechanism have been proposed under the labels chunking (Laird, Rosenbloom & Newell, 1986; Rosenbloom, 1986) and explanation-based learning (DeJong & Mooney, 1986; Minton, 1988; Mitchell, Keller & Kedar-Caballi, 1986; VanLehn & Jones, 1993).

j) Redundancy elimination: A rule set can be optimized by eliminating unnecessary steps (Neches, 1987) and by finding short cuts between intermediate results (Ohlsson, 1987b).

k) Serial-to-parallel conversion: A rule set can be replaced by a network that carries out the same computation, but in parallel (Schneider, 1984).

Finally, a repertoire of rules can be altered by *changing the priority relations among the rules*:

l) Strengthening: A rule's strength (or some other quantitative property used to rank order rules) is increased, possibly but not necessarily as a consequence of positive feedback.

m) Weakening: A rule's strength is decreased as a consequence of either decay or negative feedback. The so-called bucket brigade algorithm combines strengthening and weakening into a single priority adjustment process (Holland, 1986).

A more thorough review than can be attempted here would address many issues, including the empirical grounding of the individual mechanisms, the effects of interactions between multiple mechanisms and the completeness of the set of mechanisms explored to date. For present purposes, the feature of interest is the close relation between the space of proposed mechanisms and the underlying model of agency: How else could a rule-based system change except by adding (and deleting) rules, revising rules, optimizing sets of rules and changing the priority relations among rules? Once performance is conceptualized as a sequence of decisions, each decision involving the activation, selection and execution of rules, the space of relevant change mechanisms is implicitly specified as well.

Lesson Learned

The flowering of skill acquisition theory in the past fifteen years demonstrates the utility of the research strategy that Allen Newell and Herbert Simon outlined in the early 1970s: First model the agent; then model learning as a change in the agent. The rule-based model of agency was the key that opened the door to more powerful theories of the acquisition of competence.

Abstracting from the particulars of rule-based systems, a model of agency consists of four components: (a) a structural analysis of the relevant type of task; (b) a generic conception of what it means to solve a task of that type; (c) a formal hypothesis about how the relevant knowledge is represented in memory; and (d) a description of the control structure that retrieves and applies such knowledge.

To state the lesson in its most general form: A given system can only change in a small number of ways, so the study of change must begin by describing the system that changes. Hence, our understanding of learning cannot progress faster than our understanding of performance. When we shift our attention from competence to understanding, this lesson turns into a challenge.

Learning to Understand

A significant proportion of human knowledge has little to do with performing this or that task (Ohlsson, 1990). History is a good source of examples. The why's and the wherefore's of the French Revolution have minimal impact on any task that I perform as I go though my day and it is not easy to think of some skill that would be more or less difficult to learn depending on how much I know about, say, ancient Greece. Similar comments could be made with respect to astronomy, paleontology, sociology and many other fields. Working scientists possess the research skills that constitute expertise in these fields, but the results of their investigations are primarily descriptions of the world, its origin, history and current status. The value of those descriptions for the nonprofessional does not reside in what they enable him or her to do, but in the insights and intellectual pleasures they bring.

Much of what is known in descriptive domains consists of *facts*, i. e., assertions about particular objects or events. The number of planets, the depth of the ocean, the age of a particular fossil, the income distribution of a population of a certain country, the course of events in such and such a battle - such snippets exemplify facts. The learning of facts has been studied intensively in the fields of memory and text comprehension and the relevant mental laws can be found in any textbook on cognitive psychology: Attention, clarity of exposition, motivation, prior knowledge and repeated exposure are the main determinants of fact acquisition. However, collections of facts do not in and of themselves constitute understanding.

Facts contrast with abstract knowledge, i. e., concepts, ideas and principles that do not refer to particular objects or events but to universal features of reality. The law of gravitation is the most celebrated example of an abstract principle, closely followed in fame by the great conservation laws of physics (Feynman, 1965). These and other laws of nature do not describe any particular event. For example, the law of gravitation does not specify when and where some particular object is going to fall. Rather, it specifies the general shape of its fall, if it does fall. Similarly, the principle of natural selection does not describe the evolution of any particular species. Instead, it captures the pattern that underlies evolutionary change in general. Finally, consider the theory of the co-valent bond, one of the cornerstones of chemistry. The basic principles of this theory - e. g., that each covalent bond requires two valence electrons - are not statements about any particular substance, but about the composition of matter in general.

There is a close link between such abstract knowledge and understanding. Astronomers understand why the planets move the way they do in the sense that they know how to derive those orbits from the theory of gravitation. Chemists understand chemical reactions because they have a general theory that explains why particular reactions happen the way they do. Evolutionary biologists can be said to have understood the evolution of a particular species to the extent that they are able to fit the history of that species into the theory of natural selection; and so on. Abstract knowledge is the basis for understanding.

Unlike the case for facts and skills, there is no long-standing tradition of inquiry with respect to the acquisition of abstract knowledge. Such *higher-order learning* is the next frontier in learning research. Those who explore this frontier with the help of cognitive models need to keep the history of skill acquisition research in mind. The first lesson to be drawn from that history is that the study of learning begins with the identification of some relevant task or situation. A task is relevant if it engages the type of knowledge the researcher wants to study.

In the case of skill acquisition, this step is straightforward because there is an intrinsic connection between skill and action: To be skilled *is* to act in certain ways. For example, a skilled chess player is, by definition, someone who plays chess well. Successful performance proves the existence of practical knowledge and (consistent) failure proves its absence. In the case of abstract knowledge, these relations do not hold.

The Dissociation Between Understanding and Action

What are the tasks that exercise the understanding? When - in which situations - do people act on their knowledge of some abstract concept, idea or principle? In which types of observable behavior is such knowledge expressed? The answer to this deceptively simple question turns out to be far from obvious.

Success does not imply understanding. Almost any task can be performed well without understanding. As teachers of mathematics and physics have discovered to their horror, some students who perform well on examinations do not understand the concepts and principles (e. g., place value, the law of inertia) that the examination was supposed to assess. Those students do well because they have learned a strategy for solving examination problems, bypassing the concepts and principles that supposedly underpin that strategy.

Laboratory studies confirm this dissociation between understanding and action. For example, Krist, Fieberg and Wilkening (1993) asked both children and adults to push a ball so that it would land in a given target area and to estimate the speed required to hit the target. Although subjects at all age levels performed well on the action task, they nevertheless displayed misconceptions about mechanical motion in the judgment task. Successful task performance is not necessarily, or even frequently, a consequence of understanding.

This state of affairs is pedagogically problematic but not surprising, because competence in the absence of understanding is commonplace. We rarely understand clearly and explicitly why a familiar sequence of actions produces a desired effect. For example, static electricity can be removed from articles of clothing with a squirt of hair spray; few practitioners of this procedure can give a coherent explanation of why it works. This case is typical. In particular, we frequently use machines, from refrigerators to copiers, that we do not understand. Instead of insisting on a principled understanding of how the device works we usually settle for the procedure for using it, like school children who dispense with the principles of place value and settle for the algorithms.

The hair spray and arithmetic examples are trivial in themselves, but they illustrate a principled feature of human existence. If successful task performance were impossible without correct understanding, human culture could not have gotten started. If early hunters had had to understand transformations between kinetic and static energy before they could bend a bow, food production might never have risen to a level that enables a significant proportion of the population to spend their time thinking about such abstractions. Similarly, early farmers could not, in principle, have derived agricultural practices from a deep understanding of plant growth, because the botanic science required for such understanding is dependent upon a society with the economic surplus that agriculture makes possible.

In fact, all the technologies that brought the human race out of subsistence - metal working, leather preparation, the manufacture of cloth and glass, navigation, waterwheels and windmills, sailing boats, bread baking, brick making - had to be invented and developed in the absence of deep understanding, because such understanding has only become available since the scientific revolution, three centuries or so ago. Perhaps the most striking example of all is the boomerang. Obviously, the Australian aborigines who invented and successfully used this device did not understand how it works any more than latter day office workers understand computers and laser printers. Successful action in the absence of understanding is the normal case.

The converse is true as well.

Failure does not imply lack of understanding. Unsuccessful or inappropriate action is not necessarily a sign of faulty understanding. For example, I have an educated layman's understanding of Einstein's theory of relativity. The four-dimensional universe in which light has a fixed speed and clocks consequently behave in strange ways has figured in so many contexts, fictional and otherwise, that it has become familiar. However, my understanding does not impart any ability to carry out even the simplest task in relativity theory. Understanding the concept of relativity does not by itself engender competence in manipulating tensors and the other mathematical tools of the relativity theorist.

Other instances of understanding without competence are easy to identify. For example, my understanding of the principle of Mercator's projection does not tell me how to go about making a map. Knowledge of the operating principle of a device does not necessarily bring with it competence in its use: Knowing that the needle of a compass aligns itself with the Earth's magnetic field is not the same as knowing how to navigate. The same is true of athletic skills: Even after a ski instructor has explained why distributing the weight over the skis in such and such a way has such and such an effect on a turn, there remains to execute the maneuver correctly while careening down a steep hillside. The large number of skiers on crutches is evidence for the gap between understanding and action.

Systematic studies provide many demonstrations of the dissociation between understanding and action in symbolic domains. As a mirror image to the standard finding of correct calculations in the absence of understanding, Resnick and Omanson (1987) reported a study in which school children who had a good understanding of place value nevertheless made errors on calculation problems. Gelman and Meck (1983, 1986) and Gelman, Meck and Merkin (1986) studied young children who could not count large collections of objects and found that those children could distinguish between correct and incorrect counting performances by others (e. g., a doll), indicating that they did understand what constitutes correct counting.

The reason why understanding does not guarantee successful performance is obvious: The implications of abstract knowledge are opaque and complicated to derive. Consider the principle that the volume of a gas is inversely proportional to its pressure. This principle implies, among other conclusions, that Scuba divers had better not hold their breath while ascending, lest their lungs rupture. Needless to say, one does not train divers by teaching them the general gas law and leaving them to figure out this consequence on their own.

Returning once more to arithmetic, I once derived the standard algorithm for subtraction with regrouping from the principles of place value. This turned out to require approximately 50 pages of mathematics (Ohlsson, 1988). Obviously, school children cannot be expected to go through some mental analog of that derivation on their own, even implicitly. In general, a failure to figure out the implications for action of a given body of abstract knowledge might be due to the complexity of the derivation rather than to deficiencies in the knowledge.

Summary. The upshot of these observations is that *successful performance is neither a sufficient criterion for, nor a necessary consequence of, understanding.* On the one hand, it is possible to perform any task without understanding, by learning and doing the right actions. On the other hand, it is possible to fail while in the possession of the relevant knowledge, by failing to derive its implications. This analysis applies to any task that is solved by performing a sequence of actions.

The root of the problem is that understanding is a state of mind, not a process. There is no intrinsic connection between that state and any particular action. The consequences for the study of understanding are severe. The lack of a reliable, observable indicator of the very thing we want to study threatens to end research on higher-order learning before it begins. Researchers need to turn their attention away from goal-directed behavior; the question is where to focus instead.

Epistemic Activities

While most cognitive researchers have concentrated on goal-directed action, a small but persistent minority has insisted that *human beings employ their understanding, not in action, but in the generation of symbols* (Cassirer, 1957/1923; Gardner, 1994/1973; Goodman, 1978; Bruner, 1986). Abstract concepts, ideas and principles find their primary expression in cultural products, not in goal attainment. In particular, there is a deep connection between abstract knowledge and discourse.

The study of higher-order learning might therefore begin by asking what people do when they produce discourse. What are the canonical tasks that people carry out when they talk and write? Inspired by the work of Allan Collins (Collins & Ferguson, 1993) and David Perkins (1994) on what they call epistemic games, I suggest the following list of *epistemic tasks*:

a) *Describing*. To describe is to fashion a discourse referring to an object or an event such that a person who partakes of that discourse acquires an accurate conception of that object or event. News reports and court testimonies are familiar examples. Narratives are descriptions, but perhaps of a special kind (Bruner, 1986).

b) *Explaining*. In the canonical explanation task, the explainer is faced with an event of some sort (e. g., the sinking of the Titanic, the demise of the dinosaurs) and fashions a discourse such that a person who partakes of that discourse understands why that event happened. In science, the target of an explanatory effort is often a regularity (e. g., the orbits of the planets, rainfall) instead of a single event.

c) *Predicting*. To make a prediction is to fashion a discourse such that a person who partakes of that discourse becomes convinced that such and such an event will happen (under such and such circumstances). Predicting the weather, the outcomes of card games and the ups and downs of the stock market are three celebrated prediction problems (Casti, 1990).

d) *Arguing*. To argue is to state reasons for (or against) a particular position on some issue, thereby increasing (or decreasing) the recipient's confidence that the position is right. There are two subclasses of arguments: Arguments about what to believe and arguments about what to do.[1] Committee meetings provide many examples of arguments, to the delight of the cognitive scientist but the despair of the chairperson.

e) *Critiquing* (evaluating). To critique a cultural product is to fashion a discourse such that a person who partakes of that discourse becomes aware of the good and bad points of that product. Book reviews are familiar examples, but any cultural product can be the target of criticism, including descriptions, explanations, predictions and arguments - even critiques.

f) *Explicating*. To explicate a concept is to fashion a discourse such that the person who partakes of that discourse acquires a clearer understanding of its meaning. Parents and teachers spend a fair amount of time explicating concepts and so do philosophers, albeit for different reasons.

g) *Defining*. To define a term is to propose a usage for it. When the term already exists in the language, the boundary between defining and explicating is blurred.

This tentative taxonomy of epistemically relevant activities is short but surprisingly complete. What else do we ever do when we talk or write, over and above describe, explain, predict,

---

1. This Aristotelian distinction parallels, not accidentally, the distinction between declarative and practical knowledge.

argue, explicate and define? Although there are many other types of speech acts (e. g., to promise, request and threaten) no *epistemically relevant* extension of the taxonomy comes to mind. This should raise our hopes that the universe of epistemic activities is bounded and hence analyzable.

Is it possible to solve epistemic tasks without understanding? Perhaps argument patterns can be practiced until they become so automatic that one can find arguments for or against any position without effort. The sophistic philosophers of ancient Greece were criticized precisely because they nurtured and taught content-free argumentation skills (Billig, 1989). However, in general, intuition rebels against the idea of mindless description, explanation, prediction, argumentation, explication and definition. The understanding seems to be peculiarly exercised and engaged when we perform these tasks. The dissociation between understanding and observable behavior might still be there in principle, but it is certainly narrower than in goal-directed action. I therefore tentatively define the study of higher-order learning as the study of how people learn to perform epistemic tasks.

Towards Models of Epistemic Activities

If the first lesson from the history of skill acquisition research is that the study of learning begins with the identification of relevant tasks, the second lesson is that hypotheses about learning presuppose a model of how those tasks are performed. To construct such a model is to answer four questions: (a) What is the structure of the relevant task? (b) What, in generic terms, are people doing when they perform that task? (c) How is the relevant knowledge represented in memory? (d) What kind of control structure applies such knowledge?

We are far from having answers to these questions for any epistemic task. The stock of relevant ideas is limited to two main contenders, the deductive model and the schema model. Neither is satisfactory. They nevertheless illustrate the general thesis that conceptions of performance determines conceptions of change.

The deductive model. According to this model, the basic step in any cognitive process is an inference. To think is to deduce. This view has some face validity with respect to argument, but it has been applied to other epistemic tasks as well. For example, Hempel and Oppenheimer (1948) claimed that to explain is to prove that the target event had to happen, given the laws of nature and the facts of the case. Predictions differ from explanations only in that they are deduced before the target event happens. This conception has dominated four decades of philosophical investigation (Salmon, 1989).

The deductive model implicitly assumes that knowledge is represented in propositions. Intuitively, a proposition is what is expressed in an assertive sentence. For some reason, philosophers frequently use *the cat is on the mat* as an example. In formal logic, propositions are represented by predicate-argument constructions, e. g.,

$$On(cat, mat).$$

Psychologists prefer to talk about beliefs rather than propositions. Technically, a belief is a proposition plus a so-called propositional attitude (e. g., accepts, believes, doubts, rejects). For example, the formula

$$Doubt[\ Paul, On(cat, mat)\ ]$$

represents Paul's suspicion that the cat escaped while the philosophers were looking the other way.

If knowledge consists of beliefs (or propositions), then what are the relevant learning processes? The basic answer is that a set of beliefs can change in two ways, through the addition and deletion of beliefs from the set. The simultaneous deletion of an existing belief and the addition of a new one is usually referred to as *belief revision*. The terms "add" and "delete" should not be taken too literally in this context. The intended effect can be achieved by changing the attitude, e. g., from "doubts" to "accepts." (The cat was there after all.)

At least three branches of the cognitive sciences have attempted to explain higher-order learning in terms of belief revision. The first was the so-called cognitive consistency school, a branch of cognitive social psychology that flourished in the fifties and sixties (Abelson et al., 1968). More recently, science educators have conceptualized students' prior knowledge as systems of mistaken beliefs, so-called misconceptions, and the process of learning as the rejection of prior beliefs and the adoption of new, scientifically more accurate beliefs (Confrey, 1990; Perkins & Simmons, 1988; Posner, Strike, Hewson, & Gertzog, 1982; Strike, & Posner, 1985). In a more technical mode, research in so-called non-monotonic logic aims to develop a formal calculus for belief revision (Gördenfors, 1988; Paiva, Self & Hartley, 1994). A key problem in this field is how to keep a large belief system consistent through a sequence of additions and deletions.

Propositional theories of human cognition have been targets of tough criticism in the past two decades. Johnson-Laird (1993) and Johnson-Laird and Byrne (1991) argue strongly that human reasoning is better understood in terms of operations on mental models instead of propositions; Strike and Poser (1992) report second thoughts on science learning as belief revision; alternatives to Hempel and Oppenheimer's philosophical theory of explanation have appeared (Pitt, 1988; Rubin, 1993). The claim that people *never* reason deductively is probably overstated; see Ohlsson and Robin (1994), Smith, Langston and Nisbett (1992) and Rips (1994) for some contrary evidence. Nevertheless, the bulk of the evidence indicates that deduction is not people's most common or preferred mode of operation and propositions are not the only vehicles for representing knowledge. If so, then the study of higher-order learning needs to move beyond belief revision.

The schema model. The concept of a schema has proved useful in the analysis of a variety of cognitive processes and phenomena (Brewer & Nakamura, 1984; Rumelhart, 1980). The basic intuition is that a schema represents a larger chunk of knowledge than a single proposition. To do their work, schemas have to be abstract in some sense (Ohlsson, 1993b). Finally, because schemas are patterns, they presumably have internal structure.

According to the schema model, to think is to align patterns; more precisely, to assimilate a concrete, perceptual pattern representing a problem or situation to a more general pattern stored in memory. The elementary cognitive processes are to retrieve and to instantiate schemas. For example, to explain an event is to subsume it under an explanation pattern, a schema that defines a type of explanation (Schank, 1986; Schank, Kass & Riesbeck, 1994).

The schema model does suggest change processes that go beyond belief revision. How by what process - does a learner acquire an explanation pattern? Consider the Darwinian schema for explaining biological adaptation. It is summarized in Table 4: To explain why species G has trait P, identify some relevant dimension of the phenotype of the ancestor species, postulate inheritable variation in that dimension, identify factors in the ancestor's ecological niche that made some variants more fit than others, infer that those variants reproduced more frequently, and, finally, claim that gradual changes in the relevant trait accumulated over the course of many generations. Particular Darwinian explanations are constructed by articulating this pattern (Ohlsson, 1992a).

How does a person come to possess this explanation schema? What are the learning mechanisms that are responsible for its construction? To answer this question we need to know where the learner starts. What is the prior knowledge that constitutes the raw material, as it were, for the construction of the Darwinian schema? According to the schema hypothesis, prior knowledge should also consist of schemas; the issue is which ones.

Analysis of a corpus of several hundred written explanations collected by asking young adults to explain such adaptations as the large size of the dinosaurs and the stripes of the tiger revealed eight novice schemas (Ohlsson, 1991; Ohlsson & Bee, 1992, 1993). In an experimental test, we asked young adults to sort explanations that instantiated these eight schemas *vis-a-vis* three different adaptations (the size of the dinosaurs, the stripes of the tiger and the wings of birds) on the basis of similarity (Larreamendy-Joerns & Ohlsson, 1994, 1995). Hierarchical clustering analysis gave qualified support for five of the eight schemas identified in the previous studies, plus one additional schema. The repertoire of novice schemas that best fit the data available so far is shown in Table 5.

If we tentatively accept Table 5 as an approximate description of the learner's prior knowledge, then the question of how the expert schema in Table 4 is acquired translates into the question of what process transforms Table 5 into Table 4. Two observations are particularly relevant: First, the novice schemas are not completely wrong. Some of them, like Crossbreeding, are irrelevant for explaining evolution (but highly relevant in other contexts, e. g., animal breeding) while others, like Static Selection and Mutation, are relevant in the sense that they are parts of the target schema. Second, even the relevant schemas are overly simple. Novice explanations in this domain tend to focus on a single dimension of the problem (intra-species variations or differential fitness or mutations etc.), while the expert schema combines multiple aspects of the problem into a new structure that has more explanatory power than any of its parts.

Table 4: The schema for Darwinian explanations.

Given a species G with trait P, explain how G evolved through the following five steps:

a) Identify or hypothesize the relevant dimension along which
members of the ancestor species varied; call it V.

b) Make the case that V is inherited. In the case of physical characteristics (length, size etc.), this can usually be assumedwithout discussion.

c) Describe the survival advantage of having some value (or range of values) on V over having another value (or range of values)

d) Make the case that the differential survival rate translates intodifferential rate of reproduction.

e) Describe how small changes in V from one generation to the next accumulated into the trait P.

These observations indicate that learning the Darwinian schema is a process of assembling or--to use a Piagetian term--*coordinating* a select subset of prior schemas into a more complex schema. For example, the novice needs to hook his or her selection schema into his or her schema for fitness to get the idea of natural selection; then he or she must hook that conception into his or her schema for the accumulation of many small changes over time; and so on. In this view, learning moves from simpler knowledge structures toward more complex ones, a process that has no obvious counterpart within the deductive model. Although such combination processes have occasionally been proposed, they have received remarkable little attention in recent work on learning.

Schema-based systems are not yet as well understood as rule-based and deductive systems and there are many ambiguities. Some schemas look just like collections of propositions with variables (Hayes, 1979). It is also unclear how small a schema can be and still be a schema. For example, is

$$On(Cat: X, Mat: Y)$$

a schema for situations of the cats-on-mats type, or is it just a proposition? If schemas are nothing but collections of propositions, how does the schema model differ from the deductive model?

Another question is how a schema repertoire generates a problem solution. Although there are particular models of how schemas are activated, selected and instantiated, the space of possible control structures for schema-based systems has never been described at the same level of detail as rule-based architectures (Langley, Ohlsson, Thibadeau & Walter, 1984; Neches, Langley & Klahr, 1987). Finally, schemas can give rise to new schemas, but the ultimate origin of schemas remains unclear. It is often tacitly assumed that they are extracted from repeated encounters with related problems or situations, an idea that is afflicted with all the standard difficulties of empiricist accounts of knowledge. These problems make it difficult to specify the different ways in which schemas can change

Table 5: Novice schemas for explaining biological evolution

1. Intentional Creation
Species are created by a deity.
2. Crossbreeding
New species appear via mating between existing species.
3. Static Selection
Organisms with trait P survived while those with trait Q died; hence P dominates.
4. Mutation
New trait is a result of a sudden change in the genes.
5. Dissemination
Trait P spread gradually throughout the population because organisms with P reproduced and passed on the trait.

Summary

Viewing the acquisition of abstract knowledge through the eyeglasses provided by the history of skill acquisition research provides a particular perspective on the problems that must be confronted before cognitive models of higher-order learning become possible. The first problem is what type of task is relevant for higher-order learning. It is tentatively suggested that epistemic tasks such as explaining and arguing can play the same role in the study of higher-order learning that sequential, multi-option tasks have played in the study of skill acquisition. However, the relevant task analysis is missing. We only dimly intuit what such tasks are about.

A second, closely related problem is that we lack satisfactory models of how epistemic tasks are performed. The deductive model is not psychologically plausible and the schema model is vague. Nevertheless, the close relation between conceptions of performance and conceptions of change that is so salient in skill acquisition research appears in higher-order learning as well.

The deductive model is remarkably poor in suggestions for change mechanisms, offering little beyond the idea that individual knowledge units (beliefs or propositions) can be added and deleted. The schema model has richer implications. In particular, it strongly suggests that learning is the assembly of more complex cognitive structures out of simpler ones. However, the vagueness of the schema construct makes the space of relevant change mechanisms difficult to specify. Radical new hypotheses about how abstract declarative knowledge is encoded and how epistemic tasks are performed are likely to be needed to generate radical new hypotheses about change.

A third problem is that even if we had some new hypotheses, there is no body of phenomena against which to evaluate them. Skill acquisition models can be evaluated against well-documented regularities like the learning curve, but it is as yet unclear what a theory of higher-order learning is supposed to explain. Empirical studies of describing, explaining, predicting, arguing, critiquing, explicating or defining are usually designed to test some particular hypothesis, as opposed to finding out how people perform those tasks, and data are consequently reported in terms of the experimenter's hypothesis instead of the experimental task. The empirical basis for a science of higher-order learning does not yet exist.

One part of the problem is that the most powerful methodology for discovering and expressing regularities is quantification and discourse is more difficult to quantify than action. The most relevant aspect of a discourse is its meaning and nobody has proposed a quantitative description of meaning. Hence, researchers who collect verbal data are faced with the problem of generating objective phenomena out of a fundamentally subjective raw material.

The pragmatic solution is to convert subjects' discourse (essays, interview answers, think-aloud protocols, etc.) into frequency counts with the help of coding schemes. Over time, the obvious subjectivity of this process has been tempered somewhat by the widespread use of inter-coder reliability coefficients. It is not clear what a more principled solution would look like. One possibility is that Artificial Intelligence will come to the rescue. A language understanding program that is powerful enough to handle the fragmented discourse that subjects generate in laboratory studies would provide researchers with a tool for analyzing subjects' discourse. How soon such a tool might become available is difficult to predict.

Final Words

The flowering of skill acquisition theory in the past fifteen years have generated two broad attitudes among researchers who study learning. On the one hand, some have claimed that the successes of particular rule-based models indicate that some version of such a system could conceivably succeed as a theory of the human mind. On the other hand, those who regard the concept of a rule-based system as obviously insufficient have argued that we should abandon it and invent alternative concepts - or borrow them from biology or ethnography or European philosophy - that might afford a fresh start.

Both attitudes are equally misconceived.

On the one hand, the history of the natural sciences does not support the tendency to overstate claims that has so often marred the history of psychology. The trick of making progress in science is to slice reality into natural kinds, i. e., sets of events, phenomena and regularities that are similar in some deep sense, and to formulate small sets of mutually consistent principles to account for them. For example, mechanical motion turned out to be a natural kind for physics.

A theory for a particular natural kind is in and of itself useful and interesting. There is no need to claim that it explains everything; no theory ever does. Bounded applicability is not a weakness and it is certainly not a reason to reject a theory. Nobody would abandon Newton's theory of motion *as a theory of motion* because it does not explain heat and electricity.

Furthermore, science is a cumulative and hierarchical enterprise. Over time, low-level hypotheses and theories that explain narrow ranges of phenomena are integrated into more fundamental theories with broader ranges. Newton's derivation of Kepler's laws and the explanation of the general gas law in terms of molecular interactions are famous examples. Integration into a more fundamental theory should not be confused with rejection; physics students still study both Kepler's laws and the general gas law. Nor should integration be taken as a sign that the low-level theory was unnecessary, either conceptually or historically. Without Kepler, no Newton; without Newton, no Einstein.

The research problem posed by Edward L. Thorndike and studied so intensively in skill acquisition research - improvement in performance as a result of practice - is, I believe, a natural kind for the psychology of learning. It is a simple but fundamental fact and our understanding of learning is obviously incomplete unless we can explain it. Rule-based models do explain it with a conceptual and empirical rigor that compares favorably with explanations in other sciences. Within their intended domain of application, rule-based theories deliver everything that is claimed for them. To abandon the rule-based approach *as an explanation for skill acquisition* because it does not explain every aspect of learning is folly. On the contrary, we should celebrate the fact that at least one aspect of learning is now well understood.

On the other hand, it should be admitted that rule-based skill acquisition theories, like Newton's laws, have a bounded applicability. They explain the acquisition of one kind of knowledge and there is no reason to believe that all knowledge is of a kind. The contrasts listed in Table 1 (see introduction) strongly support the long-standing distinction between two types, variously referred to as theory and practice; science and craft; knowing *that* and knowing *how*; declarative and procedural knowledge; understanding and action; and so on (Ohlsson, 1994b).

If there are distinct types of knowledge, we should expect research to result in multiple low-level theories that explain the acquisition of particular types of knowledge before it reveals more fundamental principles that characterize all learning. To construct a theory of higher-order learning, defined as learning to perform epistemic activities such as explaining and arguing, is a reasonable goal to the extent that such activities constitute a natural kind. To pursue that goal we need not deny the successes of rule-based theories with respect to the rather different problem of explaining skill acquisition.

Acknowledgments

Preparation of this manuscript was supported, in part, by the grant for the National Research Center on Student Learning from the Office of Educational Research and Improvement (OERI), US Ministry of Education, and, in part, by Grant No. N00014-93-I-1013 from the Office of Naval Research (ONR).

References

Abelson, R.P., Aronson, E., McGuire, W.J., Newcomb, T.M., Rosenberg, M.J., & Tannenbaum, P.H., (Eds.) (1968). *Theories of cognitive consistency: A sourcebook.* Chicago, IL: Rand McNally.

Alexander, P.A., Schallert, D.L., & Hare, U.C. (1991). Coming to terms: How researchers in learning and literacy talk about knowledge. *Review of Educational Research, 61*, 315-343.

Anderson, J.R. (Ed.) (1981). *Cognitive skills and their acquisition.* Hillsdale, NJ: Erlbaum.

Anderson, J.R. (1983). *The architecture of cognition.* Cambridge, MA: Harvard University Press.

Anderson, J.R. (1987). Skill acquisition: Compilation of weak-method problem solutions. *Psychological Review, 94*, 192-210.

Anderson, J.R. (1993). *Rules of the mind.* Hillsdale, NJ: Lawrence Erlbaum.

Anderson, J.R., Kline, P., & Beasley, C.M., Jr. (1978). *A theory of the acquisition of cognitive skills* (Tech. Rep. No. 77-1). New Haven, CT: Yale University.

Anderson, J.R., Kline, P.J., & Beasley, C.M., Jr. (1979). A general learning theory and its application to schema abstraction. In G.H. Bower, (Ed.), *The psychology of learning and motivation: Advances in research and theory (Vol. 13).* New York: Academic Press.

Anzai, Y., & Simon, H.A. (1979). The theory of learning by doing. *Psychological Review, 86*, 124-140.

Billig, M. (1989). *Arguing and thinking: A rhetorical approach to social psychology.* Cambridge, UK: Cambridge University Press.

Bolc, L., (Ed.) (1987). *Computational models of learning.* Berlin, Germany: Springer-Verlag.

Brewer, W.F., & Nakamura, G.V. (1984). The nature and functions of schemas. In R. Wyer & T. Srull (Eds.), *Handbook of social cognition.* Hillsdale, NJ: Lawrence Erlbaum.

Bruner, J. (1986). *Actual minds, possible worlds.* Cambridge, MA: Harvard University Press.

Carbonell, J.G. (1983). Learning by analogy: Formulating and generalizaing plans from past experience. In R.S. Michalski, J.G. Carbonell & T.M. Mitchell (Eds.), *Machine learning: An artificial intelligence approach.* Palo Alto: Tioga.

Cassirer, E. (1957/1923). *Substance and function and Einstein's theory of relativity: Both books bound as one.* New York: Dover.

Casti, J.L. (1990). *Searching for certainty: What scientists can know about the future.* New York: William Morrow.

Chipman, S., & Meyrowitz, A., (Eds.), (1993). *Foundations of knowledge acquisition: Cognitive models of complex learning.* Boston, MA: Kluwer.

Clifford, G. J. (1984). *Edward L. Thorndike: The sane positivist.* Middletown, CT: Wesleyan University Press.

Collins, A., & Ferguson, W. (1993). Epistemic forms and epistemic games: Structures and strategies to guide inquiry. *Educational Psychologist, 28(1)*, 25-42.

Confrey, J. (1990). A review of research on student conceptions in mathematics, science, and programming. In C.B. Cazdan (Ed.), *Review of research in education (Vol. 16).* Washington, DC: American Educational Research Association.

DeJong, K. (1990). Genetic-algorithm-based learning. In Y. Kodratoff & R.S. Michalski, (Eds.), *Machine learning: An artificial intelligence approach (Vol. 3).* San Mateo, CA: Kaufmann.

DeJong, G., & Mooney, R. (1986). Explanation-based learning: An alternative view. *Machine Learning, 1*, 145-176.

Feynman, R. (1965). *The character of physical law.* Cambridge, MA: MIT Press.

Gardner, H. (1994/1973). *The arts and human development: A psychological study of the artistic process.* New York: Basic Books.

Gelman, R., & Meck, E. (1983). Preschoolers' counting: Principle before skill. *Cognition, 13,* 343-359.

Gelman, R., & Meck, E. (1986). The notion of principle: The case of counting. In J.H. Hiebert (Ed.), *Conceptual and procedural knowledge: The case of mathematics.* Hillsdale, NJ: Erlbaum.

Gelman, R., Meck, E., & Merkin, S. (1986). Young children's numerical competence. *Cognitive Development, 1,* 1-29.

Goodman, N. (1978). *Ways of worldmaking.* Indianapolis, IN: Hackett.

Gördenfors, P. (1988). *Knowledge in flux.* Cambridge, MA: MIT Press.

Hayes, P.J. (1979). The logic of frames. In D. Metzing (Ed.), *Frame conceptions and text understanding.* Berlin, Germany: Walter de Gruyter.

Hayes-Roth, F., Klahr, P., & Mostow, D. (1981). Advice taking and knowledge refinement: An iterative view of skill acquisition. In J. Anderson (Ed.), *Cognitive skills and their acquisition.* Hillsdale, NJ: Erlbaum.

Hempel, C.G., & Oppenheimer, P. (1948). Studies in the logic of explanation. *Philosophy of Science, 15,* 135-175.

Holland, J.H. (1975). *Adaptation in natural and artificial systems.* Ann Arbor, MI: The University of Michigan Press.

Holland, J.H. (1986). Escaping brittleness: The possibilities of general-purpose learning algorithms applied to parallell rule-based systems. In R.S. Michalski, J.G. Carbonell, & T.M. Mitchell (Eds.), *Machine Learning: An Artificial Intelligence Approach (Vol. 2).* Los Altos: CA: Kaufmann.

Holland, J., Holyoak, K., Nisbett, R., & Thagard, P. (1986). *Induction: The processes of inference, learning, and discovery.* Cambridge, MA: MIT Press.

James, W. (1890). *The principles of psychology (Vols. 1-2).* London: MacMillan.

Johnson-Laird, P.N. (1993). *Human and machine thinking.* Hillsdale, NJ: Erlbaum.

Johnson-Laird, P.N., & Byrne, R.M.J. (1991). *Deduction.* Hove, UK: Erlbaum.

Klahr, D., Langley, P., & Neches, R., (Eds.) (1987). *Production system models of learning and development.* Cambridge, MA: MIT Press.

Kodratoff, Y., & Michalski, R.S. (Eds.) (1990). *Machine learning: An artificial intelligence approach (Vol 3).* San Mateo, CA: Kaufmann.

Krist, H., Fieberg, E., & Wilkening, F. (1993). Intuitive physics in action and judgment: The development of knowledge about projectile motion. *Journal of Experimental Psychology: Learning, Memory, and Cognition, 19,* 952-966.

Laird, J., Rosenbloom, P., & Newell, A. (1986). Chunking in Soar: The anatomy of a general learning mechanism. *Machine Learning, 1,* 11-46.

Lane, N. (1987). *Skill acquisition rates and patterns: Issues and training implications.* New York: Springer-Verlag.

Langley, P. (1985). Learning to search: From weak methods to domain-specific heuristics. *Cognitive Science, 9,* 217-260.

Langley, P. (1987). A general theory of discrimination learning. In Klahr, D., Langley, P., & Neches, R. (Eds.), *Production system models of learning and development.* Cambridge, MA: MIT Press.

Langley, P., Ohlsson, S., Thibadeau, R., & Walter, R. (1984). Cognitive architectures and principles of behavior. In *Proceedings of the Sixth Annual Conference of the Cognitive Science Society.* Boulder, Colorado.

Larreamendy-Joerns, J., & Ohlsson, S. (1994). *The Psychological Reality of Explanation Patterns in Evolutionary Biology* (Technical Report). Pittsburgh, PA: University of Pittsburgh.

Larreamendy-Joerns, J., & Ohlsson, S. (1995). Evidence for explanation patterns in evolutionary biology. In *Proceedings of the Seventeenth Annual Meeting of the Cognitive Science Society.* Pittsburgh, PA: University of Pittsburgh. In press.

Lenat, D. B. (1983). The role of heuristics in learning by discovery: Three case studies. In R.S. Michalski, J.G. Carbonell & T.M. Mitchell, (Eds.), *Machine Learning: An Artificial Intelligence Approach.* Palo Alto, CA: Tioga.

Lewis, C. (1987). Composition of productions. In D. Klahr, P. Langley, & R. Neches (Eds.), *Production system models of learning and development.* Cambridge, MA: MIT Press.

Minton, S. (1988). *Learning search control knowledge: An explanation-based approach.* Boston: Kluwer.

Mitchell, T., Keller, R., & Kedar-Caballi, S. (1986). Explanation-based generalization: A unifying view. *Machine Learning, 1,* 47-80.

Neches, R. (1987). Learning through incremental refinement of procedures. In D. Klahr, P. Langley, & R. Neches (Eds.), *Production system models of learning and development.* Cambridge, MA: MIT Press.

Neches, R., Langley, P., & Klahr, D. (1987). Learning, development, and production systems. In D. Klahr, P. Langley, & R. Neches (Eds.), *Production system models of learning and development.* Cambridge, MA: The MIT Press.

Newell, A. (1990). *Unified theories of cognition.* Cambridge, MA: Havard University Press.

Newell, A., & Rosenbloom, P. (1981). Mechanisms of skill acquisition and the law of practice. In J. Anderson (Ed.), *Cognitive skills and their acquisition.* Hillsdale, NJ: Lawrence Erlbaum.

Newell, A., & Simon, H. (1972). *Human problem solving.* Englewood Cliffs, NJ: Prentice-Hall.

Ohlsson, S. (1983). A constrained mechanism for procedural learning. *Proceedings of the Eighth Joint International Conference on Artificial Intelligence.* Karlsruhe, Germany.

Ohlsson, S. (1987a). Transfer of training in procedural learning: A matter of conjectures and refutations? In L. Bolc (Ed.), *Computational models of learning.* Berlin, Germany: Springer-Verlag.

Ohlsson, S. (1987b). Truth versus appropriateness: Relating declarative to procedural knowledge. In D. Klahr, P. Langley, & R. Neches (Eds.), *Production system models of learning and development.* Cambridge, MA: MIT Press.

Ohlsson, S. (1988). *The conceptual basis of subtraction with regrouping: A mathematical analysis* (Technical Report No. KUL-88-02). Pittsburgh, PA: Learning Research and Development Center, University of Pittsburgh.

Ohlsson, S. (1990). Cognitive science and instruction: Why the revolution is not here (yet). In H. Mandl, E. De Corte, N. Bennett & H.F. Friedrich (Eds.), *Learning and instruction: European research in an international context: Social and cognitive aspects of learning and instruction (Vol. 2.1).* Oxford, UK: Pergamon Press.

Ohlsson, S. (1991). *Young adults' understanding of evolutionary explanations: Preliminary observations* (Technical Report). Pittsburgh, PA: University of Pittsburgh.

Ohlsson, S. (1992a). The cognitive skill of theory articulation: A neglected aspect of science education. *Science and Education, 1,* 181-192.

Ohlsson, S. (1992b). Artificial instruction: A method for relating learning theory to instructional design. In P. Winne & M. Jones (Eds.), *Foundations and frontiers in instructional computing systems.* New York: Springer-Verlag.

Ohlsson, S. (1993a). The interaction between knowledge and practice in the acquisition of cognitive skills. In S. Chipman &A.L. Meyrowitz (Eds.), *Foundations of knowledge acquisition: Cognitive models of complex learning.* Boston: Kluwer.

Ohlsson, S. (1993b). Abstract schemas. *Educational Psychologist, 28,* 51-66.

Ohlsson, S. (1994a). *Learning from performance errors* (Technical Report, KUL-94-02). Pittsburgh, PA: University of Pittsburgh.

Ohlsson, S. (1994b). Declarative and procedural knowledge. In T. Husen & T.N. Postlethwaite (Eds.), *The International Encyclopedia of Education (Vol. 3).* Oxford, UK: Elsevier Science.

Ohlsson, S., & Bee, N.V. (1992). *The effect of expository text on students' explanations of biological evolution* (Technical Report). Pittsburgh, PA: University of Pittsburgh.

Ohlsson, S., & Bee, N.V. (1993). *Constructing and reading evolutionary explanations improve (some) students' understanding of Darwin's theory.* (Technical Report). Pittsburgh, PA: University of Pittsburgh.

Ohlsson, S., Ernst, A.M., & Rees, E. (1992). The cognitive complexity of doing and learning arithmetic. *Journal of Research in Mathematics Eduation, 23(5),* 441-467.

Ohlsson, S., & Jewett, J.J. (1994). *Abstract models of learning from success and failure* (Technical Report). Pittsburgh, PA: University of Pittsburgh.

Ohlsson, S., & Jewett, J.J. (1995). Abstract computer models: Towards a new method for theorizing about adaptive agents. In N. Lavrac & S. Wrobel (Eds.), *Machine Learning: ECML-95.* Berlin, Germany: Springer-Verlag. In press.

Ohlsson, S., & Rees, E. (1991a). The function of conceptual understanding in the learning of arithmetic procedures. *Cognition and Instruction, 8,* 103-179.

Ohlsson, S., & Rees, E. (1991b). Adaptive search through constraint violation. *Journal of Experimental and Theoretical Artificial Intelligence, 3,* 33-42.

Ohlsson, S., & Rees, E. (1992). A model of knowledge-based skill acquisition. In *Proceedings of Fourteenth Annual Conference of the Cognitive Science Society.* Bloomington, Indiana: Indiana University.

Ohlsson, S., & Robin, N. (1994). The power of negative thinking: The central role of Modus Tollens in human cognition. In A. Ram & K. Eiselt (Eds.), *Proceedings of the Sixteenth Annual Conference of the Cognitive Science Society.* Hillsdale, NJ: Erlbaum.

Paiva, A , Self, I , & Hartley, R (1994) On the dynamics of learner models. In T. Cohen (Ed.), *Proceedings of the European conference on Artificial Intelligence.* London, UK: John Wiley.

Perkins, D.N. (1994). The hidden order of open-ended thinking. In J. Edwards (Ed.), *Thinking: International interdisciplinary perspectives.* Townsville, Australia: Hawker Brownlow Education.

Perkins, D.N., & Simmons, R. (1988). Patterns of misunderstanding: An integrative model for science, math, and programming. *Review of Educational Research, 58(3),* 303-326.

Pitt, J.C., (Ed.) (1988). *Theories of explanation.* New York: Oxford University Press.

Posner, G., Strike, K.A., Hewson, P.W., & Gertzog, W.A. (1982). Accomodation of a scientific conception: Toward a theory of conceptual change. *Science Education, 66(2),* 211-227.

Resnick, L., & Omanson, S. (1987). Learning to understand arithmetic. In R. Glaser (Ed.), *Advances in instructional psychology (Vol. 3).* Hillsdalen, NJ: Lawrence Erlbaum.

Rips, L.J. (1994). *The psychology of proof: Deductive reasoning in human thinking.* Cambridge, MA: MIT Press.

Rosenbloom, P. (1986). The chunking of goal hierarchies. A model of practice and stimulus-response compatibility. In J. Laird, P. Rosenbloom, & A. Newell, *Universal subgoaling and chunking: The automatic generation and learning of goal hierarchies.* Boston: Kluwer.

Rubin, D.-H. (Ed.) (1993). *Explanation.* Oxford, UK: Oxford University Press.

Rumelhart, D.E. (1980). Schemata: The building blocks of cognition. In R.J. Spiro, B.C. Bruce, & W.F. Brewer (Eds.), *Theoretical issues in reading comprehension: Perspectives from cognitive psychology, linguistics, artificial intelligence, and education.* Hillsdale, NJ: Lawrence Erlbaum.

Salmon, W.C. (1989). *Four decades of scientific explanation.* Minneapolis, MN: University of Minnesota Press.

Schank, R.C. (1986). *Explanation patterns: Understanding mechanically and creatively.* Hillsdale, NJ: Lawrence Erlbaum.

Schank, R.C., Kass, A., & Riesbeck, C.K. (1994). *Inside case-based explanation.* Hillsdale, NJ: Lawrence Erlbaum.

Schneider, W. (1984). *Toward a model of attention and the development of automatic processing* (Technical Report HARL-ONR-8402). Champaign, IL: University of Illinois.

Shrager, J., & Langley, P. (Eds.) (1990). *Computational models of scientific discovery and theory formation.* San Mateo, CA: Kaufmann.

Siegler, R.S. (1984). Mechanisms of cognitive growth: Variation and selection. In R.J. Sternberg (Ed.), *Mechanisms of cognitive development.* New York: Freeman.

Siegler, R.S. (1995). *Cognitive development: Beyond the immaculate transition.* New York: Oxford Press.

Smith, E.E., Langston, C., & Nisbett, R. (1992). The case for rules in reasoning. *Cognitive Science, 16,* 1-40.

Strike, K.A., & Posner, G.J. (1985). A conceptual change view of learning and understanding. In L. West and L. Pines (Eds.), *Cognitive structure and conceptual change.* New York: Academic Press.

Strike, K.A., & Posner, G.J. (1992). A revisionist theory of conceptual change. In R.A. Duschl & R.J. Hamilton (Eds.), *Philosophy of science, cognitive psychology, and educational theory and practice.* New York: State University of New York Press.

VanLehn, K. (1990). *Mind bugs: The origins of procedural misconceptions.* Cambridge, MA: MIT Press.

VanLehn, K., & Jones, R. (1993). Learning by explaining examples to oneself: A computational model. In S. Chipman and A. L. Meyrowitz (Eds.), *Foundations of knowledge acquisition: Cognitive models of complex learning.* Boston: Kluwer.

Machine Learning: Case Studies of an Interdisciplinary Approach

Werner Emde

Machine learning is a field in Artificial Intelligence concerned with the development of computational models of learning. This chapter presents an overview of goals and research directions in machine learning related to the issue of understanding more about the striking ability of human beings (as individuals as well as communities) to acquire knowledge from experience. Part one and part two describe research directions rooted in different areas of Computer Science. In the third part, we briefly describe some approaches influenced by research in psychology and philosophy and discuss how this research direction is able to complement the other research directions. The last part of this paper lists some open scientific questions, which reflect the need for further interdisciplinary research.

Introduction

Machine learning (ML) is a subfield of Artificial Intelligence concerned with the development of computational models of learning. The reason for such research is twofold. First, the goal is to develop methods and tools which help to construct intelligent systems, support the maintenance of such systems, and make them more reliable, more effective, and/or efficient. Second, ML is concerned with the development of computational models of learning which are able to explain aspects of learning phenomena observable in non-artificial intelligent systems. Since ML strives to develop techniques that are able to acquire the knowledge necessary in different kinds of intelligent systems (e.g., for natural language understanding systems, expert systems, intelligent robots, and tutoring systems), the field plays a central role in Artificial Intelligence research. For the same reason, ML is closely related to Knowledge Acquisition (Morik et.al., 1993), the subfield of Artificial Intelligence concerned with development of techniques that support the manual construction of knowledge bases. Using and constructing representations of domains, ML is also related to the work on knowledge representation and inference in Artificial Intelligence. As part of Computer Science the research is influenced by mathematics, logics, statistics, and philosophy. With respect to the second goal, ML belongs to Cognitive Science and is related to psychology, philosophy, and the neurosciences.

Although the motivation for building smarter computer systems and understanding more about the learning abilities of natural cognitive systems seems to be quite different, there is a close relation between the two research directions. First, due to the fact that humans possess striking learning abilities many researchers in machine learning are interested in principles of human learning in order to improve existing techniques and develop new ones. Second, in many applications it is necessary that a computer system is able to explain its behavior (e.g., in order to justify its results) and that the system is easily maintainable (e.g., in order to adjust it to changing requirements). This requires that the knowledge items and reasoning schemes used in such a system are comprehensible to humans. Therefore, insights into the structure of human conceptual knowledge and the formation of concepts in humans can help to construct explainable and maintainable intelligent adaptive systems.

The broad range of scientific results of research in ML consists of:

1. philosophical and methodological foundations (e.g., Michalski, 1994; Anderson, 1989),

2. theoretical analysis concerning the learnability of various classes of functions and the convergence of learning procedures (Kearns, 1990),

3. learning algorithms dealing with basic learning tasks,

4. integration of different learning algorithms and integration of learning algorithms and performance systems (see, e.g., Michalski & Tecuci, 1994; Morik et al., 1993),

5. experimental evaluation of learning algorithms and systems and experimental comparison with natural learning systems (see, e.g., Ahn & Medin,1992).

This paper is intended to give an idea of the research paradigm and methodology of machine learning research by describing different research directions and their relationships. First, we will present a rough taxonomy of basic learning mechanisms studied in ML. Then, we will focus on two learning algorithms dealing with different learning tasks that have been developed to support the construction of knowledge based systems. Third, we describe the goal of theoretical approaches to machine learning. In the last part, we briefly describe some approaches influenced by research in psychology and philosophy and discuss how this research direction is able to complement the other research directions.

Taxonomy of Basic Learning Mechanisms

The (common sense) term "learning" is used to denote a broad range of phenomena, ranging from acquiring motorical skills, storing and remembering past experiences efficiently and effectively, discovering regularities and causalities in data, incorporating experience into existing knowledge, becoming more efficient in solving a class of problems, recognizing analogies, to construct/revise scientific theories. All these different incarnations of learning are investigated in ML - at least to some degree - and lead to the development of various kinds of learning algorithms.

Several researchers tried to provide a definition of the term learning that is compatible with our intuition as well as philosophical considerations and, in addition, is useful to structure the field of ML. It turned out that the goal of defining the term learning is as difficult as defining the term intelligence (see, e.g., Dietterich, 1990). In a recent paper Michalski (1994) views learning as "a goal-guided process of improving the learner's knowledge by exploring the learner's experience and prior knowledge". This definition seems to fit with Newell's appealing definition of the term knowledge as "Whatever can be ascribed to an agent, such that its behavior can be computed according to the principle of rationality" (Newell, 1983). However, Michalski considers the transformation of one representation into another (e.g., more efficient) one as a form of learning. Following Newell's view, the knowledge level abstracts away from all issues of implementation, e.g., how the knowledge is represented, and the knowledge of an agent neither changes nor improves when solely the representation of that knowledge is changed (Dietterich, 1990). This means that Michalsk's use of the term knowledge is incompatible with Newell's definition. If we subscribe to Newell's definition improving representations cannot be considered as learning. Taking this one step further, even inductive processes do not realize learning, since the mechanism used to make the inductive leap is part of the agent's knowledge (Anderson, 1989). Thus, an inductive inference makes only explicit what an agent already knows in principle. The only way to acquire new knowledge is to encode representations of experience from the environment. As we acknowledge that changing representations as well as inductive processes are also forms of learning, we have to modify Michalski's definition as follows: Learning is the goal-directed process of a system that improves the knowledge or the knowledge representation of the system by exploring experience and prior knowledge.

This definition, like the one from Michalski, requires that implemented learning algorithms are regarded as part of an overall system, e.g. an implemented performance system learning, which follows some higher level goals and performs actions to achieve these goals. The learning goal is defined by the overall system and can be more or less general. A general learning goal is to increase the knowledge and to improve the representation of that knowledge. Whether or not a change of the knowledge is an improvement (and therefore regarded as 'learning') depends on the task of the overall system.

Note that we use the term knowledge representation in a very general sense covering not only declarative and procedural representations but also physical conditions. The improvement of sensors is also a special kind of learning.

Based on the above characterization of learning we are able to construct a taxonomy of basic learning mechanisms. At the top level we distinguish between mechanisms that improve the knowledge of the system and mechanisms that transform (translate) one representation into another. The improvement of knowledge can be achieved either by incorporation of new knowledge or forgetting. While forgetting is an almost ignored learning mechanism in ML, several researchers explored active and passive methods for acquiring new knowledge from the environment. Active methods deal with the problem of asking informative questions or designing informative experiments (see, e.g., Kulkarni & Simon, 1990). Passive methods deal with the problems whether and how some new information has to be incorporated into the knowledge representation of the system (see, e.g., Murray & Porter, 1989; Emde, 1987).

Most ML approaches deal with reasoning schemes that transform representations of knowledge. We distinguish between truth-preserving and not-truth-preserving transformations. A transformation is called truth-preserving if its result must be true given that the knowledge provided as input is true. Learning by truth-preserving transformations may serve the goal of improving the efficiency of the overall system (speed-up learning) or the comprehensibility of the represented knowledge. Due to the fact that resource restrictions in problem solving may hinder to find a solution with an inefficient representation, improving efficiency can also improve the effectiveness of a system. Techniques to improve the efficiency of a problem solver studied in ML include: explanation-based learning, knowledge compilation, construction of macro-operators, and reinforcement learning (see Shavlik & Dietterich, 1990, chap. 3). The development of techniques to improve the comprehensibility of represented knowledge is a relatively new research topic. Roughly, the idea is to study the inverse of the speed-up learning transformations. For example, techniques to extract logical representations out of artificial neural networks (Towell & Shavlik, 1993) can be regarded as de-compilation and rule base stratification (Sommer, 1994) is the inversion of explanation based learning.

The result of not truth-preserving transformations goes beyond the contents of the input and thus cannot be guaranteed to be correct. Suppose a system has incorporated a large number of descriptions of white swans into its knowledge representation. In addition, the systems knowledge includes an inductive procedure able to find particular regularities in descriptions of objects. The system would exhibit a not truth-preserving transformation of its representation of knowledge if it adds a rule like "If something is a swan, then its color is white" to the knowledge base. The result of such a transformation can improve the effectiveness of the system, e.g., the system becomes able to answer a question about the color of swans, and it can speed up the efficiency of the system, e.g., decrease the time to classify objects as non-swans. Obviously the result of such a transformation can be incorrect (e.g., swans can also be black), although all processed descriptions of objects were correct. We distinguish between the following types of not-truth-preserving transformations: inductive learning of concepts from examples, concept formation, abductive reasoning, learning by analogy, and knowledge revision (Shavlik & Dietterich, 1990, chap. 2, 3, and 5; Wrobel, 1994).

Learning (in the common sense meaning of word) involves usually different kinds of transformations as well as the incorporation of new knowledge from the environment. For example, learning to play chess requires storing the shape of pieces, storing the rules of chess, and acquiring declarative and procedural knowledge about good moves and chess positions. While in the past research in ML has focused on the development of learning algorithms dealing exclusively with learning tasks that require only one basic learning mechanism, there is now a growing interest in exploring the principles of multi-strategy learning systems (Michalski & Tecuci, 1994; van Someren & Reimann, 1994).

In the next section we will present two algorithms dealing with different basic learning tasks that require not-truth-preserving transformations. They represent typical pragmatic approaches to ML that are assumed to support the construction of knowledge based systems.

Heuristic Approaches to Concept Learning and Concept Formation

The learning problem which has received most attention in ML is inductive learning of concepts from examples, which can informally described as follows: A learning system is supplied with descriptions of instances (and non-instances) of a goal concept (possibly together with background knowledge) and is supposed to find a description of the goal concept that enables the system (or another system using the learning results) to classify other instances of the concept and to reject non-instances. A possible application of such a system could be, for example, to induce the description of a plant disease (i.e., the symptoms of the disease) which enables a system to distinguish plants suffering from the disease from plants not suffering from the disease. The terms concept and concept description are generally used in a very broad sense, i.e., most often it is not intended that the learned concepts show the characteristics of human concepts such as typicality effects.

One approach to concept learning from examples has been developed with the learning program FOIL by R. Quinlan (Quinlan, 1990; Cameron-Jones & Quinlan, 1994). In contrast to many other approaches, FOIL is able to deal with a powerful first-order logic (FOL) representation, i.e., the program is capable of learning concept description represented as Horn clauses from data described as a set of relations. This is an important feature as structural information which is important for many learning problems cannot be stated naturally using less expressive propositional (attribute-value) representations. On the other hand, since the FOL representation is more powerful, FOIL can also be applied to attribute-value representation learning problems. Below we will describe FOIL (version 6.0) in more detail. The program has been applied successfully to a large number of learning tasks and, therefore, can been seen as a good representative of the state-of-the-art in concept learning from examples.

Another system which we will describe in more detail is KBG from G. Bisson. Like FOIL this system is also capable of learning from relational data, but its learning task is concept formation by conceptual clustering. The input to a conceptual clustering system consists of descriptions of objects of a domain without a classification into positive and negative examples. The learning task is to aggregate the objects into an organized set of meaningful classes and to find intensional descriptions of these classes. A class is regarded as meaningful if it enables a more efficient and/or effective knowledge organization, e.g., enables a system to infer missing information for objects which are only partially described. The classes may be organized in a hierarchy or a directed acyclic graph. Conceptual clustering is a more complex learning task than concept learning from examples, because the latter can be regarded as just one step of conceptual clustering (i.e., inducing the intensional class descriptions). The aggregation of objects into classes in concept learning from examples is in this case given as learning input with, the classification of objects into positive and negative examples.

Note that learning from examples and concept formation have also studied extensively in cognitive psychology (see, e.g., Neisser & Ween, 1962; Medin & Smith, 1984; Ahn & Medin; 1992).

We will illustrate the description of FOIL and KBG using a data set which has been constructed following an application of machine learning methods to a (real-world) security policy problem in a telecommunication context (Sommer et al., 1993). We keep the examples as small and simple as possible in order to be able to restrict our attention to relevant aspects. The data set describes a few persons, possible operations on computer systems in a network, some companies managing these systems, and relations between persons, companies and computer systems. Each person described in the data set is either an operator or a manager. They are working for some company managing computer systems in a network. We assume that there are different kinds of executable computer system operations, i.e., maintenance operations (system operations) and operations on highly confidential data (confidence class operations). The data can be described by the following set of relations:

manager(jim,hal)
manager(jorge,peach)
manager(maria,neec)
manager(pierre,moon)
manager(stefan,hal)

manages(hal,node1)
manages(hal,node6)
manages(iemens,node4)
manages(moon,node2)
manages(neec,node5)
manages(peach,node3)

operator(dimitri,hal)
operator(hans,iemens)
operator(lars,peach)

system_op(op2)
system_op(op3)

conf_class_op(op1)

FOIL

FOIL learns function-free Horn clause definitions of relations. The input of FOIL consists of positive and negative examples of tuples of the target relation and sets of tuples which belong to other relations. In addition, FOIL uses a specification of the type of constants appearing in the tuples and a specification of the arguments of relations.

The goal of FOIL is to find a definition of the target relation in terms of itself and/or the other relations. The definition can consist of one or more Horn clauses of the following form:

$$P(X_1,X_2,... ,X_k) \leftarrow L_1, L_2, ... , L_n$$

Each literal L_i on the right-hand side of a clause has one of the following forms:

- $Q(W_1,W_2,... ,W_m)$ or $not(Q(W_1,W_2,... ,W_m))$, where Q is a relation and Wi are variables, at least one of which must have occurred on the left-hand side of the clause or within a preceding literal,

- $X_s = X_t$, $X_s \neq X_t$, $X_s > X_t$, $X_s \leq X_t$, that compare the values of existing variables X_s and X_t,

- $X_s = c$, $X_s \neq c$, $X_s > c$, $X_s \leq c$, that compare the value of an existing variable X_s with a constant c, e.g., a real number.

The learning task of FOIL is to induce a definition of the target relation covering (nearly) all positive examples of tuples of the target relation and covering (nearly) no negative examples. The meaning of "nearly" has to be specified by the user as a parameter (minimum accuracy of a clause).

In our example domain, we have chosen the relation *legal* to be the target relation.:

legal(dimitri,op2,node6)   not(legal(dimitri,op1,node6))
legal(hans,op2,node4)   not(legal(dimitri,op3,node2))
legal(jim,op1,node1)   not(legal(maria,op3,node5)
legal(lars,op2,node3)   not(legal(stefan,op1,node5))
legal(pierre,op1,node2)
legal(stefan,op1,node6)

The relation describes which person is allowed to perform which operation on a particular computer system. The learning goal is to find an intensional description of the relation in terms of the relations *manages, manager, operator, system_op,* and *conf_class_op*. These relations are the background knowledge in our learning task. An induced concept definition could be used, for example, in a computer system to automatically check and/or determine access/operation rights of people. The positive examples describe some specific cases which are classified as *legal* (the positive examples) and not *legal* (the negative examples), e.g., *Dimitri* is allowed to execute operation *op2* on system *node6*, and it is *illegal* if *Dimitri* executes operation *op1* on the system *node6*. Note that the structure of this learning task in an artificial domain is very similar to many real world learning tasks which have to be solved by children and adults. For example, children have to learn which operation they are allowed to perform on objects owned by other people with or without asking for permission. Suppose the goal of a child named Dimitri is to perform the operation "take out and consume" on an object "lowly" contained in a bag owned by a person Mary, his grandmother. In order to decide if it is necessary to ask for permission Dimitri might use a general rule that allows determine if the operation he wants to perform is a legal one.

Search for a Definition

FOIL follows a covering algorithm in order to achieve this goal. Beginning with the complete set of examples, FOIL constructs a Horn clause which covers at least some of the positive examples. Then, FOIL continues to find another clause "explaining" some of the remaining positive examples until (nearly) all positive examples are covered. At the end, FOIL reviews the set of all clauses, discards redundant clauses, orders the remaining ones by moving recursive clauses to the end, and outputs the result.

If FOIL is applied to the data set described above, it will output the following rules (uppercase letters denote variables):

   (1) *legal(A,B,C)* ← system_op(B), manages(D,C), operator(A,D)

   (2) *legal(A,B,C)* ← conf_class_op(B), manages(D,C), manager(A,D)

A person A is allowed to perform operation B on a system C, if either (1) the person is an operator of a company D which manages system C and the operation is a system operation, or (2) if the person is manager of a company D which manages system C and the operation is a confidence class operation.

Search for a Clause

In order to construct a single clause, FOIL follows a general-to-specific search strategy. It begins with the most general clause with an empty right-hand side covering all positive as well as all negative examples of the target relation. This clause is specialized by adding a literal to the body of the clause. This specialization step is repeated as long as the clause covers a negative example or the clause becomes too complex.

The interesting question now is: Which relation should be used and with which arguments to specialize a overly-general clause? Note that even if the data set contains a small number of relations, the search space can be very large. FOIL uses a weighted information-gain heuristic to guide the search for new literals.

The information needed to signal that a tuple in a training set T_i is positive is $I(T_i) = -\log_2((T_i^+ + c) / (|T_i| + c))$, where T_i^+ is the number of positive tuples in T_i, $|T_i|$ is the total number of positive and negative tuples, and c is the constant 0. After a new literal L_i has been added to the current clause leading to a new set of positive and negative tuples T_{i+1}, the information needed is $I(T_{i+1}) = -\log_2((T_{i+1}^+ + c) / (|T_{i+1}| + c))$. The information gained by adding the literal L_i is given by:

$$Gain(L_i) = T_i^{++} * (I(T_i) - I(T_{i+1})).$$

The difference is multiplied by the number of positive tuples in Ti which are also represented by one or more tuples in Ti+1 giving credit to literals covering a larger number of positive tuples. Instead of using zero as constant c in the formulas, FOIL uses the constant 1. Otherwise, FOIL would never be able select a literal leading to the same proportion of positive tuples to the total number of tuples, e.g., if there are 10 positive and 20 negative tuples in Ti and 5 positive and 10 negative tuples in Ti+1, then the gain would be zero. The reason for the using c=1 is that it is easier to filter out a small set of negative tuples than a large set.

In general, FOIL selects the literal with the highest information gain. Using this heuristic, FOIL explores only a very small part of possible combinations of literals to build a clause, which is the main reason for its efficiency. The system includes different backtracking mechanisms, but once a literal has been selected, alternative literals usually need not be investigated. FOIL deviates from the information gain heuristic when only literals with a low information gain are available to specialize a clause, i.e., there is no literal really helpful to exclude unwanted negative tuples. In this case, FOIL will add all available determinate literals to the body of the clause. These literals obtain zero information gain, but introduce one or more new variable. A literal L_j is determinate with respect to a partial clause, if L_j introduces one or more new variable, but there is only one possible instantiation of these variables with respect to the other variables in preceding literals (or the left-hand side of the clause) and the corresponding relation. For example, if FOIL starts to specialize the most-general clause

legal(A,B,C) <=

which covers all of the 6 positive and all of the 4 negative tuples::

jim,op1,node1: +
pierre,op1,node2: +
lars,op2,node3: +
hans,op2,node4: +
dimitri,op2,node6: +
stefan,op1,node6: +

maria,op3,node5: -
dimitri,op1,node6: -
stefan,op1,node5: -
dimitri,op3,node2: -

Then, there are only two literals with non-zero information gain: *conf_class_op(B)* and *system_op(B)*. If one of these literals is added to the right-hand side of the clause, the clause will cover 3 positive and 2 negative tuples of the training set. Thus the information gain would be

3 * (-log2((6+1)/(10+1) - (-log2((3+1)/(5+1))))) = 0.2

This is less than the information gain required by a corresponding default parameter value used for this example. Therefore, FOIL will select the determinate literal *manages(D,C)*. The literal is determinate, because there is only one possible instantiation of the variable *D* in the manages-relation for a given instantiation of the variable *C* (which appears on the left-hand side of the clause). Therefore, the resulting clause

legal(A,B,C) ← manages(D,C)

also covers the 6 positive and all of the 4 negative tuples. Due to the new variable, FOIL includes the corresponding instantiations of the variable *D* in the tuple set:

jim,op1,node1,hal: +   maria,op3,node5,neec: -
pierre,op1,node2,moon: +   dimitri,op1,node6,hal: -
lars,op2,node3,peach: +   stefan,op1,node5,neec: -
hans,op2,node4,iemens: +   dimitri,op3,node2,moon: -
dimitri,op2,node6,hal: +
stefan,op1,node6,hal: +

The next literal *operator(E,D)* is chosen according to the information gain heuristic. This literal with an information gain of 2.1 also includes a new variable. Therefore, the new tuple set contains fewer negative tuples:

jim,op1,node1,hal,dimitri: +   dimitri,op1,node6, hal, dimitri: -
lars,op2,node3,peach,lars: +
hans,op2,node4,iemens,hans: +
dimitri,op2,node6,hal,dimitri: +
stefan,op1,node6,hal,dimitri: +

The next literal with the highest gain (0.7) is *system_op(B)*. This literal contains a variable also contained in the left-hand side of the clause. Therefore, this literal could also have been used as the first literal on the right-hand side. In order to exclude the possibility that all literals together are more specific than necessary, FOIL decides at this point to "regrow" the clause with *system_op(B)* as the first literal. In the next steps, FOIL adds *manages(D,C)* (as determinate literal) and *operator(A,D)* (having the highest information gain, now 1.8). This completes the clause

legal(A,B,C) ← system_op(B), manages(D,C), operator(A,D)

as all negative tuples are excluded with the last literal. Before FOIL tries to find another clause, the system examines if one literal of the clause can be dropped without any loss of accuracy, but in this example, each literal is necessary in order to prevent covering of negative tuples. The second clause (already shown above) which covers the remaining positive tuples of the target relation is then build very similar to the first clause. Finally, FOIL checks if one of the clauses is redundant. As this not the case in this example, FOIL outputs both rules as definition of the relation legal.

Final Remarks on FOIL

We have now described the main ideas behind FOIL, a program that constructs function-free Horn clause definitions of relations from examples and extensionally defined background knowledge. A more complete description (of previous versions) of the system can be found in Quinlan (1990) and Cameron-Jones and Quinlan (1994). Although FOIL is still under development, the system has already been applied successfully to many different relational (and propositional) concept learning problems. Due to the success of the system, many other systems have been developed using similar ideas or extending the approach, e.g., the system FOCL (Pazzani & Kibler, 1992) is able to take advantage of intensional definitions of relations (potentially including the target relation) which are specified as additional input to the learning system.

Despite the fact that FOIL has been applied successfully to many different learning tasks, it is always possible to find a learning problem where FOIL will fail to find a definition of a target relation, no matter how the diverse learning parameters of the system are set. The use of the information gain heuristic, which is responsible for the efficiency of FOIL in many domains, hinders FOIL from exploring some parts of the hypothesis space. If the definition of the concept lies somewhere in these parts, the system has no chance to find it. For example, FOIL will never use a non-determinate literal (introducing new variables) with zero information gain, if there is a literal with small but positive information gain, although such a literal can later turn out to be useful and necessary.

FOIL is one instance of a large class of approaches developed in machine learning concerned with the induction of concepts from examples. These approaches differ, for example, in the kind of representation formalism used to represent the learning input and learning output, and the search strategy in the hypothesis space (see Schlimmer & Langley, 1993). Some algorithms require that the complete learning input is available at the beginning of a learning process, other algorithms are able to refine their learning results in the light of new information. Learning algorithms can also be classified according to the extent to which they are able to take advantage of different kinds of background knowledge. Also, different methods have been developed to deal with imperfect data sets (containing noisy data or missing data), to handle numerical data, and to deal with large data sets. Hence, it is sometimes difficult to identify the most effective and most efficient algorithm for a given learning problem. A relatively well understood problem is the induction of decision trees from examples, each described by a list of values for a fixed set of attributes (Quinlan, 1986); corresponding programs have already achieved practical relevance for the construction of knowledge based systems.

It should be noted that successful applications of programs that induce concept descriptions from examples are usually not obtained by running a program only once. Instead it is necessary to adjust the system parameters, reformulate the learning input, and inspect the learning result several times until the learning output can be released for the use in another system. This is a consequence of the fact that the learning input describes usually only a very small fraction of instances of the concept which has to be learned, such that it is possible to find many hypotheses which "explain" the learning input. Therefore, the learning input and/or the learning algorithm must contain some constraints (learning bias) which prohibit the output of useless learning results. The analysis of different kinds of learning biases is one of the most important research topics (see Shavlik & Dietterich, 1990, pp. 45).

KBG

KBG-2 is a conceptual clustering system (Bisson, 1992b) intended to support the construction and organization of a knowledge base. Given a set of descriptions of objects in a domain and a domain theory, KBG constructs a directed-acyclic graph of new concepts, which are intensionally described by an organized set of rules. Using the explanation module of the system, the user is able to inspect the learning result and to adjust system parameters until the user is satisfied with the learning output. This learning result is added to the knowledge base and can be used in subsequent learning steps with new sets of descriptions of objects to explore other parts of the domain.

KBG requires as input a case-oriented representation, i.e., a set of object descriptions each in form of a conjunct of ground literals and, optionally, a set of rules as domain theory. The following set of object descriptions from our example domain is used to illustrate the representation and generalization approach implemented in KBG:

D1: *operation(jim,op1,node1), manager(jim,hal), conf_class_op(op1), manages(hal,node1)*

D2: *operation(pierre,op1,node2), manager(pierre,moon), conf_class_op(op1), manages(moon,node2)*

D3: *operation(lars,op2,node3), operator(lars,peach), operator(lars,moon), system_op(op2), manages(peach,node3)*

D4: *operation(hans,op2,node4), operator(hans,iemens), system_op(op2), manages(iemens,node4)*

D5: *operation(dimitri,op2,node6), operator(dimitri,hal), system_op(op2), manages(hal,node6)*

D6: *operation(stefan,op1,node6), manager(stefan,hal), manager(stefan,peach), conf_class_op(op1), manages(hal,node6)*

D7: *operation(maria,op3,node5), manager(maria,neec), system_op(op3), manages(neec,node5)*

D8: *operation(dimitri,op1,node6), operator(dimitri,hal), conf_class_op(op1), manages(hal,node6)*

D9: *operation(stefan,op1,node5), manager(stefan,hal), conf_class_op(op1), manages(neec,node5)*

D10: *operation(dimitri,op3,node2), operator(dimitri,hal), system_op(op3), manages(moon,node2)*

For example, D1 is a description of the event in which operator *Jim* working for *HAL* executed a security operation *Op1* on a computer system *Node1* managed by *HAL*. In contrast to the set of facts supplied to FOIL, the events are not classified as *legal* or *illegal;* the predicate *operation* is used instead of *legal*. KBG constructed the hierarchy of classes from these descriptions shown in Figure 1. The nodes represent classes built by KBG. The leaves are the identifiers of object descriptions followed by a '+' if the event was described to FOIL as a positive example of the relation legal, or '-' otherwise.

Although KBG was not supplied with a classification of the objects, the system built two classes (class-3 and class-4), which correspond to the rules induced by FOIL: class-3 covers all events with a confidence class operation (described as legal to FOIL) and class-4 covers all legal system operation events. The intensional descriptions of the classes constructed by KBG consists of a system of rules, i.e., a sub-class is described by a reference to the super-class and a list of additional literals describing the specialization. If each reference to a super-class in the rules is replaced by the intensional description itself, the descriptions of class-3 and class-4 are equivalent to the corresponding rules induced by FOIL.

The conceptual clustering of KBG can be divided into three successive steps. In the first step, the description of the examples are saturated using a domain theory which can be specified optionally. In the second learning step, a set of generalization and clustering operators are

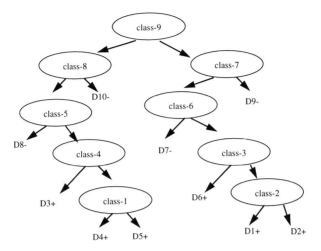

Figure 1: Hierarchy of classes constructed by KBG

applied iteratively in a bottom-up fashion guided by similarity measures in order to build a graph of generalizations. The last step aims at building a hierarchical system of rules from the generalization graph. In this step, KBG drops all premises in the class descriptions which are not necessary to discriminate between the instances of different classes. In the following only the conceptual clustering step of KBG is described in more detail, for a description of the other steps see Bisson (1992a, 1992b).

Construction of a Directed Acyclic Graph of Classes

In the above example KBG has constructed a hierarchy of classes. Each class captures a similarity among its instances. Usually the system outputs a directed acyclic graph (DAG) of classes, i.e., some objects are instances of more than one class, each capturing a different view (similarity) on the set of objects.

In order to construct a DAG of classes, KBG follows a bottom-up clustering method which can be roughly described as follows. Using a similarity measure, which will be discussed in the next section, KBG computes the similarity between all pairs of objects described in the input. Those objects which are very similar to each other, i.e., whose similarity exceeds a certain threshold parameter, are grouped into one class. The corresponding object descriptions are then generalized, e.g., by dropping literals from the original object descriptions and turning constants into variables. Such generalizations are not only used later in the rule construction step, but also to compute generalized object descriptions by turning variables back into constants. These descriptions are added to the conceptual clustering learning input, while the objects description which were generalized are deleted. Then, KBG computes the similarity between the new generalized object descriptions and all remaining object descriptions and repeats the steps described above until there is only one object description left in the learning input.

In our example, the descriptions of D1 and D2 and the descriptions of D3 and D4 are judged to be very similar by KBG. The generalization of D1 and D2 is used to compute the new generalized description NGD1:

   NGD1: *operation(p1,o1,n1), manager(p1,c1), conf_class_op(o1),   manages(c1,n1).*

This new description is judged to be very similar to D6 and KBG builds class-3 covering the objects D1, D2, and D3. The arguments of the predicates in NGD1 can be regarded as synonyms of entities involved in one instance of class-2.

Computation of the Similarity Between Objects

Computing the similarity between objects is relevant for the clustering of objects as well as the construction of generalizations from object descriptions. While the resulting numerical values determine which objects are grouped together, intermediate results are used to determine how the corresponding descriptions are generalized.

For example, KBG needs to know which entities in the descriptions of D6 and NGD1 correspond to each other in order to be able to construct a generalization of both descriptions:

D6: *operation(stefan,op1,node6), manager(stefan,hal), manager(stefan,peach), conf_class_op(op1), manages(hal,node6)*,

NGD1: *operation(p1,o1,n1), manager(p1,c1), conf_class_op(o1),manages(c1,n1)*.

In this example, the problem is caused by the fact that D6 contains two literals built with the predicate *manager* and NGD1 contains only one such literal. Therefore, KBG has at least the choice either to assume that the company *hal* corresponds to *c1* and the relation between *stefan* and *peach* is irrelevant in the context of the learning task, or KBG could assume that *peach* corresponds to company *c1* and the relation between *stefan* and *hal* is irrelevant. In the first case, the system would deliver following generalization of D6 and NGD1: G1: Class-3 is the set of operation events with a confidence class operation, which is executed by a manager of a company managing the node on which the operation was executed,

and in the second case the generalization would be G2: Class-3 is the set of operation events with a confidence class operation, which is executed by a manager of a company on a computer system managed by the same or another company.

This matching problem - which only occurs when dealing with representation formalisms powerful enough to represent relational information - is dealt with in KBG by choosing those matches between entities of descriptions which are most similar to each other. For example, KBG computes a high similarity value for D6 and NDG1, because everything what is stated about the person *stefan* (the company *hal*, the operation *op1*, and computer system *node6*) in D6 is very similar to what is known about person *p1* (company *c1*, operation *o1*, and computer system *n1*) in description NGD1. Consequently, the generalization delivered by KBG is the first one (G1) based on the assumption that *hal* corresponds to *n1*.

In order to compute the similarity between two object descriptions, KBG considers the similarity between all entities involved in both descriptions. Two descriptions are completely similar if both descriptions refer to the same number of entities related in the same way to each other. KBG uses a recursive schema to compute the similarity between the arguments of the predicates. For example, the similarity SIM of *stefan* and *p1* which both occur as first argument of the predicate *operation* and the predicate *manager* is computed by taking into account the similarity between the other arguments of these predicates and the specification of the weights of the predicates used in the descriptions.

SIM(*stefan,p1*) = f(SIM(*op1,o1*),... , SIM(*hal,c1*), predicate-weight(*operation*),...,
      predicate-weight(*manages*)),

$SIM(op1,o1) = f(SIM(stefan,p1),...,SIM(hal,c1)$, predicateweight($operation$),...,
predicate-weight($manages$)).

KBG uses an iterative method to compute the similarities between entities. Starting with a rough estimate of the similarity between the different entities, the system refines these values by taking into account the similarities between the other entities computed in the previous iteration. The number of iterations performed by KBG has to be specified by the user. The similarity between two descriptions is defined as the average of the similarity between the most similar entities. The similarity measures used to compute the similarities between entities and descriptions and more details about the method used to compute these values are described in (Bisson, (1992a).

Final Remarks on KBG

KBG is a conceptual clustering system which forms a structured set of classes (concepts) from (unclassified) descriptions of objects in a domain. KBG's knowledge representation formalism is based on first-order logic (without negation and function symbols) with some extensions, e.g., for dealing with numerical values. Unlike other well-known conceptual clustering systems like UNIMEM or COBWEB (see Gennari, Langley & Fisher, 1989), KBG can also be applied if relational information is important. Like FOIL, the system follows a heuristic approach, as the generalization process of the system is directed by a similarity measure. Due to this fact the search of KBG is very efficient, i.e., the computational complexity is polynomial in the number of descriptions. The rule building module of the system is able to construct rules which allow to deduce missing information about partially described objects, thus KBG supports the organization and refinement of knowledge bases.

KBG has been applied in various domains and the learning results were useful - at least in the sense that some of the classes of the clustering results could be used successfully by another learning system (Emde, 1994). A general evaluation of KBG's conceptual clustering results is difficult, because important criteria like comprehensibility or quality of knowledge organization are ill-defined or difficult to evaluate.

Conceptual clustering systems like COBWEB, UNIMEM (see Gennari et al., 1989) and KBG tend to produce an increasing number of classes if the number of descriptions of objects is increased. The evaluation of the utility of the new concepts is more or less well-defined and more or less well-justified (see Gennari et.al., 1989). Other approaches to concept formation also carefully evaluate the advantages of new concepts before they are introduced into the representation (e.g., see Wrobel, 1994e; Kietz & Morik, 1993). Nevertheless, there is an important difference in that approaches to conceptual clustering presuppose an idea of knowledge representation and organization which is hard to relate to other knowledge representation schemes developed in Artificial Intelligence. An important exception are representations developed in the research on case-based reasoning (see Kolodner, 1993). While usually a concept is introduced because there is a need to refer to a particular set of objects, conceptual clustering systems construct a concept for other reasons, e.g., because information about concept membership allows a system to predict missing data (Gennari et al., 1989) or the known instances are similar to each other (as it is the case in KBG). An approach which only incorporates those "concepts" constructed by conceptual clustering necessary to refer to a particular set of instances is described in (Emde, 1994). Future research has to deal with the question how different representations used inside and outside of current machine learning systems are related to each other and what the knowledge representation and organization of integrated learning systems should look like.

Final Remarks on FOIL and KBG

KBG and FOIL represent approaches dealing with different and important learning tasks: inductive learning of concepts from examples and conceptual clustering. Both approaches rely on the use of heuristics to deal with the computational complexity of the learning tasks. Neither FOIL nor KBG can be regarded as models of human concept learning (although information gain as well as similarity might also play a role in human learning). Instead they should be regarded as tools able to support the construction of knowledge based systems. Due to the fact that they are not integrated systems which contain modules able to handle other learning tasks like knowledge revision, these system require the help of a user in order to be able to deliver useful learning results. Future work is necessary to continue the research on integrating different learning approaches and integrating learning systems with performance systems. A collection of papers describing approaches concerned with other learning tasks (e.g., the improvement of the efficiency of problem solvers) or hybrid learning systems can be found in (Shavlik & Dietterich, 1990).

Theoretical Approaches

In the last section we have seen that FOIL is able to induce concept descriptions from examples very efficiently in many cases, but sometimes the systems fails or becomes inefficient. A question which immediately comes to mind is: Is it possible to implement an efficient system which can be guaranteed to find a concept description. A description covering (most of) the positive examples and (nearly) no negative examples, if it exists and can be represented by function-free Horn clauses.

Such and related questions are studied under the topic *theory of learnability* with two main research directions: *inductive inference* (Angluin & Smith, 1982) and *computational learning theory* (Valiant, 1984; Kearns, 1990; Haussler, 1990). The central paradigm of inductive inference is the notion of *identification in the limit* and deals with time convergence of learning procedures. We will restrict our attention to computational learning theory which addresses issues of practical relevance such as learning approximate concepts, learning from noise, polynomial time complexity, and number of training examples necessary to learn concepts. In contrast to inductive inference, the main concern of computational learning theory is the computational complexity of learning tasks.

Most approaches in the field of computational learning theory are based on a framework introduced by L. Valiant called *Probably Approximately Correct* (PAC) learning. Originally, this framework has been defined to analyze complexity issues in learning Boolean formulae, but has recently been extended, e.g., such that it is possible to analyze learning of first-order Horn clauses from examples and background knowledge (see Kietz & Dzeroski, 1994) or learning of exemplar-based representations.

The basic problem of analyzing learning by example tasks is the following. Inductive learning systems cannot be guaranteed to be correct, because any attempt of inducing a general concept description from a limited number of training examples can result in a description that wrongly classifies a few or even almost all instances of the concept. In Valiant´s PAC framework this problem is dealt with by allowing learning algorithms to produce descriptions that are good approximations of the target concepts with a high probability. In order to be *approximately correct*, the probability that a learning result produces a mis-classification must equal or less than a small constant called the error parameter. A learning algorithm solves a learning problem *probably approximately correct* if the probability to produce an approximately correct result is equal to or greater than a large constant called the confidence parameter.

This idea serves as basis to analyze various classes of learning problems (usually defined by the language of possible learning results) by taking in consideration all possible learning algorithms: A class of learning problems is called *PAC-learnable* if there exists an algorithm that can solve all problems of the class probably approximately correct. Based on this framework various properties of classes of learning problems could be proven. For example, is was possible to show that some apparently simple classes of problems are not efficiently learnable, i.e., PAC-learnable in polynomial time. Other results concern the number of examples required to guarantee PAC learning or the rate of noise that can be tolerated.

Many of the obtained results are disappointing in the sense that it turned out that even if the target concepts are known to have a very restricted form, the learning problems are not polynomially PAC-learnable. For example, if the language to represent concepts is restricted to Horn clauses with non-determinate literals and with variables of depth one and with literals of arity of at most two, the learning problem is not PAC-learnable unless a widely assumed conjecture of computational complexity theory is false (see Kietz & Dzeroski, 1994). This also means that is not possible to implement a learning program that is able to find all target concepts representable with function-free Horn-clauses efficiently. This explains why FOIL fails on some learning tasks.

On the other hand, such negative results turned out to be useful, because they inspired to prove the polynomial PAC-learnability of (sometimes only slightly) more restricted concept classes. This is of practical interest, e.g., because sometimes it is possible to tolerate such restrictions.

Alternatives to Valiant's framework have also been developed and it has been shown that the computational complexity of concept learning problems can be reduced by supplying additional information to a learning system, e.g., by allowing the system to ask particular kinds of questions (see Kearns, 1990). These are important results, because they justify the hypothesis that concept learning in natural systems is not a mystorious process, but simply somewhat different from what is studied within the PAC learning framework, e.g., humans are able to learn efficiently and effectively, because they can take advantage of different kinds of background knowledge.

In summary theoretical approaches to machine learning have already lead to valuable insights into the computational complexity of learning. Future work in this field will help to identify and to analyze new (or recently proposed) learning biases.

Computational Models of Human Learning

We have already stated that learning in FOIL and KBG can hardly be described as models of human learning. These and many other approaches are exclusively rooted in computer science and related fields, e.g., information theory and data analysis. There are also approaches which try to take advantage of the great deal of research in disciplines related to cognitive science. Especially the work on computational models of scientific discovery has been inspired by cognitive psychology, developmental psychology, and the philosophy of science (see Langley, 1987; Shrager & Langley, 1990). Also, research on the structure and the formation of human concepts in psychology has attracted many researchers in machine learning in their attempts to overcome shortcomings and limitations of early approaches to concept learning and concept formation (Wrobel, 1994 contains a recent overview). In the following I will briefly survey research issues of some approaches which are influenced by research in psychology and philosophy.

Most machine learning approaches to concept learning are based on the idea that a concept is defined by a set of features that are individually necessary and jointly sufficient. This classical view on concepts cannot explain various psychological phenomena (Smith & Medin, 1981). Other models which have been developed in psychology are the probabilistic model, the exemplar model, and hybrid models. In the probabilistic model, concepts are represented by combinations of weighted features which allows to represent disjunctive concepts. A machine learning system whose representation is based on this model is COBWEB (Fisher, 1987). Also, neural net approaches can be assigned to this model (see Hinton, 1989). Although the probabilistic model explains more phenomena than the classical model, there are still some experimental results - for instance, context effects - which cannot be explained without further assumptions.

In the exemplar model, a concept is represented by a (sub-)set of instances of the concept rather than by a generalized description. An example of a learning system which describes concepts using this kind of concept representation is PROTOS (Bareiss, Porter & Wier, 1988). An hybrid approach has been developed by Michalski (Michalski, 1990). His two-tired representation consists of a propositional description and an evaluation function used to determine the degree of membership.

These approaches are (more or less) cognitively adequate models of learning with respect to the representation formalisms. They may also be cognitively adequate with respect to the learning results they are able to achieve, i.e., humans might achieve the same learning result from the same learning input as the learning systems. A learning approach can also be (more or less) cognitively adequate with respect to the learning processes carried out by the learning system, e.g., humans might follow the same line of reasoning steps.

One research area which is very often described to have the goal of developing "computational models of human learning" is the research on scientific discovery. Following activities of scientific discovery have been explored:

- the generation of hypotheses (theories) using different reasoning schemes (e.g., inductive, deductive, or analogical inference) and different kinds of representations (e.g., quantitative and qualitative models),

- the evaluation of hypotheses (theories) including the design of experiments,

- the prediction of observations from an experimental setting and a hypothesis (theory), and

- the revision of hypotheses (theories).

One of the most notable discovery systems which has been developed in the research area is the KEKADA system (Kulkarni & Simon, 1990). It integrates prediction, theory revision, experimentation, and evaluation. Therefore, the system is able to perform successive steps of a discovery process and to repeat these steps in a cycle until all hypotheses which could improve the acquired knowledge any further are ruled out. In contrast to many other discovery systems, KEKADA has been evaluated by comparing its behavior to the behavior of scientists. Unfortunately, a detailed justification of the positive result of this comparison is not presented by the authors. Therefore, we prefer to stay on the safe side and will not describe KEKADA as a cognitively adequate model of scientific discovery.

Scientific discovery is one of the most ambitious goals of machine learning. This explains why current systems still ignore many important aspects of scientific discovery, e.g., the collaboration, competition, and communication among scientists or phenomena like "confirmation bias" (see Tweney, 1990; cf. Emde, 1987); and it becomes understandable that up to now there is no machine learning system which can truly be regarded as model of human scientific discovery - neither with respect to the representation, the learning results, nor the lines of reasoning. Instead we might say that machine learning has already been successful in converting findings from cognitive science research into learning systems for scientific domains.

Final Remarks and Conclusions

In this paper we have described different research directions of machine learning. Machine learning techniques have been applied successfully in a large number of real-world domains. Many of these applications can only be regarded as case studies which demonstrate the applicability of the techniques, but there are also cases where automatically generated knowledge is used in applications systems (see, e.g., Giordana et al., 1993) or has turned out to be scientifically relevant and was published in top scientific journals of their research area (see, e.g., Muggleton et al., 92). Recent progress in the theoretical analysis of the computational complexity of machine learning algorithms lead to insights for the design of new/practical algorithms. Machine learning can now truly be regarded as an experimental science. Publications on new or improved techniques are now usually required to include a description of experimental results unless the claims made by the authors are justified by a theoretical analysis. A large collection of publicly available machine learning data sets allows the systematic analysis of new methods and their comparison with existing methods.

The paper is far away from giving a broad overview of the whole field of machine learning. Many research topics such as learning in artificial neural nets (see Hinton, 1989), genetic algorithms (see Booker et al.., 1989), and reinforcement learning have been omitted. Also numerous details of and alternatives to approaches described in this paper have not been discussed. An excellent overview with a different bias is (Dietterich, 1990). For a broader overview see Schlimmer and Langley (1993). Collections of important articles are Shavlik and Dietterich (1990) and Carbonell (1990).

The conclusion which should be drawn from this paper is: The research in the field of machine learning requires much more interdisciplinary research - and cognitive science can benefit from machine learning research and vice-versa.

Machine learning offers:

- support in the formal representation of psychological models and their implementation in computer programs,

- experience in the experimental evaluation of computational models of learning, and

- methods to determine the computational complexity of learning problems and convergence of learning algorithms.

Machine learning requires from cognitive psychology, development psychology, philosophy of science, education, cognitive neuroscience, linguistics, history of science, sociology of science, etc.:

- careful evaluation of current approaches (some good examples are described in (Medin et al., 1987; Ahn & Medin, 1992)),

- ideas on how existing approaches can be improved by new (and old) ideas, e.g., how to make learning systems more efficient and effective,

- help from psychology in order to be able to analyze the comprehensibility of machine learning results, and

- advice how to improve the comprehensibility of machine learning processes.

Acknowledgments

I would like to thank Saso Dzeroski, Peter Reimann, Edgar Sommer, Dietrich Wettschereck, and Stefan Wrobel for comments on drafts of this paper. I would like to thank Gilles Bisson for making KBG available and explaining the secrets of his system. This work was partially supported by the European Community ESPRIT program under contract 6020 (Inductive Logic Programming).

References

Ahn, W.-K., & Medin, D.L. (1992). A Two-Stage Model of Category Construction. *Cognitive Science, 16,* 81-121.

Angluin, D., & Smith, C. H. (1982). *A Survey of Inductive Inference: Theory and Methods.* Technical Report 250. Yale University.

Bareiss, E. R., Porter, B. W., & Wier, C. C. (1988). PROTOS: An Exemplar-Based Learning Apprentice. *International Journal of Man-Machine Studies, 29(5),* 549-561.

Bisson, G. (1992a). Conceptual Clustering in a First Order Logic Representation. *Proceeding of the 10th ECAI.*

Bisson, G. (1992b). Learning in FOL with a Similarity Measure. *Proceedings of the AAAI-92.* AAAI Press.

Booker, L. B., Goldberg, D. E., & Holland, J. H. (1989). Classifier Systems and Genetic Algorithms. *Artificial Intelligence, 40.*

Cameron-Jones, R. M., & Quinlan, J. R. (1994). Efficient Top-down Induction of Logic Programs. *SIGART Bulletin, 5 (1),* 33-24.

Carbonell, J. G. (1990). *Machine Learning: Paradigms and Methods.* Cambridge, MA: MIT Press.

Dietterich, T.G. (1990). Machine Learning. In J.Traub (Ed.), *Annual Review of Computer Science. Vol. 4.*

Dietterich, T. G., & Michalski, R. S. (1983). A Comparative Review of Selected Methods for Learning from Examples. In R. S. Michalski, J. G. Carbonell, & T. M. Mitchell (Eds.), *Machine Learning - An Artificial Intelligence Approach, Vol. I.* Los Altos, CA: Morgan Kaufmann.

Dzeroski, S., & Kietz, J.-U. (1994) Inductive Logic Programming. *SIGART Bulletin, 5(1),* 22-32.

Emde, W. (1987). Non-Cumulative learning in METAXA.3. Proceedings of the Tenth International Joint Conference On Artificial Intelligence (IJCAI-87). Morgan Kaufmann.

Emde, W. (1994). Inductive Learning of Characteristic Concept Descriptions from Small Sets of Classified Examples. In F. Bergadano & L. De Raedt (Eds.), *Machine Learning: ECML-94, European Conference on Machine Learning, Vol. 784 of Lecture Notes in Artificial Intelligence.* Berlin: Springer.

Fisher, D. H. (1987). Knowledge acquisition via incremental conceptual clustering. *Machine Learning, 2,* 139-172.

Gennari, J. H., Langley, P., & Fisher, D. H. (1989). *Models of Incremental Concept Formation. Artificial Intelligence, 40,* 11-61.

Giordana, A., Saitta, L., Bergadano, F., Brancadori, F., & De Marchi, D. (1993). ENIGMA: A System that Learns Diagnostic Knowledge. *IEEE Transactions on Knowledge and data Engineering, 5(1).*

Haussler, D. (1990). Applying Valiant's Learning Framework to AI Concept Learning Problems. In Y. Kodratoff & R. S. Michalski (Eds.), *Machine Learning - An Artificial Intelligence Approach, volume III.* San Mateo: Morgan Kaufmann.

Hinton, G. E. (1989). Connectionist Learning Procedures. *Artificial Intelligence, 40,* 185-234.

Kearns, M. J. (1990). *The Computational Complexity of Machine Learning.* Distinguished Dissertation. Cambridge, Mass: MIT Press .

Kietz, J.-U., & Morik, K. (1994). A Polynomial Approach to the Constructive Induction of Structural Knowledge. *Machine Learning, 14,* 193-217.

Kolodner, J. L. (1993). *Case-Based Reasoning.* Los Altos, CA: Morgan Kaufmann.

Kulkarni, D., & Simon, H. A. (1990). Experimentation in Machine Discovery. In J. Shrager & P. Langley (Eds.), *Computational Models of Scientific Discovery and Theory Formation.* Los Altos, CA: Morgan Kaufmann.

Medin, D.L. & Smith, E.E. (1984). Concept and Concept Formation. *Annual Review of Psychology, 35,* 299-339.

Medin, D.L., Wattenmaker, W.D., & Michalski, R.S. (1987). Constraints and Preferences in Inductive Learning: An Exerimental Study of Human and Machine Performance. *Cognitive Science, 11,* 299-339

Michalski, R.S. (1990). Learning Flexible Concepts: Fundamental Ideas and a Method Based on Two-Tiered Representation. In Y. Kodratoff & R. S. Michalski (Eds.), *Machine Learning - An Artificial Intelligence Approach, Vol. III.* San Francisco: Morgan Kaufmann.

Michalski, R.S. (1994). Inferential Theory of Learning: Developing Foundations for Multistrategy Learning. In R.S. Michalski & G. Tecuci (Eds.), *Machine Learning - A Multistrategy Approach, Vol. IV.* San Francisco: Morgan Kaufmann.

Michalski, R.S., & Tecuci, G. (Eds.). (1994). *Machine Learning - A Multistrategy Approach, Vol. IV.* San Francisco: Morgan Kaufmann.

Morik, K., Wrobel, S., Kietz, J.-U., & Emde, W. (1993). *Knowledge Acquisition and Machine Learning: Theory Methods and Applications.* London, New York: Academic Press.

Muggleton, S. & Feng, C. (1990). Efficient Induction of Logic Programs. *Proceedings of the 1st Conference on Algorithmic Learning Theory.*

Muggleton, S., King, R. D., & Sternberg, M. J. E. (1992). Protein Secondary Structure Prediction using Logic-based Machine Learning. *Protein Engineering, 5(7),* 647-657.

Murray, K.S., & Porter, B.W. (1989). Controlling Search for the Consequences of New Information During Knowledge Integration. In B. Spatz (Ed.), *Proceedings of the 6th Int. Workshop on Machine Learning.* Palo Alto: Morgan Kaufmann.

Neisser, U., & Weene, P. (1962). Hierarchies in concept attainment. Journal of Experimental Psychology.,64, 640-645.

Newell, A. (1982). The Knowledge Level. *Artificial Intelligence, 18(1),* 87-127.

Pazzani, M., & Kibler, D. (1992). The Utility of Knowledge in Inductive Learning. *Machine Learning, 9(1).*

Quinlan, J. R. (1986). Induction of Decision Trees. *Machine Learning, 1 (1),* 81-106.

Quinlan, J. R. (1990). Learning Logical Definitions from Relations. *Machine Learning, 5 (3),* 239-266.

Schlimmer, J.C., & Langley, P. (1993). Machine Learning. In S.C. Shapiro (Ed.), *Encyclopaedia of Artificial Intelligence. 2nd Edition. Volume 1.* New York: John Wiley & Son.

Shavlik, J. W., & Dieterich, T. D. (Eds.). (1990). *Readings in Machine Learning.* Los Altos, CA: Morgan Kaufmann.

Shrager, J., & Langley, P. (Eds.). (1990). *Computational Models of Scientific Discovery and Theory Formation*. Los Altos, CA: Morgan Kaufmann.

Smith, E. E., & Medin, D. L. (1981). *Categories and Concepts*. London, UK: Harvard University Press.

Sommer, E. (1994). FENDER: An Approach to Theory Restructuring. In N. Lavrac & S. Wrobel (Eds.). *Machine Learning: ECML-95. Lecture Notes in Artificial Intelligence, Vol. 912*. Berlin: Springer.

Sommer, E., Morik, K., Andre, J. M., & Uszynski, M. (1993). What On-line Learning Can Do for Knowledge Acquisition - A Case Study. *Knowledge Acquisition, 6,* 435-460.

Towell, G.G.,& Shavlik, J.W. (1994). Refining Symbolic Knowledge Using Neural Networks. In R.S. Michalski & G. Tecuci (Eds.), *Machine Learning - A Multistrategy Approach, Vol. IV*. San Francisco: Morgan Kaufmann.

Tweney, R. D. (1990). Five Questions for Computationalists. In J. Shrager & P. Langley (Eds.), *Computational Models of Scientific Discovery and Theory Formation*. Los Altos, CA: Morgan Kaufmann.

Valiant, L. G. (1984). A Theory of the Learnable. *Communications of the ACM, 27(11),* 1134-1142.

van Someren, M., & Reimann, P. (1994). Multi-Objective Learning with Multiple Representations. In this book.

Wrobel, S. (1994). *Concept Formation and Knowledge Revision*. Kluwer Academic Publishers, Dordrecht, Netherlands.

Mental and Physical Artifacts in Cognitive Practices

Roger Säljö[1]

Introduction

For most researchers in the areas of cognition and learning, thinking was, until recently, construed as "an individual act bounded by the physical facts of brain and body." (Resnick, 1991, p. 1). This assumption entered into research as the self-evident point of departure and, as Resnick so aptly puts it, "it was there largely by past consensus and implicit definition." (*ibid*.). In some obvious manner the object of inquiry in studies of human cognition had to be the individual mind, since thinking is located in the mental machinery of the body; what goes on in thinking must go on inside the brain. This delimitation of human cognition is thus not a theoretical assumption in the sense of being an explicitly formulated presupposition for scholarly analysis, it is part of a much wider web of taken-for-granteds and pre-theoretical assumptions regarding mind-body relationships and the fundamentally individual nature of cognition and action (Taylor, 1989; Wertsch, 1991).

The corollaries of these assumptions regarding the nature of cognition are readily observable in research. In a cognitivist perspective, cognition is decontextualized from physical (and communicative) action and treated as a mental entity that causes action but is somehow not part of it. As Harré and Gillett (1994) put it, "the theorists behind the cognitive revolution were mentalists, in the sense that they took for granted that there were mental processes behind what people could be observed to do" (p. 8). And understanding cognition implies primarily clarifying what people think, since "all action follows from thought" (Shotter, 1991, p. 57). In a similar vein, culture, context and social life in general have been conceived as entities that 'influence' cognition, but they have not been seen as constitutive elements of human thinking - it is not by means of cultural resources (including physical artifacts), contextual cues and social situatedness that people think and act; rather these dimensions can be added on to our understanding once we understand fully "how the brain processes information" (Barsalou, 1992, p. 9).

As a consequence of the perspectives launched within what is codified as the cognitive revolution, current research builds on a foundation on which cognition has been reinstated as a legitimate and significant phenomenon to study, yet where the assumptions regarding human thinking restrict the kinds of issues that can be addressed. The social situatedness and sensitivity of human sense-making and action that have been brought into focus in so much research in various fields during the past years, remain inexplicable, and context is still widely considered "a nuisance variable" rather than "an integral aspect of cognitive events." (Rogoff, 1984, p. 3, cf., e.g., Chaiklin & Lave, 1993; Nunes, Schliemann & Carraher, 1993). At a general level the present situation in cognitive research implies that the relationship between the social and collective levels of human activity on the one hand, and individual action on the other is difficult to address. In research, cognition is posited as first and foremost a property of the individual mind, and research implies modelling this entity as such. The ability to formulate models that prove consistency of thought-patterns across situations and transfer of what is learned between contexts is still the expected outcome of successful theorizing.

---

1. This article was written while the author was a fellow at the Swedish Collegium for the Advanced Study of the Social Sciences (SCASSS), Uppsala. The research reported here has been financed by the Swedish Council for Research in the Humanities and Social Sciences.

Cognition And Human Practices: A Sociocultural Approach

There are many ways to formulate the differences between a sociocultural approach to human cognition and communicative action on the one hand, and those assumptions that dominate mainstream cognitivist approaches on the other. A full account of these differences would result in an extensive discussion of the philosophical underpinnings and epistemological positions of different approaches to research. In the present context, however, I will focus on some specific issues that concern how human cognition and learning can be understood within the framework of a sociocultural approach in which such phenomena are viewed as integral elements of situated practices in complex societies.

Following the suggestions made by Vygotsky (1986) and later developed by Wertsch (1985, 1991) and several others, human thinking is fundamentally a product of social interaction. During ontogenesis, the *"nature of the development itself changes*, from biological to socio-historical" (Vygotsky, 1986, p. 94; italics in original). Thus, "verbal thought is not an innate, natural form of behavior, but is determined by a historical-cultural process and has specific properties and laws that cannot be found in the natural [i.e. earlier and pre-verbal] forms of thought and speech." (ibid.). This assumption of the fundamental interdependence between 'verbal thought' and social and cultural processes, Vygotsky also formulated in his famous and often quoted 'genetic law of cultural development'. Thus, "any function in the childs cultural development appears twice, or on two planes. First it appears on the social plane, and then on the psychological plane." (1981, p. 163). Thus, categories that are used between people in discursive practices to account for the world (inter-psychological categories), will appear as tools for thinking within individuals (i.e., as intra-psychological categories). Through formulations such as these, Vygotsky attempted to create the foundations for an understanding of thinking that is not premised on the assumption that cognition is exclusively a private and internal mental process disconnected from action in social life. Instead thinking relies on the use of modes of understanding the world - intellectual tools and signs - that are collective in nature, and it is in itself a social practice in which these tools are put to use for specific purposes. Thinking is thus not something that lies 'behind' or 'under' individual action, it is an integral part of human practices.

Thinking and the Use of Tools

One of the significant features of a sociocultural perspective on human thinking and learning that makes it stand out as an alternative to dualist positions within cognitivism is the assumption of the centrality of *mediation* and the role of *tools* - psychological as well as technical - in human practices. The concept of mediation refers to the fact that our relationship with the outside world is always mediated by signs and artifacts. We do not encounter the world as it exists in any neutral and objective sense outside the realm of human experience. We learn to interact with it by means of the signs and tools provided by our culture and in terms of which phenomena make sense. In this sense, human cognitive socialization - learning and development - is a process of appropriating concepts that originate in communicative practices in our culture. In other words, the world is pre-interpreted for us by previous generations, and we draw on the experiences that others have made before us.

Tools serve as mediational means, i.e., they - metaphorically speaking - stand between the individual and the world. The most important psychological tool is language, which is the prime device for rendering the world intelligible and for communicating our intentions to others. Language here does not refer to a formal system but should be conceived as a semiotic resource providing signs that can be flexibly and creatively used in social practices. "In contrast to many, contemporary analyses of language, which focus on the structure of sign systems independent of any mediating role they might play, a sociocultural interpretation presupposes that one conceives of language and other sign systems in terms of how they are a part of and *mediate* human action." (Wertsch, 1991, p. 29; italics in original).

An important corollary of this position is that language is first and foremost a system that serves purposes of coordinating human activities; it is a means of action and a practical resource rather than a device for contemplating the world *in vacuo* (Marková, 1982; Silverman & Torode, 1980). Concepts and words do not mean anything in and by themselves, language use and the construction of meaning are always social processes dependent on people who interact, and meaning is always relative to options and constraints that are present in social situations. "A word is a bridge thrown between myself and another" as Voloshinov (1973, p. 86) puts it. And consequently, if "one end of the bridge depends on me, then the other depends on my addressee. A word is a territory shared by both addresser and addressee, by the speaker and his interlocutor." (ibid). Communication is thus always a two-sided affair in which speakers (or writers) and listeners (or readers) actively contribute to create what can be "conceived of as an *inter-subjectively established social reality.*" (Rommetveit, 1973, p. 25; italics in original). Communication in this perspective is never an issue of simply reproducing meaning but rather is an active and in some sense creative process in which past experiences are brought to bear on whatever is talked about.

The concept of mediation and the role of language in this context have obvious links to current discussions within various constructivist positions on the nature of human concept formation as well as to concepts such as representation and processing used in cognitivist traditions. In cognitivist approaches, representation is held to be an inner image or a mental model (Johnson- Laird, 1983) that the mind creates when confronted with an object or an event and that matches this object. An additional tenet is that "cognitive representations are perceptually based, and that perception is basically realistic" (Edwards & Potter, 1992, p. 19), which implies that representations are often conceived as copies of whatever is out there. In contrast to this, a sociocultural approach would emphasize how discourse enters into our perceptions and thinking, and how conceptualizations of phenomena reflect distinctions that are discursive in origin rather than present in objects as such (Bergqvist & Säljö, 1994; Säljö & Bergqvist, in press). The somewhat archaic expression 'verbal thinking' that Vygotsky uses points to the continuity between communication and thinking that reflects this position. As the individual is socialized into a particular culture, there is a "close correspondence between thought and speech" (1986, p. 80). Thinking implies operating with psychological tools that originate in language and that allow for adequate and sensitive evaluations of what are situationally appropriate modes of describing or understanding an object or a phenomenon. There is no assumption of decontextualized and unverifiable correspondences between mental images and an outside reality.

An obvious implication of the perspective outlined above is thus that thinking to a large extent is achieved through talk. Thus, not only can we assume that there is a continuity between what goes on inside and outside the heads of individuals in terms of the semiotic resources used for thinking, it is also obvious that talk is a mode of thinking that is vital in almost every setting. As Hutchins & Palen (in press) put it, "natural language as a medium for creating representations is a language of thought." (p. 2). The obviousness of the fact that thinking goes on between individuals and by means of discourse often escapes researchers as a result of the sharp line of division maintained within a dualist position where thinking is construed as pursued in brain structures rather than by means of linguistic resources. Consider as an example the following two excerpts taken from a classroom in which students in secondary school are working on the problem of producing a statute-book in which the "*laws that were considered to be of primary importance for living safely in our society.*" (Bergqvist, 1990, p. 94, italics in original) were to be listed and discussed. In the first excerpt (see Figure 1) we find the students cooperating on this task by enumerating different kinds of offences that the statute book should specify.

Table 1: Excerpt of dialogue about statues

2	Hanna 1	Burglary, should I write that down? Should I write burglary?
3	Nina 1	Yes! (impatiently) Wait! Assault, murder, theft, robbery. That's only this kind of thing ... Is there no other ... eh (laughs) eh ... embarrassing, no bu
4	Hanna 2	Eh ... eh ... well, hit and run. Hit and run, we talked about that earlier on.
5	Nina 2	Well traffic and such.
6	Hanna 3	Drunken driving.
7	Nina 3	Lets just write down lots ... dru ... drunkenness. (giggling)
8	Hanna 4	Dangerous ... drunken ...
9	Nina 4	Shoplifting, yes.
10	Hanna 5	Dangerous driving, or whatever its called (Berqvist, 1990, p. 98)

The two girls Nina and Hanna here operate in a manner which could equally well be conceived as an internal dialogue within one individual. They coordinate their thinking within the context of a shared institutional activity, and they negotiate what is considered as significant contributions and valid representations of a criminal act. Their talking can be conceived as thinking, and their thinking is very clearly carried out by means of sociocultural resources which are linguistic in nature. When Nina in her first statement in this excerpt establishes with some embarrassment that they have been limiting themselves to violent activities and wants to change their line of thinking, her interlocutor responds by suggesting 'hit and run' as another example of a candidate crime. This particular example, which is an adequate contribution, however, can also be conceived as representing an act of physical violence. Nina therefore continues by taking 'hit and run' as additional example, but also by exploiting it as a resource for moving the conversation into the area of traffic, where they should be able to find lots of other offences that would fit into the task they have to do. Thus, the dynamics of thinking and dialogical reasoning are in many respects parallel and contain creative components in which different semantic potentials (Rommetveit, 1992) of expressions and utterances are exploited in productive manners.

Thinking is thus socially distributed by means of language (and other tools; cf. below), and talk is a most productive and significant vehicle for cognitive activities. It should not be conceived merely as a medium in which whatever is 'inside' the cognitive system of an individual is represented, as is so often done in research, for instance when collecting data through interviews, 'think-aloud' protocols or when conducting experiments (cf. Grossen, 1993; Elbers, & Kelderman, 1994; Elbers, 1991). Another example from the same corpus of data that further illustrates how thinking is a discursive process and has to be understood as occurring between individuals is shown in Tabelle 2. Here a group of four secondary school students working on the same issue as above are engaged in the activity of finding a technical term for a particular offence. Robert in his first comment gives a description in everyday language of this offence - destruction - but at the same time he makes clear that there is a term which in technical, legal parlance is the expected one. What triggers this discussion is a cognitive - and communicative - situation which comes close to the so-called tip-of- the-tongue phenomenon (cf. Brown & McNeill, 1966; Howard, 1983, p. 159ff) discussed in the literature

lang + gesture
reading + writing
systems of calculation
social interaction

through which we make meaning,
form concepts, construct representations

demonstrate self-awareness

Table 2: Excerpts from a dialogue on statute law (Bergqvist, 1990, p. 101)

729	Robert 181	What's destruction called? Its called something special.
730	Eva 218	We already have destruction once.
731	Inga 163	Offence.
732	Robert 182	No-o.
733	Eva 219	Well, it does have a special name.
734	Robert 183	Ye-es.
735	Inga 164	Damage.
736	Robert 184 Ralf 154 Eva 220	Yes!!
737	Eva 221	Good Inga!
738	Robert 185	Damage!! Oh, thats good Inga!!

Again, this interactive sequence can very well be understood as somehow representing what would go on within an individual in a similar problem solving situation. When attempting to find the term that they are searching for, individuals oscillate between internal 'verbal' thinking and externalizing their thoughts in explicit language to make what they think public. There is no sense in which our psychological understanding of interactions of this kind would be improved by positing internal thinking as somehow being pursued at a totally different level of description in terms of processes and mechanisms that would lie 'under' or 'behind' discursive action.

Psychological Tools and Learning

① doing ③ concept
② making construction
② meaning representation
(A) self aware

The role of psychological tools in human learning is thus fundamental. **By acquiring concepts and discursive tools, we appropriate ways of understanding reality that have developed within particular discursive practices in different sectors in a complex society.** When faced with identical problems or situations, people differing in expertise will construe the objects very differently depending on the conceptual frameworks they are familiar with and are able to draw upon. What is a chaotic and completely unintelligible picture to an outsider, as in the case of an X-ray, is highly meaningful and relevant for action for the expert nurse or physician. Even though individuals may be exposed to identical stimuli, these will mean very different things depending on experiential backgrounds and the conceptual resources we bring to the situation when deciphering the X-ray or any other cultural tool.

A very interesting example of the significance of psychological tools can be found in the work by De Groot (1965) on the nature of expertise in chess playing. De Groot made a series of controlled studies and experiments in which expert players (Masters and Grand Masters) and less expert, although quite competent, players (experts) were exposed to chess boards with on-going games for very brief intervals only. The task given to the participants was to reproduce as many as possible of the positions of the pieces on the board. The results show that there were very marked differences in the abilities of these groups to reproduce the positions. In particular, if the positions of the pieces could be seen as representing situations that are likely to appear in games amongst skilled players, experts (Masters and above) were much more accurate in their ability to describe the positions than were their less skilled colleagues (while previous research had shown that this difference did not appear if the pieces were placed in a random or atypical manner on the board). Thus, what this example illustrates is the fundamental mode in which psychological tools enter into the mode in which objects and processes are constituted for us. Again, these groups had access to identical stimuli, but what differed was the mode in which meaning was read into the patterns appearing on the chessboard. The Masters were able "to pick up the *essential relations between the pieces*, their mobility and capturing possibilities, their co-operation or opposition." (p. 331, italics in original). Thus, the Masters were able to construe the visual stimuli in terms of coherent and dynamically evolving patterns that followed the logic of skilled chess playing and in which there were potentials, threats and tensions rather than individual pieces placed next to each other.

These examples illustrate that representation is not a passive process of creating a mental image in a picture-like fashion. Rather, conceptual resources constitute objects and events for us in accordance with criteria utilized in specific human practices. Furthermore, conceptual knowledge is action-oriented and developed to serve as functional devices in social practices; "applying a concept to something enables me to act in ways that I otherwise could not." (Harré & Gillett, 1994, p. 41). Since modern society is characterized by a multitude of social and institutional practices in activity systems such as production, science, bureaucracies, schools, health care and many others, events and objects are construed in many different ways to serve different purposes. To learn is to appropriate psychological tools and conceptual resources that fit certain needs in on-going activities rather than to internalize a 'neutral' image of the world.

Artifacts and Cognition[1]

The Vygotskian analogy between psychological and technical tools is suggestive but should be taken with some caution (cf. Wertsch, 1985, p. 77ff). Yet, it is obvious that there are striking parallels between how technological devices and linguistic expressions serve as mediational means in social practices. Tools such as paper and pencil, newspapers and books and the wonders of modern information technology mediate reality for us in a wide range of activities; in an obvious sense our actions are performed by means of technical tools rather than by direct intervention in physical reality. Thus, we remember by writing things down in notebooks and calendars, and whenever we need to retrieve a telephone number, a code for the teller machine or whatever, we consult our notebook. When counting the money in our cheque account, there is nowhere we can go to count the money, rather we consult the record of the cheque account produced by the bank or we look in the cheque book that we keep ourselves. The use of a computer and software in a problem-solving situation may alter the nature of cooperation between learners in joint problem-solving and facilitate "co-construction of knowledge" (Light, Littleton, Messer & Joiner, 1994; cf. Barbieri & Light, 1992) by offering representations that provide concrete backgrounds for verbal interaction on how to plan, negotiate and so on.

The potential of the computer to transform both the nature and organization of the classroom is discussed by Cole and Griffin (1987) who contrast two metaphors for computer-student interaction. The first metaphor they discuss assumes that the computer is an agent, operating as a "partner in dialogue". This view implies that the student-computer system can be viewed as an analogue to the student-teacher system with the computer replacing the teacher. Within the framework provided by this perspective it is important to look at the computer's potential for providing structured hints, well timed feedback, and a wealth of factual knowledge. It is this metaphor, they suggest, that underlies the bulk of research on computers and education at the present time. The second metaphor they discuss is of the computer as a 'medium', not replacing

---

1. I am grateful to Paul Light and Karen Littleton, Department of Psychology, University of Southampton, for substantial contributions to this section.

people, but "reorganizing interactions among people", creating new environments in which children can be educated and grow by discovering and gaining access to the world around them. This metaphor emphasizes the potential of computers for re-organizing instruction within the classroom and for making possible the extension of education beyond the classroom (Cole & Griffin, 1987, pp. 45-46).

It is this second metaphor, that of computer as 'medium', which is of interest from the point of view of a sociocultural approach to psychology. Clearly, cultural psychology is not interested in computer technology simply as a new vehicle for transmitting knowledge or as a new way of providing exploratory environments. Rather, it is concerned with how computers uniquely transform the way in which human cognitive activity is organized. To date there has been very little research on this, thus there is a pressing need to consider the special relevance of computers for re-ordering the contexts of education by re-organizing interactions among people. For example, we need to understand how the use of educational software serves to reorganize the social processes of children's joint problem solving (Crook, 1992). Keogh and Barnes (1994) have started to investigate this issue by comparing the nature of the talk and joint activity observed in same or mixed-gender pairs of children engaged in an identical language problem solving task (involving the assembly of a poem from a jumbled collection of phrases) presented either on or off the computer. Their findings highlight the impact that the presence of the computer has on the activity of the mixed gender pairs: boys dominate the task when it is presented on the machine, whereas the activity is distributed more equally between the pair members when the task is off computer.

We also need to know how such technology reorganizes es the interactions among pupils and teachers. As Mercer notes, "the quality of understanding that learners acquire through the use of information technology in the classroom is not, and never will be, determined by the quality of the 'interface' between the learner and the technology. Quality of understanding, the nature of educational knowledge, is determined by a much more complex contextual system which is inseparable from how education is defined in our culture ... this culturally-based contextual system is continually created and re-created in the classroom through interactions between teachers and learners." (Mercer, 1993, p. 37).

When it comes to computer use, however, many children know more than their teacher. One investigation of 'expert' children and 'novice' teachers (Shrock & Stepp, 1991) took the form of a naturalistic study of the social interaction surrounding a microcomputer in an American elementary school classroom. The teacher was relatively inexperienced in computer use and so designated a child 'expert' as the resource person for students learning to use the computer. The observed negative effects on the role definition of 'teacher' and the frequency of interactions not conducive to learning led the researchers to warn of the potential danger of child experts becoming 'gate-keepers' of knowledge and competing authority figures in the classroom. Clearly, then, the use of technology in the classroom may facilitate a different kind of social dynamic between pupil and teacher, and future research will need to pay particular attention to the teacher/pupil discourse in classroom settings where new technology is taken as a focal point (Crook, 1992, p. 225).

As well as re-organizing interactions between people, computer technology has the potential to create new educational environments. Consider, for example, the opportunities offered by computer-mediated communication. Here computer technology can support joint activity which may need to be separated in time and space. In this situation the network provides a common storage area which can be referred to by collaborating pupils in different groups or from different classrooms. It may allow different generations of pupils to 'leave tracks' that become a resource for new cohorts.

In an interesting sense this configuration furnishes new media for the organization of common knowledge within the community of learners. Pupils are thereby given new opportunities to participate within that community - this might apply to networking infra-structures related at the level of primary school or at the level of undergraduate departments. Such technology also opens up the possibility for the extension of education beyond the classroom. As Crook (1992, p. 221) puts it, this "form of communication opens up exchanges between children who are growing up and learning in, perhaps, very different cultural contexts", and "it can also create real audiences for their work and a real possibility of intellectual co-ordination with peers in pursuit of joint projects."

But although computers have the potential to reorganize learning interactions in a variety of significant ways, everyday experience suggests that social institutions have a remarkable capacity for 'neutralizing' the effects of new developments, technological or otherwise. Classrooms may prove to be too well 'buffered' to be much affected by computers and indeed may assimilate computers entirely into their existing ways of doing things. Only time will tell whether computer technology will radically alter the ways in which children's thinking is developed and extended (cf. Cole, 1991).

In a very fundamental sense, we think with and through artifacts. In human practices there is an intricate interplay between tools and physical activities. The experienced carpenter attempting to establish how much wood that will be needed when repairing the wall of a wooden house will make a drawing of the building and make his calculations by means of this paper and pencil version of the house. There will be no need to measure the wall more than once, since the drawing - if done with adequate precision - mediates the wall in a functional manner. Most further reasoning can be done without measuring the real object.

Technical tools thus extend, or rather transform, the capacities for physical and intellectual action that were bestowed upon human beings by nature, as it were. With tools such as paper and pencil, calculators, binoculars, computers and telephones, tasks that would be burdensome, maybe even impossible to perform become manageable. In the creation of human culture, tool-making can be seen as one of the most powerful achievements.The difference between digging with ones hands and with a shovel of some kind or between hunting by throwing stones and using a bow and an arrow are profound also from a psychological point of view. Changing tools alters the structure of work activity (Scribner & Cole, 1981, p. 8) and, thus, the cognitive and communicative requirements of our actions. Through the use of tools, the human environment is fundamentally transformed and new modes of organizing habitats and social life become possible. We no longer have to follow the rhythms and demands of nature, rather we can actively transform and control the physical environment to the needs we perceive.

In parenthesis it can be noted that many scholars argue that tool-making is not an exclusively human talent. Even non-human primates show signs of using tools to adapt to demands of certain habitats and to avail themselves of resources they would otherwise not be able to utilize. Thus, chimpanzees have been found to use sticks for activities such as ant-dipping and termite-fishing (Boesch & Boesch, 1993), and they also use stones for cracking nuts that they would otherwise not be able to open. Furthermore, they not only use tools but also produce them; thus wild chimpanzees make tools using six different methods (Boesch & Boesch, 1993, p. 162) which include cutting objects (sticks, stalks, etc.) to be of certain lengths and also shaping them to fit the demands of the situation in which they are to be used (which includes using artifacts for body care!). The argument for conceiving such achievements as almost culture-like, gains momentum from observations that indicate that primates that belong to the same species and that are genetically identical, vary considerably in the tools they utilize. Thus, there are substantial local differences in tool behavior in each chimpanzee population even though the basic conditions for tool use (potential tool material and food source) are present in the habitat. (Sugiyama, 1993, p. 183).

Human tool use is of course much more sophisticated and the range of activities in which we make use of tools is impressive. In fact, there are few activities in which human-made artifacts do not play a decisive role. And as tools develop, increasingly complex and demanding activities can be carried out by means of artificial resources. What is interesting from the point of view of cognition and learning is that tools cannot be conceived as external to cognition, on the contrary they are integral parts of our cognitizing as well as of our physical action. An illuminating example of this has been given by Bateson (1972), which is discussed at some length by Wertsch (1991, p. 33ff) and Goodwin and Duranti (1992, p. 4ff), of the blind man using a stick. The stick and the blind man operate together as one functional and cognitive system in a particular activity, and the stick is an extension of the intellectual and sensory capacities of its user. However, the stick has no power to communicate signals outside its use by a human being, it gains its power as a device for orienting oneself and for relating to the environment only when integrated into a human practice and when used by a cognitizing subject engaged in a purposeful activity. The tool and the human being operate in a system that cannot be divided if one wants to understand cognition and practical action, rather there is a seamless co-functionality in which the mediational means form part of actions in situated practices.

Situating Thinking in Human Practices

It follows from what has been said above that learning in a sociocultural perspective can be described as the appropriation and mastery of communicative (including conceptual) and technical tools that serve as mediational means in social practices. These tools are the products of culture and they thus represent the experiences made by previous generations. At the same time, however, even physical artifacts contain knowledge that is of a conceptual and thus discursive origin. When interacting with the world by means of an instrument such as a compass or a watch, these tools contain symbolic resources that represent the world in categories that are clearly human in origin; the compass gives directions in degrees and the watch in units such as seconds, minutes and hours. Even technical devices can thus to a large extent be seen as extensions of what was originally human conceptual tools, although these resources have now been built into physical equipment.

In recent research by scholars such as Suchman (1987; Suchman & Trigg, 1993), Hutchins (1994), Goodwin (in press), and many others, this perspective of studying cognition as situated action and as tool mediated has been taken further in interesting ways. In a series of studies, Hutchins (Hutchins & Palen, in press) has explored the interdependence between human action and technological tools in environments such as cockpits and when navigating in the pilot house on board modern naval ships. In the latter context, Hutchins points out how the long history of navigation implies a continuity in the psychological and even some technological tools that are used. The task of navigating a modern ship is socially distributed and divided between individuals performing actions that imply reading instruments, coordinating information and making decisions on a continuous basis whenever the ship is at sea. Instruments such as nautical charts, an alidade, telephones and other communication devices, watches, echo-sounding equipment and several others are necessary ingredients in this complex activity, which involves up to six people working intensely when navigating in narrow waters. The cognitive part of this work is very clearly achieved by thinking, by communicating and by consulting instruments that account for the world in a manner that is productive for this particular activity. Thus, the task of navigating and "its computational properties are determined in large part by the structure of the tools with which the navigators work." (p. 43), and the cognitive dimension is precisely what unites people and instruments in a socially organized practice. Thought is shaped by and implemented in a collective activity in a particular setting, and we will learn little about cognition in real world events if we assumed that "cognitive activity has to be crammed into the individual mind" (p. 62) and described in a language that refers to hypothetical entities and processes that in mysterious ways differ from what can be observed in interaction. As Hutchins argues, "the properties of groups of minds in interaction with each other, or the properties of the interaction between individual minds and artifacts in the world, are frequently at the heart of intelligent human performance." (ibid.), and there is nothing more fundamental to cognition than that.

In a similar study of sophisticated mediational devices used in an aircraft, Hutchins & Palen (in press) illustrate how different such mediational resources are employed in parallel and as multilayered resources for coordinating action. In this case, the analysis concerns the activities of an airline crew with three members discovering a fuel leak during a simulated flight. The authors show how the technological devices (among other things the panel with the fuel gauge and other relevant instruments) mediate what happens in the aircraft in a manner which is typical of modern technology. The "fuel system itself as a collection of physical components cannot actually be seen from any real vantage point, but the pilots can 'see' the fuel system by seeing through the panel. In fact, it is only through seeing the fuel panels and diagrams... that pilots have any experience of the fuel system." (p. 20). The pilots thus interact with a mediated version of the tanks and the rest of the components of the fuel system, they have no immediate physical contact with it outside their operations on the panel. As is evident from the title of the work, 'Constructing Meaning from Space, Gesture, and Talk', the authors show how the instruments and the equipment of the cockpit, the gestures and non-verbal signals and talk produce meaning in the task of attempting to master the problem of the failure in the fuel system. Thus, when pointing to the instruments on the panel in shared practical activities, "the gestures acquire their meaning by virtue of being superimposed on the meaningful spatial layout of the fuel control panel". Furthermore, "enacted over the panel, ..., these gestures take on meanings such as turning off the pumps and [as indicating] the newly established path along which fuel is flowing", while the "same gestures produced in the absence of the panel would, of course, be quite meaningless." (p. 21). Thus, the "properties of the crew and cockpit as a cognitive system are in part determined by the patterns and richness of communication among them" (p. 22), and talk, gestures, instruments, and cognition are intimately intertwined and mutually supportive and contribute to the creation of a functional unit. The robustness of this unit is produced partially by the complementarity of the resources available; while "gesture by itself is always action in the present, the verbal layer of the representation does things that cannot be done in the other layers" (p. 21), for instance "to control conceptual and temporal relationships" (p. 22).

Conclusions

Throughout this chapter, I have been arguing for understanding human learning and cognition by means of unit that is identical to what Goodwin (in press), following Goffman, refers to as a "situated activity system" (p. 6). In such systems, cognition and learning have to be accounted for by analyzing a socially purposeful and situated activity which is maintained through practices that integrate physical tools and instruments, communicative (including cognitive) activities, rules and traditions of participant roles and contributions, and criteria of success and failure. Thinking will be understood as pursued in conjunction with artifacts, and the exact modes in which cognition and practical action are shared between actors and mediational means become objects of analysis rather than something that can be taken for granted by means of *a priori* restricting cognition to what takes place inside the heads of individuals.

By analyzing learning in terms of the roles and responsibilities given to people within situated activity systems, it becomes possible to understand how individuals expand their intellectual repertoires and practical skills through participation in collective activities rather than through absorbing information *in vacuo*. Expertise will be seen as something that is publicly displayed and shaped within the context of socially meaningful activities, rather than as something that is of a strictly internal and mental nature.

Following such a path will also enable us to reconsider the modes in which our understanding of learning is hampered by past restrictions. One notable such example concerns the issue of transfer of knowledge. Through the analysis presented above, it becomes possible to understand why the framing of learning problems in terms of transfer - as traditionally conceived - is too limited (cf. Lave, 1988; Lave & Wenger, 1991; see also Gruber et al., this volume). The assumption that individuals carry knowledge, procedures and skills from one context to the other to apply them to new problems represents an unreasonable position. As has been argued above, thinking is part of a situated activity system, and as the situation changes so will the mediational means and the modes in which problems are structured and perceived. In situated activity systems, the constitution of a problem is a creative and most significant activity, and the determination of what is problematic about an instance is not necessarily visible by analyzing the problem as such. Encountering a task inside or outside the work place or the school may dramatically transform our perceptions of it and the range of solutions that appear reasonable. In fact, whether we encounter a problem in the context of a math lesson or a social science lesson may alter our assumptions of what are appropriate modes of dealing with it (Säljö & Wyndhamn, 1993).

Thus, the apparent fact that human beings are able to learn cannot be understood by means of the highly limiting assumptions regarding the decontextualized nature of knowledge that characterizes the idea of transfer, which confuses rather than clarifies the issues. The concept itself risks putting us into a paradoxical situation; at the same time as much research that has been specifically designed to study transfer fails to demonstrate any significant effects (cf. Lave, 1988, for extensive discussion), we know that what people are able to do must in some sense reflect their past experiences. The task for a systematic research approach to the issue of learning in complex settings becomes precisely one of studying how a problem is understood and constituted, and what kinds of structuring resources that individuals rely on when dealing with it (cf. Newman, Griffin & Cole, 1984). We will learn little by continuing to assume that learning can be understood as a simple process in which decontextualized pieces of information and conceptual knowledge are taken from one context to the next in a mechanical fashion. Modern situated activity systems are far too dynamic and complex to allow for such simple assumptions to serve as productive and inspiring theoretical guidelines.

References

Barbieri, M.S., & Light, P. (1992). Interaction, gender and performance on a computer-based problem-solving task. *Learning and Instruction, 2(3)*, 199-214.

Barsalou, L.W. (1992). *Cognitive psychology.* Hillsdale, NJ: Erlbaum.

Bateson, G. (1972). *Steps to an ecology of mind.* New York: Ballantine.

Bergqvist, K. (1990). Doing schoolwork. Task premises and joint activity in the comprehensive classroom. *Linköping Studies in Arts and Science, 55*. Linköping: University of Linköping.

Bergqvist, K., & Säljö, R. (1994). Conceptually blindfolded in the optics lab. Dilemmas of inductive learning. *European Journal of Psychology of Education, 9(2)*, 149-158.

Boesch, Ch., & Boesch, H. (1993). Diversity of tool use and tool-making in wild chimpanzees. In A. Berthelet & J. Chavaillon (Eds.), *The use of tools by human and non-human primates.* Oxford: Clarendon.

Brown, R., & McNeill, D. (1966). The tip-of-the-tongue phenomenon. *Journal of Verbal Learning and Verbal Behaviour, 5*, 325-337.

Chaiklin, S., & Lave, J. (1993). *Understanding practice. Perspectives on activity and context.* Cambridge, Ma.: Cambridge University Press.

Cole, M. (1991). A cultural theory of development: What does it imply about the application of scientific research? *Learning and Instruction, 1(3)*, 187-200.

Cole, M., & Griffin, P. (1987). *Contextual factors in education: Improving science and mathematics education for minorities and women.* Madison: Wisconsin Center for Education Research.

Crook, C. (1992). Cultural artefacts in social development: The case of computers. In H. McGurk (Ed.), *Childhood social development: Contemporary perspectives.* Hove: Lawrence Erlbaum.

De Groot, A. (1965). *Thought and choice in chess.* The Hague: Mouton.

Edwards, D., & Potter, J. (1992). *Discursive psychology.* London: Sage.

Elbers, E. (1991). The development of competence and its social context. *Educational Psychology Review, 3*, 73-99.

Elbers, E., & Kelderman, A. (1994). Ground rules for testing: Expectations and misunderstandings in test situations. *European Journal of Psychology of Education, 9 (2)*, 111-120.

Goodwin, C. (in press). The blackness of black: Color categories as situated practice. In C. Pontecorvo, L. Resnick, & R. Säljö (Eds.), *Discourse, tools, and reasoning:Situated cognition and technologically supported environments.* (preliminary title). New York: Springer.

Goodwin, C., & Duranti, A. (1992). Rethinking context: An introduction. In A. Duranti & C.Goodwin (Eds.), *Rethinking context. Language as an interactive phenomenon.* Cambridge: Cambridge University Press.

Grossen, M. (1993). Negotiating the meaning of questions in didactic and experimental contracts. *European Journal of Psychology of Education, 8(4)*, 451-471.

Harré, R., Gillett, G. (1994). *The discursive mind.* London: Sage.

Howard, D.V. (1983). *Cognitive psychology. Memory, language, and thought.* New York: MacMillan.

Hutchins, E. (1994). *Cognition in the wild.* Cambridge, MA: The MIT Press.

Hutchins, E., & Palen, V. (in press). Constructing meaning from space, gesture, and talk. To appear in C. Pontecorvo, L. B. Resnick, & R. Säljö (Eds.), *Discourse, tools, and reasoning: Situated cognition and technologically supported environments.* (preliminary title). New York: Springer.

Johnson-Laird, P. (1983). *Mental models.* Cambridge, MA: Harvard University Press.

Keogh, T., & Barnes, P. (1994, September). Computers versus paper; girls versus boys. Paper presented at the *International Conference of Group and Interactive Learning*, University of Strathclyde.

Lave, J. (1988). *Cognition in practice.* Cambridge: Cambridge University Press.

Lave, J., & Wenger, E. (1991). *Situated learning. Legitimate peripheral participation.* Cambridge: Cambridge University Press.

Light, P., Littleton, K., Messer, D., & Joiner, R. (1994). Social and communicative processes In computer-based problem solving. *European Journal of Psychology of Education, 9 (2)*, 93-110.

Marková, I. (1982). *Paradigms, thought, and language.* Chichester: Wiley.

Mercer, N. (1993). Computer-based activities in classroom contexts. In P. Scrimshaw (Ed.), *Language, classrooms and computers.* London: Routgledge.

Newman, D., Griffin, P., & Cole, M. (1984). Social constraints in laboratory and classroom tasks. In B. Rogoff & J. Lave (Eds.), *Everyday cognition: Its development in social context.* Cambridge, MA: Harvard University Press.

Nunes, T., Schliemann, A., & Carraher, D. W. (1993). *Street mathematics and school mathematics.* Cambridge: Cambridge University Press.

Resnick, L.B. (1991). Shared cognition: Thinking as social practice. In L. Resnick, J.M. Levine, & S. Teasley (Eds.), *Perspectives on socially shared cognition.* Washington, DC: American Psychological Association.

Rogoff, B. (1984). Introduction: Thinking and learning in social context. In B. Rogoff & J. Lave (Eds.), *Everyday cognition: Its development in social context.* Cambridge, MA: Harvard University Press.

Rommetveit, R. (1973). *On message structure.* London: Wiley.

Rommetveit, R. (1992). Outlines of a dialogically based social-cognitive approach to human cognition and communication. In A. Heen-Wold (Ed.), *The dialogical alternative: Towards a theory of langauge and mind.* Oslo: Scandinavian University Press.

Säljö, R., & Bergqvist, K. (in press). Seeing the light. Discourse and practice in the optics lab. To appear in C. Pontecorvo, L. B. Resnick, & R. Säljö (Eds.), *Discourse, tools and reasoning: Situated cognition and technologically supported environments.* (preliminary title). New York: Springer.

Säljö, R., & Wyndhamn, J. (1993). Solving everyday problems in the formal setting: An empirical study of the school as a context for thought. In S. Chaiklin & J. Lave (Eds.), *Understanding practice. Perspectives on activity and context.* Cambridge: Harvard University Press.

Scribner, S., & Cole, M. (1981). *The psychology of literacy.* Cambridge, MA: Harvard University Press.

Shotter, J. (1991). The rhetorical-responsive nature of mind: A social constructionist account. In A. Still & A. Costall (Eds.), *Against cognitivism. Alternative foundations for cognitive psychology.* London: Harvester-Wheatsheaf.

Shrock, S., & Stepp, S. (1991). The role of child micro-computer experts in an elementary classroom: A theme emerging from a naturalistic study. *Journal of Research on Computing in Education, 23*, 545-559.

Silverman, D., & Torode, B. (1980). *The material word.* London: Routledge & Kegan Paul.

Suchman, L. (1987). *Plans and situated actions. The problem of human machine communication.* Cambridge: Cambridge University Press.

Suchman, L., & Trigg, R. (1993). Artificial intelligence as craftwork. In S. Chaiklin & J. Lave (Eds.), *Understanding practice. Perspectives on activity and context.* Cambridge: Cambridge University Press.

Sugiyama, Y. (1993). Local variation of tools and tool use among wild chimpanzee populations. In A. Berthelet & J. Chavaillon (Eds.), *The use of tools by human and non-human primates.* Oxford: Clarendon.

Taylor, C. (1989). *Sources of the self: The making of modern identity.* Cambridge, MA: Harvard University Press.

Voloshinov, V.N. (1973). *Marxism and the philosophy of language.* [L. Matejka &I. R.Titutnik, Trans.]. New York: Seminar Press.

Vygotsky, L.S. (1981). The genesis of higher mental functions. In J.V. Wertsch (Ed.), The concept of activity in Soviet psychology. Armonk, NY: Sharpe.

Vygotsky, L.S. (1986). *Thought and language.* [A. Kozulin, Trans.] Cambridge, MA: The MIT Press.

Wertsch, J.V. (1985). *Vygotsky and the social formation of mind*. Cambridge, MA: Harvard University Press.

Wertsch, J.V. (1991). *Voices of the mind*. Cambridge, MA: Harvard University Press.

Learning Theory and Instructional Science

Erik De Corte

Introduction

Three major components can be distinguished in a theory of learning from instruction, namely a theory of expertise describing the knowledge structures and skills underlying competent performance in a domain, an acquisition theory explaining the processes of learning and development necessary to achieve expert performance, and a theory of intervention describing appropriate and effective teaching methods and instructional strategies for eliciting those processes (see also Resnick, 1983).

While the study of learning was a central issue in psychological research in the behavioristic tradition, the rise and breakthrough of cognitive psychology starting in the late 1950s led to a shift in focus toward the analysis of expertise and an almost deliberate neglect of acquisition processes. But in recent years researchers in the field have become again interested in learning phenomena (Glaser, 1992b; Shuell, 1986). This renewed interest has been stimulated by work aiming at the design of powerful learning environments, but also by research focussing on the development of models of machine learning.

Because understanding of competent performance is relevant and useful in view of studying the processes necessary to acquire expertise, the aptitudes involved in skilled learning, thinking and problem solving will first be described briefly. Next an overview will be given of some major characteristics of effective learning in humans that derive from recent research in instructional psychology. A major and topical issue in research on learning and instruction will then be discussed, namely transfer of knowledge and cognitive skills. Finally, some implications for the design of instruction will be presented.

Aptitudes Involved in Skilled Learning and Thinking

There is emerging a research-based consensus that skilled performance in solving new problems and approaching challenging learning tasks in a variety of content domains requires the acquisition of four categories of aptitudes. The term "aptitude" is used here in the broad sense as advocated recently by Snow (1992), namely to refer to any characteristic of the student which can influence his or her learning and problem-solving activity and achievement. Those four categories of aptitudes, which can be conceived of as the primary goals of cognitive learning in a variety of instructional and training settings, are the following:

1. Flexible application of a well-organized, domain-specific knowledge base, involving facts, symbols, conventions, definitions, formulas, algorithms, concepts, and rules which constitute the substance of a subject-matter field (see e.g., Glaser, 1991).

2. Heuristic methods, i.e. systematic search strategies for problem analysis and transformation, such as carefully analyzing a problem specifying the knowns and the unknowns, decomposing a problem into subgoals, finding an easier related or analogous problem, working backward from the intended goal or solution (see e.g., Schoenfeld, 1992). Although heuristic methods do not guarantee that one will find the solution of a problem, they increase substantially the probability of success because they induce a systematic and planned approach to the task.

3. Metacognitive knowledge and skills, involving knowledge concerning one's own cognitive functioning, on the one hand, and activities relating to the self-monitoring and regulation of one's cognitive processes, on the other. The latter include such skills as planning a solution process; monitoring an ongoing solution process; evaluating and, if necessary, debugging an answer or solution; and reflecting on one's learning and problem-solving activities (Brown, Bransford, Campione, & Ferrara, 1983).

4. Affective components, involving beliefs, attitudes, and emotions which reflect the whole range of affective reactions to learning, and vary in the degree of affect involved, namely from rather cold for beliefs to hot for emotions (McLeod 1990). Recent work, for instance in the domain of mathematics learning, has especially focused on the identification of beliefs many of which are induced by teaching, and have a rather negative effect on student learning and problem solving, such as "being able to solve a problem is largely a question of luck", or "solving a problem should not take more than a few minutes".

The available literature shows also that in expert problem solving those different categories of aptitudes are applied integratively and interactively (De Corte, Greer & Verschaffel, in press). Moreover, it has recently been argued by Perkins, Jay and Tishman (in press) that mastering the appropriate aptitudes is not enough to guarantee productive thinking and problem solving, but that this requires in addition a disposition to do so. Perkins et al. (in press) distinguish three components of such a disposition: inclination, sensitivity, and ability. Inclination is defined as the tendency to engage in a given behavior due to motivation and habits. Sensitivity refers to the feeling for opportunities for implementing the appropriate behavior. Ability constitutes the actual skill to deploy the behavior, and corresponds largely to the aptitudes mentioned above. In other words, while cognitive aptitudes as well as affective, motivational components are important aspects of a disposition, this notion involves more; this view is based on the observation that students often have the necessary aptitudes to perform certain tasks or solve certain problems, but do not exercise them because of lack of spontaneous inclination and sensitivity.

Major Features of Effective Learning

If one endorses the preceding dispositional view of skilled learning and thinking, the question arises as to what kind of acquisition processes are conducive to the attainment in learners of the intended disposition and the aptitudes it involves.

The negative answer to the latter question is that this disposition cannot be acquired through learning processes that consist of the passive and often decontextualized absorption of knowledge gained and institutionalized by past generations. Although often implicitly, this view is still prevailing in today's educational practice; the conception of learning as the acquisition of formally taught explicit knowledge also underlies many intelligent tutoring systems that derive from mainstream cognitive science (Brown, 1990).

Without attempting to be exhaustive, I will outline a series of important, research-based features of (effective) learning processes that provide a sound basis for instructional design. Those characteristics can be summarized in the following definition of learning: it is a constructive, cumulative, self-regulated, intentional, situated and collaborative process of knowledge and meaning building (see e.g., Cobb, in press; Shuell, 1986, in press; Brown, Collins, & Duguid, 1989).

Learning is constructive (Cobb, in press; De Corte, 1990; Glaser, 1991). This major and overarching characteristic that is supported by a substantial body of research, involves that learners are not passive recipients of information, but that they construct their own knowledge and skills. Some scholars in the field of learning and instruction, for instance in the domain of mathematics education, take an extreme or radical position in this respect, claiming that all knowledge is a subjective and purely idiosyncratic cognitive construction and not at all the reflection of an objective reality "out there" (see e.g., von Glasersfeld, 1991). Other researchers, however, represent a more moderate or realistic standpoint. The constructivist view certainly implies that acquiring new knowledge and skills is an active process, in the sense that it requires cognitive processing from the side of the learner (Shuell, 1986, in press). Referring to Salomon and Globerson (1987) one can say that effective learning is a mindful and effortful activity. Recent research in a variety of content domains has shown that this constructive learning activity is not always successful, but results rather frequently in the acquisition of misconceptions or deficient skills (see e.g., Perkins & Simmons, 1988).

Learning is cumulative (Dochy, 1992; Shuell, 1986, in press; Vosniadou & Brewer, 1987). This means that learners construct new knowledge on the basis of their prior - formal as well as informal - knowledge: starting from what they already know and can do, learners process actively the information they encounter, and, as a consequence, derive new meanings and acquire new skills. Taking into account that learners are sometimes afflicted with misconceptions and deficient skills the impact of prior knowledge on future learning can be negative and inhibitory instead of positive and facilitating. In this respect, it is important to mention that misconceptions have been found to be often very resistant to change (see e.g., Perkins & Simmons, 1988).

Learning is self-regulated (Corno, 1986; Shuell, in press; Simons, 1989). This characteristic refers to the metacognitive aspects of effective learning, especially the managing and monitoring activities of the learner. According to Simons (1989) this involves: "being able to prepare one's own learning, to take the necessary steps to learn, to regulate learning, to provide for one's own feedback and performance judgements and to keep oneself concentrated and motivated". (p. 16) The more learning becomes self-regulated the more students take control over their own learning; correlatively, they are less dependent on instructional support for performing these regulatory activities.

Learning is goal-oriented (Bereiter & Scardamalia, 1989; Shuell, in press). Although learning can also occur incidently, there is now a wide consensus that effective, meaningful learning is facilitated by explicit awareness of and orientation toward a goal. Taking into account its constructive and self-regulated nature, it is plausible to assume that learning will be most successful when students determine and state their own goals. But learning can also be successful when predefined objectives are put forward by a teacher, a textbook, a computer program, etc., assuming, however, that those goals are endorsed and adopted by the students (Shuell, in press). Bereiter and Scardamalia (1989) have introduced the term intentional learning to refer to those cognitive processes that have learning itself as a goal.

Learning is situated (Brown, Collins, & Duguid, 1989; Greeno, 1991; Lave & Wenger, 1991). The notion that learning and cognition are situated has emerged in reaction to the "strong" information-processing view, that considers learning and thinking as processes that take place within the mind, and knowledge as representations of facts, concepts, relations, principles, procedures stored and encapsulated in the head - the static pieces of furniture of the mind (Hall, 1881) that can be activated and used to carry out a task or solve a problem. In contrast, the situated view conceives learning in terms of increasing participation in communities of practice (Lave & Wenger, 1991), and knowledge as fundamentally distributed, i.e. "stretched over, not divided among -- mind, body, activity and culturally organized settings (which include other actors)" (Lave, 1988, p. 1). In a further elaboration of this environmental view, Greeno (1991) has compared learning a knowledge domain with learning to live in an environment in which one has to learn how to move around, what the available resources are, and how to use them in carrying out tasks and activities successfully. The person's knowledge, then, "is in his or her abilities to find and use the resources, not in having mental versions of maps and instructions as the basis for all reasoning and action" (Greeno, 1991, p. 175). A major implication of this view of learning and knowledge is the need to anchor learning in authentic, real-life social and physical contexts that are representative of the situations in which students will have to use their knowledge and skills afterwards (Brown et al., 1989).

Learning is collaborative (Brown et al., 1989; Vygotsky, 1978). The situated view of learning as participation in social practice involves already the collaborative character of productive learning. The notion that learning is essentially a social process is also central in the conception of many radical constructivists, and is used to explain how the almost idiosyncratic processes of knowledge construction can lead to the acquisition of common concepts and skills among learners. For example, Wood, Cobb, and Yackel (1991) consider social interaction as essential for mathematics learning, individual knowledge construction occurring throughout processes of interaction, negotiation, and collaboration through which students become acculturated members of a mathematical community and culture. The impact of social interaction on knowledge acquisition and on cognitive development is also supported by recent developmental research (see e.g., Perret-Clermont & Schubauer-Leoni, 1989).

Transfer: A Holy Grail?

The importance of being able to transfer acquired knowledge and cognitive skills to new learning tasks and problem situations is recognized with respect to schooling, but also in non-school educational and instructional settings. This issue is obviously not only of theoretical significance, but is also of utmost practical importance, as has been clearly voiced by McKeachie (1987): "Nonetheless, many researchers and educators, as well as hordes of businessman, government officials, and others, hope to find ways of teaching and learning general problem-solving skills. If we grant that prior knowledge is necessary for effective problem solving in most areas, the question becomes one of whether or not problem-solving skills developed in one field can be taught in ways that enable the skills to be transferred to other fields in which the individual has some prior knowledge." (p. 445) Taking this into account it is not surprising that considerable attention has been paid to the topic in the recent literature (see e.g., Clark, 1992; Cormier & Hagman, 1987; De Corte, 1987; Detterman & Sternberg, in press; Mayer, 1988; Perkins & Salomon, in press; Prawat, 1989; Salomon & Perkins, 1989; Singley & Anderson, 1989). However, the available research shows that transfer is a very complex phenomenon, that transfer effects do not occur spontaneously, and are even difficult to obtain deliberately (see e.g., Butterfield & Nelson, 1989; Clark, 1992; Perkins & Salomon, 1989). The latter findings have been accounted for in the recent literature by a robust result of the analysis of expertise in a variety of domains, namely that competence in a certain field depends to a large extent on the availability of a well-organized domain-specific knowledge base (see e.g., Glaser, 1987). And, this interpretation was reinforced by the emerging notion that learning is situated (Brown et al., 1989), and thus context-bound. However, another explanation does not deny the importance of domain-specific knowledge for skilled performance, but stresses that the lack of positive transfer results is mainly due to the absence of appropriate conditions needed for transfer (De Corte & Verschaffel, 1986; Perkins & Salomon, 1989; Perkins & Salomon, in press). Those conditions relate to characteristics of the learners (subject variables), to features of the tasks (task variables), and to the nature of the instruction (instructional variables) (see also De Corte, Verschaffel, & Schrooten, 1991).

Concerning the subject variables the extensive research program of Brown, Campione, and their coworkers (see e.g., Brown, 1989; Campione & Brown, 1990) has shown that skilled learners distinguish themselves from their less skilled fellows with respect to one of the four categories of aptitudes involved in competent learning and problem solving mentioned before, namely metacognitive skills. This confirms the self-regulated nature of learning discussed in the previous section. Recently Campione & Brown (1990) have summarized their findings as follows: "More efficient learners and more flexible transferrers spend more time planning, and analyzing and classifying the problems before they attempt to offer an answer. They are more likely to take advantage of opportunities to check their reasoning during the course of working on a problem. They are better able to engage in a number of efficient fix-up strategies when they seem to be getting off track. Poorer performers, in contrast, begin generating solutions much more quickly. They try out alternative rules in a fairly random order, trying to see if it works, and when informed that they are wrong, moving on to another one, etc. When beginning to work on a new problem, they are less likely to refer back to prior problems. Overall, the global learning and transfer indices do appear to reflect the operation of an array of monitoring and self-regulatory skills, or weak but general methods" (p.168). In terms of Kuhl's (1985) theory of self-regulation one could say that skilled learners and transferrers are characterized by a high level of action control, i.e. a systematic and persistent orientation toward a preconceived objective; this implies that the person is constantly monitoring his activity, and, when necessary, makes the required corrections. These findings are the more interesting because they question the currently prevailing standpoint that individual differences in competency as well as differences between developmental levels are mainly determined by domain-specific knowledge.

As far as the task variables are concerned it is rather generally accepted that far transfer is more difficult to obtain than near transfer. This notion of transfer distance relates to the degree to which the transfer task is remote or novel in comparison with the original learning task. However, also here recent work suggests that reality is more complex. Indeed, Bassok & Holyoak (1989) have reported asymmetric results: while they found substantial transfer effects from algebra to physics, the opposite outcomes did hardly occur. These findings were interpreted in terms of the degree of content-specific embedding of the original learning outcomes, in the sense that physics is a semantically more rich domain than algebra. But a later study by Bassok (1990) showed that this does not provide a sufficient explanation for the lack of transfer from physics to algebra; indeed, she observed transfer from economy - which is also a content-rich domain - to algebra. All these results lead to the conclusion that as far as the task aspects are concerned, the probability of transfer cannot be reduced to the distance variable, but that more qualitative task features and their mutual relations influence the occurrence of transfer.

A major aspect that has to be taken into account when explaining the disappointing findings in many transfer studies, is their lack of an intentional and systematic orientation toward instruction for transfer. In these investigations, it was often more or less implicitly assumed that learning would produce transfer in a rather direct and automatic way. However, on the basis of the acquired research experience on the one hand, and the transfer literature in general on the other, this assumption is now disposed as "wishful thinking". Indeed, it has been shown over and over that concepts and skills learned in one domain are not spontaneously generalized to other content domains (Gick & Holyoak, 1983; Pressley, Snyder, & Cariglia-Bull, 1987). Most investigators nowadays share the standpoint that in order to achieve cognitive transfer in learners, it is necessary to teach explicitly and intentionally for transfer. This implies that the teacher has to show students how the skills learned in one context can be usefully applied in other problem situations, to teach them how to do so, and to give them experiences in applying their skills in different contexts. Recent research, especially a series of studies relating to transfer from learning to program (De Corte, Verschaffel, & Schrooten, 1992; Mayer, 1988), in which more attention has been paid to the design of transfer-oriented learning environments, have indeed shown transfer effects, albeit that in most cases only near transfer has been achieved, i.e. transfer to tasks that are closely related to the original learning task. This raises the question as to which are the instructional variables that have facilitated the occurrence of transfer in successful studies? In line with the preceding results on the subject variables, transfer-oriented instruction should aim at fostering the metacognitive skills and the action control of the learners. Simultaneously initial learning of the knowledge and skills the transfer of which is aimed at, has to result in thorough mastery through extensive and diverse practice (Gick & Holyoak, 1987; Perkins & Salomon, in press; Salomon & Perkins, 1989; Simons, 1990). To pursue more directly and intentionally the transfer of certain knowledge and skills, the so-called high road to transfer as described by Salomon and Perkins (1989) has to some degree been adopted in the successful studies referred to above. This involves mainly the following two aspects: Mindful abstraction of the skills one wants to transfer, and decontextualisation of these skills by demonstrating their usefulness in other situations (Salomon & Perkins, 1987). This distinction is echoed in the discrimination of two instruction components proposed by Littlefield (1988), namely: Framing, involving "the act of relating a specific set of behaviors to a broader framework of problem solving"; and bridging, involving "the act of relating processes that occur within one context to similar processes occurring elsewhere" (Littlefield, Delclos, Lever, Clayton, Bransford, & Frank, 1988, p. 356).

A new theoretical account of transfer that can orient future research to further unravel the underlying processes, has recently emerged - maybe somewhat unexpectedly - from the perspective of situated cognition and learning. According to Greeno, Smith, and Moore (in press) transfer should not be conceived of in terms of applying mental representations acquired in one context to more or less new situations and problems. Instead they present a view of transfer based on affordances and invariants. What a learner acquires in a learning situation is an activity in response to affordances of that situation, i.e. properties of the situation that elicit and support certain activities. Transfer of an activity to a new situation involves a transformation of the initial situation and an invariant interaction of the learner in the new context. Transfer of the activity can occur when the transformed situation contains the same or similar affordances as the initial learning context that are perceived by the learner. According to Greeno et al. (in press) representations can, but are not necessarily involved in transfer: "affordances can be perceived without there being a symbolic representation of the properties that specify the affordances" (p. 7).

Learning Theory and the Design of Powerful Learning Environments

Taking the dispositional view of competent learning and problem solving, and the preceding features of effective learning and transfer processes as a starting point, instructional science faces a challenging task, namely the elaboration of a coherent framework consisting of research-based principles for the design of powerful learning environments, i.e. situations eliciting in students the learning processes that are conducive to the acquisition and transfer of the intended aptitudes and disposition.

This challenge is approached in different ways. A first approach is usually referred to as instructional design, and aims at the elaboration of rather specific and applicable prescriptions for designing educational practice, that are based on descriptive theory, empirically validated, and framed within a more encompassing design model. Such a design model involves design parameters, design procedures and design/development processes (Elen, 1992). This approach is primarily practice oriented: through offering validated prescriptions for instruction the optimization of student learning is hoped for. Therefore, it draws heavily on learning research and theory, but it does not intend to contribute directly to the further development of learning theory. The question raises whether this will not easily lead to a kind of recipe approach to the design of learning environments, which is rather in contradiction with the constructivist view of learning. In this respect, Duffy (1990) has remarked that prescriptions as such are not useful at all, due to their limited and fragmented character which leads easily to rigid and inappropriate use.

A second approach can be called the knowledge acquisition and utilization model, and starts in some respect from the preceding criticism on instructional design. Taking into account that the teaching-learning process is too complex to specify in advance, and that instruction as problem solving is mediated by teachers thinking and decision making, it is considered inappropriate to provide prescriptions. It is argued that a more valuable approach is to make the research-based theoretical knowledge about students' learning and thinking available to teachers, and to help them to use this knowledge base in order to make informed and situation-bound instructional decisions (Duffy, 1990). An example of this approach is Cognitively Guided Instruction (CGI) developed at the University of Wisconsin by Carpenter, Fennema and their colleagues (see e.g., Carpenter & Fennema, 1992) with respect to the teaching of addition and subtraction word problem solving in the first grade of the primary school. A substantial amount of research has resulted in a fine-grained analysis of the varied repertoire of informal strategies that children use to solve such problems, and provides descriptions of the stages in the acquisition of more advanced solution procedures. A number of studies on CGI carried out with volunteering teachers, supports the hypothesis that acquiring this theoretical knowledge base helps teachers to better understand children's solution processes, and to use this knowledge as a basis for appropriate instructional decision making. Whether this seemingly productive approach would work equally well at other grade levels, with less motivated teachers, and in more complex content areas for which research-based knowledge is less specified and less robust remains an open question.

A third approach is represented by scholars who carry out so-called design experiments, and aim at the development of a design science of education (Brown, in press; Collins, 1992). According to Collins (1992) "a design science of education must determine how different designs of learning environments contribute to learning, cooperation, and motivation" (p. 15). As a result a design theory should emerge that can guide the implementation of educational innovations by specifying the variables influencing their success or their failure. In contrast to traditional instructional design described above, this approach is not oriented toward the elaboration of specific prescriptions, but tries to create in real classrooms - in narrow cooperation with practitioners as co-investigators - complex instructional interventions that embody the characteristics of effective learning processes (see e.g., Brown, in press). While this intervention approach intends to contribute to the optimization of educational practice, it is important to mention that the primary goal is to advance theory building. The underlying idea is that one productive way to better understand the processes and outcomes of learning is to create environments that elicit and produce them (Glaser, 1992b). This orientation toward theory building requires the elaboration of an appropriate methodology for designing experiments in complex classroom settings in such a way that theoretically valid conclusions can be drawn from the empirical data (see Collins, 1992, for a number of guiding principles for the development of such a methodology).

Although each of the three approaches to the design of powerful teaching-learning environments has its merits and restrictions, the third approach looks the most promising and productive one, especially because of its explicit orientation toward theory building in partnership between researchers and practitioners. This partnership idea implies a bidirectional relationship: while practitioners can help to translate theory into practice and, thus, to make practice more research-based, their partner role should also result in making research more practice-driven. In this respect Glaser (1992a) has recently stated: "In a mature science, work on basic theory is often invigorated by goal-oriented technology, and perhaps at this time in the history of the study of learning, the close coupling of theorizing and practical development will encourage fundamental science, as well as improvements of education and training" (p. 256).

In the domain of computational learning intelligent tutoring systems represent attempts to create instructional environments that can serve at the same time as a test-bed for theoretical principles of learning. The question raises whether the existing ITS are in accordance with the major features of effective learning processes described above. Indeed, "traditional" intelligent tutors that base their instructional decisions on a detailed diagnosis of students' knowledge, can easily lead to a preponderance of highly structured, directive and relatively constrained learning environments lacking sufficient opportunities for active and collaborative learner involvement and participation. Anderson's Geometry Tutor (Anderson, Boyle, & Reiser, 1985), one of the most frequently quoted examples of an ITS, is an illustration of such a directive system. As remarked by Kaput (1992), suggested attempts to make the tutor more flexible and education-ally adjustable will not change its underlying epistemology: "the knowledge and the underlying authority of the tutor reside in the computer." (p. 545) Paraphrasing Papert (1990) who opposes "constructionism" to "instructionism", one could say that the Geometry Tutor will continue to reflect an "instructivist" rather than a "constructivist" view of learning.

The now prevailing constructivist conception of learning and the problems confronting the design of ITS, have fostered the emergence of the view that computer-based learning environments should not so much involve the knowledge and intelligence to guide and structure learning processes, but that they should rather create situations and offer tools that stimulate students to make maximum use of their own cognitive potential (Scardamalia, Bereiter, McLean, Swallow, & Woodruff, 1989). In this connection Kintsch (1991) has launched the idea of unintelligent tutoring: "A tutor should not provide the intelligence to guide learning, it should not do the planning and monitoring of the student's progress, because those are the very activities the students must perform themselves in order to learn. What a tutor should do is to provide a temporary support for learners that allows them to perform at a level just beyond their current ability level." (p. 245) It is obvious that Vygotsky's (1978) notion of the zone of proximal development underlies this view about the optimum nature of the interventions to support constructive learning processes.

In line with this evolving conception of computer-based learning (see also Brown, 1990), there is a clear shift toward supportive systems that are less structured and less directive, that are more focussing on coaching than on tutoring, that involve student-controlled tools for the acquisition of knowledge, and that attempt to integrate both, tools and coaching strategies, in collaborative learning environments (see also Kaput, 1992). Successful examples of such environments have already been developed (see e.g., De Corte, Linn, Mandl, & Verschaffel, 1992). In those environments the New Information Technology is not anymore just an add-on to an existing and unchanged classroom setting, but is embedded in powerful teaching-learning environments. Embedding means that the computer is judiciously integrated in the environment capitalizing on its strength and potential to present, represent, and transform information (e.g., simulations of phenomena and processes), and to induce effective forms of interaction and cooperation (e.g., through exchanging data, information and problems via a network) (De Corte, 1993). Those environments aim at the elicitation of constructive acquisition processes, and make ample use of student interaction and cooperative learning (for a discussion of recent research on cooperative learning with computers see Mevarech & Light, 1992). Developmental work and investigations relating to such environments, based on the available knowledge accumulated in the domain of research on learning and instruction, can contribute to realize gradually the aspirations expressed by Kolodner (1991) in her editorial statement in the first issue of The Journal of the Learning Sciences: "But rather than trying to use computers to solve all of education's problems, we need concrete guidelines about what kinds of educational environments are effective in what kinds of situations, and based on those guidelines, we need to develop more innovative ways to use computers." (p. 2)

References

Anderson, J.R., Boyle, C.F., & Reiser, B.J. (1985). Intelligent tutoring systems. *Science, 228,* 456-462.

Bassok, M. (1990). Transfer of domain-specific problem-solving procedures. *Journal of Experimental Psychology: Learning, Memory and Cognition, 16,* 522-533.

Bassok, M., & Holyoak, K.J. (1989). Interdomain transfer between isomorphic topics in algebra and physics. *Journal of Experimental Psychology: Learning, Memory and Cognition, 15,* 153-166.

Bereiter, C., & Scardamalia, M. (1989). Intentional learning as a goal of instruction. In L.B. Resnick (Ed.), *Knowing, learning, and instruction. Essays in honor of Robert Glaser.* Hillsdale, NJ: Lawrence Erlbaum Associates.

Brown, A.L. (1989). Analogical learning and transfer : What develops? In S. Vosniadou & A. Ortony (Eds.), *Similarity and analogical reasoning.* Cambridge: Cambridge University Press.

Brown, A.L. (in press). Design experiments : Theoretical and methodological challenges in creating complex interventions in classroom settings. *The Journal of the Learning Sciences.*

Brown, A.L., Bransford, J.D., Ferrera, R.A., & Campione, J.C. (1983). Learning, remembering, and understanding. In P.H. Mussen, J.H. Flavell, & E.M. Markman (Eds.), *Child psychology. Volume III: Cognitive development.* New York: John Wiley.

Brown, J.S. (1990). Toward a new epistomology for learning. In C. Frasson & J. Gauthiar (Eds.), *Intelligent tutoring systems : At the crossroads of artificial intelligence and education.* Norwoord, NJ: Ablex.

Brown, J.S., Collins, A., & Duguid, P. (1989). Situated cognition and the culture of learning. *Educational Researcher, 18(1),* 32-42.

Butterfield, E.C., & Nelson, G.D. (1989). Theory and practice of teaching for transfer (ERIC Annual Review Paper). *Educational Technology Research and Development, 37(3),* 5-38.

Campione, J.C., & Brown, A.L. (1990). Guided learning and transfer : Implications for approaches to assessment. In N. Frederiksen, R. Glaser, A. Lesgold, & M.G. Shafto (Eds.), *Diagnositic monitoring of skill and knowledge acquisition.* Hillsdale, NJ: Lawrence Erlbaum Associates.

Carpenter, T.P., & Fennema, E. (1992). Cognitive Guided Instruction : Building on the knowledge of students and teachers. *International Journal of Educational Research, 17,* 457-470.

Clark, R.E. (1992). Facilitating domain-general problem-solving : Computers, cognitive processes and instruction. In E. De Corte, M. Linn, H. Mandl, & L. Verschaffel (Eds.), *Computer-based learning environments and problem solving. (NATO-ASI Series F: Computer and Systems Sciences. Vol. 84.)* Berlin: Springer-Verlag.

Cobb, P. (in press). Constructivism. In T. Husen & T.N. Postlethwaite (Eds.), *International encyclopedia of education. (Second edition).* Oxford, England: Pergamon Press.

Collins, A. (1992). Toward a design science of education. In E. Scanlon & T. O'Shea (Eds.), *New directions in educational technology. (NATO-ASI Series F: Computers and Systems Sciences, Vol. 96.)* Berlin: Springer-Verlag.

Cormier, S.M., & Hagman, J.D. (Eds.) (1987). Transfer of learning. *Contemporary research and applications. (Educational Technology Series.)* San Diego, CA: Academic Press.

Corno, L. (1986). The metacognitive control components of self-regulated learning. *Contemporary Educational Psychology, 11,* 333-346.

De Corte, E. (Ed.) (1987). Acquisition and transfer of knowledge and cognitive skills. *International Journal of Educational Research, 11,* 601-712.

De Corte, E. (1990). Acquiring and teaching cognitive skills : A state-of-the-art of theory and research. In P.J.D. Drenth, J.A. Sergeant, & R.J. Takens (Eds.), *European perspectives in psychology. Volume 1.* London: John Wiley.

De Corte, E. (1993). Psychological aspects of changes in learning supported by informatics. Keynote lecture to be presented at the *IFIP Open Conference on "Informatics and Changes in Learning"*, Gmunden, Austria.

De Corte, E., Greer, B., & Verschaffel, L. (in press). Mathematics. In D. Berliner & R. Calfee (Eds.), *Handbook of educational psychology.* New York: Macmillan.

De Corte, E., Linn, M.C., Mandl, H., & Verschaffel, L. (Eds.) (1992). *Computer-based learning environments and problem solving (NATO-ASI Series F: Computer and Systems Sciences, Vol. 84).* Berlin: Springer.

De Corte, E., & Verschaffel, L. (1986). Effects of computer experience on children's thinking skills. *Journal of Structural Learning, 9,* 161-174.

De Corte, E., Verschaffel, L., & Schrooten, H. (1991). Transfer van kennis en cognitieve vaardigheden (Transfer of knowledge and cognitive skills). In *Onderwijskundig lexicon (2de editie, A 3300 - 1-19).* Alphen aan den Rijn: Samson.

De Corte, E., Verschaffel, L, & Schrooten, H. (1992). Kognitive Effekte computergestützten Lernens : Zum Stand der Forschung. *Unterrichtswissenschaft: Zeitschrift für Lernforschung, 20,* 12-33.

Detterman, D., & Sternberg, R. (Eds.) (in press). *Transfer on trial.* Norwood, NJ: Ablex.

Dochy, F.J.R.C. (1992). *Assessment of prior knowledge as a determinant for future learning.* Utrecht, The Netherlands: Lemma.

Duffy, T.M. (1990). Toward aiding the text design process. Paper presented at the Annual Meeting of the *American Educational Research Association,* Boston, MA.

Elen, J. (1992). *Toward prescriptions in instructional design: A theoretical and empirical approach. (Dissertation.)* Leuven: University of Leuven, Faculty of Psychology and Educational Sciences.

Gick, M.L., & Holyoak, K.J. (1983). Schema induction and analogical transfer. *Cognitive Psychology, 15,* 1-38.

Gick, M.L., & Holyoak, K.J. (1987). The cognitive basis of transfer. In S.M. Cormier & J.D. Hagman (Eds.), *Transfer of learning. Contemporary research and applications. (Educational Technology Series.)* San Diego, CA: Academic Press.

Glaser, R. (1987). Learning theory and theories of knowledge. In E. De Corte, H. Lodewijks, R. Parmentier, & P. Span (Eds.), *Learning and instruction. European research in an international context. Volume 1.* Oxford/Leuven: Pergamon Press/Leuven University Press.

Glaser, R. (1991). The maturing of the relationship between the science of learning and cognition and educational practice. *Learning and Instruction, 1,* 129-144.

Glaser, R. (1992a). Learning, cognition, and education : Then and now. In H. L. Pick, Jr., P. van den Broek, & D.C. Knill (Eds.), *Cognition: Conceptual and methodological issues.* Washington, DC: American Psychological Association.

Glaser, R. (1992b). Learning theory and instruction. Invited lecture presented at the *25th International Congress of Psychology*, Brussels, Belgium.

Greeno, J.G. (1991). Number sense as situated knowing in a conceptual domain. *Journal for Reserach in Mathematics Education, 22,* 170-218.

Greeno, J.G., Smith, D.R., & Moore, J.L. (in press). Transfer of situated learning. In D. Detterman & R. Sternberg (Eds.), *Transfer on trial.* Norwood, NJ: Ablex.

Hall, G.S. (1881). The contents of children's minds. *Princeton Review, 11,* 249-272.

Kaput, J.J. (1992). Technology and mathematics education. In D.A. Grouws (Ed.), *Handbook of research on mathematics teaching and learning.* New York: Macmillan.

Kintsch, W. (1991). A theory of discourse comprehension : Implications for a tutor for word algebra problems. In M. Carretero, M. Popoe, R.J. Simons, & J.J. Pozo (Eds.), *Learning and instruction : European research in an international context. Volume 3.* Oxford, UK: Pergamon Press.

Kolodner, J.L. (1991). Editorial : "The Journal of the Learning Sciences": Effecting changes in education. *The Journal of the Learning Sciences, 1,* 1-6.

Kuhl, J. (1985). Volitonal mediators of cognition-behavior consistency : Self-regulatory processes and action versus state orientation. In J. Kuhl & J. Beckman (Eds.), *Action-control: From cognition to behavior.* Berlin: Springer-Verlag.

Lave, J. (1988). *Cognition in practice: Mind, mathematics and culture in everyday life.* Cambridge: Cambridge University Press.

Lave , J., & Wenger, E. (1991). *Situated learning. Legitimate peripheral participation.* Cambridge: Cambridge University Press.

Littlefield, J., Delclos, V.R., Lever, S., Clayton, K.N., Bransford, J.D., & Franks, J.J. (1988). Learning LOGO: Method of teaching, transfer of general skills, and attitudes toward school and computers. In R.E. Mayer (Ed.), *Teaching and learning computer programming. Multiple research perspectives.* Hillsdale, NJ: Lawrence Erlbaum Associates.

Mayer, R.E. (Ed.) (1988). *Teaching and learning computer programming: Multiple research perspectives.* Hillsdale, NJ: Lawrence Erlbaum Associates.

McKeachie, W.J. (1987). The new look in instructional psychology: Teaching strategies for learning and thinking. In E. De Corte, H. Lodewijks, R. Parmentier, & P. Span (Eds.), *Learning and instruction. European research in an international context. Volume 1.* Oxford/Leuven: Pergamon Press/Leuven University Press.

McLeod, D.B. (1990). Information-processing theories and mathematics learning: The role of affect. *International Journal of Educational Research, 14,* 13-29.

Mevarech, Z., & Light, P. (Eds.) (1992). Cooperative learning with computers. *Learning and Instruction, 2,* 155-285 (Special issue).

Papert, S. (1990). An introduction to the 5th anniversary collection. In I. Harel (Ed.), *Constructionist learning: A 5th anniversary collection of papers.* Cambridge , MA: MIT Media Laboratory.

Perkins, D.N., Jay, E., & Tishman, S. (in press). Beyond abilities: A dispositional theory of thinking. *The Merril-Palmer Quarterly.*

Perkins, D.N., & Salomon, G. (1989). Are cognitive skills context-bound ? *Educational Researcher, 18(1),* 16-25.

Perkins, D.N., & Salomon, G. (in press). Transfer of learning. In T. Husen & T.N. Postlethwaite (Eds.), *International encyclopedia of education (Second edition).* Oxford, England: Pergamon Press.

Perkins, D.N., & Simmons, R. (1988). Patterns of misunderstanding: An integrative model of science, math, and programming. *Review of Educational Research, 58,* 303- 326.

Perret-Clermont, A., & Schubauer-Leoni, M. (Eds.) (1989). Social factors in learning and teaching. *International Journal of Educational Research, 13,* 573-684.

Prawat, R.S. (1989). Promoting access to knowledge, strategy, and disposition in student : A research synthesis. *Review of Educational Research, 59*, 1-41.

Pressley, M., Snyder, B.L., & Cariglia-Bull, T. (1987). How can good strategy use be taught to children? Evaluation of six alternative approaches. In S.M. Cormier & J.D. Hagman (Eds.), *Transfer of learning. Contemporary research and applications. (Educational Technology Series.)* San Diego, CA: Academic Press.

Resnick, L.B. (1983). Toward a cognitive theory of instruction. In S. Paris, G. Olson, & H. Stevenson (Eds.), *Learning and motivation in the classroom.* Hillsdale, N.J. : Lawrence Erlbaum Associates.

Salomon, G., & Globerson, T. (1987). Skill may not be enough: The role of mindfulness in learning and transfer. *International Journal of Educational Research, 11*, 623-637.

Salomon, G., & Perkins, D.N. (1987). Transfer of cognitive skills from programming: When and how ? *Journal of Educational Computing Research, 3*, 149-169.

Salomon, G., & Perkins, D.N. (1989). Rocky roads to transfer: Rethinking mechanisms of a neglected phenomenon. *Educational Psychologist, 24*, 113-142.

Scardamalia, M., Bereiter, C., McLean, R.S., Swallow, J., & Woodruff, E. (1989). Computer-supported intentional learning environments. *Journal of Educational Computing Research, 5*, 51-68.

Schoenfeld, A.H. (1992). Learning to think mathematically: Problem solving, metacognition, and sense-making in mathematics. In D.A. Grouws (Ed.), *Handbook of research on mathematics learning and teaching.* New York: Macmillan.

Shuell, T.J. (1986). Cognitive conceptions of learning. *Review of Educational Research, 56*, 411-436.

Shuell, T.J. (in press). Designing instructional computing systems for meaningful learning. In M. Jones & P.H. Winne (Eds.), *Foundations and frontiers of adaptive learning environments.* New York: Springer-Verlag.

Simons, P.R.J. (1990). *Tranfervermogen. (Transfer ability). (Inaugurale rede).* Nijmegen: K.U. Nijmegen.

Simons, P.R.J. (1989). Learning to learn. In P. Span, E. De Corte, & B. van Hout Wolters (Eds.), *Onderwijsleerprocesses: Strategien voor de verwerking van informatie.* Amsterdam/Lisse: Swets & Zeitlinger.

Singley, M.K., & Anderson, J.R. (1989). *The transfer of cognitive skill.* Cambridge, MA: Harvard University Press.

Snow, R.E. (1992). Aptitude theory: Yesterday, today, and tomorrow. *Educational Psychologist, 27*, 5-32.

von Glaserfeld, E. (Ed.) (1991). *Radical constructivism in mathematics education.* Dordrecht, The Netherlands: Kluwer.

Vosniadou, S., & Brewer, W.F. (1987). Theories of knowledge restructuring in development. *Review of Educational Research, 57*, 51-67.

Vygotsky, L.S. (1978). *Mind in society. The development of higher psychological processes.* Cambridge, MA: Harvard University Press.

Wood, T., Cobb, P., & Yackel, E. (1991). Change in teaching mathematics. *American Educational Research Journal, 28*, 587-616.

Knowledge Representation Changes in Humans and Machines

Lorenza Saitta, F. Neri, M.T. Bajo, J. Cañas, S. Chaiklin, F. Esposito, D. Kayser, C. Nédellec, G. Sabah, A. Tiberghien, G. Vergnaud, S. Vosniadou

Introduction

Learning is a fundamental activity of any intelligent agent, either natural or artificial. For every task the agent has to perform, it needs to acquire the appropriate means in the form of declarative/procedural knowledge or of perceptual/motor skills. This process involves both the reasoning abilities of the agent and an analysis of the already available and target knowledge at various levels.

In solving a task, first of all the *ontology* of the domain has to be specified, i.e., the entities involved in the phenomena under consideration and the relationships among them. Then, the *types* of background and target knowledge must be selected, namely whether they need to be, for example, causal models, shallow classificatory knowledge, stimulus-response association, time-dependent knowledge, and so on. Once these more basic aspects have been clarified, suitable *representation formalisms* and specific *knowledge contents,* depending both upon the domain and the task, are to be chosen to make concrete the preceding abstract notions. Especially when the task to be performed is complex, multiple choices are usually possible for any of the mentioned aspects, in order to design the learning component both at the algorithmic and at the data manipulation level. In Machine Learning the ontologies of the domain and the available background knowledge are usually considered given, and the important choices involve the knowledge representation formalisms for the target knowledge and the data. However, these choices cannot be made in isolation, because they partly depend upon the specific paradigm (e.g., symbolic, connectionist, evolutionary, case-based, reinforcement-based) in which the learning problem has been cast. For example, the connectionist paradigm (Rumelhart & McClelland, 1986) cannot currently handle hypotheses expressed in first order-logic (FOL), whereas logic-based paradigms (Michalski, 1983; Mitchell et al., 1986; Muggleton, 1991) are not naturally amenable to deal with noisy or numerical data.

Even after a specific paradigm has been selected, a large room for alternatives is left for the choice of a specific hypothesis representation language, i.e. the *language bias* (Mitchell, 1982). This choice has a strong impact on the amount of computational resources needed for learning. For instance, hypotheses expressed in FOL may have to be found in excessively large search spaces, and some operations on them are inherently exponential. Also, disjunctive hypotheses may require too many training examples (Nédellec & Rouveirol, 1993). On the other hand, not every learning methodology is uniformly applicable to any type of target knowledge. A typical example, in this respect, is time-dependent knowledge, such as the one needed for describing the behavior of a dynamical system. Recently, some authors have investigated the impact that the language bias may have on complex learning problems, such as the ones found in molecular biology (Craven & Shavlik, 1995; Hirsch & Japkowicz, 1994).

The problem of selecting a suitable representation for a problem is not limited to automated learning, but is a general issue in any type of problem solving. The relevance of the representation has been early on stressed by Newell (1965), who presented examples of problems susceptible of alternative representations. A classical work on representation changes is the one by Korf (1980), who considered this problem as a search task in the space of possible representations. Two dimensions of this space are *information structure,* whose changes are described as isomorphisms, and *information quantity,* whose changes are described as homomorphisms.

In order to cope with the complexity issue in learning, the hypothesis representation language L is kept as simple as possible. This is usually done by imposing constraints on the target knowledge syntax, limiting thus the expressive power of L. This kind of restriction may prove effective in obtaining, for instance, polinomial learnability, as showed by the COLT approach (Valiant, 1984); but, on the other hand, increases the probability of loosing better hypotheses, if these last cannot be represented in the reduced language. Another important aspect is comprehensibility for a human end-user; in fact, too low-level languages may not be immediately graspable by the intuition of the user. In some kinds of applications this factor may severely limit the acceptability of automatically acquired knowledge.

An important dichotomy, in this respect, is the one between propositional (descriptions consisting of attribute-value pairs) and first-order logic (i.e., relational) representation languages. Using a FOL language, many problems, such as matching (Haussler, 1989) or testing for subsumption, become computationally intractable, and even the very notion of "generality" may acquire more than one meaning (Plotkin, 1970; Buntine, 1988; Helft, 1989; Console& Saitta, 1992). As a consequence, more severe restrictions have to be imposed on the language syntax (e.g., use only determinate literals) or semantics (e.g., only one-to-one variable : constant unification), in order to keep computational complexity within acceptable bounds. Interesting limits in the syntax allowing for tractable subsumption algorithms have been investigated in Donini et al. (1991).

Another important aspect concerning the choice of a representation language is the level of detail to be considered in the descriptions of data and hypotheses. Too detailed descriptions may generate an excessive fragmentation of important aspects, which become thus unrecognizable; furthermore, they tend to be incomprehensible and may render problem solving and learning intractable. On the other hand, too concise descriptions may let essential distinctions disappear, making a problem unsolvable (Valtorta & Zahid, 1990). For the above reasons, the process of defining a well suited representation language for a given learning problem becomes, in a natural way, an iterative one, in which the current choice is evaluated, criticized and possibly modified. This "try-and-modify" cycle may last long and be very costly, because it is currently performed manually by the designer of the learning system. Even for a human learner the process of modifying his/her own model of the world may require a large cognitive effort, which increases with the complexity of the currently hold model and the extension and depth of the necessary changes.

One possibility of reducing the costs inherent in the mentioned selection process would be that of (partly) automating it, providing the learning system with the ability of adjusting by itself, during learning, its representation language. In this way, the initial choice would be much less critical and the revision cycle could be avoided. Another possibility consists in providing the user of the ML system with explanations that help him/her to understand what are the consequences of the input knowledge representation on the learning results and then make him/her able to perform the appropriate alterations (Saitta, Botta & Neri, 1993; Nédellec & Kodratoff, 1994).

For solving the above mentioned problems, results from studies on human conceptual change can provide useful insights, especially for systems devoted to incremental learning. On the other hand, machine learning can provide computational models of learning processes (e.g., Pazzani, 1991), whose predictions can be afterwards tested by means of psychological experiments. Hypotheses about the structure and content of the mental models people are supposed to hold provide suggestions for appropriate selection of a more realistic language bias in automated learning systems.

Representation Changes in Humans

According to a French psychologist, the notion of *representation* may have several meanings (Bresson, 1987). One for instance indicates the structures of knowledge in long-term memory and another refers to the circumstantial knowledge construction, depending on a particular context, with specific goals, and in a given situation, with the aim of performing a task (Richard, 1990). Both notions of representation are used by cognitive scientists, who generally assume that performance in different cognitive tasks is in part determined by the way in which knowledge is organized and represented. Performing a task or solving a problem in a specific domain involves the construction of a mental representation which is determined by the properties or attributes of the concepts involved, by the interrelationships among them and the *naive theories* within which these concepts are embedded, and the situation (or the task) itself. Research has shown that success in problem solving depends on the quality of these representations as well as on the specific procedures and processes used to perform a given task (Chi, Feltovich & Glaser, 1981; Larkin, 1981; Anzai & Yokohama, 1984). Therefore, learning and acquisition of knowledge imply modifications of knowledge structures at different levels of organization as well as modifications in the procedures used to solve a problem. Three issues, related to the way knowledge is organized and represented in the knowledge base, will be considered in the following: concepts and conceptual structures, naive theories and mental models (see also Vosniadou, this volume).

Concepts and Conceptual Structures

Access to conceptual knowledge is needed to determine which concepts are involved in a given problem and to infer their properties and relations with other concepts, in the specific domain in which the problem is thought to belong. Natural concepts are at least partially organized in terms of underlying dimensions and properties. There are substantial research findings which suggest that *categorization* is a flexible process in which background knowledge and task demands determine which attributes and dimensions should be considered (Barsalou, 1991; Lambert, 1994). Hence, the categorization process should change as new knowledge is acquired. Researchers investigating the novice-expert shift have shown that the organization of the knowledge of experts differs from that of novices in that experts represent more and different relations among concepts than do novices, and also in that experts organize their knowledge in terms of abstract properties that are not available to novices (Goldsmith, Johnson & Acton, 1991; Gonzalvo, Cañas & Bajo, 1994; Schoenfeld & Herrman, 1982; Schvaneveldt et al., 1985). For example, Gonzalvo, Cañas & Bajo (1994) compared students' organization of important concepts, in their knowledge regarding the history of psychology, with that of their instructors. The research showed that students organized their conceptual knowledge in terms of superficial dimensions such as "global familiarity", whereas experts organized their concepts in terms of abstract properties such as "degree of mentalism". As students acquired more knowledge about the discipline (after taking a history of psychology course), their knowledge of the structural relations among the main concepts became more like that of experts. In other words, the students used abstract principles that were not available to them prior to instruction. These changes in knowledge organization have been observed in domains as varied as computer programming (Cañas, Bajo & Gonzalvo, 1993), statistics (Goldsmith, Johnson & Acton, 1991), and air-navigation (Schvaneveldt et al., 1985).

Another, more radical form of conceptual reorganization happens when concepts move from one ontological category to another (Chi, 1992; Chi, Slotta & Leeuw, 1994), a kind of change that has also been referred to as *tree branching* or *tree switching* (Thagard, 1992). Such kinds of reorganization are observed in the history of science when radical theory changes are taking place (as, for example, in the case of the differentiation between heat and temperature, or between force and pressure).

Theories

Recent experimental findings (e.g., Rips,1989) have challenged the view that concepts are grouped together to form categories on the basis of similarity. It has instead been suggested that conceptual coherence can be explained if we assume that concepts are embedded in theories (Medin & Wattenmaker, 1987). Concepts seem to be organized in the context of naive theories of the world that are based on everyday experience. This background knowledge constrains the type of attributes considered for categorization (Medin, Goldstone & Gentner, 1993). A series of studies by Vosniadou and Brewer (1992, 1994) have shown how children start by believing that the earth belongs to the category of physical object and then proceed to apply to it their naive theories about physical objects. Vosniadou and Brewer have described such "theories" in terms of certain presuppositions and beliefs which are derived by the human cognitive system on the basis of observation and instruction. Such presuppositions and beliefs constrain the knowledge acquisition process and determine in important ways the kinds of representation of situations that individuals form. Conceptual changes often require the revision of presuppositions and beliefs of the naive theory as well as changes from one ontological category to another.

Accounts of conceptual change in terms of theory change are also found in explanations of adults' misconceptions in science (e.g., (Clement, 1982; McCloskey, 1983;Vosniadou, 1994)). For example, McCloskey (1983) had subjects think out aloud while solving motion problems and later interviewed them about their answers. Analyses of these data suggested that most of his subjects used a naive "impetus" theory of motion, and that most of the errors could be accounted for as stemming from that theory. The finding that similar errors are made by different individuals in different situations have made investigators propose that misconceptions are not random or idiosyncratic but based on a more general system of beliefs (Vosniadou, 1994).

Mental Representations

Based on how they categorize a given task, and depending on the nature of the theoretical beliefs associated with that category, individuals are assumed to construct a mental representation which contains all the information that is needed for the execution of the task. Research comparing the representations of physics problems used by novices and experts has shown that experts tend to represent physics problems in abstract terms (e.g., point, mass, massless-strings, frictionless surfaces) whereas novices use surface features (e.g., blocks ropes, slopes) that are more related to real world situations (Anzai & Yokoyama, 1984; Chi, Feltovich & Glaser, 1981). Also, diagrams of physical problems seem to be used and interpreted differently by experts and novices. Experts seem to be proficient in drawing physics diagrams and making inferences from them, while novices are not (Anzai, 1991).Vosniadou (1994) has assumed that representations of knowledge about the physical world take on the form of mental models. Mental models do not have a unique definition (Richard 1990; Gentner & Stevens, 1983; Johnson-Laird, 1983), but they have in common quite important points. Vosniadou hypothesizes that mental models are constructed on the spot to deal with the demands of specific situations and are constrained by the underlying beliefs and presuppositions associated with a given domain. As an example, in physics learning, the model is the link between the theory the learner holds and the objects and events involved in his/her experience: the model is an "intermediary between the theoretical aspects and the ostentive aspects" (Bachelard, 1989).

Vosniadou & Brewer (1992, 1994) have found that only a small number of relatively well defined generic mental models of the earth were used by the elementary school children in their studies to represent the earth and the day/night cycle. These mental models differed in the extent to which they incorporated scientific elements about astronomical phenomena provided through instruction. Thus, some first-grade children represented the earth as a flat rectangle or a flat circle, supported by ground, with solar objects and the sky located above its top. Fifth-grade children were more likely to represent the earth as a sphere, but were still confused as to exactly where the people lived on this sphere; for example, they were uncomfortable with the idea that people lived "down", "at the bottom of the earth" without falling.

Procedural Knowledge

A complete account of the expert/novice shift must undeniably take into consideration shifts in procedural knowledge used to solve a given task. It appears that there are substantial differences between novices and experts in the heuristics or strategies they use in applying domain knowledge in order to derive a solution (Simon & Simon, 1978; Larkin et al., 1980; Reimann & Chi, 1989).

Quantitative representations are opposed to qualitative ones, and intuition, based on associative patterns, is contrasted to solutions of mathematical equations. Experience in problem solving induces a gradual shift from quantitative to qualitative problem analysis, which implies not only different mental representations, but also the existence of means to link the two in a coherent model of the world. For instance, Plötzner and Spada (1992) present a framework that describes learning in physics as a sequence of multiple levels of mental domain representations ranging from qualitative to quantitative.

Moreover, experts usually start inference processes from the information available in the problem. This forward reasoning procedure is very dependent on domain specific knowledge. It relies heavily on the individual's ability to classify the problem according to the principles that can be applied to the given variables in order to get closer to a solution. In contrast, novices tend to use backward procedures that start the inference process from the expected final solution, searching for appropriate data to satisfy the goal. Results suggest that novices' solving procedures are weak and generic, while experts use specific procedures (Larkin et al., 1980; Larkin, 1981).

Computational Models

Several aspects of the process of constructing and shifting cognitive representations for solving problems have been described by means of computer and formal modelling. For example, Kayser (1988) presents an approach to concept representation, called *variable-depth representation,* which introduces a description of rules and facts such that the rules are all considered at the same level, whereas the facts may be at different ones. Properties of entities may vary from level to level and entities may also disappear at some level. The paper also discusses how the depth of a fact can be computed and shows how this flexible representation can be used in reasoning. This approach bears resemblance with abstraction mechanisms.

Another relevant approach in AI is described in Sabah & Vilnat (1993). The main goal of this study was to introduce some flexibility into the semantic representations used in natural language understanding systems. In fact, a universal list of cases, useful in different applications, is quite impossible to define, and, even inside a given application, the representation level may have to be varied according to various needs. In order to overcome this difficulty, conceptual graphs are used to represent the semantic knowledge used by a syntactic-semantic parser. The rules of the parser take into account a hierarchy of relational types and construct various representations of the same sentence at various levels, providing a way to achieve representation changes. Moreover, the canonical knowledge base contains refined types of relations, which allows contraction and expansion operations to be performed, adding flexibility to the representation.

Other models have tried to provide an account of the backward-forward procedural shifts (Larkin, 1981; Lambert, 1990). Lambert (1990) discusses a hybrid model in which a distributed memory module is linked to a classical production system. The distributed memory module is used to represent the information that is known from the problem statement, the final goal, and a set of subgoals. The database of the production system is used to represent a set of principles and the conditions under which they are applicable. The subgoals in the memory module guide the inference process carried out by the production system. As the system learns to associate subgoals to specific input patterns, backward reasoning is used more and more rarely, and models tend to focus on other aspects of the representational shift that occurs with learning (Reif, 1987; Larkin et al., 1988).

An Educational Perspective

It has been hypothesized that learning takes places by modifications in long-term memory, and that these modifications occur through the construction of representations, whatever their form may be (Lautrey 1993). Moreover, social psychology assures us that the representation is the place and the support of congruencies where the psychological and the social are intertwined (Vignaux, 1992). This point is shared by both psychology and didactics and is of crucial importance when education is concerned. Consequently, the study of representation change is of fundamental importance in human learning. More than this, representations changes can be considered *per se* as indicators of learning.

From this perspective, a satisfactory theory of representation needs a notion that can plausibly be the representational counterpart of situations: the concept of "scheme" (Vergnaud, 1992) could provide such a notion. A "scheme" is the invariant organization of behavior for a certain class of situations. It is a dynamic entity that consists of four kinds of elements: *goals* and anticipations, *rules of action, operational invariants* (concepts-in-action and theorems-in-action), and *inference* mechanisms. Any of the four kinds of elements may be changed by learning and experience. Operational invariants are the core of concept formation: their cognitive function is to select the relevant information and support inferences to choose or generate rules of action and subgoals. Concepts-in-action are essential in the selection, identification and interpretation of information, but they are not sufficient conditions for a computation to take place. Computation requires propositions that can be true or false; therefore, theorems-in-action, which are propositions hold to be true, are necessary ingredients of the theory. Some relevant concepts-in-action are those of state, transformation, initial/final, cardinal (for the states), positive and negative (for the transformations).

From experiments on how children learn arithmetic, it was argued that it is impossible to study the learning/development of a concept independently of the situations that make a concept meaningful. The *conceptual field* theory provides a framework to study, analyze and classify the learning/development of a whole set of interconnected concepts and theorems, in relationship with the progressive mastering of an increasing set of situations, duly analyzed from both a cognitive and an epistemological point of view. Examples of such fields are additive and multiplicative structures, and elementary dynamics (Vergnaud,1990; Weil-Barsi & Vergnaud, 1990).

Useful insights into the human learning mechanisms can be gained from the interpretation of difficulties in physics learning. By taking the point of view of didactics, the role of knowledge in physics is to be introduced explicitly in the analysis of learning. There appears to be a gap between the meaning constructed by the learner and certain aspects of physics knowledge, particularly concerning physical quantities, their relationships and their meaning in the framework of physics. Then, it is necessary to take into account the relation between the learner's knowledge acquisition and the physics education. In order to clarify the "meaning" the learner constructs when interpreting and/or predicting material situations, several hypotheses about the learner's cognitive activities can be put forward.

One hypothesis assumes that when interpreting (or predicting) material situations, the learner constructs a "model" of the situation (analogical and/or propositional), depending on his/her own point of view (Tiberghien, 1994). In this modelling process the learner is assumed to select the objects and events according to his/her own theory. Underlying such a hypothesis is the assumption that the learner is coherent from his/her point of view with respect to the situation, including social context. This hypothesis agrees with the findings of psychological research (Brown, 1989; Carey, 1985; Vosniadou, 1989). For example, Brown (1989) states that young children not only can transfer their knowledge on a "deeper bases than mere-appearance matches", but also that they can use relational information in which causality plays a fundamental role. For Brown, "… a theory would be defined as a coherent explanatory network of interrelated concepts …" and "… a causal explanation would refer to a principled understanding of part of a larger system, such as the fact that inanimate objects need to be pushed, pulled, or propelled into action …". The hypothesis that the learner's modelling is based on learner's theory is confirmed by the observation of causal explanation in even young children's knowledge processing.

For example, in everyday life the main constraint on a model of an action is the perceived result of the action, which is related to a cause in a linear relation (Guidoni, 1985). This model can be constructed *ad hoc* with the situation and still compatible with linear causal reasoning, which belongs to the learner's theory (Tiberghien, 1989). Thus, in the case of young learners, who acquired their knowledge in the context of everyday life, the meaning of words, such as "heat" and "temperature", may be radically different from that in the physics framework, even if, in some specific situations, the meaning seems similar. This leads to hypothesize a *theory* level and a *model* level and to investigate the relations between them.

Another approach, related to representation changes, deals with the role of *external* representation as tools for thinking and then for constructing *internal* representation. This approach is particularly interesting in school-based learning (Chaiklin & Hedegaard, 1989). The significance of these external representations can be expressed from several theoretical perspectives.Within many intellectual traditions, especially within mathematics and the natural sciences (but also to some extent in the humanities), the use of models is a fundamental element in the subject's matter. One cannot practice disciplinary traditions without models; they are a necessary part of learning an intellectual tradition.

A second sense of models or external representations comes from dialectical philosophy (Ilyenkov, 1977). This philosophy has inspired a research tradition that uses the philosophical theory of knowledge as a guideline for analyzing subject matter for teaching (Davydov, 1988 a,b,c, 1990; Aidarova, 1982; Hedegaard, Hakkarainen &Engeström, 1984; Hedegaard, 1988; Vos, 1991). An important principle in this tradition is the idea of a genetically primary relation, sometimes also called a "germ cell". The primary relation is the basic relationship that is used to understand concrete phenomena. Teaching aims to start with forming this basic, abstract relationships.The hypothesis or assumption is that abstract relationships are easier to understand because they necessarily eliminate many of the complex details of concrete, specific examples. The teaching task is to help students learn to use the basic relationship to explore concrete phenomena that are within the subject-matter domain. This use of abstraction, in an instructional context, may be a potentially fruitful meeting point for the existing research on the use of abstractions in machine learning.

A third sense of model is found is a variety of pedagogical research that has used models as part of instruction. As a simple example, the balance scale has been used as a physical model for teaching the statistical concept of weighted average (Hardiman, Well & Pollatsek, 1984). More extensive uses of models can be found in specific teaching sequences (Smith, Snir & Grosslight, 1992; Steinberg &Wainwright, 1993; White & Frederiksen, 1987). General perspectives about using models in physics instruction are also available (Halloun & Hestenes, 1987; Hestenes, 1987, 1992; Karplus, 1969).

These approaches are the more interesting for research in human learning, because of the need of a theory of representation giving a comprehensive view of the way learning can take place, both in ordinary environments and in specific classroom situations.

Representation Changes in Machines

In a broad sense, any concept learning system may be thought of as undergoing knowledge representation changes during its activity. However, we have limited the current review to a stricter interpretation of this notion, namely to changes that occur only in the *representation languages* for the data and the target knowledge. Two possible ways of coping with this problem of automated shift of bias (Utgoff, 1986a) have been proposed so far in Machine Learning (ML): *constructive learning,* i.e., a dynamic definition of the hypothesis representation language, according to the needs emerging during learning, and *abstraction,* broadly intended as a mechanism to build up a "simpler" representation language than the one in which the problem had been originally formulated.

An important pre requisite to implement automatic shift of representation is the elicitation of the biases (e.g., the control knowledge) used by the ML systems so that the restrictions applied to the hypothesis space become clear (Russell & Grosof, 1990; Nédellec & Rouveirol, 1994). Methods to automatically shifting bias are very difficult to control because there exist no efficient heuristic to identify the deep cause of the language insufficiency and to remedy it. This is the reason why most of the work on shift of bias focuses on the definition of a *language bias* that the user may shift by himself (Ade et al., 1995; Tausend, 1994; Feldman & Nédellec, 1994).

Finally, the ability of a system to be "self-aware" and reflective could be an important feature to help automating the selection of appropriate representations. In fact, an automatic system that performs a complex learning task should have the capability to reason about its own behavior and to use explicit knowledge about its knowledge limits as well as about the various tasks it can perform (see also the chapter by Van Someren & Reimann, this volume). If the analogy between the behavior of a complex system and mental activity is accepted, having knowledge about its own activity may correspond to an implementation of a partial "consciousness" (Minsky, 1985).

To this goal, Distributed Artificial Intelligence may prove to be a useful paradigm, allowing learning to be considered as an interactive activity going on among a set of agents, each one being a reflective system, holding beliefs about its own knowledge and the one of other agents. It is then necessary to have a clear distinction between the agent level and the self-representation the agent uses: the meta-representation is an abstract description of the system behavior (Newell, 1982). In order to maintain a self-representation, a reflective system has to use an architecture with a meta-level, containing a partial representation of the initial system. Furthermore, by considering meta-systems themselves as usual agents, the "mechanism" can be applied recursively at different levels, resulting in a hierarchical organization of the agents.

A system well suited to concretize these ideas is CARAMEL (Sabah, 1990; Sabah & Briffault, 1993), which is able to perform various tasks using natural language understanding. It is based on a new architecture that combines the advantages of *blackboard* systems (Erman et al., 1980; Hayes-Roth, 1985; Nii, 1986) and *message passing* (Hewitt, 1977; Agha & Hewitt, 1986; Lesser & Corkill, 1983; Hewitt, 1986), without their drawbacks. The system extends the blackboard model by including a continuous control system (made possible by a parallel implementation), allowing a sophisticated management of the processes and of their interruption by message passing through a hierarchy of active agents.

Constructive Learning

Constructive learning has been defined by Michalski (1983) as the process of building up descriptors to be used during learning which are new with respect to those introduced in the initial language. These descriptors are features (attributes, predicates), which may be defined in terms of the original ones or suggested by a domain theory. Constructive induction has been mostly addressed in symbolic learning approaches, even though some kinds of artificial neural networks may be considered as being able to perform it as well, by dynamically changing their structure and not only the weights associated to their connections.

Constructive induction is also known under the name "predicate invention", because constructivity mostly consists, as mentioned before, in introducing new predicate names in the language. Predicate invention is actively investigated in the Inductive Logic Programming framework (Muggleton, 1991), beginning with the definition, in the system DUCE (Muggleton, 1987), of a set of *constructive operators* for changing propositional languages, and its extension, in CIGOL (Muggleton & Buntine, 1988), of some of these operators to FOL languages. Within the same framework, Rouveirol (1994) presents two new kinds of representation changes, namely *flattening,* which transforms a logic program with function symbols into one without them, and *saturation,* which completes an example description with relevant information, using background knowledge.

One way of creating new descriptors is to examine the input data, searching for possible relationships among them and suggesting meaningful grouping. Of this kind are the systems exemplified by BACON (Langley et al., 1986). Another form of constructive induction has been realized integrating statistical techniques for synthesizing new descriptors in the symbolic learning system RES (Esposito, Malerba & Semeraro, 1993a).

Other systems work in a cycle, by analyzing generated hypotheses at one step, introducing new predicates and iterating learning. FRINGE (Pagallo & Haussler, 1990) and CITRE (Matheus & Rendell, 1989) work in this way for generating decision trees by introducing combinations of attribute-value pairs. Carpineto (1992) suggests to use a hierarchy of languages within creasing complexity. In the same line, an approach, currently using a manual construction method, has been proposed by Hirsh & Japkowicz (1994).

Joint exploitation of both examples and background knowledge can also be employed to change the language bias. This is the case of STABB, a system which has been embedded into LEX (Utgoff, 1986b), of CLINT (De Raedt & Bruynooghe, 1991), and of AQ17.HCI (Wnek & Michalski, 1994).

A new method for concept formation is presented in Wrobel (1994), and a polynomial time algorithm to perform constructive induction in a relational domain is used in the system KLUSTER (Kietz & Morik, 1994). Also suited for relational domains is the proposal by Aronis & Provost (1994), which combines examples and domain knowledge into an inheritance network, from which new relations are suggested. Finally, the system APT also proposes, among various revision operators, an original predicate invention operator that specializes overly general concept definitions (Nédellec,1992).

A related topic, which definitely influences the shift of representation, is revision of background theory. Many ML methods have also tackled the problem of automatically revising incorrect and/or incomplete background knowledge. They mostly exploit examples: new incoming examples reveal incorrectness and/or incompleteness in a theory. Validation and correction are then part of learning (Pazzani, 1991; Ginsberg, 1989; Bergadano & Giordana, 1990; Ourston & Mooney, 1990; Nédellec, 1992). The additional examples are usually provided to the system by a teacher (data-driven learning), either asked for by the system whenever it suspects an insufficiency in the theory, or resulting from experiments performed by the system. The examples are generally considered as correct; they thus help to identify the type of the problem and guide the correction.

A novel specialization operator for revising incorrect theories has been proposed in Esposito, Malerba & Semeraro (1993b): it relies on the automated introduction of the negation operator in the representation language, when no positive concept definition does exist. The operator has been implemented in an incremental learning system which adopts a model of generalization whose formal properties have been investigated in Esposito, Malerba & Semeraro (1994a). The advantages of this model with respect to other generalization models used to learn logical definitions from relations have been presented in Esposito, Malerba & Semeraro 1994b).

An alternative way of approaching the problem is to exploit deep models of the domain, in order to explain why errors occurred (Cain, 1991; Saitta, Botta & Neri, 1993; Baroglio, Botta & Saitta, 1994).

Abstraction

Constructive learning can be considered as a special case, applied to learning, of a more general mechanism for generating and handling intermediate-level concepts in world descriptions, i.e., *abstraction*. Abstraction is the ability to change the level of details of a representation and is a fundamental aspect of human thought, one so frequently and pervasively used that we barely notice it (Plaisted, 1981). Very different ideas have been associated with the notion of abstraction. For instance, objects in a universe may collapse into *indistinguishable sets,* if no relevant predicates in the domain of interest can distinguish them (Hobbs, 1985). A similar approach is taken by Imielinski (1987), who proposes a domain abstraction, based on an equivalence relation. Introducing fuzzy sets (Zadeh, 1965) on continuous-valued domains can be seen as another way of obtaining a more abstract view of the world.

In Artificial Intelligence, abstraction has been mainly applied in planning (Knoblock, Tenenberg & Qiang, 1990; Martin & Allen, 1990) and problem solving (Benjamin et al., 1990; Subramanian, 1990; Yoshida & Motoda, 1990; Ellman, 1993; Mostow, Ellman & Prieditis, 1990). More recently, several other kinds of tasks have received benefits from this idea. For instance, abstraction is useful in qualitative physics (Falkenhainer & Forbus, 1990; Iwasaki, 1990; Williams, 1990; Ling & Steinberg, 1992), temporal reasoning (Choueiry & Faltings, 1992) and in databases (Imielinski & Dalal, 1990).

More oriented toward software engineering, Lowry (1988, 1990) describes the system STRATA, which reformulates problem class descriptions for algorithm synthesis. Furthermore, the introduction of several level of abstraction in the knowledge used to perform hierarchical model-based diagnosis has been proved to increase the efficiency in this kind of task (Mozetic, 1990; Struss, 1992).

Only recently has the Machine Learning community started to pay attention to the abstraction mechanism (Drastal, Czako & Raatz, 1989; Knoblock, 1989; Veloso & Carbonell, 1991;

Giordana & Saitta, 1990; Giordana, Saitta & Roverso, 1991; Giordana, Lo Bello & Saitta, 1993; Keller, 1990; Fisher et al., 1992). Abstraction, dealing with transformations between representation spaces, offers a new perspective to learning, in that it may give solutions to the fundamental dilemmas involving the trade-off between knowledge simplicity and predictive power, knowledge meaningfulness and task-dependency.

In learning, abstraction has been explicitly used in the system MIRO (Drastal, Czako & Raatz, 1989), which constructs new attributes to be used by an inductive learner, through a deduction process from a domain theory. Abstraction has to be distinguished from generalization (Giordana & Saitta, 1990), and is in no way intended as an alternative mechanism to it; on the contrary, generalization and abstraction have complementary properties and goals. Generalization has been, and remains, the basic mechanism for hypothesis formation, whereas abstraction provides a mechanism for representing these hypotheses on a hierarchy of levels. In other words, abstraction is basically an *organizational* mechanism, which imposes a *structure* on the world, in such a way that a "meaning" can be easily associated to the component parts of the structure, reducing thus the cognitive effort for handling the world representation.

Giordana, Saitta and Roverso (1991) argue that generality is an extensional property of concepts and is based on instance set inclusion. Abstraction is an intensional property and is based on hypothesis information content. Then, a useful notion of abstraction in learning is one that preserves both the *more-general-than* relation and the extensional properties of concepts (i.e., their coverage) across hierarchical levels of representation spaces. This amounts to the fact that any hypothesis, generated inside any representation space, is guaranteed to be extensionally equivalent to the same hypothesis, represented in any other more or less abstract space. Another important aspect of abstraction is that it allows simple, yet meaningful and useful descriptions to be obtained.

A semantic abstraction (Tenenberg, 1987; Giordana, Saitta & Roverso, 1991), preserving concept extension is somewhat in contrast with most definitions proposed in AI. On the other hand, it is well on the line of the Abstract Data Types (ADT) theory, used in structured programming, in program specification and analysis and as a basic concept in object-oriented languages. Moreover, the ADT theory has a feature which is missing from the abstraction view, common in AI. Artificial Intelligence research has been only concerned with changes in the language predicate set, whereas in the ADT approach one builds up "objects" (i.e., the data types), defined in terms of properties and interactions with the external world and other objects; each object has to be addressed as a whole, disregarding its internal structure and actual implementation. The process of building up compound conceptual objects, synthesizing groups of elementary pieces of information available in the ground world, and, then, hiding their internal structure in the abstracted world, is the central core of the abstraction mechanism in learning. This idea has been used in pattern recognition, especially in image analysis.

For the reasons mentioned above, not only new predicates (Muggleton & Buntine, 1988), but also new terms as compound objects have to be invented (Giordana & Saitta, 1990). Building up new "data types", representing intermediate concepts useful to describe higher-level ones, is the key both for obtaining meaningful, human-like concept representations and for reducing the combinatorial complexity of the learning process. The introduction of term abstraction is a key difference between the notion of abstraction proposed in Giordana, Saitta & Roverso (1991) and the notion of constructive induction reviewed in the preceding section.

In psychology, the idea of abstraction plays a key role in perception, there being related to the concept of "Gestalt" and being concerned with holistic properties of objects and events. It may also be considered as a possible basis for analogy (Vosniadou & Ortony, 1989).

An interesting question is whether abstraction can play a role in connectionist approaches, by associating "individuality" with specific sub-nets, in such a way that they could be used as building blocks to construct larger networks. If this question would be answered in the affirmative, on could ask further whether this internal structuring spontaneously emerges as a consequence of increasing the size of the networks. If this would be the case, we could explain the natural creation of symbols from the sub-symbolic representation level by arguing that this takes place for the sake of saving cognitive efforts.

Research Directions

We conclude in describing two research projects that go beyond the state of the art outlined in the previous sections, and that are pursued in the context of the "Learning in Human and Machine" programs (Reimann & Spada, this book).

Computational-Cognitive Modelling of Representational Change in Elementary Dynamics

The purpose of this project is to better understand the mutual influences and interrelationships between computational and psychological representational formalisms for better modelling the processes involved in conceptual change. We have chosen to work in the domain of elementary Dynamics and to model the problem solving behavior of subjects at different ages and levels of expertise.

From a psychological point of view, the project will attempt to provide a description of the mental representations used by subjects and to capture the differences in the organization of the knowledge base that underlies them. More specifically, the project will try to understand how different mental representations are related to different ways in which information is categorized as well as to different theoretical beliefs within which conceptual structures are embedded. While at present there are some proposals regarding the ways in which mental representations can be constrained by underlying beliefs and presuppositions, and how concepts are embedded in theories that make them cohere, we have not yet seen the development of theoretical frameworks that tie these types of knowledge organization and representation together or relating them to specific knowledge acquisition mechanisms.

From a computational point of view, the representation schemes and machine learning algorithms that can be used as tools for modelling cognitive changes will be specified. The project will also try to take advantage of linguistic analysis to better understand the nature of conceptual change, including shifts in representation and meaning that are taking place with the acquisition of expertise. The final challenge is to implement a computer system that learns to solve problems in the domain of elementary dynamics by making representational shifts and using problem solving procedures that are similar to those of humans. The construction of such a system should help us understanding some of the mechanisms of conceptual change that are difficult to study through empirical methods.

Formation and Evolution of Mental Models of Physical Phenomena in a Restricted Set of Situations

People acquire in their lifetime models of the world which they use to interpret data, to explain phenomena and to make predictions. These models usually evolve when new information is gathered, and their evolution may entail changes in the way knowledge is organized and encoded inside the models themselves. The aim of this project is to analyze, both from a cognitive and from a computational point of view, the conceptualizations and reasoning processes involved in the required representation changes. In order to make the task feasible, we will limit the study to the formation and modification of mental models in simple physical domains, based on a set of controlled experiments, performed under restricted and explicitly stated conditions.

A bottom-up methodological approach, consisting in working on a concrete and delimited problem of heat transfer and to try to generalize the results to other domains has been chosen. At the beginning, existing machine learning systems will be used as tools for testing, on a body of already available experimental data, models of the learning processes going on in humans. The evaluation of obtained results will be exploited as feedback to improve either the cognitive models or the machine learning systems or both. To the human learning sciences the project will provide means for verifying mechanisms hypothesized to underly, cognitive processes such as knowledge acquisition and explanation of observations, for suggesting critical experiments, and to quickly explore the effects of possible variations of parameters in the experimental setting.

Special attention will be given to the protocol of information transfer from the teacher to the learner (be it a human disciple or a machine), in such a way that useful hints for educational sciences may result. The deep interaction between computational and cognitive modelling of the learning processes should lead eventually to improvements of the used machine learning systems, both in terms of increased performance and competence, and in terms of enhanced cognitive plausibility. This shall be achieved through a grasping of the human ability to change representations in response to new information to explain and/or to a new goal to reach.

Conclusions

Although there are specific proposals, regarding the ways in which mental models can be constrained by underlying beliefs and presuppositions (Vosniadou, 1994), and even though some accounts of categorization make strong connections between conceptual organization and theories (e.g., Medin, Goldstone & Gentner, 1993), there are not theoretical frameworks tying these three types of representation together or relating them to specific procedures. Computational models and interdisciplinary research can be of great help in bringing different lines of research together.

The pilot projects shall provide the test-beds for bringing together competencies and ideas from cooperative fields in a truly interdisciplinary approach.

References

Ade, H., De Raedt, L., & Bruynooghe, M. (1995). Declarative Bias for Specific-to-General ILP Systems. *MachineLearning,* Special Issue on Declarative Bias. To appear.

Agha, G. and Hewitt, C. (1986). *Actors: A Model of Concurrent Computation in Distributed Systems.* MIT Press. Cambridge, MA.

Aidarova, L. (1982). *Child Development and Education.* (L. Lezhneva, Transl.). Progress. Moscow. (Original work published in 1982).

Anzai, Y. (1991). Learning and Use of Representations for Physics Expertise. In A. Ericsson and J. Smith (Eds.). *Toward a General Theory of Expertise.* Cambridge University Press, Cambridge, MA.

Anzai, Y., & Yokohoma, T. (1984). Internal Models in Physics Problem Solving. *Cognition and Instruction, 1*, 397-450.

Aronis, J.M., & Provost, F.J. (1994). Efficiently Constructing Relational Features from Background Knowledge for Inductive Machine Learning. *Proceedings of AAAI Workshop on KnowledgeDiscovery in Databases .* Stanford, CA.

Bachelard, S. (1989). Quelques Aspects Historiques des Notions de Modèle et de Justification des Modèles. In P. Delattre & M. Thellier (Eds.), *Elaboration et Justification des Modèles, Vol. 1.* Maloine, Paris, France.

Baroglio, C., Botta, M. & Saitta, L. (1994). WHY: A System that Learns Using Causal Models and Examples. In R. Michalski & G.Tecuci (Eds.), *Machine Learning: A Multistrategy Approach, Vol. IV.* Morgan Kaufmann, San Francisco, CA.

Barsalou, L.W. (1991). Deriving Categories to Achieve Goals. In G.H. Bower (Ed.), *The Psychology of Learning and Motivation: Advances in Research and Theory.* Academic Press, New York, NY.

Benjamin, D.P., Dorst L., Mandhyan, I.., & Rosar, M. (1990). An Algebraic Approach to Abstraction and Representation Change. *Proceedings of the AAAI Workshop on Automatic Generation of Approximations and Abstractions.* Boston, MA.

Bergadano, F., & Giordana A. (1990). Guiding Induction with Domain Theories. In Y. Kodratoff & R. Michalski (Eds.), Machine Learning: An Artificial Intelligence Approach, Vol. III. Morgan Kaufmann, Los Altos, CA.

Bresson, F. (1987). Les Fonctions de Représentation et de Communication. In J. Piaget, P. Mouloud, & J.P. Bronkart (Eds.), *Psychologie.* Encyclopédie de la Pléiade. Paris, France.

Brown, A.L. (1989). Analogical Learning and Transfer: What Develops?. In S. Vosnadiou & A. Ortony (Eds.), *Similarity and Analogical Reasoning.* Cambridge University Press, Cambridge, MA.

Buntine, W. (1988). Generalized Subsumption and Its Applications to Induction and Redundancy. *Artificial Intelligence, 36.*

Cain, T. (1991). The DUCTOR: A Theory Revision System for Propositional Domains. *Proceedings of the. 5th International Machine Learning Workshop.* Evanston, IL.

Cañas, J.J., Bajo, M.T., & Gonzalvo, P. (1994). Mental Models and Computer Programming. *International Journal of Human-Computer Studies, 40,* 795-811.

Carey, S. (1985). *Conceptual Change in Childhood.* MIT Press, Cambridge, MA.

Carpineto, C. (1992). Version Spaces of Concept Languages. *Proceedings of the Workshop on Approximation and Abstraction of Computational Theories.* San José, CA.

Chaiklin, S., & Hedegaard, M. (1989). Educational Activity: An Approach to Teaching and Learning in School. Paper presented to the *8th International Human Science Research Conference.* Aarhus, Denmark.

Chi, M.T.H. (1992). Conceptual Change within and across Ontological Categories: Examples from Learning and Discovery in Science. In R. Giere (Ed.), *Cognitive Models of Science.* Minnesota Studies in the Philosophy of Science, University of Minnesota Press, Minneapolis, MN.

Chi, M.T.H., Feltovich, P.J., & Glaser, R. (1981). Categorization and Representation of Physics Problems by Experts and Novices. *Cognitive Science, 5,* 121-152.

Chi, M.T.H., Slotta J.D., & de Leeuw, N. (1994). From Things to Processes: A Theory of Conceptual Change for Learning Science Concepts. *Learning and Instruction, 4,* 27-43.

Choueiry, B.Y., & Faltings, B. (1992). Building Temporal Abstractions. *Proceedings of the Workshop on Approximation and Abstraction of Computational Theories.* SanJosé, CA.

Clement, J. (1982). Students' Preconceptions in Introductory Mechanics. *American Journal of Physics, 50,* 66-71.

Console, L., & Saitta, L. (1992). Abduction, Induction and Inverse Resolution. *Proceedings of the First Compulog Net Workshop on Logic Programming in AI.* London, UK.

Craven, M., & Shavlik, J. (1995). Investigating the Value of a Good Input Representation. In T. Petsche, S. Judd, & S. Hanson (Eds.). *Computational Learning Theory and Natural Learning Systems, Vol. 3*. MIT Press, Cambridge, MA.

Davydov, V.V. (1988a). Problems of Developmental Teaching. I. *Soviet Education, 30(8)*, 6-97.

Davydov, V.V. (1988b). Problems of Developmental Teaching. II. *Soviet Education, 30(9)*, 3-83.

Davydov, V.V. (1988c). Problems of Developmental Teaching. III. *Soviet Education, 30(10)*, 3-41.

Davydov, V.V. (1990). Types of Generalization in Instruction: Logical and Psychological Problems in the Structuring of School Curricula. (J. Teller, Transl.). In J. Kilpatrick (Ed.), *Soviet Studies in Mathematics Education. Vol. 2*. National Council of Teachers of Mathematics. Reston, VA. (Original work published 1972).

De Raedt, L., & Bruynooghe, M. (1991). CLINT: A Multistrategy Interactive Concept Learner and Theory Revision System. *Proceedings of the First International Workshop on Multistrategy Learning*. Harpers Ferry, WV.

Donini, F., Lenzerini, M., Nardi, D.,& Nutt, W. (1991). Tractable Concept Languages. *Proceedings of the 12th International Joint Conference on Artificial Intelligence.*

Sydney, Australia.

Drastal, G., Czako, G., & Raatz, S. (1989). Induction in an Abstraction Space. *Proceedings of the 11th International Joint Conference on Artificial Intelligence*. Detroit, MI.

Ellman, T.(1993). Synthesis of Abstraction Hierarchies for Constraint Satisfaction by Clustering Approximately Equivalent Objects. *Proceedings of the International Conference on Machine Learning*. Amherst, MA.

Erman, L.D., Hayes-Roth, F., Lesser, V., & Raj Reddy, D. (1980). The HERSAY-II Speech Understanding System: Integrating Knowledge to Resolve Uncertainty. *Computing Surveys, 12*, 213-253.

Esposito, F., Malerba, D., Semeraro, G. (1993a). Incorporating Statistical Techniques into Empirical Learning Systems. In D. Hand (Ed.), *Artificial Intelligence Frontiers in Statistics*. Chapman & Hall, London, UK.

Esposito, F., Malerba, D., Semeraro, G. (1993b). Negation as a Specializing Operator. *Lecture Notes in Artificial Intelligence, Vol. 728*, 166-177.

Esposito, F., Malerba, D., Semeraro, G., Brunk, C. and Pazzani, M. (1994a). Avoiding Non Termination when Learning Logical Programs. *Lecture Notes in Computer Science, Vol. 883.*

Esposito, F., Malerba, D., Semeraro, G., Brunk, C., & Pazzani, M.(1994b). Traps and Pitfalls when Learning Logical Definitions from Relations. *Lecture Notes in Artificial Intelligence, Vol. 869*, 376-385.

Falkenhainer, B., & Forbus, K.D. (1990). Compositional Modeling of Physical Systems. *Proceedings of the AAAI Workshop on Automatic Generation of Approximations and Abstractions*. Boston, MA.

Feldman, R., & Nédellec, C. (1994). A Framework for Specifying Explicit Bias for Revision of Approximate Knowledge Bases. In B. Gaines & M. Musen (Eds.), *Knowledge Acquisition Workshop*.

Fisher, D., Carnes, R., Yang, H., & Yoo, J. (1992). Basic Levels of Problem Solving and Other Phenomena. *Proceedings of the. Workshop on Approximation and Abstraction of Computational Theories*. San José, CA.

Gentner, D., & Stevens, A.L. (Eds.) (1983). *Mental Models*. Lawrence Erlbaum Associates Inc., Hillsdale, NJ.

Ginsberg, A. (1989). Theory Revision via Prior Operationalization. Proceedings of the National Conference on Artificial Intelligence.

Giordana, A., & Saitta, L. (1990). Abstraction: a General Framework for Learning. *Working Notes of Workshop on Automated Generation of Approximations and Abstractions.* Boston, MA.

Giordana, A., Saitta, L., Roverso, D. (1991). Abstracting Concepts with Inverse Resolution, Proceedings of the *8th Int. Machine Learning Workshop.* Evanston, IL.

Giordana, A., Lo Bello, G., & Saitta, L. (1993). Abstraction in Propositional Calculus. *Proceedings of the Workshop on Knowledge Compilation and Speed Up Learning.* (Amherst, MA).

Goldsmith, T.E., Jonhson, P.J., &Acton, W.H. (1991). Assessing Structural Knowledge. *Journal of Educational Psychology, 83,* 88-96.

Cañas, J.J., & Bajo, M.T. (1994). Structural representations in knowledge acquisition. *Journal of Educational Psychology, 86.* In press.

Guidoni, P. (1985). On natural thinking. *European Journal of Science Education, 7,* 133-140.

Halloun, I.A., & Hestenes, D. (1987). Modeling Instruction in Mechanics. *American Journal of Physics, 55,* 455-462.

Hardiman, J., Well, P.T., & Pollatsek, A.D. (1984). The Usefulness of the Balance Model in Understanding the Mean. *Journal of Educational Psychology.*

Haussler, D. (1989). Learning Conjunctive Concepts in Structural Domains. *Machine Learning,* 7-40.

Hayes-Roth, B.(1985). A Blackboard Architecture for Control. *Artificial Intelligence, 26,* 252-321.

Hedegaard, M. (1988). *The Development of Schoolchildren's Personality Viewed through the Social Science Subjects.* Aarhus Universitet, Aarhus,Denmark. (In Danish).

Hedegaard, M., Hakkarainen, P., & Engeström, Y. (Eds.) (1984). *Learning and Teaching on a Scientific Basis: Methodological andEpistemological Aspects of the Activity Theory of Learning and Teaching.* Psykologisk Institut, Aarhus Universitet, Aarhus, Denmark.

Helft, N. (1989). Induction as Nonmonotonic Inference. *Proceedings of the 1st Conference on Knowledge Representation and Reasoning.* Boston, MA, 1989.

Hestenes, D. (1987). Toward a Modelling Theory of Physics Instruction. *American Journal of Physics, 55,* 440-454.

Hestenes, D. (1992). Modeling Games in the Newtonian World. *American Journal of Physics, 60,* 732-748.

Hewitt, C. (1977). Viewing Control Structure as Patterns of Passing Messages. *Artificial Intelligence, 8,* 343-364.

Hewitt, C. (1986). Offices are Open Systems. *ACM Transactions, 4,* 271-287.

Hirsch, H., & Japkowicz, N. (1994). Bootstrapping Training-Data Representations for Inductive Learning: A Case Study in Molecular Biology. *Proceedings of the 12th National Conference on Artificial Intelligence.* Seattle, WA, 1994.

Hobbs, J. (1985). Granularity. *Proceedings of the International Joint Conference on Artificial Intelligence* .Los Angeles, CA, 1985.

Ilyenkov, E.V. (1977). *Dialectical Logic: Essays on its History and Theory.* (H.C. Creighton, Transl.). Progress, Moscow: (Original work published in 1974).

Imielinski, T. (1987). Domain Abstraction and Limited Reasoning. *Proceedings of the International Joint Conferences on Artificial Intelligence.* Milano, Italy, 1987.

Imielinski, T., & Dalal, M. (1990). Your Time is Up: Approximate Query Answering in Deductive Databases. *Proceedings of the AAAI Workshop on Automatic Generation of Approximations and Abstractions.* Boston, MA.

Iwasaski, Y. (1990). Reasoning with Multiple Abstraction Models. *Proceedings of the AAAI Workshop on Automatic Generation of Approximations and Abstractions.* Boston, MA.

Johnson-Laird, P.N. (1983). *Mental models: Towards a Cognitive Science of Language, Inference, and Consciousness.* Harvard University Press, Cambridge, MA.

Karplus, R. (1969). *Introductory Physics: A Model Approach.* W. A. Benjamin, New York, NY.

Kayser, D. (1988). What Kind of Thing is a Concept? *Computational Intelligence, 4,* 158-165.

Keller, R.M. (1990). Learning Approximate Concept Descriptions. Proceedings AAAI Workshop on Automatic Generation of Approximations and Abstractions. Boston, MA.

Kietz, J.U., & Morik, K. (1994). A Polynomial Approach to the Constructive Induction of Structural Knowledge. *Machine Learning, 14,* 193-218.

Knoblock, C. (1989). Learning Hierarchies of Abstraction Spaces. *Proceedings of the 6th International Workshop on Machine Learning.* Ithaca, NY.

Knoblock, C., Tenenberg, J., & Yang Qiang (1990). A Spectrum of Abstraction Hierarchies for Planning. *Proceedings of the AAAI Workshop on Automatic Generation of Approximations and Abstractions.* Boston, MA.

Korf, R.E. (1980). Toward a Model of Representation Changes. *Artificial Intelligence, 14,* 41-78.

Lamberts, K. (1990). A Hybrid Model of Learning to Solve Physics Problems. *The European Journal of Cognitive Psychology, 2,* 151-170.

Langley, P., Zytkow, J.M., Simon, H.A., & Bradshaw, G.L. (1986). Search for Regularity: Four Aspects of Scientific Discovery. In R. Michalski, J. Carbonell, &T. Mitchell (Eds.), *Machine Learning: An AI Approach, Vol. II.* Morgan Kaufmann, Los Altos, CA.

Larkin, J.H. (1981). Enriching Formal Knowledge: A Model for Learning to Solve Textbook Physics Problems. In J. Anderson (Ed.), *Cognitive Skills and their Acquisition.* Erlbaum, Hillsdale, N.J.

Larkin, J.H., McDermott, J., Simon, D.P., & Simon, H.A. (1980). Models of Competence in Solving Physics Problems. *Cognitive Science, 4,* 317-345.

Larkin, J.H., Reif, F., Carbonell, J., & Gugliotta, A. (1988). A Flexible Expert Reasoner with Multi-Domain Inferencing. *Cognitive Science, 12,* 101-138.

Lautrey, J. (1993). Structure and Variability : A Plea for a Pluralistic Approach to Cognitive Development. In R. Case & W. Edelstein (Eds.), *The New Structuralism in Cognitive Development. Contribution in Human Development, Vol. 23,* 101-114. Karger, Base.

Lesser, V., & Corkill, D. (1983). The Distributed Vehicle Monitoring Testbed: A Tool for Investigating Distributed Problem Solving Networks. *AI Magazine, Fall Issue.*

Ling, R., & Steinberg, L. (1992). Model Generation from Physical Principles: A Progress Report. *Proceedings of the Workshop on Approximation and Abstraction of Computational Theories.* San José, CA.

Lowry, M. (1988). STRATA: Problem Reformulation and ADT. *Proceedings of the 1st International Workshop on Change of Representation and Induction Bias.* Briarcliff, NY, 1988.

Lowry, M.R. (1990). Abstracting Domains with Hidden States. *Proceedings of the AAAI Workshop on Automatic Generation of Approximations and Abstractions.* Boston, MA.

Martin, N.G., & Allen, J.F. (1990). Abstraction in Planning: A Probabilistic Approach. *Proceedings of the AAAI Workshop on Automatic Generation of Approximations and Abstractions.* Boston, MA.

Matheus, C., & Rendel,l L. (1989). Constructive Induction on Decision Trees. *Proceedings of the International Joint Conference on Artificial Intelligence.* Detroit, MI, 1989.

Mc Closkey, M. (1983). Naive Theories of Motion. In D.H. Gentner & A.L. Stevens (Eds.). *Mental Models.* Erlbaum, Hillsdale, N.J.

Medin, D.L., Goldstone, R.L., & Gentner, D. (1993). Respects for Similarity. *Psychological Review, 100*, 238-254.

Medin, D.L., & Wattenmaker, W.D. (1987). Category Cohesiveness, Theories, and Cognitive Archeology. In U. Neisser (Ed.), *Concepts and Conceptual Development: Ecological and Intellectual Factors in Categorization.* Cambridge University Press, New York, NY.

Michalski, R. (1983): A Theory and Methodology of Inductive Learning. In R. S. Michalski, J. G. Carbonell, & T. Mitchell (Eds.), *Machine Learning: An Artificial Intelligence Approach, Vol. I.* Morgan Kaufmann. Los Altos, CA.

Minsky, M. (1985). *The Society of Mind.* Simon & Schuster, New York, NY.

Mitchell, T. (1982): Generalization as Search. *Artificial Intelligence, 18*, 203-226.

Mitchell, T., Keller, R.M., Kedar-Cabelli, S. (1986). Based Generalization: A Unifying View. *Machine Learning, 1*, 47-80.

Mostow, J., Ellman, T., & Prieditis, A. (1990). A Unified Transformational Model for Discovery Heuristics by Idealizing Intractable Problems. *Proceedings of the AAAI Workshop on Automatic Generation of Approximations and Abstractions.* Boston, MA.

Mozetic, I. (1990). Abstractions in Model-Based Diagnosis. *Working Notes of the Workshop on Automated Generation of Approximations and Abstractions.* Boston, MA.

Muggleton, S. (1987): Duce, an Oracle Based Approach to Constructive Induction. *Proc IJCAI-87.* Milan, Italy.

Muggleton, S. (1991). Logic Programming. *New Generation Computing, 8,* 295-318.

Muggleton, S., & Buntine, W. (1988). Machine Invention of First-Order Predicates by Inverting Resolution. *Proceedings of the 5th International Conference on Machine Learning.* Ann Arbor, MI.

Nédellec, C. (1992). How to Specialize by Theory Refinement. *Proceedings of the European Conference on Artificial Intelligence.* Vienna, Austria.

Nédellec, C., & Rouveirol, C. (1993). Biases for Incremental Hypothesis-Driven Systems. *Proceedings of the AAAI Spring Symposium on Training Issues in Incremental Learning.* Stanford, CA.

Nédellec, C., & Rouveirol, C. (1994). Specification of the HAIKU System. *Research Report 928.* Université de Paris-Sud, Orsay, France.

Nédellec, C., & Kodratoff, Y. (1994). *Proceedings of ECAI-94 Workshop on Integration of Machine Learning and Knowledge Acquisition.* Amsterdam, Netherlands.

Newell, A. (1965). Limitations of Current Stock of Ideas about Problem Solving. In A. Kent & O. Taulbee (Eds.), *Electronic Information Handling.* Spartan Book, Washington, DC.

Newell, A. (1982). The Knowledge Level. *Artificial Intelligence, 18*, 87-127.

Nii, P. (1986). Blackboard Systems: the Blackboard Model of ProblemSolving and the Evolution of Blackboard Architectures. *AI Magazine*, 82-106.

Ourston, D., & Mooney, R.J. (1990). Changing the rules: A comprehensive approach to theory refinement. Proceedings of the National Conference on Artificial Intelligence.

Pagallo, G., & Haussler, D. (1990). Boolean Feature Discovery in Empirical Learning. *Machine Learning,* 71-99.

Pazzani, M. (1991). Influence of Prior Knowledge in Concept Acquisition: Experimental and Computational Results. *Journal of Experimental Psychology: Learning, Memory, and Cognition, 17,* 416-432.

Plaisted, D. (1981). Theorem Proving with Abstraction. *Artificial Intelligence, 16,* 47-108.

Plotkin, G. (1970). A Note on Inductive Generalization. *Machine Intelligence, 5,* 153-163.

Plötzner, R., & Spada, H. (1992). Analysis-based Learning on Multiple Levels of Mental Domain Representation. In E. de Corte, M. Linn, H. Mandl, & L. Verschaffel (Eds.), *Computer-Based Learning Environments and Problem-Solving.* Springer, Berlin, Germany.

Reif, F. (1987). Interpretation of Scientific or Mathematical Concepts: Cognitive Issues and Instructional Implications. *Cognitive Science, 11,* 395-416.

Reimann, P., & Chi, M.T.H. (1989). Human Expertise. In K.J. Gilhooly (Ed.), *Human and Machine Problem Solving.* Plenum Publ. Co.

Richard, J.F. (1990). Introduction. In J. Richard, C. Bonnet, & R. Ghiglionne. *Traité de Psychologie Cognitive, Vol. II.* Dunod, Paris, France.

Rips, L.J. (1989). Similarity, Typicality, and Categorization. In S. Vosniadou & A. Ortony (Eds.), *Similarity and Analogical Reasoning.* Cambridge University Press, New York, NY.

Rouveirol, C. (1994). Flattening and Saturation: Two Representation Changes for Generalization. *Machine Learning, 14,* 139-168.

Rumelhart, D., & McClelland, J. (1986). *Parallel Distributed Processing.* MIT Press, Cambridge, MA.

Russell, S., & Grosof (1990). A Sketch of Autonomous Learning Using Declarative Bias. In P. Brazdil & K. Konolige (Eds.), *Machine Learning, Meta-Reasoning and Logics.* Kluwer Academic Publishers.

Sabah, G. (1990). CARAMEL: A Flexible Model for Interaction Between the Cognitive Processes Underlying Natural Language Understanding. *Proceedings of Coling.* (Helsinki, Finland).

Sabah, G., & Briffault, X. (1993). CARAMEL: A Step Towards Reflection in Natural Language Understanding Systems. *Proceedings of IEEE International Conference on Tools with Artificial Intelligence.* Boston, MA.

Sabah, G., & Vilnat, A. (1993). A Hierarchy of Relational Types in Conceptual Graphs to Handle Natural Language Parsing. *Proceedings of the International Conference on Conceptual Structures.* Québec, Canada.

Saitta, L., Botta, M., & Neri, F. (1993). Multistrategy Learning and Theory Revision. *Machine Learning, 11,* 153-172.

Schoenfeld, A.H., & Herrman, D.J. (1982). Problem Perception and Knowledge Structure in Expert and Novice Mathematical ProblemSolvers. *Journal of Experimental Psychology: Learning, Memory and Cognition, 8,* 484-494.

Schvaneveldt, R.W., Durso, F.T., Goldsmith, T.E., Breen, T.J., Cooke, N.M.,Tucker, R.G., & DeMaio, J.C. (1985). Measuring the Structure of Expertise. *Inernational Journal of Man-Machine Studies, 23,* 699-728.

Simon, D.P., & Simon, H.A. (1978). Individual Differences in Solving Physics Problems. In R.S. Siegler (Ed.), *Children's thinking: What Develop?* Erlbaum, Hillsdale, N.J.

Smith, C., Snir, J., & Grosslight, L. (1992). Using Conceptual Models to Facilitate Conceptual Change: The Case of Weight-Density Differentiation. *Cognition and Instruction, 9,* 221-283.

Steinberg, M. S., & Wainwright, C. L. (1993). Using Models to Teach Electricity: The CASTLE Project. *ThePhysics Teacher, 31.*

Struss, P. (1992). An Application of Model Simplification and Abstraction to Fault Localization in Power Transmission Networks. *Proceedings of Workshop on Approximation and Abstraction of Computational Theories.* San José, CA.

Subramanian, D. (1990). Automation of Abstractions and Approximations: Some Challenges. *Proceedings of the AAAI Workshop on Automatic Generation of Approximations and Abstractions.* Boston, MA.

Tausend, B. (1994). Representing Biases for Inductive Logic Programming. *Proceedings of European Conference on Machine Learning.* Catania, Italy.

Tenenberg, J. (1987). Preserving Consistency across Abstraction Mappings. *Proceeding of IJCAI-87.* Milan, Italy.

Thagard, P. (1992). *Conceptual Revolutions.* Princeton University Press, Princeton, MA.

Tiberghien, A. (1989). Learning and Teaching at Middle School Level of Concepts and Phenomena in Physics. The Case of Temperature. In H. Mandl, E. de Corte, N. Bennett, & H.F. Friedrich (Eds.), *Learning and Instruction. European Research in an International Context, Volume 2.1.* Pergamon Press, Oxford, UK.

Tiberghien, A. (1994). Modelling as a Basis for Analysing Teaching-Learning Situations. *Learning and Instruction, 4,* 71-87.

Utgoff, P. (1986a). *Machine Learning of Inductive Bias.* Kluwer Academic Publ., Norwell, MA.

Utgoff, P. (1986b). Shift of Bias For Inductive Concept Learning, In R. Michalski, J. Carbonell, &T. Mitchell (Eds.), *Machine Learning: An AI Approach, Vol. II.* Morgan Kaufmann, Los Altos, CA.

Valiant, L. G. (1984). A Theory of the Learnable. *Communications of the ACM, 27,* 1134-1142.

Valtorta, M., & Zahid, M.I. (1990). Some Heuristics Cannot be Derived from Simplified Models. *Proceedings of the AAAI Workshop on Automatic Generation of Approximations and Abstractions.* Boston, MA.

Veloso, M., Carbonell, J. (1991). Learning by Analogical Replay in PRODIGY: First Results. *Proceeding of European Working Session on Learning.* Oporto, Portugal.

Vergnaud, G. (1990). Epistemology and Psychology of Mathematics Education. In Kilpatrick &Nesher (Eds.), *Mathematics and Cognition.* Cambridge University Press, Cambridge, MA.

Vergnaud, G. (1992). Conceptual Fields, Problem-Solving and Intelligent Computer-Tools. In E. de Corte, M. Linn, H. Mandland, & L. Verschaffel (Eds.), *Computer-Based Learning Environments and Problem-Solving.* Springer, Berlin, Germany.

Vignaux, G. (1992). *Les Sciences Cognitives. An Introduction.* Paris, France.

Vos, H. (1991). Development of Germ Learning for Transfer and Generalization: Models and Sequencing. *Proceedings of the 4th Annual Meeting of the European Association for Research on Learning and Instruction.* Turku, Finland.

Vosniadou, S. (1989). Analogical Reasoning in Knowledge Acquisition. In S. Vosnadiou & A. Ortony (Eds.), *Similarity and Analogical Reasoning.* CambridgeUniversity Press, Cambridge, MA.

Vosniadou, S., & Brewer, W.F. (1992). Mental Models of the Earth: A Study of Conceptual Change in Childhood. *Cognitive Psychology, 24,* 535-585.

Vosniadou, S., & Brewer, W.F. (1994). Mental Models of the Day/Night Cycle. *Cognitive Science 18,* 123-183.

Vosniadou, S. (1994). Capturing and Modeling the Process of Conceptual Change. *Learning and Instruction, 4,* 45-69.

Vosniadou, S., & Ortony A. *Similarity and Analogical Reasoning.* Cambridge University Press, New York, NY.

Weil-Barsi, A., & Vergnaud, G. (1990). Student's Conceptions in Physics and Mathematics: Biases and Helps. In J.P. Caverni, J.M. Fabre, & M. Gonzalez (Eds.), *Cognitive Biases.* North Holland, Elsevier Science Publ.

White, B.Y., & Frederiksen, J. R. (1987). Causal Model Progressions as a Foundation for Intelligent Learning Environments. *Technical Report No. 6686.* BBN Laboratories, Cambridge, MA.

Williams, B.C. (1990). Capturing How Things Work: Constructing Critical Abstractions of Local Interactions. *Proceedings of the AAAI Workshop on Automatic Generation of Approximations and Abstractions.* Boston, MA.

Wneck, J., & Michalski, R. (1994). Hypothesis-Driven Constructive Induction in AQ17-HCI: A Method and Experiments. *Machine Learning, 14,* 139-168.

Wrobel, S. (1994). Concept Formation during Interactive Theory Revision. *Machine Learning, 169-192.*

Yoshida, K., & Motoda, H. (1990). Towards Automatic Generation of Hierarchical Knowledge Bases. *Proceedings of the AAAI Workshop on Automatic Generation of Approximations and Abstractions.* Boston, MA.

Zadeh, L. (1965). Fuzzy Sets. *Information and Control, 8,* 338-353.

Multi-objective Learning With Multiple Representations

Maarten van Someren and Peter Reimann

Introduction

It is evident that human learning involves a variety of representations. Important inputs to learning such as experience and teaching materials come in a variety of forms. Acquiring problem solving skills and knowledge about a domain from such a variety requires different ways of learning. A single problem solving task often involves reasoning with multiple representations and therefore knowledge in each of these representations must be acquired, and somehow integrated, to bring the knowledge to bear on a task. People are able to use knowledge for a wide range of tasks rather than a single task. In addition to the variety in "input" from which we learn, we change the knowledge during learning into different internal forms. We do not simply store the input but we generalize it, represent it in a more efficient form, modify it from new experience and so on. These changes are partially determined by the task for which knowledge is used. A physics principle that was read in descriptive form (e.g. Pressure * Volume / Temperature is constant) can be used to acquire a heuristic to predict the effect of certain events (e.g. if the temperature increases and the volume remains the same, the pressure will increase too).

Most current machine learning systems follow a single learning strategy: they are usually only able to use one type of input (examples, say) in a fixed representational format (e.g., feature lists), apply one learning strategy to the input (e.g., induction based on learning a discrimination tree) and are only able to acquire knowledge for one goal (for instance, to improve classification performance). This is also true of the currently most advanced proposals for complete cognitive architectures for problem solving and learning: ACT-R (Anderson, 1993) and SOAR (Newell et al., 1989; Newell, 1990). ACT-R distinguishes declarative memory structures from procedural knowledge (or skills). Handling the variety in representations and learning tasks is considered part of the "knowledge" rather than the architecture and it is therefore not part of the ACT-R architecture. The same is true of SOAR. It is even more radical in having a single representation form and explicitly postulating a single learning mechanism, chunking.

None of this work explicitly addresses the issues of learning with multiple representations for multiple purposes. Only recently the machine learning community has begun to work on multistrategy learning programs (see Michalski & Tecuci, 1994, for an overview). The chapters by Saitta et al. and by Emde in this book discuss machine learning methods for changing representations to make them fit better with observations and general facts that are supplied to the learner or to remove redundant elements from the knowledge. Here we focus on learning in the context of problem solving and in particular on the following main issues:

- What is the role of multiple representations in problem solving? One of the characteristics of human problem solving is the flexibility in using of different representations. For example, if we need to predict our arrival time for a planned trip, we can use our experience with similar trips or we can use an estimate of travel speed with geographical and mathematical knowledge. Some tasks are performed by combining knowledge in different forms. For example, medical reasoning tasks often involve anatomical, pathophysiological, biological and experiential knowledge. This raises first of all the question of the role of different representations in problem solving.

- The second main question concerns learning processes in systems that use multiple representations. It is useful here to distinguish two aspects of learning: improving knowledge from interaction with the environment and from active exploration of the environment.

A system that must learn from different representations and that uses multiple representations in problem solving faces the problems of single representation systems, such as the credit assignment problem, the problem of selecting good generalizations and of handling the complexity of incremental learning. However, in addition to these it faces some problems that are due to multiple representations:

- Unifying different representation by identifying common meaning: to combine knowledge in different representations in a single problem solving process requires some common ground between these representations.

- Deciding in which form to store new knowledge. If multiple representations are used then new information can be stored in different forms with very similar effects on performance. How is this controlled?

- Finding the right form for asking questions. If knowledge appears to be missing then there are different ways to search for new information. Finding a good question (or a good experiment) requires the question to be posed (or the experiment to be generated) in a form that takes the source of information into account.

- Finding the appropriate form for output of problem solving. Similarly, output must sometimes be stated in a form that is required by the environment, which may involve special reasoning.

Our perspective on learning and problem solving with multiple representations focuses on the role of goals. We propose to explain both problem solving, learning and the use of multiple representations in a functional perspective, as a goal-driven process. This means that we search for cognitive architectures and knowledge that can relate learning to problem solving and can take into account the relation between these to the task demands.

This perspective draws together several lines of research. Machine learning researchers have realized that intelligent systems cannot, in general, "bootstrap" themselves solely by induction from experience. Without "bias" it is very difficult to find correct generalizations in realistic complex learning situations and the knowledge that is acquired in this way does not support common forms of communication, such as providing explanations or taking advice (e.g. Van de Merckt and Decaestecker, 1995). This means that machine learning must address a new kind of learning tasks: learning from data other than examples. In cognitive and educational psychology the role of the learner in directing the learning process is the topic of growing interest (e.g. De Corte, in this book). We may expect that discrepancies between representations cause difficulties during problem solving and learning.

In the area of knowledge acquisition for expert systems, the role of multiple representations is also becoming a topic of interest. Constructing a knowledge-based system is often to some extent a matter of translating (and completing) knowledge that exists in the form of texts or even formalized or implemented representations. However, "translating" knowledge and adapting it to the problem solving task of the new system is a task that is not yet well understood.

Ultimately we want to be able to explain the role of multiple representations in problem solving and learning and to use this knowledge to design and build systems that are as flexible as people in the range of problem solving and learning tasks that they can perform. In this chapter, we attempt to sketch a picture of the state of the art both in psychology and machine learning concerning issues of multi-objective learning with multiple representations by identifying crucial recent research issues and illustrating them with prototypical research projects. We first address learning with multiple representations, then learning with multiple goals and finally the issues of learning strategies. Each section addresses its issue in general and then summarizes the most relevant work in cognitive psychology and machine learning. In the final section, we identify the main issues in learning with multiple goals and multiple representations.

Multiple Representations

Intuitively it is clear that problem solving and learning involve a wide range of representations. Much of our learning takes place in the context of actions but obviously we also learn from expository sources such as teachers and textbooks. The form in which information for learning is available varies considerably.

Unfortunately, the term "representation" has different meanings. Rather than attempting a theoretical treatment of this topic, we define informally a few notions that help to distinguish different representations. These notions are "medium", "representation language", "vocabulary", "ontology" and "knowledge". Medium refers to the physical form of information, for instance sound, visual or electronic information. Following the terminology in Artificial Intelligence and machine learning, by "representation language" we mean "formal representation language". Examples of formal representation languages are "first-order predicate logic" or "production rules with certainty factors", "cases represented as feature-value vectors". Some frequently used representation languages are decision trees, rule-based languages and recently probabilistic languages and qualitative calculi (e.g. Forbus, 1988). For an introduction see an introduction to Artificial Intelligence (e.g. Rich and Knight, 1991). Associated with such a formal representation language are methods for reasoning with the knowledge.

The "vocabulary" of the knowledge is not part of the representation language, nor is the content of the representation. A vocabulary instantiates a representation language. Often it is useful to characterize a representation not only by its vocabulary but also by the way in which words can be combined to make meaningful expressions. For example, if we represent a problem as an "object" with associated "speed", "direction", "weight" and "location" then for example "a car with speed 10 m.p.h., heading north with weight 500 kilo and location starting 10 miles south of Strasbourg" is a meaningful expression but it does not make sense to describe for example the speed as "10 miles south of Strasbourg". To characterize a representation beyond its representation language and its vocabulary we define a "lexical structure" or "ontology". The notion of "ontology" corresponds more or less to the notion of "language bias" in machine learning (see Saitta et al., this book). As indicated above, the notions of "representation language", "vocabulary" and "ontology" are used to define ever more specific objects. A "piece of knowledge" can be viewed as an instance of a language *cum* vocabulary *cum* ontology. Language, vocabulary and ontology define a collection of possible "pieces of knowledge". They can therefore be viewed as part of the formulation of learning goals. It is useful to also have a word for a particular "representation language + vocabulary + ontology". We shall call this "language". In this view a "piece of knowledge" corresponds to a text in language.

In cognitive psychology, these distinctions between different aspects of representations are not normally made and the term representation may refer to formal language, vocabulary or ontology. The reason is probably that in people, unlike in machines, we cannot observe the formal language and have only indirect access to vocabulary and ontology. Data about this are verbal reports and for example concept sorting data. This makes it difficult to study representations in detail.

Here are some examples of representations. Many problem solving skills are initially acquired from texts with examples and then refined and optimised by experience with problem solving. This involves at least the following three representations:

- a set of specific events/experiences (i.e., "cases" in contrast to general knowledge): in the context of problem solving this refers to specific problems and experience with solving them. Problem solving with this representation involves some form of analogy reasoning. If experience grows then retrieving relevant experiences can become a problem.

- Recognition rules: an alternative class of representations consists of recognition rules that relate problems directly to solutions, without intermediate knowledge or intermediate reasoning steps. Note that "direct recognition rules" is a class of languages. There can be different forms of direct recognition rules.

- Models: a third class of representations are models. These are structured representations of a domain that are used for step-wise solving problems about the domain. These models may be acquired from textbooks or other expository sources. They may need to be transformed into procedural form before they can be used in problem solving.

Other differences in the representation language are related to forming abstractions. In many domains problems are presented in "raw" terms. For example, a description of complaints by a patient or a description of an transport problem to an engineer. This is then transformed into qualitative, abstract terms, from medicine or from physics, which makes its possible to apply general scientific knowledge to the problem. There is evidence that constructing such abstract problem descriptions is a key factor in competent problem solving (e.g., Reif & Heller, 1982). From a computational viewpoint such abstractions can make computations much more efficient because irrelevant data and knowledge do not have to be considered.

Problem solving utilizing multiple languages, vocabularies or ontologies differs from problem solving within a single representation because it involves transformation of information or communication between components. For example, if problem data are supplied in the form of a text and a diagram then the information in these two forms must be combined by transforming one into the other or by constructing a new representation into which both are transformed. Many problem solving processes involve the abstraction of "raw" problem data into a form that makes it possible to apply knowledge to them. For example, problem solving in medical domains involves transformation of patient data into medical terms, physics problem solving often involves formalizing descriptions of natural processes or states into physics terms and architectural design involves transformation of requirements into architectural terms. After such transformations knowledge can be applied to actually solve the problem.

In Artificial Intelligence there are two architectural solutions to the problem of reasoning with multiple representations: the "interlingua" architecture, in which all representations are translated into a single language and the output is translated out of this language into the required form, and the "distributed problem solving architecture" in which "agents" perform specific tasks and the form of information that is exchanged between components is specific for the communication channel.

Psychological Research

Different Input Representations

Data from the outside world are perceived by humans in many forms. In psychology, typically distinctions drawn are those according to the channel used (audio, visual, audiovisual), the hardware that carries the data (book, TV, radio), and most importantly, according to the symbol system that is employed (language, pictures, numbers). For purposes of learning, the different symbol systems have different strengths and weaknesses, the details of which are not well known and depend to a large degree on what information is to be conveyed to the learner and with which instructional goal. For instance, in order to train motor skills, providing for video and animation input may in general be more effective than a purely verbal description.

Rather than looking into the strengths and weaknesses of the various possible input formats, let us mention some of the problems that occur when a learner has to coordinate several presentation formats. Ward & Sweller (1990) report that worked examples (i.e., the combination of problems with their solution) are effective teaching devices only to the degree that they direct attention to the appropriate features of the solution and reduce cognitive load. This, they claim, is not the case for examples in which different representational formats are used, e.g., diagrams combined with text. For instance, in kinematics, worked solutions contain text, diagrams and equations. Ward and Sweller found that the typical kinematics example does not improve learning in the same way as algebra examples do. In algebra, examples lead to superior learning results when compared with problem solving (e.g., Sweller & Cooper, 1985), in kinematics no advantage of examples over problem solving can be observed. Similar findings were made in the area of geometry, where examples mix equations and diagrams (Tarmizi & Sweller, 1988). When Ward and Sweller (1990) constructed kinematics examples in which equations and diagrammatic information were strongly integrated, subjects learned better from them than from problem solving only. These empirical findings receive theoretical support from the simulation study of Larkin & Simon (1987), for instance. A similar effect was found by Tabachnek, Koedinger, & Nathan (1994). Both experts and students in economy were able to understand principles of economy in verbal and in graphical representations but only experts were able to combine the two types of reasoning in problem solving and explanation.

In addition to these problem solving studies, the relation between examples and explanatory text has also been the focus of a study conducted by Marton & Wenestam (1978), looking onto this issue from a text comprehension perspective. They found that human learner come to an understanding of the relation between text and example that is often quite different from the one the textbook author intended. In the eye of textbook authors, examples serve an illustration function: to illustrate more abstract and general notions and/or procedures mentioned in the text. Students, however, often see no relation between examples and text, or they judge the examples as more relevant for problem solving (see also LeFevre & Dixon, 1986). Recent computational studies on how students acquire knowledge from worked examples (VanLehn, Jones & Chi, 1992; Reimann, Schult & Wichmann, 1993) provides us with functional accounts why this may be the case. For instance, these studies show that extensive processing (in the form of elaborations that go beyond the information given) of examples is required in order to connect them to the principles delineated in the textbook, the kind of processing mostly shown only by high achievers.

This suggests that relating knowledge that is represented in different representations is an important aspect of real life problem solving and learning tasks.

Instructional Issues.   With the rise of computers in instruction, the possibilities for using multiple and alternative presentational formats for the same subject matter have become dramatically improved. This is witnessed for instance by the increasing utilization of computer simulations to convey instruction (De Jong, 1991; Opwis, Stumpf & Spada, 1991; Moyse & Reimann, 1995). Other instructional applications include the use of graphs to show complex information (e.g., Hollan et al., 1984) and the use of graphical means to clarify the structure of declarative and procedural information in a system (e.g., Richer & Clancey, 1985). In what can be considered the most advanced form of providing alternative representations these are used in a manner that relate more directly to problem solving. For instance, Nathan, Kintsch, & Young (1992) have build a system that explicates the structure of algebra word problems by animated graphics; for related work in geometry see Koedinger & Anderson (1990). Along a similar line, Cheng (1993) introduces the concept of Law Encoding diagrams, a representation that correctly encodes the underlying relations of a (quantitative) law in the structure of a diagram one can "reason with" (see also Dobson, 1993, for related work on logic rules).

Different Mental Representations

Humans do not only rely on representational formats that are provided from the outside, as in the case where geometry principles are accompanied by diagrams. Often, they construct their own representations, form and content being dependent on knowledge and context (e.g., task demands). Psychologists became recently interested in changes of representations and the coordination of different representations since it has been observed that this is a critical feature accounting for many differences between experts and novices performance (for an overview see Reimann & Chi, 1989; VanLehn, 1989)[1].

Expert-Novice Research. One of the striking differences between novices and experts in formal domains such as physics and math is that novices attempt to develop their solution backwards from the unknown term by means of a general, domain independent problem solving strategy called Means-Ends-Analysis (Simon & Simon, 1978; Larkin, McDermott, Simon & Simon, 1980), whereas experts start with the values known and derive new values, "miraculously" leading to the correct solution. That this difference cannot be attributed to a general strategy difference between experts and novices becomes clear when analyzing what experts are doing when confronted with non-routine problems: They then, too, have to rely on so-called weak problem solving methods, for instance means-ends analysis and analogical reasoning. Hence, what enables experts to reason in a forward chaining manner is their superior domain knowledge. This has been demonstrated empirically in the seminal work of Chi, Feltovich & Glaser (1981) who showed that physics experts do not only posses more knowledge, but have it also differently organized. This allows them to represent problems on a level that is directly related to their solution. The research conducted by Chi et al. (1981) showed that experts make use of quantitative information (equations and numbers) differently from novices. But this is not the only difference.

Different Representational Levels for Physics Problem Solving. It was in particular Jill Larkin (McDermott & Larkin, 1978, Larkin, 1983) who looked into the role qualitative knowledge plays when experts are solving (physics) problems and how this compares with novices' behavior. From observing experts, she found three different forms of representations for a problem: naive (e.g., sketches of the problem situation), qualitative-scientific (including abstract physical concepts such as masses and forces), and quantitative-scientific (e.g., algebraic equations). Novices also developed a naive and a scientific-quantitative representation, but there was little evidence that they developed a qualitative-scientific one. For purposes of problem solving, the qualitative-scientific representation is very useful since it imposes constraints on the quantitative solution and enables the problem solver to classify the problem in theoretical terms, thereby pointing directly to a solution method. Both empirical work and simulation studies lend credi-

---

1. From a different but related perspective, study of representation changes has a long history in developmental psychology, starting with the seminal work of Piaget; for an overview of recent research, see Carey (1985).

bility to the advantage of reasoning qualitatively about a problem before phrasing it in quantitative terms (e.g., Roschelle, 1991; Plötzner, 1993).

Different Representations of Medical Knowledge.   Another area where the use of different representations has been extensively studied is medical reasoning (for an overview see Evans & Patel, 1989). Mental representations of medical knowledge have been described as existing in three basic formats, either in parallel or in a developmental sequence (Schmidt, Norman & Boshuizen, 1990). The first format is a causal network representation in which nodes cover physiological, anatomical and clinical concepts and links between the nodes capture mainly causal ("produces", "results in", "has effect") relations, but also temporal and other kinds of relationships. Such causal networks cover well the extensive declarative knowledge students of medicine acquire through formal training conveyed in lectures and textbooks. When students are supposed to reason with this knowledge, for instance in order to come up with a diagnosis for a patient, they produce long and detailed, but not necessarily correct explanations, depicting many steps from the symptoms and signs back to the disease. After some amount of clinical training, students begin to develop shortcut rules in their diagnostic reasoning, i.e., they begin to associate symptoms and signs directly with diseases or at least with disease classes. This associational knowledge is best represented in terms of rules or more complex forms of knowledge chunks, such as schemata and scripts. After an extensive amount of experience with a medical domain, doctors seem to organize more and more of their knowledge in a case-based format, meaning that specific experiences with specific patients override the more general knowledge structures contained in causal networks and rules or schemata. Diagnostic reasoning is now performed similarity-based, by analogical reasoning from the current case to similar cases with known diagnosis.

Interesting problems occur if these three representational formats need to be coordinated. For instance, how can an experienced physician who commands over a lot of associational and/or case-specific knowledge explain to a medical novice how to perform a diagnosis? As an extreme example, the expert may not know anymore the exact patho-physiological process behind the disease, even so he or she excels in making correct diagnosis. However, it is rather improbable that this occurs often. A more appropriate model is a two (or multi)-tired representation where general knowledge is enhanced but not replaced by more specific knowledge (see for instance Portinale et al., 1993).

Why do humans use multiple representations, thereby also often combining external and internal ones? For instance, when solving math problems, people manipulate internally an linguistic representation of a problem, and externally algebraic and/or graphical symbol system. The answer is that the combination of different representations is in many cases more powerful than working with a single one. If all goes well, the different advantages of the representational systems can be combined synergistically, the disadvantages cancel each other out. For instance, in a study of the use of multiple representational formats for solving word algebra problems, Tabachnek, Koedinger & Nathan (1994) classify the different representational formats according to distance from situation (as given in the problem description), computational efficiency, and working memory demands. When students, as observed, combine a verbal-mathematical and an algebraic representation for solving problems, they make implicitly use of the fact that the verbal representation because of being close to the situational description can be used to keep the semantics of the solution attempts straight, whereas the algebraic representation has a high computational efficiency. The verbal representation imposes high demands on memory, whereas the algebraic one, when externalized on paper, makes comparatively low memory demands. Koedinger & Tabachnek (1994) observed that the use of multiple strategies leads to increased problem solving success in this domain.

It is obvious that research into the computational features of different representational systems that are used by humans and into the effects of combining theses representations will have impact on instructional practice. While research focuses currently on the advantages for problem solving, research on consequences for *learnability* should be next on the agenda.

Machine Learning

Basic machine learning methods are usually defined in terms of a single formal representation language. The vocabulary for the knowledge to be learned is also given. However, many ML techniques do use additional knowledge besides specific examples. Here we review some of these representations and their role in learning. Learning in this case involves the acquisition of both the numerical and the abstract knowledge.

For instance, some expert systems use different formal language for intermediate representations. There is some evidence that for example qualitative abstractions of numerical problems make it possible to efficiently find an abstract solution and then use the abstract solution as a plan for calculating the numerical solution. This can be more efficient than solving the problem in a numerical representation (Mozetic, 1990). Learning in this case involves the acquisition of both the numerical and the abstract knowledge.

Along similar lines, some exploratory work has been done on reasoning and learning in the context of visual and diagrammatic representations. For instance, Cheng and Simon (1992) studied scientific discovery from diagrams and animations. Knowledge about physics can be expressed in graphical form and techniques for extrapolating structures in graphical representations can be used to discover new regularities. Tabachnek et al. (1994) describe a model of teaching and learning that involves both graphical and verbal representations. This enables her to explain some of the differences in the way experts and novices use graphical representations.

These examples illustrate the role of multiple languages in problem solving and reasoning. Now let us consider the role of multiple languages in learning. First we look at the role of multiple languages in finding generalizations and then we look at multiple languages in speedup learning.

Multiple Representations in Finding Generalizations. If we need to generalize from specific examples to a wide range of problems then the formal representation language and the vocabulary allow a large number of hypotheses. Several learning methods restrict this using knowledge about acceptable hypotheses. This is called "language bias".

There are many different forms of language bias in machine learning research. Bias can be general, preferring or requiring knowledge of a particular grammatical form, or it can be specific, addressing the content of knowledge that is to be acquired. A form of general language bias consists of a preference for hypotheses that are conjunctions of descriptive terms over hypotheses that are disjunctions or that use negations. This bias was noted by Bruner et al. (1956) in the context of learning artificial concepts defined over drawings. In a domain of objects with shapes, colors sizes, etc. a concept like "green circle" (the conjunction of "green" and "circle") is found more quickly than "green or red", "circle or rectangle" or than "green, no rectangle" (see also Medin et al. (1987)). Another general bias that is very strong and that plays an important role in machine learning is simplicity or simply size. Simple hypotheses are considered before complex hypotheses. (Note that it is not the same as bias for conjunctive hypotheses.) The hypothesis "green circle" is easier than "green or red" although as expressions they are of equal size.

A form of specific bias consists of an ordering defined on the terms that can appear in the knowledge that is learned. These terms may be ordered from most to least relevant. Hypotheses with relevant terms are considered first. A more complex form of specific language bias involves descriptions of the content of knowledge. For example, when learning about the diagnosis of persons who complain about chest pain, we may know that if a person has had these complaints before than the possible medication for these complaints is relevant information. If a person has complaints for the first time, medication for them will not be relevant. Several languages have been designed and used to represent this language bias. Some examples are discussed in Russel and Grosof (1990) and Morik et al. (1993). See also below in the section of learning goals.

All these forms of language bias define an order over the knowledge that is to be learned. During generalizations, hypotheses are considered following this order thus resulting in the best hypothesis.

Another form of generalization that involves multiple representations combines cases (specific experiences) and intensional representations. Problem solving can either use specific cases or intensional knowledge. When learning from experience, generalization can exploit both forms of learning by initially collecting cases but later generalizing from specific cases to general, intensional knowledge. Because both forms of problem solving are available, generalization can be postponed until enough cases are collected. Architectures based on this principle are described in e.g. Golding and Rosenbloom (1991), Wrobel (1994), Portinale, Torasso, Ortalda and Giardino (1993), and Helsper and van Someren (1995).

To sum up, in the process of acquiring generalizations multiple representations thus play the role of "language bias", describing the form of the knowledge that is to be acquired and the role of temporary knowledge that await generalization.

Multiple representations in speedup learning. By changing the representation of knowledge it can be brought into a form that allows faster use of the knowledge. This can be in the same formal representation language or it can involve "compilation" into a different formal language. The latter form is studied in machine learning only between closely related formal languages. The basic idea behind different representations for efficiency is to cut out knowledge that is only used for intermediate steps. If this can be replaced by knowledge that directly allows the solution to be found from the input then this can result in faster problem solving. In this case the learned representation can be a special form of the initial representation. Anderson (1983) introduced this idea in psychology to explain learning by practice phenomena in human skill acquisition.

After Minton (1988) showed that this method does not always actually lead to shorter processing, research has concentrated on a closer examination of the costs of reasoning and the selective use of Explanation-Based Learning techniques to actually achieve a speedup effect (Etzioni, 1992). Speedup learning is generally studied in the context of a single performance task and also it involves a one way traffic from (slow) reasoning knowledge to (fast) recognition knowledge. However, what if a person or system must use its reasoning knowledge - either for a different task than for which knowledge was optimized or for communication?

Issues in Learning with Multiple Representations

In this section we identify several issues that deserve further research. One is, How do people relate knowledge that is represented in different forms (e.g. particular observation vs. scientific principles, verbal, graphical and mathematical representations)? The importance of this task is reasonably well documented and several studies (e.g. by Karmirloff-Smith, 1992; Larkin, 1983; Tabachnek et al., 1994; Nathan et al., 1992) suggest or even demonstrate that knowing the relation between different representations is an important factor in a cognitive skill, in addition to knowledge in the different representations. Because expert performance on a task requires problem solving with multiple representations and knowledge is acquired initially in different languages, is it necessary to relate or translate knowledge into the form in which it can be used for problem solving. Failure to achieve this integration gives the effect of "knowing" something but not using this "knowledge".

Another important issue is the role of intermediate abstractions in problem solving. Both machine learning and cognitive psychology suggest that learners optimize the use of resources (such as memory) when satisfying performance goals (such as speed and error rate). This raises the question how this type of learning is controlled: if knowledge can be acquired in different forms, how can the optimal form be found? The main ideas are that compact representations are good because they use little memory, are usually (but not always) fast and because they are likely to be good generalizations. However, as noted by Van de Velde (1988), in some problem solving architectures there is trade-off between speed, compactness and accuracy. Simple, abstract models lack precision and detailed, accurate models are large and slow.

These issues have direct implications for education. The form in which information is presented to a learner must be such that (a) communications runs smoothly and fast and (b) the learner is able to relate the information to the other knowledge that is uses in problem solving.

Learning Goals

As we saw in the previous section, multiple representations in problem solving and learning are often associated with different input and output representations and with complex reasoning processes that make it profitable to construct and maintain internal representations. In both cases learning is a relatively complex task. A useful concept to understand complex learning processes is the notion of a learning goal. Although much learning takes place implicitly and automatically as a side effect of other activities, learning can also be a conscious, goal directed activity (e.g. Leake & Ram, 1993). People can decide to take actions with the purpose of learning something and computer systems can be given explicit learning tasks or, more importantly, come up with such ones by themselves (e.g., Ram, 1991; Krulwich, 1991). Outside of school, we are usually not provided with learning goals, but have to come up with them on our own. This holds both for overarching learning goals (such as: prepare for a degree) as well and even more for those learning goals that arise from impasses in problem solving and acting: A situation occurs where the agent needs to improve his knowledge in some way to complete an act, solve a problem, or be able to provide an explanation. Learning goals are crucial for the formulation of learning strategies and for determining when learning should start and stop.

In its explicit form, a learning goal is a description (in some representation language) of knowledge that a person (or a computer) wants to acquire. For example, in order to be able to solve physics problems, one needs to know the meaning of basic physics concepts, the laws of physics, their algebraic formulations, and basic algebra skills. Vocabulary and ontology can thus be used to represent learning goals. Learning goals, like goals in general, can also be represented implicitly by referring to a number of constraints the goal state must satisfy. For instance, one may have the learning goal to be able to solve m tasks in n minutes. This formulation of a learning goal does not specify the knowledge necessary for accomplishing the tasks nor does it say anything about the representational format and structure of that knowledge. It does, however, guide selection of a learning strategy, massed practice for instance.

In order to distinguish goal-driven learning from other forms of learning, it is essential not only that the learning goal is represented *explicitly* (either as a goal state or in form of constraints on the goal state) as part of the learning systems declarative knowledge, but also that the system *dynamically* adapts its learning behavior to its learning goals, which in turn adapt dynamically to the changing learning demands. This requires that the learning system can reason about the information it needs (cf. Leake & Ram, 1993)

The information needs are to a large degree determined by the kind of activity a system is engaged in at any point in time, for instance: problem solving with its various special forms (e.g., Wielinga et al., 1992; Breuker & van de Velde, 1994). Corresponding to the various knowledge demands different problem solving methods impose, different learning goals may arise. Formulation of learning goals is part of the following general decision process a multi-strategy learner is constantly engaged in (cf. Ram & Cox, 1994):

- What are learning opportunities?
- How can knowledge gaps be identified (blame assignment problem)?
- How are learning goals formed (decision what to learn)?
- How are learning strategies selected (decision how to learn)? This includes the decision with which representational format to learn.

Identifying Learning Opportunities.   The question of When learning should ensue needs to be answered because under realistic conditions learning needs to be coordinated with other performance processes an organism is engaged in. With the exception of very basic learning processes that run automatically, learning puts demands on cognitive and motivational resources. Therefore, learning cannot always be the default reaction. Both for human and machine learning, the constraint most often employed is that learning takes predominantly place under conditions where the organism encounters a problem. A problem can take many forms: an impasse in problem solving or in constructing an explanation for an event, or the occurrence of an unexpected event, even unexpected success. Learning should only take place when the cause for the problem is supposedly a reasoning failure, i.e., has been caused by an incomplete or incorrect internal ("mental") model of the respective aspects of the external environment. Mere "slips" should not trigger learning efforts.

Blame assignment problem.   When a learning system encounters a problem, it needs to determine the cause(s) of the underlying reasoning failure. In general terms, reasoning failures can occur because the relevant background knowledge is incomplete, or in other words, because the situation is (partially) novel. In this case, the system will have no expectations (and no explanations) for an event. Another class of problems arise when the background knowledge is incorrect. In this case, expectation failures will occur. The knowledge bears on the task, but does not always lead to correct expectations and/or performance. Thirdly, knowledge can be mis-indexed: The knowledge that when utilized would have avoided the failure is part of the background knowledge but was not activated. Again, on the performance level expectation errors arise. These three classes have been suggested by Ram & Cox (1994). For a similar, more fine-grained classification see Michalski (1994).

Forming learning goals.   In general, having identified a cause for a reasoning failure reduces the number of things that should be learned, but it does not determine completely what needs to be learned. Furthermore, a single reasoning failure may have multiple causes, or it is not clear which out of a multitude of possible causes is actually responsible. Therefore, after having identified the potential cause(s) for a reasoning failure, it is still not trivial to pin down what needs to be learned. Goal formulation will furthermore be dependent on the current situation of the agent, to be described in terms of concurrent goals and states of the cognitive system resources (e.g., leisure vs. highly demanding activities), his current background knowledge, and prior goals. Even so the learner may be able to formulate a learning goal, he may decide to suspend it and reactivate it when conditions are better. If the learning problem is complex, the learning goal will be a complex structure, a plan coordinating a sequence of learning steps to be taken.

How learning goals are achieved is discussed below in the section on learning strategies.

Psychological Research

In the educational literature, when discussing the influence of goals on learning, an often discussed distinction is the one between learning goals and performance goals. This distinction is based on the observation that while some students perform tasks with the goal to advance their knowledge and skill, others are more concerned with social considerations: avoiding blame, looking good, making an impression on the teacher and the like (Dweck, 1989; Marshall, 1988; Nolen, 1988). In general, it is not clear whether the difference between these two goal orientations actually influences learning and learning outcomes, and if so, whether it is of direct influence or just a mediating variable (Ng & Bereiter, 1991). Only a few psychological studies have by now addressed the question of how learning goals causally and in detail influence learning performance and outcome.

A study by Ng and Bereiter (1991) is among the few which look on a more detailed level into the relation between goals and learning. They observed how students, all of them volunteers, worked through a self-paced, computer-based BASIC programming course. The manner this course was introduced guaranteed that only subjects with an intrinsic learning interest entered the course: There were no credits to be gained nor was there any money to be earned. Despite this intrinsic learning orientation, Ng and Bereiter found stable and marked differences between the goals subjects set for themselves during the course. Three goal orientations could be distinguished: (a) task-completion goals: get the tasks whether self-chosen or assigned done; (b) instructional goals: get a grasp of the nature of the learning materials; (c) knowledge-building goals: relate the learning materials with the personal learning agenda. The relationship between the goal types is an hierarchical one: Many learning activities of students may be influence by task-completion goals, some by instructional goals, and few by knowledge-building goals. Given this hierarchical relationship, it is not astonishing that Ng and Bereiter found in the verbal protocols of their subjects many instances of task-oriented goals and only few instances of knowledge-building goals. As for effects on programming performance, goal orientation turned out to be a sufficient but not necessary factor for good problem solving. On a post-test with nine standard items, all of those subjects that had shown a knowledge-building orientation performed well, but so did others who showed little or none of this orientation.

Outside of research on learning, the influence of goals on cognitive processing has been studied in many areas: self perception, dissonance theory, person perception, decision making, and scientific reasoning, for instance (for an review see Kunda, 1990).

Questions of how humans form goals and how these goals influence cognition and performance are also central to the psychology of motivation and acting. However, with some important exceptions (e.g. Kuhl, 1985), this line of research has not produced process analysis. Hence, little is known about the mechanisms that construct goals and mediate their influence on cognitive processing. This is not to say that these theories are of no relevance for the study of goal-directed learning. One way to make them productive for our endeavour is realized in current research on autodidactic learning (e.g., Zimmermann, 1989; Friedrich & Mandl, 1990). Autodidactic learning refers to forms of learning who's direction and means are controlled by the individual rather than by an agenda imposed form the outside. Central research questions comprise how people organize their learning (time management, use of resources, sequencing, outcome evaluation) and how they coordinate it with other activities (job, household). Psychological theories bearing on these issues are motivational psychology (e.g, goal selection as a process of evaluating value, subjective success probability, and instrumentality) and the psychology of action control. For instance, Kuhl (1985) describes in his action control theory a group of cognitive processes that can be used to shield an active, behavior guiding intention from competing, possibly incompatible intentions. In short, research on autodidactic learning analysis processes of goal formation, planning (strategy selection), and execution control (e.g., monitoring) on a macroscopic level, whereas machine learning research begins to analyze these on a microscopic level yielding detailed process models.

Machine Learning

Basic ML techniques are mostly directed at general goals such increasing the generality of knowledge (increasing the range of problems that can be solved) or the speed. An important subsidiary goals is size: many methods minimize the size of the knowledge base. This is implicitly motivated by the assumption that a "small" generalization is, in general, also more likely to be correct than a "big" generalization. The status of this assumption is subject of research (e.g. Wolff, 1993). Only recently work was done on functional models of learning systems and on reflective architectures for learning and problem solving (in the context of multistrategy learning).

Describing Learning Goals

A few recent publications address the topic of controlling learning using explicit representations of the goal of learning. The language bias that we discussed in a previous section, in particular specific language bias, can be viewed as a kind of learning goal: it make it possible to express the form of what is to be learned. The representation of different forms of bias is an important research topic in Machine Learning. Suppose that we explicitly represent possible vocabularies that can be used to construct generalizations. One of these vocabularies can be used as bias in generalization but at the same time it is possible to reason about extending or reducing the vocabulary. The use of explicitly represented bias is of course not restricted to the vocabulary. Other techniques gradually relax bias on the structure of the knowledge to be acquired, allowing ever more complex hypotheses to be considered.

Reflective architectures: A different way to specify learning goals is in terms of the problem solving architecture. For example, if we know that the procedure for solving a new problem consists of three subprocesses (1) retrieve a similar old problem, (2) analyze the differences and (3) accept or modify the old solution, then this means that we need to learn the knowledge for each of these subprocesses. A problem solving architecture consists of a representation language for knowledge and a mechanism for using this knowledge to solve problems. The representation language determines the form of the knowledge that is to be acquired. As we discussed in the previous section, this can be specified further by some form of language bias. However, the problem solving architecture also specifies the form of the knowledge by its dynamic behavior. Suppose that a system is learning from a training problem (a problem with a correct solution that could not have been found by the system using only its current knowledge). The new knowledge must of course be in the representation language of the architecture but it must also enable the problem solving mechanism to find the solution to the training problem. This means that it is possible to make a rather specific description of the missing knowledge on the basis of the data of the training problem, the correct solution and the problem solving architecture.

Fully reflective architectures: Examples of learning systems that are based on reflective architectures are described by Carbonell et al. (1991), Ram and Cox (1994), and Plaza et al. (1993). An older example is Wilkins' system ODYSSEUS (Wilkins, 1990). All these techniques are based on the idea that a failure to solve a problem is described in terms of the problem solving mechanism. This is then used to characterize the missing knowledge and to generate a question to the user or an experiment (e.g. see Carbonel et al., 1991).

Van Dompseler and van Someren (1994; see also Thomas et al., 1993) describe a system that uses an explicit model of the problem solving process that can represent language bias in terms of this process. For each step the system contains abstract descriptions of the input and output. For example, it may know which knowledge is needed to find a medical interpretation of a complaint, what possible complaints are and what possible medical interpretations are. Then it may also know that the next type of reasoning step is to find a physiological cause for the interpreted complaints and again it can represent possible causes, and a description of the knowledge relating interpreted complaints to causes. This is then used as language bias. In this system *lacunae* in the knowledge are not just characterized in terms of an explicit model of the problem solving process that specifies the structure of the reasoning process in addition to the vocabulary and lexical structure, but also by the problem solving architecture and dynamic knowledge constructed during problem solving.

All these techniques apply to an impasse-driven learning situation: After an unsuccessful attempt was made to solve a problem, this problem is then characterized in terms of the problem solving step and the failing or false knowledge that is used at that step. For example, at the level of general representation languages, if a solution cannot be found in a production rule system we look for a production rule that has been missing or for a rule that was too specific (had too many conditions) to be applied. If we have a more specific ontology, distinguishing for example between symptoms, complaints, causes, diseases and therapies and knowledge for inferring one from the other, then we can describe the missing knowledge as a missing relation between for example complaint and cause or between disease and therapy.

These techniques focus the learning process using a model of the problem solving mechanism and problem solving experience. This can be combined with language bias. Together these elements make it possible to formulate learning goals. Research along this line is relatively new and is connected to research on knowledge acquisition for knowledge based systems (e.g. Thomas et al., 1993; van Dompseler and van Someren, 1994; Morik et al., 1993). This approach has been applied mostly to learning generalization but recently it can also be used for speedup learning. In this case the problem solving architecture is used to identify sources of computational costs.

Issues in Goal-Directed Learning

The concepts and techniques from Machine Learning appear to provide a basis to understand part of the role of learning goals in problem solving and learning with multiple representations. One important issue is to obtain a better view of the learning goals that people have: how can we describe what we do not know? Another issue is the knowledge that is required for achieving such goals. What do we need to know about our own knowledge and about the sources of information to achieve learning goals? Further issues concern taxonomies for learning goals: Which goals do human learners distinguish? Which ones should machine learning systems distinguish? What gives rise to the formulation of learning goals? How, in detail, do learning goals affect the learning process? How are interactions between learning goals handled? It is obvious that such questions are of high relevance not only for basic research in human and machine learning, but are also of concern for instructional settings. They are in particular related to fostering self-regulative and strategic competencies in learners, a theme we turn to in the following section.

Learning Strategies

Coordinating multiple representations and multiple learning goals is a challenging task for humans, let alone for machine learning systems. In order to cope with this complexity, the learning system must embody strategic knowledge. Knowledge that controls complex learning processes is labelled a learning strategy. A learning strategy could for instance comprise the following steps: plan experiments -> carry them out -> identify trends in the data -> memorize the relevant trend information. In general, a learning strategy is a knowledge structure that contains among other things information on what the input to the learning mechanism proper must be[1], how it is to be represented (for instance, in abstracted form), which inferences to apply, and how the results should be represented and used. It also contains contextual information beyond logical requirements: not only under which circumstances the strategy can be evoked, but also when it *should* be excited. And it contains various descriptions of the strategy: how cognitively demanding it is (memory burden), how long it takes to execute, given prototypical input, how precise and valid the learning results are, and so on. All this knowledge is required to make an informed decision between a number of available learning strategies in order to find one that is as much as possible adapted to the learning goal(s) and the situation the learner finds himself in. While this is normatively true, it is another question whether it is pragmatically feasible (for instance, because of computational demands) and empirically the rule. Hence, in particular with respect to strategy selection we have to be careful to not confuse the competence of a learning system with the factors involved in performance. It is probable, for instance, that in many cases learning systems do not consciously consider all the knowledge they have about the situation and about the learning strategies they command because they have learned to employ specific strategies in specific situations. In other words, the decision making process has been cached into a memory structure and does not need to be repeated all the time.

Strategy execution. Since a realistic cognitive system will be engaged in following a multitude of possibly competing goals at any given time and on top of that has to monitor its environment for unexpected and possibly threatening events, having decided for a learning strategy does not imply that the strategy will be carried out immediately. Its initiation may be delayed, its execution interrupted and resumed later on, or be completely abandoned. These monitoring and control issues have to be dealt with at the level of cognitive architecture.

Learning in the context of multiple representations that are associated with different ways of using the knowledge (different problem solving tasks, communication) implies that learning involves more than generalizing experiences. Improved performance of a task may be the result of an adequate generalization from experiences but it can also be due to other types of reasoning such as translation between representations of abductive reasoning.

Psychology

Even though it is almost taken as tautological that human learners employ multiple learning methods, taking into account multiple forms of prior knowledge and available knowledge sources and using multiple representations, one finds little psychological research that deals with the phenomenon in its full complexity. The rule both in experimental psychology and in cognitive modelling is to study single strategies and single representations in isolation, or, since it is convenient for experimental work, to compare two approaches. What is left out are many of

---

1. If the input is not simply provided by the environment, a learning strategy may also refer to an information search strategy, i.e., descriptions of methods to search for and organize information.

the crucial problems that lie at the heart of multistrategy learning: How are multiple strategies and representations coordinated? How are they adapted to the task, in particular, to the learning goals?

Learning strategies have received a great deal of attention in psychology. Let us become clear what is meant with this notion. A strategy serves the purpose to help accomplish some goal. Hence, a learning strategy serves to accomplish a learning goal. Weinstein & Mayer (1985) define learning strategies as "cognitions or behaviors that a learner engages in during learning that are intended to influence the encoding process so as to facilitate the acquisition, retention, and retrieval of new knowledge". They categorize learning strategies into the following eight categories: basic and complex rehearsal strategies, basic and complex elaboration strategies, basic and complex organizational strategies, affective strategies, and comprehension monitoring strategies. This is a taxonomy based on functional differences. Other taxonomies have been proposed, for example by Danserau (1978, 1985). He distinguishes on the top level between primary strategies that are employed for encoding, storing, retrieving, and using (text) information, and support strategies which are used to help the learner maintain a suitable mind set for learning .

Both taxonomies (and all others we know about) distinguish between two aspects: knowledge about learning strategies, and the ability to control the employment of these strategies. It seems appropriate to label the first aspect tactical knowledge, knowledge about learning actions (operators). This tactical knowledge becomes only useful for learning if is supported by strategic knowledge, i.e., knowledge about when to employ the learning actions and how to monitor their progress. It has been empirically demonstrated that students of nearly all ages know or can be taught basic learning methods such note taking, outlining, rehearsing, but what distinguishes successful learners from the rest is their strategic knowledge. Successful training of learning strategies (e.g., Palinscar & Brown, 1984) therefore has to aim at three areas in parallel: "(a) training in the use of task-specific strategies (tactics); (b) `awareness` training, explicit instruction concerning the significance of tactics and the range of their utility (metacognitive knowledge); and (c) instruction in how to orchestrate and oversee tactic deployment (self-regulation strategies)" (Derry & Murphy, 1986, p. 13).

Under the perspective of employing multiple learning strategies for multiple learning goals, research on comprehension monitoring is most relevant. To pin it down in a definition: "Comprehension monitoring involves establishing learning goals, assessing the degree to which those goals are being met and, if necessary, modifying the strategies being used so as to more closely meet the goals" (Weinstein & Rogers, 1985, p. 620). It was found that many learners, even after years of schooling, have difficulties in identifying learning goals and monitoring the progress they make towards these goals (e.g, Brown, 1980, for an review). Why might this be the case? We think that two factors can account for this. One is that students in school settings are not required to perform these two functions because they are to a large degree taken over by the teacher. When entering the university, where students are supposed to be independent learners, or when entering the work place, where independent learning is increasingly often required, difficulties arise due to the lack of experience in independent studying. A second factor that makes comprehension monitoring a tough problem is that it is to a large extent dependent on proficiency in the domain learning takes place in. Being proficient in an (academic) domain - being an expert - means to have (a) higher order, systematic knowledge structures, (b) explicit knowledge of the organizational structure of the knowledge involved in a discipline, and (c) knowledge on a level detailed enough so that expectations can be generated on side of the learner (Weinstein & Rogers, 1985). Features (a) and (b) help to not getting lost in the subject materials, (c) helps to monitor comprehension on a more fine grained level, in paragraph and sentence processing for instance.

The Novices are faced with a conundrum here: By definition, they do not command over the domain knowledge that would be required for optimal comprehension monitoring; since this hinders knowledge acquisition, the chances are reduced that they will ever reach the required knowledge level. In order to step out of this potentially vicious cycle, learners need to be able to employ learning strategies that are not completely specific to the domain but are also not so general that their application in a domain becomes very difficult. Students need to know learning strategies that are suitable for important types of learning materials and situations. It may therefore be appropriate to speak about learning strategies in terms of strategies to learn from simulations, to learn from examples, to learn from mathematical exercises, from prose text of a specific genre, and so forth. In order to define more precisely what the right abstraction level should be and what the most important methods on that level are, more research is needed that analysis learning from particular types of input information and their co-ordination.

Machine Learning

Recently several publications have appeared under the heading "multistrategy learning". The idea is to combine elements from existing learning techniques (or even complete learning systems) into a method (and system) that can perform a wider range of learning tasks or to combine basic learning operators with other types of reasoning. For example, several systems combine techniques for forming new concepts with generalization. The new concepts then help to structure the search for good generalizations. An example of combining learning processes with other inference is the NeoDISCIPLE system (Tecuci, 1991). This constructs "plausible justifications" for observations that it cannot fully explain. This in contrast to more strict justifications. Plausible justifications are found by a general technique for plausible reasoning. The plausible justification can then added to the knowledge which gives the effect of learning or it can be generalized.

Another example of the use of multiple learning methods is ML-SMART (Bergadano, Giordana, & Saitta, 1988). This program uses inductive reasoning from observations combined with deductive reasoning from initial background knowledge to learn knowledge that is consistent with the background knowledge and generalizes the observations.

The MUSKRAT system (Graner, 1993) is one of the few ML systems that use multiple representations. It has a simple reflective architecture with an explicit representation of the problem solving method and the representations of components of the method. This is used to select and apply acquisition operators to construct a system by acquiring the knowledge for each component. In this way the architecture is filled with knowledge by learning systems that are appropriate for the representation and learning goal. Acquisition can be done automatically (if training examples are available) or by interviewing a domain expert.

These systems all employ learning techniques as means to the construction of knowledge-based systems. A different approach to multistrategy learning is to integrate machine learning and problem solving in the design of "adaptive" systems. These are systems that both solve problems and learn. The results of research in machine learning are usually presented as algorithms and systems. For the process of designing complex systems, models at an intermediate level of abstraction are needed. This is common practice in software engineering and more recently also in knowledge engineering. Designing and building complex systems that have learning as one of their tasks, has drawn attention to the issue of abstract models of learning behavior that can be used in the design of complex systems. Currently only some initial work has been done on this topic. Van de Velde & Slodzian (1994) present an example of a functional model of techniques for learning decision trees. The functional analysis shows how various decision tree algorithms can be configured from functional components.

In the field of knowledge acquisition research is taking place that is also relevant for the issue of learning strategies. For example, Wielinga, Schreiber & Breuker (1992) define a language for specifying problem solving methods and predefined domain ontologies that make it possible to configure and refine abstract descriptions of knowledge. This is used in the process of acquiring knowledge from human experts and other sources such as text books, manuals, records, etc. A model is constructed and gradually refined and used to set for example topics for interviews with experts or for a document search.

Issues

The general issue here is the performance of learning tasks that are complex in the sense that they involve learning from multiple sources, directed at specific learning goals (that may be created dynamically during learning or problem solving). Not much is known yet about the knowledge and reasoning processes that play a role in complex learning tasks. Which knowledge is required for intelligent active learning where learning involves not only storage and generalization of experience but also other forms of acquiring new knowledge (such as transformation or restructuring) and active exploration of available sources of information? To what extent is it possible for a learner to control complex learning processes and even to plan ahead for learning? Intricate problems arise for the architecture of the cognitive system that hosts these complex decisions processes. We consider it probable that much of the planning and control processes will not take place solely in the mental medium ("in the head"), but that resources the learning environment offers will be utilized. For instance, a learner can arrange to associate the (re-)activation of learning goals with certain constellations in her physical environment and hence be *reminded* of the learning goal by environmental features instead of having to *memorize* a list of open learning goals. In other words, complex learning may be in the same manner distributed between the agent and her social and physical environment as is the case for other complex problem solving and planning tasks (e.g. Suchman, 1987).

The architecture and the knowledge that are needed for intelligent learning are relevant both for the study of both machine learning and human learning. They may help to explain the differences in learning rate between people and the effect of educational environments and they will be the basis of adaptive computer systems that actively try to improve their performance

Conclusions

In this chapter we review several key issues in learning with multiple representations and multiple goals in the context of problem solving. We end this chapter with a note on the methodology for collaboration between machine learning, psychology and education.

Let us recapitulate the relationships that proved critical for the understanding of complex learning behavior. Humans and increasingly often machines use multiple representations of perceived and inferred information because this results in an increased inferencing power. Humans and increasingly often machines generate and utilize learning goals to guide (bias) and control (monitor) learning because of the inherent complexities of instructionless learning and because often requirements are such that multiple goals need to be satisfied (e.g., problem solving and explanation giving). The learning goals should help to constrain the kind of domain representation most suitable for a kind of learning goal. For instance, when the goal is a speed-up in performance, a procedural, lean knowledge structure is most suitable. In order to coordinate the accomplishment of learning goals and the usage of multiple representational formats, the need for control structures arise. Hence, learning goals suggest learning strategies which in turn satisfy learning goals when executed properly. Learning strategies may contain information about the representational format most suitable for their execution, either explicitly, or implicitly because their applicability description matches only against a specific representational for- mat. The utilization of multiple representations, goals and strategies for learning requires a reflexive or meta-cognitive architecture, one where cognitive states and processes can become the object of deliberation.

Research Issues

The Role of Multiple Representations in Problem Solving

Some representations are directly associated with the form of input and output, both with regard to learning and with regard to problem solving. Some problem solving takes place directly in these representations. However, these representations may have different performance charac- teristics such as memory size and speed. Research in both psychology and machine learning suggest that this may motivate selective use of different representations for sub-tasks, construc- tion of special representations and selective learning in a particular representation. However, empirical evidence and analysis do not at this stage make it possible to evaluate the potential of this type of explanation. A complication is that knowledge may be relevant for more than one problem solving task. In this case, optimization should take all these into account. A compact representation for one task may for example result in very slow reasoning for another task. Compare also the analysis by Van de Velde (1988) on the trade off between accuracy, speed and compactness.

The research issue is if it is possible to use this approach to explain the appearance of differ- ent representations in problem solving and learning.

Teaching Multiple Representations

If the role of representations in problem solving is known, this can be used to teach knowledge in a form that generates adequate problem solving. For several tasks and domains representa- tions have been identified that are not generally used by learners, but that are known to be useful (from studies of experts) and that constitute effective teaching material (e.g. for physics prob- lem solving: Larkin, 1983; for logical syllogisms, see Dobson, 1993).

Following Anderson's approach (e.g. Anderson, 1990), experiments with teaching that is based on detailed cognitive models of the learning task in turn provide feedback on the models and indirectly on the architecture.

Representing Learning Goals

The notion of learning goal is to some extent paradoxical: if we would know exactly what to learn, we would not need to learn it anymore. This raises the question How we can describe what we do not know and What we want to learn. Machine learning research focuses on the idea that goals are stated in terms of the problem solving process, in particular of the problem solv- ing architecture. Knowledge acquisition research introduced the notion of predefined ontologies that can be used as a richer representation of learning goals. In psychology some evidence was found for the effect of explicit learning goals on learning performance, but not much detail is known about the role of learning goals in learning and problem solving.

An important research issue appears to be the relation between these different types of lear- ning goals and the role that learning goals play in learning and problem solving.

Identifying the Knowledge and Strategies for Performing Complex Learning Tasks

In complex problem solvers, the initial motivation for learning is usually some performance failure or an initial learning goal. Due to the multiplicity of representations, sources of information and feedback and the multiplicity of possible learning activities some strategic control over the learning process appears to be necessary. Not much is known now about the knowledge involved in controlling such processes.

A Methodological Note

Answering the questions above requires a collaborative effort that uses both computational techniques and empirical methods. These can be combined using the notion of "task analysis" (Anderson, 1990; van Someren et al., 1994). A task analysis specifies how a task can be performed "rationally" with respect to certain assumptions about the cognitive architecture and knowledge involved. For example, if we want to explain the role of qualitative models in physics problem solving we can conduct a task analysis. This means that we specify which knowledge and which methods are needed to solve a physics problem. Obviously there is no unique way to perform such a task but task analysis searches for the most efficient way to find a correct solution (assuming knowledge and a cognitive architecture that is plausible). If this analysis would suggest that a qualitative model is redundant and would reduce efficiency or threaten correctness of the solution, then it is likely that one of our assumptions about architecture or knowledge is incorrect. Constructing a task analysis closely parallels research in machine learning. In this field also optimal architectures and knowledge is pursued for solving learning problems, however, the assumptions about the architecture are based on those of computer systems rather than of humans. However, we believe that machine learning techniques can often be used as the basis of a task analysis and that cognitive psychology studies many learning tasks that are outside the scope of those studied by machine learning research.

References

Anderson, J.R. (1983). *The architecture of cognition*. Cambridge, MA: Harvard University Press.

Anderson, J.R. (1990). *The adaptive character of thought*. Hillsdale, NJ: Lawrence Erlbaum Associates.

Anderson, J.R. (1993). *Rules of the mind*. Hillsdale, NJ: Lawrence Erlbaum

Bergadano, F., Giordana, A., & Saitta, L. (1988). Concept acquisition in an integrated EBL and SBL environment. In Proceedings of the European Conference on Artificial Intelligence. London: Pitman.

Breuker, J.A., & van de Velde, W. (Eds.). (1994). *CommonKADS library for expertise modelling: reusable problem solving components*. Amsterdam: IOS Press.

Brown, A.L. (1980). Metacognitive development and reading. In R.J. Spiro, B.C. Bruce, & W.F. Brewer (Eds.), *Theoretical issues in reading comprehension*. Hillsdale, NJ: Erlbaum.

Bruner, J.S., Goodnow, J.J., & Austin, G.A. (1956). *A study of thinking*. New York: Wiley and Sons.

Carbonell, J.G., Knoblock, C.A., &Minton, S. (1991). PRODIGY: An integrated architecture for planning and learning. In K. VanLehn (Ed.), *Architectures for Intelligence. The Twenty-Second Carnegie Mellon Symposium on Cognition*. Hillsdale, NJ: Erlbaum.

Carey, S. (1985). *Conceptual change in childhood*. Cambridge, MA: MIT Press.

Cheng, P.C-H. (1993). Multiple interactive structural representation systems for education. In R. Cox, M. Petre, P. Brna, & J. Lee (Eds.), *Proceedings of the workshop of graphical representations, reasoning and communication of the AI-Ed 93 World conference on Artificial Intelligence in Education*. Edinburgh: Univ. of Edinburgh.

Cheng, P.C.-H., &Simon, H.A. (1992). The right representation for discovery: finding the conservation of momentum. In D. Sleeman & P. Edwards (eds), *Proceedings of the Tenth International Workshop on Machine Learning (ML92)*.

Chi, M.T.H., Feltovich, P., & Glaser, R. (1981). Categorization and representation of physics problems by experts and novices. *Cognitive Science, 5*, 121-152.

Danserau, D.F. (1978). The development of a learning strategy curriculum. In H.F. O'Neill (Ed.), *Learning strategies*. New York: Academic Press.

Danserau, D.F. (1985). Learning Strategy Research. In J.W. Segal, S.F. Chipman, & R. Glaser (Eds.), *Thinking and learning skills (Vol. 1)*. Hillsdale, NJ.: Erlbaum.

Derry, S.J., & Murphy, D.A. (1986). Designing systems that train learning abilities: form theory to practice. *Review of Educational Research, 56*, 1-39.

Dobson, M. (1993). Learning Through and by Visualisation: A Case of Inter-media Translation. In Proceedings *Uses of Computer Visualisation in Higher Education*. Elsevier.

Dompseler, H.J.H. van, & Someren, M.W. van. (1994). Using models of problem solving as bias in automated knowledge acquisition. In A. Cohn (ed), *ECAI 94 11th European Conference on Artificial Intelligence*. London: John Wiley & Sons.

Dweck, C.S. (1989). Motivation. In A. Lesgold & R. Glaser (Eds.), *Foundations for a psychology of education*. Hillsdale, NJ: Erlbaum.

Etzioni, O. (1992). Acquiring search-control knowledge via static analysis. *Artificial Intelligence, 62*, 255-301.

Evans, D., & Patel, V. (Eds.). (1989). *Cognitive science in medicin: biomedical modeling*. Cambridge, MA: MIT Press.

Forbus, K.D. (1988). Qualitative Physics: Past, Present and Future. In H. E. Shrobe (ed.), *Exploring Artificial Intelligence*. San Mateo, California:Morgan Kaufmann.

Friedrich, H.F., & Mandl, H. (1990). Psychologische Aspekte autodidaktischen Lernens (Psychological aspects of autodidatic learning). *Unterrichtswissenschaft, 18*, 197-218.

Golding, A.R., & Rosenbloom, P.S. (1991). Improving Rule-Based Systems through Case-Based Reasoning. In Proceedings of *AAAI-91*. MIT Press.

Graner, N. (1993). The MUSKRAT system. In Proceedings *second workshop on multistrategy learning*. George Mason University.

Helsper, E., & Someren, M.W. van. (1995). Lazy revision by explanation-based indexing of failure. Proceedings *NAIC-95*. Erasmus Universiteit Rotterdam.

Hollan, J.D., Hutchins, E.L, & Weitzman, L. (1984). STEAMER: an interactive inspectable simulation-based training system. *AI Magazin, 5(2)*, 15-27.

Jong, T. de. (1991). Learning and instruction with computer simulations. *Education and Computing, 6*, 217-229.

Karmirloff-Smith, A. (1992). *Beyond modularity. A developmental perspective on cognitive science*. Cambridge, MA: MIT Press.

Koedinger, K.R., & Anderson, J.R. (1990). Abstract planning and perceptual chunks - elements of expertise in geometry. *Cognitive Science, 14*, 511-550.

Koedinger, K.R., & Tabachnek, H.J.M. (1994). *Two strategies are better than one: multiple strategy use in word problem solving*. Paper presented at the AERA Meeting 1994, New Orleans.

Krulwich, B. (1991). Determining what to learn in a multi-component planning system. In (Eds.), Proceedings of the *1991 Cognitive Science Conference*.

Kuhl, J. (1985). Volitional mediators of cognition-behavior consistency: self-regulatory processes and action versus state orientation. In J. Kuhl & J. Beckmann (Eds.), Action control. From cognition to behavior. Berlin: Springer.

Kunda, Z. (1990). The case for motivated reasoning. *Psychological Bulletin, 108*, 480-498.

Larkin, J.H. (1983). The role of problem representations in physics. In D. Gentner & A. L. Stevens (Eds.), *Mental models*. Hillsdale, NJ: Erlbaum.

Larkin, J.H., & Simon, H.A. (1987). Why a diagram is (sometimes) worth ten thousand words. *Cognitive Science, 11*, 65-99.

Larkin, J.H., McDermott, J., Simon, D.P., & Simon, H.A. (1980). Models of competence in solving physics problems. *Cognitive Science, 4*, 317-345.

Leake, D., & Ram, A. (1993). Goal-driven learning: fundamental issues. *AI Magazine, 14(4)*, 67-72.

LeFevre, J.-A., & Dixon, P. (1986). Do written instructions need examples? *Cognition and Instruction, 3*, 1, 1-30.

Marshall, H.H. (1988). Work or learning: Implications of classroom metaphors. *Educational Researcher, 17(9)*, 9-16.

Marton, F., & Wenestam, C.G. (1978). Qualitative differences in the understanding and retention of the main point in some texts based on the principle-example structure. In M.M. Gruneberg, P.E. Morris, & R.N. Snykes (Eds.), *Practical aspects of memory*. London.

McDermott, J., & Larkin, J.H. (1978). Representing textbook physics problems. In (Eds.) Proceedings of the *second national conference of the canadian society for computational studies of intelligence*. Toronto: University of Toronto Press.

Medin, D.L., Wattenmaker, W.D., & Michalski, R.S. (1987). Constraints and preferences in inductive learning: An experimental study of human and machine performance. *Cognitive Science, 11*, 299-339.

Michalski, R.S., & Tecuci, G. (Eds.) (1994). *Machine Learning a multistrategy approach*. San Mateo: Morgan Kaufmann.

Minton, S. (1988). *Learning effective search control knowledge: An explanation-based approach*. Dordrecht: Kluwer.

Morik, K., Wrobel, S., Kietz, J.-U., & Emde, W. (1993). *Knowledge acquisition and machine learning*. London: Academic Press.

Moyse, R., & Reimann, P. (Eds.) (1995). *Simulations for learning: design, development, and use* (Technical Report No. 110). Freiburg, Germany: University of Freiburg, Department of Psychology.

Mozetic, I.. (1990). Abstractions in Model-Based Diagnosis. *Working Notes of the Workshop on Automated Generation of Approximations and Abstractions*. (Boston, MA).

Nathan, M.J., Kintsch, W., & Young, E. (1992). A theory of algebra-word-problem comprehension and its implications for the design of learning environments. *Cognition and Instruction, 9*, 329-389.

Newell, A. (1990). *Unified Theories of Cognition*. Cambridge, Ma:Harvard University Press.

Newell, A., Rosenbloom, P.S., & Laird, J.E. (1989). Symbolic architectures for cognition. In M. I. Posner (Ed.), *Foundations of Cognitive Science*. Cambridge, Mass.:MIT Press.

Ng, E., & Bereiter, C. (1991). Three levels of goal orientation in learning. *Journal of the Learning Sciences, 1*, 243-271.

Nolen, S.B. (1988). Reasons for studying: Motivational oriantations and study strategies. *Cognition and Instruction*, *5*, 269-287.

Opwis, K., Stumpf, M., & Spada, H. (1991). Domain respresentation and student modeling in a microworld for elastic impacts. *Mental Models and Human-Computer Interaction*, *2*, 361-372.

Palinscar, A.S., & Brown, A.L. (1984). Reciprocal teaching of comprehension fostering and comprehension-monitoring activities. *Cognition and Instruction*, *1*, 117-175.

Plaza, E., Aamodt, A., Ram, A., van de Velde, W . & van Someren, M. (1993). Integrated Learning Architectures. In P. Brazdil (Ed.), *Machine Learning: ECML-93*. Berlin: Springer-Verlag.

Plötzner, R. (1993). *The integrative use of qualititative and quantitative knowledge in physics problem solving*. Unpublished doctoral thesis.

Portinale, L., Torasso, P., Ortalda, C., & Giardino, A. (1993). Using case-based reasoning to focus model-based diagnostic problem solving. *European Conference on Case-Based Reasoning*. New York: Springer.

Ram, A. (1991). A theory of questions and question asking. *The Journal of the Learning Sciences*, *1*, 273-318.

Ram, A., & Cox, M. (1994). Introspective reasoning using meta-explanations for multistrategy learning. In R. Michalski & G. Tecuci (Eds.), Machine Learning: A multistrategy approach. San Mateo, CA.: Morgan Kaufmann.

Reif, F., & Heller, J.I. (1982). Knowledge structure and problem solving in physics. *Educational Psychologist*, *17*, 102-127.

Reimann, P., & Chi, M.T.H. (1989). Human expertise. In K.J. Gilhooly (Ed.), *Human and Machine Problem Solving*. London, New York: Plenum Press.

Reimann, P., Schult, T. J., &Wichmann, S. (1993). Understanding worked-out examples: A computational model. In G. Strube & K. F. Wender (Eds.), *The cognitive psychology of knowledge*. Amsterdam: Elsevier.

Rich, E., & K. Knight (1991). *Artificial Intelligence* (second edition). Singapore: McGraw-Hill.

Richer, M.H., & Clancey, W.J. (1985). GUIDON-WATCH: A graphical interface for viewing a knowlegde-based system. *IEEE Computer Graphics and Applications*, *5(11)*, 51-64.

Roschelle, J. (1991). *Students' construction of qualitative physics knowledge: Learning about velocity and acceleration in a computer microworld*. Unpublished doctoral dissertation, Berkeley, CA: University of California.

Russel, S., &B. Grosof (1990). A sketch of autonomous learning using declarative bias. In P. Bradzil, & K. Konolige (eds.), *Machine Learning, meta-reasonig and logics*. Dordrecht: Kluwer.

Schmidt, H.G., Norman, G.R., & Boshuizen, H.P.A. (1990). A cognitive perspective on medical expertise: theory and implications. *Academic Medicine*, *65*, 611-621.

Simon, D.P.; Simon, H.A. (1978). Individual differences in solving physics problems. In R. Siegler (Ed.), *Children's thinking: What develops?* Hillsdale, NJ.: Erlbaum.

Someren, M.W. van, Barnard, Y, & Sandberg, J. (1994). *The think aloud method - a practical approach to modelling cognitive processes*. London: Academic Press.

Suchman, L.A. (1987). *Plans and situated actions*. Cambridge, MA: Cambridge University Press.

Sweller, J., & Cooper, G.A. (1985). The use of worked examples as a substitute for problem solving in learning algebra. *Cognition and Instruction*, *21*, 59-89.

Tabachnek, H.J.M., Leonardo, A.M., & Simon, H.A. (1994). How does an expert use a graph? A model of visual and verbal inferencing in economics. In Proceedings *Cognitive Science Conference 1994.*

Tabachnek, H.J.M., Koedinger, K.R., & Nathan, M.J. (1994). Toward a theoretical account of strategy use and sense-making in mathematics problem solving. In A. Ram & K. Eiselt (Eds.), *Proceedings of the Sixteenth Annual Conference of the Cognitive Science Society.* Hillsdale, NJ: Erlbaum.

Tarmizi, R.A., & Sweller, J. (1988). Guidance during mathematical problem solving. *Journal of Educational Psychology, 804,* 424-436.

Tecuci, G. (1991). A multistrategy learning approach to domain modelling and knowledge acquisition. In Y. Kodratoff (ed.), *Proceedings European Working Session on Learning 1991,* Berlin:Springer-Verlag.

Thomas, J., Laublet, P., & Ganascia, J.G. (1993). A machine learning tool designed for knowledge-based knowledge acquisition approach. In N. Aussenac, G. Boy, B. Gaines, M. Linster, J.-G. Ganascia, & Y. Kodratoff (eds), *Knowledge Acquisition for Knowledge Based Systems, Proceedings of the 7th European Workshop EKAW-93.* Berlin: Springer-Verlag.

Van de Merckt, T., & Decaestaecker, C. (1995). Multiple-Knowledge Representations in Concept Learning. In S. Wrobel & N. Lavrac (eds), Proceedings *European Conference on Machine Learning,* 1995.

VanLehn, K. (1989). Problem solving and cognitive skill acquisition. In M.L. Posner (Ed.), *Foundations of Cognitive Science.* Cambridge, MA: MIT Press.

VanLehn, K., Jones, R.M., & Chi, M.T.H. (1992). A model of the self-explanation effect. *Journal of the Learning Sciences, 2,* 1-59.

Velde, W. van de (1988). Quality Of Learning. In Proceedings of the *8th European Conference on Artificial Intelligence.*

Velde, W., & van de Slodzian, A. (1994). Configuring decision tree learning algorithms with KresT. In W. van de Velde (ed), Proceedings *Workshop on Knowledge Level models of machine learning,* Catania.

Ward, M., & Sweller, J. (1990). Structuring effective worked examples. *Cognition and Instruction, 7,* 1-39.

Weinstein, C.E., & Mayer, R.E. (1985). The teaching of learning strategies. In M.C. Wittrock (Ed.), *Handbook of research on teaching* (3rd edition). New York: Macmillan.

Weinstein, C.E., & Rogers, B.T. (1985). Comprehension monitoring as a learning strategy. In G. d'Ydewalle (Ed.), *Cognition, information processing and motivation.* Amsterdam: Elsevier.

Wilkins, D.H. (1990). Knowledge Base Refinement as Improving an Incorrect and Incomplete Domain Theory. In Y. Kodratoff & R. S. Michalski (eds), *Machine learning: an Artificial Intelligence Approach (Vol. III).* San Mateo: Morgan Kaufmann.

Wielinga, B.J., Schreiber, A.Th., & Breuker, J.A. (1992). KADS: A Modelling Approach to Knowledge Engineering. *Knowledge Acquisition, vol.1,* reprinted in: B. Buchanan, & D. Wilkins (eds.), (1992), *Readings in Knowledge Acquisition and Learning.* San Mateo: Morgan Kaufmann.

Wolff, J.G. (1993). Computing, cognition and information compression. *AI Communications, 6(2),* 107-127.

Wrobel, S. (1994). Concept formation during interactive theory revision. *Machine Learning, 14,* 169-192.

Zimmermann, B.J. (1989). A social cognitive view of self-regulated academic learning. *Journal of Educational Psychology, 81,* 329-339.

Order Effects in Incremental Learning

Pat Langley

Introduction

Intelligent agents, including humans, exist in an environment that changes over time. Thus, it seems natural that models of learning in such agents take into account the fact that this process also takes place over time. We often refer to such agents as *incremental* learners, in that the temporal nature of experience leads them to incorporate that experience in a piecemeal fashion.

In this chapter we discuss the notion of incremental learning from three perspectives - machine learning, instructional theory, and experimental cognitive psychology. These fields share a concern with the incremental nature of learning and with the effects of training order on the acquired knowledge. However, the literature has often been imprecise and sometimes inconsistent about the definition and nature of incremental learning, suggesting the need for a clearer treatment of the issues that arise in this context.

We attempt to clarify the situation in the following section by presenting some definitions of incremental learning and introducing some distinctions among types of order effects. We then turn to a more detailed discussion of two such types of effects from the vantage points of the different fields, briefly reviewing some relevant work in each case. Finally, we outline some directions for future research on this intriguing topic.

The Nature of Incremental Learning

Most research on incremental learning rests on three assumptions, which are often implicit in the literature in this area. Each of these assumptions appears to hold for human learners, and they seem equally desirable for artificial ones. First, the agent should be able to use its learned knowledge to carry out its performance task at any stage of learning. Second, the incorporation of experience into memory during learning should be computationally efficient. Finally, the learning process should not make unreasonable space demands, so that memory requirements increase as a tractable function of experience[1].

Definitions of Incremental Learning

The literature also contains different definitions of incremental learning, sometimes implicit, which seem tied to the above assumptions. We should briefly review these alternatives, in hopes of deciding which one is most appropriate for our current analysis. Perhaps the most common definition deals only with the first of the above assumptions.

> Definition 1. A learner L is *incremental* if L inputs one training experience at a time.

Clearly, for any learner of this sort, one can interrupt the training process and ask the agent to use its acquired knowledge to make predictions or carry out some other task. Such a learner certainly appears incremental to an external viewer.

---

1. In most of examples, the term "experience" translates to "training instance". But because we will see other senses of the former term elsewhere in the chapter, we will use it in our definitions.

However, note that one can easily adapt *any* learning algorithm to fit this definition, including ones that process many instances at a time, by simply storing the instances observed so far and running the method on them. For example, Schlimmer and Fisher (1986) describe such a variant of Quinlan's (1986) nonincremental ID3 algorithm for decision-tree induction. This system simply runs ID3 as a subroutine on the first training case, the first two cases, the first three cases, and so on, thus mimicking the external behavior of an incremental learner. One can adapt this idea to make any nonincremental learning algorithm appear incremental by our first definition. In fact, the above definition says more about the nature of the learning task than about the learner itself. Within the machine learning literature, particularly that on computational learning theory, this situation is sometimes referred to as an *on-line* learning problem (Littlestone, 1987).

Clearly, it seems desirable to distinguish between arbitrary methods that handle on-line tasks and ones that better reflect our intuitions about incremental processing. A more plausible definition would incorporate not only the first assumption but also the second one given above.

> Definition 2. A learner L is *incremental* if L inputs one training experience at a time and does not reprocess any previous experiences.

This version actually places a constraint on the learning mechanism itself, in that it can process each experience only once. We might relax this constraint somewhat to allow limited reprocessing, provided we do so cautiously. The important idea is that the time taken to process each experience must remain constant or nearly so with increasing numbers, in order to guarantee efficient learning of the sort seen in humans.[1]

Although this definition is a considerable improvement, it still violates some important intuitions. For example, Mitchell's (1982) candidate elimination algorithm for learning logical conjunctions processes instances one at a time and does not need to reprocess them. However, it accomplishes this feat by retaining in memory a set of competing hypotheses that summarize the data, and it reprocesses these hypotheses upon incorporating each training case. This presents no problem by itself, but Haussler (1987) has shown that the number of such hypotheses can grow exponentially with the number of training items, which seems contrary to our notions of incrementality.

We can avoid the inclusion of such algorithms by incorporating the third of the above assumptions into our definition.

> Definition 3. A learner L is an *incremental* if L inputs one training experience at a time, does not reprocess any previous experiences, and retains only one knowledge structure in memory.

This formulation rules out learning methods that retain competing descriptions, such as the candidate elimination algorithm, as well as methods like Winston's (1975) that carry out explicit backtracking. Learners that are incremental in this sense retain no set of alternatives and no memory of where they have been; they can only incorporate the next training item and move forward in response. For this reason, Langley, Gennari, and Iba (1987) refer to them as *incremental hill climbing* approaches to learning.

---

1. Note that even when learning method is incremental in this sense, one may not use it in an on-line fashion. For example, the weight-updating scheme used in backpropagation for neural networks does not reprocess instances by itself, yet researchers typically rerun the algorithm over the training set many times, thus violating our second assumption about reprocessing.

We will restrict ourselves to this third definition of incremental processing in the remainder of this paper. We maintain that any viable theory of human learning must be based on this definition, and we will see that many common learning methods satisfy it, though they are seldom presented in these terms. We can loosen our definition somewhat to allow storage of a few competing knowledge structures, or to allow a current structure with a number of possible successors, from which one is then selected. These variations still restrict memory to a manageable size.

Definitions of Order Effects

Learning mechanisms that rely on incremental hill climbing have one central characteristic that has received considerable attention: their behavior tends to be affected by the *order* of experience. We can state this notion more precisely:

> Definition 4. A learner L exhibits an *order effect* on a training set of experiences T if there exist two or more orders of T for which L produces different knowledge structures.

The origin of such effects is best understood in terms of search through the space of knowledge structures. An incremental learning method must make decisions about which path to follow (which structure to create) based on samples of the data. Different early samples may lead the learner down quite different paths, and later experiences may not be sufficient to counteract them[1]. Figure 1 (a) shows the paths through the space of knowledge structures for two different orders of the same experiences; because the learner arrives at different structures, this constitutes an example of an order effect. In contrast, the paths in Figure 1 (b) diverge initially but lead to the same structure, meaning no order effect has occurred.

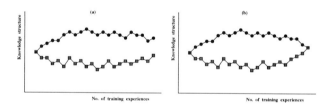

Figure 1: The knowledge structures generated by an incremental learner for two different orders of training experiences when (a) an order effect produces two different structures and (b) when the absence of an order effect produces the same structure

Our definition of order effects focuses on particular training sets and their presentation order, but we can rephrase things to emphasize the algorithm itself:

---

1. We must distinguish between behavior differences that result from order effects on a given training set and the quite distinct ones that result from different samples of data. The latter can occur even with the most nonincremental of learning methods.

Definition 5. An learner L is *order sensitive* if there exists a training set T on which L exhibits an order effect.

Similarly, we can say that a learner is *order independent* if it never exhibits an order effect. This formulation takes an all-or-none stance, but clearly one can also talk about degrees of order sensitivity, in terms of the number of training sets and the number of orders in which such effects occur, as well as the resulting distance between the learned structures.

One can also talk about the implications of order effects on behavior, using some performance measure M that reflects the usefulness of the knowledge learned from experience, such as accuracy on test cases. It seems reasonable to assume that some order effects, although producing different knowledge structures, have relatively little impact on performance.

Definition 6. An order effect for learner L on training set T is *benign* with respect to measure M if all orders of T produce knowledge structures of (nearly) equal scores on M.

In contrast, we can say that an order effect is *malignant* if different orders produce quite different results on the performance measure. Naturally, malignant order effects hold greater interest for most learning researchers, especially those with prescriptive rather than descriptive goals.

Levels of Order Effects

There exist at least three different levels at which order effects can occur, and thus three different ways in which we can instantiate the term *experience* in the previous definitions. Recall that most learning research deals with the acquisition of *concepts* from training *instances* that are described in terms of *attributes* or *features*. Incremental processing can occur, and thus order effects can result, with respect any of these levels, as depicted in Figure 2.

At the finest temporal resolution, the agent can process the attributes of each instance one at a time. In some frameworks, such as discrimination networks, attribute order can affect both performance and learning. Clearly, humans have limited attentional resources, so that one might expect that researchers would give high priority to modeling the effect of attribute order. Nevertheless, though many systems give different importance to different attributes, only a few (e.g., Feigenbaum, 1963; Gennari, 1991) acknowledge that they can be observed in different orders, and even these do not explicitly examine the effects of observation order on learning. For this reason, we will not have much to say on the topic here.

At the intermediate level, the agent can process training instances one at a time. This is clearly the most common interpretation of both incremental learning and order effects within the literature, and we consider it at some length in the next section. We will see that there exist machine learning algorithms that process instances in an incremental manner, psychological studies of the effects of instance order, and hypotheses about the uses of instance order in education, each of which sheds a different light on the nature of incremental processing.

At the highest level, the agent can learn distinct concepts one at a time, and their order of acquisition can make the learning task more or less difficult. There exists some work on this topic within machine learning and cognitive psychology, but it has received perhaps the most attention within the education paradigm, where courses of instruction typically order concepts in some principled fashion. We devote a later section to the incremental learning of different concepts.

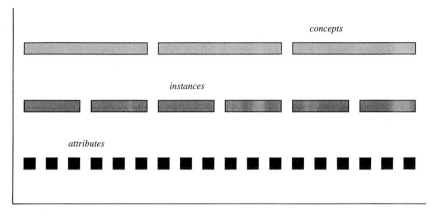

concepts

instances

attributes

Order of processing experience

Figure 2: Incremental processing can occur at three levels of temporal resolution: with respect to the attributes used to describe to instances, for instances of the concepts being learned, and for the concepts themselves.

The Effects of Instance Order

Research on the effects of instance order can approach the problem from different perspectives. Much of the work takes a prescriptive slant, treating order effects either as something to be eliminated or something to use profitably. Another alternative is to treat order effects as a phenomenon to be studied from a purely descriptive angle. Below we consider each of these vantages in turn.

Mitigating the Effects of Instance Order

If one's aim is to engineer an autonomous agent that learns from experience in a robust manner, then the effects of instance order - at least malignant ones - are undesirable. For this reason, many machine learning papers on incremental methods discuss schemes for eliminating or mitigating the order sensitivity of induction algorithms. Researchers have explored a variety of approaches to this issue within the framework of incremental hill climbing that we defined in the former section.

The simplest scheme involves making strong assumptions about the nature of the target concept, so that different orders of the same training data always produce the same result. For example, some early work on the induction of logical concepts focused on *conjunctive* concepts, and algorithms for this task which move from specific to general hypotheses show no order sensitivity, at least when used on attribute-value descriptions. Similarly, the naive Bayesian classifier (Langley, Iba, & Thompson, 1992) assumes both a single probabilistic summary for each class and independence among attributes; this lets it use a simple learning method that updates counts for each observed combination of class and attribute value, which makes it completely insensitive to training order. Within the area of grammar induction, Angluin (1977) describes an incremental algorithm for learning the restricted class of k-reversible grammars; this technique adds a new chain of states to an existing finite-state machine for each sentence it encounters, then merges states in a way that also guarantees against order effects.

However, some researchers find such representational restrictions distasteful (despite their excellent performance on many domains), and so have considered other responses to the problem. An alternative approach relies on background knowledge to constrain the learning process and thus to mitigate order effects[1]. When used to improve classification accuracy, explanation-based methods constitute an extreme version of this idea (e.g., Flann & Dietterich, 1989). In this scheme, each training case leads to the creation of one rule, and the order in which they are added to memory does not affect the result. Less extreme variations of this approach are also possible. For example, McKusick and Langley (1991) show that providing a partial concept hierarchy can reduce order effects in incremental clustering systems, and we expect similar results would occur with other learning methods. Cornuejols (1993) presents an insightful formal analysis of the conditions under which background knowledge reduces order effects.

Yet another response incorporates bidirectional learning operators that can undo early decisions that were based on nonrepresentative data. For example, many logical induction methods include both operators for making rules more general and more specific (e.g., Iba, Wogulis, & Langley, 1988), and algorithms for hierarchical clustering often include both operators for merging and splitting nodes in a taxonomy, as shown for Fisher's (1987) COBWEB algorithm in Figure 3. Such dual operators give learners the ability to emulate backtracking in certain situations, even though they have no memory of their previous knowledge structures. Gennari et al. (1989) present evidence that such operators reduce order effects in one clustering system, and their inclusion in other systems suggests their usefulness there as well.

A fourth framework takes a more conservative approach, retaining a current hypothesized knowledge structure and a manageable set of potential successor hypotheses, then waiting until one has observed enough training cases to determine with confidence the best successor. For example, Schlimmer and Fisher's (1986) approach to incremental decision-tree induction retains statistics on alternative attributes and extends the tree downward only when one attribute appears statistically better than the others. In a similar manner, Iba (1987) collects statistics on macro-operators, making sure they will aid problem-solving efficiency before adding them to memory. Greiner (1992) describes a very general formulation of this idea; his approach to incremental hill climbing needs no bidirectional operators because it collects enough training cases to (nearly) always makes the right decision at each step in the search process.

Another class of methods attempts to reduce order effects by storing multiple, complementary descriptions in memory. Like the previous approach, this relies on the idea that one should not commit to a single knowledge structure early on, before the training data clearly indicate that one is better than the others. For example, some clustering systems create directed acyclic graphs that can sort instances in multiple ways (e.g., Levinson, 1985; Martin & Billman, 1994). In its extreme form, this approach violates the spirit of incremental hill climbing in that the size of the knowledge structure can grow very rapidly as a function of the number of training cases. However, placing restrictions on the number of complementary descriptions can ensure manageable memory while retaining the benefits of a least-commitment approach.

---

1. Of course, because incremental methods process experiences sequentially, the results of learning from the first n instances constitutes a form of background knowledge for the n + 1st instance. Here we refer to knowledge that is available before the learning process begins.

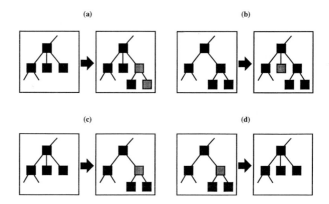

Figure 3: Learning operators used by Fisher's (1987) COBWEB to modify the structure of a probabilistic concept hierarchy: (a) extending the hierarchy downward; (b) creating a new sibling at the current; (c) merging two existing concepts; and (d) splitting an existing concept. Operators (c) and (d) are explicitly designed to reduce order effects.

A final approach concerns the notion of distributed representations in multilayer neural networks. The standard method for learning in such networks, backpropagation, is typically run through the training set many times, rather than altering the network to master each case before presenting the next one. McClosky and Cohen (1989) and Ratcliff (1990) have shown that, when trained in this latter mode, backpropagation exhibits "catastrophic interference", in that learning each new item causes the network to forget those learned previously. French (1993) argues that this effect results from the distributed representation of knowledge embodied in the network's hidden units. He shows that one can reduce this order effect by encouraging backpropagation to produce weights that give less distributed activations among hidden units. French also suggests that Kruschke's (1993) approach, which uses an inverse exponential activation function, avoids catastrophic interference for the same reason.

Instance Order in Instructional Design

Not all researchers view order effects as something to eliminate; some instead see them as given constraints that one must take into account during instruction. This attitude is especially prevalent among those in education who study instructional design, but it also occurs in some work on machine learning. Research in this tradition involves the design of presentation orders that will maximize the rate or quality of learning by simplifying the acquisition task.[1]

One simple technique along these lines involves the idea of a *near miss*, which is a negative instance of some concept that almost but does not quite satisfy the concept's definition. Winston

---

1. One should not confuse the positive use of order effects during instruction with the notion of benign effects discussed above. In fact, malignant effects are most relevant for instructional design.

(1975) posits that presenting a positive training case followed by near misses will simplify the induction process, as this lets the learner easily detect individual differences between the positive instance and the negative ones that are necessary to the concept definition. Unfortunately, this technique makes sense only for concepts with logical definitions, making it inapplicable to many natural categories and to many learning methods. Neri and Saitta (1993) describe a more general technique for selecting training cases to increase learning rates.

Another variant on this approach assumes that learners will fare better if presentation order alternates among instances of different categories than if presented with many cases of one category followed by those of another. The intuition here is that observation of contrasting training cases will encourage introduction of the appropriate distinctions. McKusick and Langley (1991) show that this training regimen increases the learning rate for a probabilistic clustering method by encouraging the creation of proper distinctions high in the concept hierarchy. A related idea underlies the standard 'epoch' training for backpropagation in neural networks, which iterates through training cases many times in order to avoid the "catastrophic interference" described earlier.

VanLehn (1987) observes that, in teaching complex concepts and procedures, many textbooks present them "one disjunct at a time". That is, if the target structure involves a number of distinct components that cover different situations, these components are presented separately, with each one being learned before turning to the next. The assumption here is that learning a number of simple concepts or procedures, when identified as such, is easier than acquiring a single complex structure. Superficially, at least, this advice seems to conflict with the alternation strategy recommended above, though VanLehn focused on procedural tasks and the alternation scheme comes from work on concept learning.

In some domains, training cases can themselves have different levels of complexity. Porat and Feldman (1991) take advantage of this fact to simplify the problem of grammar induction by presenting simple sample sentences before more complex ones. Like the "one disjunct" strategy, this training order lets the learner master parts of the target grammar on simple cases before being challenged by harder ones. Elman (1991) uses a similar training regimen for connectionist learning of phrase structure grammars, in which he gradually increases the proportion of complex sentences in the training set. This approach also seems recommended for memory-limited agents (including humans), as it lets them establish chunks during the early phases that aid retention during later periods.

Rendell (1986) and Iba (1989) draw on a similar insight in their work on learning problem-solving strategies. Their systems are initially presented with relatively easy problems which they can solve with little domain knowledge; they then use the resulting solution as material for learning. Once the systems have acquired some knowledge in this manner, they are given more difficult problems to drive further learning. This "bootstrapping" approach would seem generally useful whenever the agent must learn from the results of some search process.

Another approach to instruction hypothesizes an *accretion* theory of learning in humans (Rumelhart & Norman, 1978), in which new knowledge is added to existing structures. According to this theory, new experiences that have some connection with known memory structures are stored and accessible, whereas experience that makes little or no contact is effectively lost. This suggests a training regimen in which one first presents information about core ideas, then gradually presents elaborations that build the learner's knowledge base outward around the edges.

Finally, some research emphasizes the power of letting the learner select its own experiences. For instance, Carbonell and Gil (1987), Gross (1991), and Scott and Markovitch (1991) show the advantages of experimental control for automated learning systems. The basic insight behind this approach is that the learner often knows more about its own hypotheses, and thus about the areas of uncertainty, than does the instructor. Thus, learner-selected instances can provide more information and thus faster acquisition than teacher-selected experience.

Instance Order and Human Behavior

Until now, we have focused on techniques for reducing order effects in machine learning systems and intuitively plausible approaches for taking advantage of such effects during instruction. Both of these perspectives have a prescriptive flavor. However, there also exist experimental results about the effect of instance order on human learning, though descriptive studies of this sort have been relatively rare.

The literature on human memory touches on order effects, though not as directly as one might like. There is clear evidence of both retroactive inhibition (e.g., Müller & Pilzecker, 1900) - that learning on later items can hurt retrieval of ones mastered earlier - and the related phenomenon of proactive inhibition - that items mastered early on can inhibit learning on later ones. Both forms of interference are more likely when the items are similar in some fashion, thus allowing confusion. Studies of mass vs. distributed practice are also somewhat relevant to order effects, though they were not designed with this issue in mind. Most important, studies of this sort have emphasized rote memorization rather than concept acquisition or similar forms of induction.

A few studies of category learning have dealt with order effects more explicitly. Elio and Anderson (1984) considered two presentation orders of training instances for categories with graded structure, in which some cases were more typical than others. In one condition, they first presented a sample of highly typical instances, followed by a sample containing a mixture of typical and less typical cases, and finally a sample that was fully representative of the category. In another condition, each successive training sample was representative. The authors found that, when instructed to formulate explicit hypotheses, subjects learned the target concepts better (in terms of accuracy and typicality ratings) from purely representative samples. In contrast, when told to simply remember the individual instances, they did better when first seeing only typical samples. In later work, Elio and Lin (1994) modeled this interaction effect with two distinct learning strategies, one involving rule induction and the other using an instance-based mechanism.

Clapper and Bower (1994) report interesting results on an unsupervised learning task involving two simple logical conjunctions, using a performance criterion measuring ability to distinguish attributes with constant values for each category from those which vary. They found that subjects given training cases from one category followed by those from the other category learned more rapidly than did subjects given training instances that interleaved the two categories. Clapper and Bower suggested that the first presentation order lets the learner acquire norms for one category, and then be surprised when instances from the second category depart from those norms. Note that this finding directly contradicts the alternation method discussed earlier, which was found to aid some machine learning algorithms; thus, it suggests that these methods provide poor models of human learning, at least in this domain.

Studies of human problem solving have also revealed some intriguing effects of problem order. Luchins' (1942) experiments with the water jug task showed that, when given a set of training problems that had only one solution, subjects later solved other problems that had alternative solutions in the same way. However, this *Einstellungs* effect did not occur when they encountered both types of problems early in training. The order of problem presentation also influenced the time it took subjects to extinguish this behavior. Jones (1989), Langley and Allen (1991), and others provide computational accounts of Luchins' basic phenomena in terms of early acquisition of search-control knowledge and subsequent use of that knowledge to bias problem solving.

In summary, experimental psychology has given less attention to the effects of instance order than machine learning or educational theory, but the studies that have been reported call into question some of the assumptions of the latter two fields. Clearly, a fuller descriptive account of the incremental nature of human learning would complement, and possibly redirect, the prescriptive work in other areas.

The Effects of Concept Order

As we noted earlier, one can impose an ordering not only the training cases provided for learning, but also on the concepts that are to be learned. This issue arises only in more complex learning tasks, where some concepts can be defined or grounded in terms of other concepts[1]. Work in this tradition has focused almost exclusively on the advantages of certain presentation orders, rather than on the effects of different orders or on techniques for overcoming them.

From Simple to Complex Concepts

Most research in this area has assumed that the preferable training order moves from simple to complex concepts. That is, if some high-level concept can be formulated in terms of lower-level ones, then learning will be aided if one masters the simpler concepts first. A number of machine learning efforts build on this idea. For example, Sammut and Banerji (1986) describe an incremental approach that first learns simple logical concepts from supervised data, then uses the learned rules to re-express instances of more complex concepts at higher levels of abstraction. Elio and Watanabe (1991) report another learning algorithm that operates along similar lines. In both cases, the intuition is that augmenting the instance description with new features, which must first be learned themselves, can ease the task of learning complex concepts.

The educational theorist Gagne (1966) proposed that human learning occurs in a similar manner, and recommended the design of instructional sequences in which students mastered component skills before attempting to learn about the more complex procedures that require them[2]. For the domain of solving first-order algebraic equations, he presented a skill hierarchy with eight distinct levels, ranging from symbol recognition and number use at the lowest tier, through intermediate skills like simplifying functional expressions and adding numbers to both sides, to equation solving at the highest level. However, as Singley and Anderson (1989) note, experimental support for Gagne's theory has generally been difficult to obtain. In particular, some "scramble" studies have failed to find any differences between training regimens that incorporate the component-first scheme and ones that order skills randomly.

From Complex to Simple Concepts

Not all researchers have assumed that components are best learned before composite concepts or skills. Shapiro's (1987) technique of *structured induction* recommends exactly the opposite, at least in the use of decision-tree induction to construct knowledge bases. He found that

---

1. We intend the term "concept" here in the broadest sense possible, to cover not only static structures but also temporal ones like procedures and grammars.

2. Some theories of human learning, such as Rosenbloom and Newell's (1987) chunking account, assume that simple concepts are learned before more complex ones but take no position on the effect of training order.

domain experts could provide examples for use as training cases, but that they preferred to describe them in terms of high-level attributes. After constructing a decision tree from these cases, one could then get experts to provide lower-level examples as training data for concepts that defined the initial attributes. The result of this top-down process is a recursively defined decision tree that eventually grounds out in observable features. Langley and Simon (in press) note that structured induction has been used to construct a number of fielded knowledge bases.

Some educational psychologists have proposed analogous training sequences for human instruction. For example, both Bruner's (1966) spiral curriculum and Reigeluth and Stein's (1983) elaboration theory recommend that students first be taught very general skills, and only them be shown techniques for instantiating them. There have been fewer experimental evaluations of such top-down organizations than for bottom-up ones like Gagne's, but clearly they deserve equal attention, as do mixed instructional strategies.

Directions for Research on Incremental Learning

The study of incremental learning and order effects clearly has important implications for both the construction of artificial intelligent agents and the design of instructional sequences for humans. The work to date has revealed some promising approaches in both areas, but much more remains to be done before we understand the full nature of incremental learning. We can group the important lines of research still needed into three main classes.

First, the field needs better measures for detecting order effects in incremental learners, whether human or machine. Learning curves, which describe performance as a function of the number of training experiences, will likely occupy a central role in this effort. Typically, the mean values of learning curves are used to reveal the rate of learning, but they such curves also suggest the presence of order effects. Briefly, one can expose learners to the same training data in different orders, then examine not the mean but the variance along the resulting curve; a high variance suggests a strong sensitivity to training order in the learner. However, this is only one promising technique, and others may prove just as useful.

We also need better descriptive languages for characterizing the paths taken by incremental learners through the space of knowledge structures, and better techniques for identifying the choices responsible for order effects. For this, we need to look more closely at individual training orders and to compare the behaviors they produce in the learner. If order effects are absent within certain subsets set of training orders but present across these subsets, then the differences among those sets may be useful in describing the cause of the effects. Again, this approach is only one among many possible methods for analyzing sequential behavior in learning.

Finally, we need better theories about the sources of order sensitivity that hold across broad classes of incremental learners. Existing accounts revolve around notions of alternating vs. batch orders, typical vs. atypical instances, and simple vs. complex problems. These provide reasonable starting points, but they are more like simple hypotheses than coherent theories. The view of incremental learning as hill-climbing search through a space of knowledge structures, with decisions affected by the most recent experience, holds the most promise for a unified account of order effects, though the exact nature of this account remains far from clear.

We encourage researchers from education, cognitive psychology, and machine learning to look more closely at the nature of incremental processing, and to build on the growing body of work in this area. We hope that a joint effort by scientists from all three disciplines will lead to insights that would not be possible by studying the effects of training order from a single perspective.

Acknowledgments

Thanks to members of the ESF Task Force on Sequencing Effects for enlightening discussions that led to many of the ideas presented in this chapter. This work was supported in part by a grant from the European Science Foundation on Learning in Humans and Machines, and in part by Grant F49620-94-1-0118 from the Computer Science Division of the U.S. Air Force Office of Scientific Research.

References

Angluin, D. (1977). Inference of reversible grammars. *Journal of the Association for Computing Machinery, 29*, 741-765.

Bruner, J. (1966). *Towards a theory of instruction.* New York: W. W. Norton.

Carbonell, J.G., & Gil, Y. (1987). Learning by experimentation. *Proceedings of the Fourth International Workshop on Machine Learning.* Irvine, CA: Morgan Kaufmann.

Clapper, J.P., & Bower, G.H. (1994). Category invention and unsupervised learning. *Journal of Experimental Psychology: Learning, Memory, and Cognition, 20*, 443-460.

Cornuejols, A. (1993). Getting order independence in incremental learning. *Proceedings of the 1993 European Conference on Machine Learning.* Vienna: Springer-Verlag.

Elio, R., & Anderson, J.R. (1984). The effects of information order and learning mode on schema abstraction. *Memory & Cognition, 12,* 20-30.

Elio, R., & Lin, K. (1994). Simulation models of the influence of learning mode and training variance on category learning. *Cognitive Science, 18*, 185-219.

Elio, R., & Watanabe, L. (1991). An incremental deductive strategy for controlling constructive induction in learning from examples. *Machine Learning, 7*, 7-44.

Elman, J.L. (1991). Distributed representations, simple recurrent networks, and grammatical structure. *Machine Learning, 7*, 195-225.

Feigenbaum, E.A. (1963). The simulation of verbal learning behavior. In E.A. Feigenbaum & J. Feldman (Eds.), *Computers and thought.* New York: McGraw-Hill.

Fisher, D.H. (1987). Knowledge acquisition via incremental conceptual clustering. *Machine Learning, 2*, 139-172.

Flann, N.S., & Dietterich, T.G. (1989). A study of explanation-based methods for inductive learning. *Machine Learning, 4*, 187-226.

French, R.M. (1993). Using semi-distributed representations to overcome catastrophic forgetting in connectionist networks. *Proceedings of the AAAI Spring Symposium on Training Issues in Incremental Learning.* Stanford, CA: AAAI Press.

Gagne, R.M. (1966). *The conditions of learning.* New York: Holt, Reinhart, & Winston.

Gennari, J.H. (1991). Concept formation and attention. *Proceedings of the Thirteenth Conference of the Cognitive Science Society.* Chicago: Lawrence Erlbaum.

Gennari, J.H., Langley, P., & Fisher, D.H. (1989). Models of incremental concept formation. *Artificial Intelligence, 40,* 11-61.

Greiner, R. (1992). Probabilistic hill-climbing: Theory and applications. *Proceedings of the Ninth Canadian Conference on Artificial Intelligence.* Vancouver: Morgan Kaufmann.

Gross, K.P. (1991). *Concept acquisition through attribute evolution and experimental selection.* Doctoral dissertation, School of Computer Science, Carnegie Mellon University, Pittsburgh, PA.

Haussler, D. (1987). Bias, version spaces, and Valiant's learning framework. *Proceedings of the Fourth International Workshop on Machine Learning.* Irvine, CA: Morgan Kaufmann.

Iba, G.A. (1989). A heuristic approach to the discovery of macro-operators. *Machine Learning, 3*, 285-317.

Iba, W., Wogulis, J., & Langley, P. (1988). Trading off simplicity and coverage in incremental concept learning. *Proceedings of the Fifth International Conference on Machine Learning.* Ann Arbor, MI: Morgan Kaufmann.

Jones, R. (1989). *A model of retrieval in problem solving.* Doctoral dissertation, Department of Information & Computer Science, University of California, Irvine.

Kruschke, J.K. (1992). Alcove: An exemplar-based connectionist model of category learning. *Psychological Review, 99*, 22-44.

Langley, P., & Allen, J.A. (1991). Learning, memory, and search in planning. *Proceedings of the Thirteenth Conference of the Cognitive Science Society.* Chicago: Lawrence Erlbaum.

Langley, P., Gennari, J.H., & Iba, W. (1987). Hill-climbing theories of learning. *Proceedings of the Fourth International Workshop on Machine Learning.* Irvine, CA: Morgan Kaufmann.

Langley, P., Iba, W., & Thompson, K. (1992). An analysis of Bayesian classifiers. *Proceedings of the Tenth National Conference on Artificial Intelligence.* San Jose, CA: AAAI.

Langley, P., & Simon, H.A. (in press). Applications of machine learning and rule induction. *Communications of the ACM.*

Levinson, R. (1985). *A self-organizing retrieval system for graphs.* Doctoral dissertation, Department of Computer Sciences, University of Texas, Austin.

Littlestone, N. (1987). Learning quickly when irrelevant attributes abound: A new linear threshold algorithm. *Machine Learning, 2*, 285-318.

Luchins, A.S. (1942). Mechanization in problem solving: The effect of Einstellung. *Psychological Monographs, 54*, 248.

Martin, J.D., & Billman, D.O. (1994). Acquiring and combining overlapping concepts. *Machine Learning, 16*, 121-155.

McClosky, M., & Cohen, N.J. (1989). Catastrophic interference in connectionist networks: The sequential learning problem. In G.H. Bower (Ed.). *The psychology of learning and motivation, Vol. 24.* San Diego, CA: Academic Press.

McKusick, K.B., & Langley, P. (1991). Constraints on tree structure in concept formation. *Proceedings of the Twelfth International Joint Conference on Artificial Intelligence.* Sydney: Morgan Kaufmann.

Mitchell, T.M. (1982). Generalization as search. *Artificial Intelligence, 18*, 203-226.

Müller, G.E., & Pilzecker, A. (1900). Experimentalle Beiträge zur Lehre vom Gedächtnis. *Zeitschrift für Psychologie, 1.*

Neri, F., & Saitta, L. (1993). Exploiting example selection and ordering to speed up learning. *Proceedings of the AAAI Spring Symposium on Training Issues in Incremental Learning.* Stanford, CA: AAAI Press.

Porat, S., & Feldman, J. A. (1991). Learning automata from ordered examples. *Machine Learning, 7*, 109-138.

Quinlan, J.R. (1986). Induction of decision trees. *Machine Learning, 1*, 81-106.

Reigeluth, C.M., & Stein, F.S. (1983). The elaboration theory of instruction. In C.M. Reigeluth (Ed.), *Instructional design theories and models.* Hillsdale, NJ: Lawrence Erlbaum.

Ratcliff, R. (1990). Connectionist models of recognition memory: Constraints imposed by learning and forgetting functions. *Psychological Review, 2*, 285-308.

Rendell, L.A. (1986). A new basis for state-space learning systems and a successful implementation. *Artificial Intelligence, 20,* 369-392.

Rosenbloom, P., & Newell, A. (1987). Learning by chunking: A production system model of practice. In D. Klahr, P. Langley, & R. Neches (Eds.). *Production system models of learning and development.* Cambridge, MA: MIT Press.

Rumelhart, D.E., & Norman, D.A. (1978). Accretion, tuning, and restructuring: Three modes of learning. In J.W. Cotton & R. Klatzky (Eds.), *Semantic factors in cognition.* Hillsdale, NJ: Lawrence Erlbaum.

Sammut, C., & Banerji, R.B. (1986). Learning concepts by asking questions. In R.S. Michalski, J.G. Carbonell, & T.M. Mitchell (Eds.). *Machine learning: An artificial intelligence approach, Vol. 2. S*an Mateo, CA: Morgan Kaufmann.

Schlimmer, J.C., & Fisher, D. (1986). A case study of incremental concept induction. *Proceedings of the Fifth National Conference on Artificial Intelligence.* Philadelphia, PA: Morgan Kaufmann.

Scott, P.D., & Markovitch, S. (1991). Representation generation in an exploratory learning system. In D.H. Fisher, M.J. Pazzani, & P. Langley (Eds.). *Concept formation: Knowledge and experience in unsupervised learning.* San Mateo, CA: Morgan Kaufmann.

Shapiro, A.D. (1987). *Structured induction for expert systems.* Wokingham, UK: Addison-Wesley.

Singley, M.K., & Anderson, J.R. (1989). *The tansfer of cognitive skill. C*ambridge, MA: Harvard University Press.

VanLehn, K. (1987). Learning one subprocedure per lesson.*Artificial Intelligence, 31,* 1-40.

Winston, P.H. (1975). Learning structural descriptions from examples. In P.H. Winston (Ed.), *The psychology of computer vision.* New York: McGraw-Hill.

Situated Learning and Transfer

Hans Gruber, Lai-Chong Law, Heinz Mandl, and Alexander Renkl

Transfer occurs rather seldom. Empirical evidence for this claim has been provided by experimental cognitive research. A brief sketch of it is the starting point of our chapter. In the second part, we discuss the theoretical and epistemological positions of five prominent researchers from the situated cognition camp with respect to transfer. Part three deals rooted in structional models situated learning. The potentials and pitfalls of the employment of computer-based learning environments for situated learning for transfer is discussed in part four. Finally, some open question for further research are presented.

Recognition of the Problem: Lack of Transfer in Learning

The phenomenon of lacking transfer can reliably be found when subjects' problem solving behavior is analyzed. When solving a problem, most subjects cannot make use of the feasibility to refer to the experiences with former problems requiring similar solution procedures. For instance, Gick and Holyoak (1980, 1983) showed that the solution rate in working with the Duncker radiation problem amounts to about five to ten percent. The same rate can be observed when subjects try to solve the analogous fortress problem which can be solved by the same principle. A measure of transfer can be devised using the amount of additional correct solutions in working on the fortress problem after presentation of the radiation problem and its solution. Ample evidence is available to show that such transfer doesn't happen frequently. However, learning conditions can be varied by manipulating contexts and contents of problems to be worked on, so that transferability of knowledge can be dramatically increased (Catrambone & Holyoak, 1989).

To interpret such experimental research outcomes one can refer to theories of induction (Holland, Holyoak, Nisbett & Thagard, 1986; Holyoak, 1985; Holyoak, Koh & Nisbett, 1989), analogical thinking (Sternberg, 1977), or schema theory (Kintsch & van Dijk, 1978; Rumelhart, 1975). Several similar terms have been used to describe the transfer processes, such as analogical problem solving (Gick & Holyoak, 1980), analogical transfer (Gick, 1985; Gick & Holyoak, 1983; Holyoak, 1985), knowledge transfer (Gick & Holyoak, 1987), or problem-solving transfer (Bassok, 1990; Bassok & Holyoak, 1989, 1990; Catrambone & Holyoak, 1989). Even though the concepts are not completely compatible, they converge to the same ideas.

One central aspect of many transfer approaches is that pragmatic aspects are considered. In particular, the problem solver's goals and the situational context have to be considered. Therefore, a close conceptual connection can be found between experimental research on transfer and situated learning approaches (see also the chapters by Vosniadou, by De Corte, and by Säljö in this volume). Up to now, however, this connection has seldom been explicitly expressed. So to say, the spontaneous transfer from research on transfer to situated learning theory has occurred only rarely.

The low solution rates in experimental laboratories as well as in classroom instruction raise the problem of how to design learning environments so that knowledge application - in other words: transfer - becomes probable. One requirement is the analysis of problem solving processes and the identification of conditions that facilitate transfer. The problem solving processes involved in analogical reasoning are often modelled as a four-part sequence: (a) constructing mental representations of source problems and target problems; (b) selecting source problems as candidates for being transferred onto target problems; (c) performing mapping processes analyzing several components of source problems and target problems; (d) extending the mapping processes to generate solutions. The critical phases within this model are (a) how relevant source problems can efficiently be found and (b) how relevant features can be identified that serve to trigger mapping processes in order to develop a model of the target problems.

Experimental research has identified several components that facilitate successful transfer. Gick and Holyoak (1980) found that retrieving from memory aspects relevant for drawing analogies occurred more often when hints had been given. Of the two phases of spontaneous transfer, noticing an analogy and applying the analogy in the solution process, the former one seems to be the main problem. Elucidating possibilities to transfer from source problems to target problems therefore is a central task of instruction. The situated learning approaches claim to achieve exactly this function, in the way of increasing the probability of successful transfer.

Holyoak and Koh (1987) showed that transfer could be facilitated by creating generalized rules or schemas. However, the existence of schemas alone did not produce increased transfer, but the schemas' quality was of importance. Schema quality substantially correlated with the amount of spontaneous transfer; high quality schemata which were based on the deep structure of problems instead of surface similarities increased transfer. Gick and Holyoak (1983) stimulated their subjects to induce solution schemata by (a) presenting an abstract of the source problems, (b) presenting a verbal description of the basic principle, (c) presenting a diagrammatic picture of the basic principle. In none of these conditions transfer could be increased. Only when multiple source problems were presented and additionally a solution schema was provided, could transfer be increased. Concordantly, it was found that the rate of spontaneous transfer was also increased if multiple source problems were presented without presenting a solution schema. Presumably, subjects themselves inductively constructed problem schemata which afterwards were used to solve the target problems (Catrambone & Holyoak, 1989; Gick & Holyoak, 1983, 1987). Presenting problems from multiple perspectives as well as fostering subjects' activity in constructing coherence between examples, which have proved to be crucial determinants of transfer in experimental research, are also central concepts in situated learning approaches.

Other components have been identified which are important in determining the amount of transfer. These components mainly refer to the encoding and retrieval conditions, for instance, memory organization (Bassok & Holyoak, 1989; Ross, 1989), mode of presenting information (multimodality: Gick & Holyoak, 1983; visual support: Gick, 1985), pre-knowledge and expertise (Chi, Feltovich & Glaser, 1981; Chi, Glaser & Rees, 1982; Gick & Holyoak, 1983; Novick, 1988).

Many of the components identified in experimental studies have been implemented in computer simulations. It could be shown that the same mechanisms that were used in modelling human learning could be used to account for machine learning processes as well. Examples for the implementation of human analogical processing are the Structure-Mapping Engine (Falkenhainer, Forbus, & Gentner, 1989) and the Analogical Constraint Mapping Engine (Holyoak & Thagard, 1989). The latter is a formal theory of Holyoak's model of analogical reasoning described above. The central algorithm integrates structural, semantic, and pragmatic constraints so that even "human" characteristics like pragmatism have been successfully integrated in the simulation.

The research reported above belongs to the traditional cognitive paradigm. In this context, knowledge is regarded as an abstract entity that resides in the heads of individuals. The problem of transfer is a problem of application of these abstract entities in situations that are different from the learning context. The approaches reported give some explanations why relevant knowledge is not transferred, although it is present in the mind of the problem solver or learner. A completely different view on transfer is held by the situated cognition camp. Knowledge is not conceived as an abstract entity that is independent of situations. On the contrary, knowledge is principally bound to situations. The question then is how transfer can occur at all. In the next section we provide an overview about the positions of five prominent researchers from the situated cognition movement.

Situated Cognition And Learning: Review of Theoretical Frameworks

Transfer, being an elusive problem, has fallen in and out of the central focus several times in the history of psychological research (Singley & Anderson, 1989). Situated cognition, with its main focus on the interactions between people and the historically and culturally constituted contexts in which they are embedded, has emerged as a new school of thought in cognitive science in recent years. This section sets out to explore the main arguments of five representative views put forward respectively by Jean Lave (cognitive anthropology), Barbara Rogoff (cognitive anthropology), James Greeno (ecological psychology), Lauren Resnick (socio-cognitive approach) and William Clancey (neuropsychology). Each of these situationists conceives situated cognition and transfer differently according to his/her own philosophical orientation. Therefore, a spectrum of views of transfer can be identified. Indeed, the diversifications hinge crucially on the interpretations of specific theoretical constructs including representation, knowledge, learning and culture.

Lave's Theory of Cognition in Practice

Based on her commitments to anthropological perspectives, neo-Marxist social theories as well as Frankfurt School philosophy, Lave poses a strong oppositional stance against the presuppositions that ground mainstream cognitive science (Pea, 1990), particularly assailing perspectives on transfer (Lave, 1988). To take her extreme position, Lave objects the use of the term "transfer" because it suggests that knowing is a matter of mechanically re-applying inert concepts in different situations. Lave's arguments pertaining to transfer revolve around three central issues.

Issues Pertinent to Transfer

The first issue is continuity of cognitive activity across contexts which is assumed to be a function of knowledge stored in memory and general cognitive processes. Lave questions such an assumption and argues that person-acting, arenas, and settings appear to be implicated together in the very constitution of activity. More to the point, Lave (1988) comments that "... transfer is characterized as occurring across unrelated, or analogically related, or remotely related situations, but never across settings complexly interrelated in activity, personnel, time, space or their furnishings" (p. 40). By the same token, Lave strictly criticizes functional psychological theory which treats school as "the decontextualized (and hence privileged as well as powerful) site of learning that is intended for distant and future use" (p. 9). For the sake of supporting her postulations, Lave assembles a diversity of evidence for situationally specific arithmetic practice and concludes that there appear to be qualitatively different practices of arithmetic in different settings (e.g., supermarket, grocery shops, and small stores). In short, she commends an analytic approach as the explanation of continuity of cognitive activity across contexts which is a matter of social reproduction, and thus of dialectical relations between the constitutive order (including semiotic systems, political economy and social structure) and the experienced lived-in world.

The second issue is nature of knowledge. The learning transfer research rests on the assumption of cultural uniformity which is entailed in the concept of knowledge domains whose boundaries and internal structures are presumably independent of individuals. Lave refutes such a notion which suggests that knowledge has no interactive, generative or action-motivating prop-erties. Another problematic notion is "knowledge-as-a-tool" which implies the dissociation between cognition and sociocultural context.

The third issue is learning process and communities of practice. To substantiate her situated view of learning by investigating apprenticeship training forms which appear in various forms in different contexts (e.g., Vai tailors, Yucatec midwives, butchers), Lave (1991) concludes that learning is not to be identified with the acquisition of structures or in gaining a discrete body of abstract knowledge, but takes place through legitimate peripheral participation in ongoing social practice (Lave & Wenger, 1991); the process of changing knowledgeable skill is sub-sumed in processes of changing identity in and through membership in a community of practi-tioners; and mastery is an organizational, relational characteristic of community of practice. Taken together, Lave advocates a move away from the learning transfer genre to a social theory by which dialectic relations among persons, their activities, and contexts are implicated in suc-cess (and failure) of portability of learned skills across situations rather than merely cognitive strategies.

Implications for Schooling and Instruction

Lave (1988, 1990a,b, 1991) insistently emphasizes the power of everyday practice and that pro-cesses of learning should be embedded in the communities of practice in which the centripetal participation of apprentices are the pivotal concern. Unfortunately, she has not stated explicitly how transfer of appropriated skills across contexts can be facilitated and the mechanisms so involved have not been unambiguously specified. On the other hand, she ardently advocates cooperative learning because the sociological mechanisms so involved lead to equitable knowl-edge accessibility. She also remarks that analyses of learning in and out of school should be used as a basis for generating research design. More to the point, she stresses that an under-standing of social organization in school should be a central theme both in curricular design and in teacher training. Nonetheless, Lave and other's (e.g., Brown, Collins, & Duguid, 1991a,b) challenge the assumption that schools are privileged sites for learning is a radical one that many find disturbing and thus have dismissed it as unrealistic and therefore irrelevant to the present social conditions (e.g., Palinscar, 1989; Wineburg, 1991).

In sum, one of Lave's central achievements is recasting problem solving from "a cognitive psychological perspective that tends to treat problems as givens, to a dialectical one that sees problem-solving activity in everyday situations as arising from conflict-generating dilemmas that require resolution" (Pea, 1990, p. 29). Moreover, critical insight can be obtained from her method of close observational research *in situ*. Her work can impose a striking urge on cognitive psychologists as well as educationalists to reconsider the orthodox explanations of cognitive processes in general and traditional ways of teaching in particular.

Rogoff's Theory of Apprenticeship in Thinking and Transfer of Learning

The central tenet of Rogoff's theory is that children's cognitive development is inseparable from the social milieu in which children learn according to a cultural curriculum; from their earliest days, they augment skills and perspectives of their society with the aid of other people. In fact, apart from the influences of her anthropological background, many of her ideas are originated from Vygotskian notion of Zone of Proximal Development which has exerted consequential influences on developmental psychology (Rogoff & Wertsch, 1984). Moreover, her theory extends one step further by including nonverbal communication as well. Guided participation is the kernel concept of Rogoff's theory. Such conception implies that both guidance and participation in culturally valued activities are essential to children's apprenticeship in thinking. Guidance is either tacit or explicit, and participation may vary in the extent to which children or caregivers are responsible for its arrangement. Underlying the processes of guided participation is inter-subjectivity: a sharing of focus and purpose between children and their more skilled partners and their challenging and exploring peers (Rogoff, 1990).

Mechanisms of Transfer - Bridging from Known to New

Transfer of knowledge is conventionally interpreted as to hinge upon the similarities between novel and old situations that should be subjectively recognized by an agent. However, even more important than the active role of the individual in linking contexts is the part played by other individuals and cultural scripts for problem solution in guiding the individual's application of information and skills to a new situation (Rogoff, Gauvain, & Ellis, 1991). Children, who are supposed to play their active part, may seldom be independently responsible for discovering the connections between problems or transforming available knowledge to fit new problems (D'Andrade, 1981). The building of bridges between the known and the new is thus assumed to be predominantly supported through adult-child interactions. For instance, adults helping children to make connections may specify how the new situation resembles the old. Parallels between two situations (e.g., a laboratory task and a more familiar real-life context) are drawn or highlighted to foster the transfer of the related skills and relevant information (Rogoff, 1984). Formal instruction and informal social interaction provide the child with a model of an expert applying appropriate background information to a new problem, thereby giving the child experience in the skillful generalization of knowledge to new problems. Nevertheless, the research data regarding the enhancement of cognitive skills through guided participation are rather inconsistent (see e.g., Gardner & Rogoff, 1990; Gauvain & Rogoff, 1989). The enabling effects of guidance are age-dependent, and are related to the readiness of the expert partners to take up their leading role (cf. the problem of sequestration experienced by apprentices in Lave's (1988) studies) as well as to the motivational problem of both partners involved in the participation (Rogoff, 1991).

In fact, as mentioned in the foregoing discussion, the claim that analogical transfer can be enhanced by giving individuals explicit hints or evoking in them a process of comparing old and new information is evident by some empirical data (see e.g., Spencer & Weisberg, 1986). These facilitation strategies are analogous to bridging instructions adopted in apprenticeship learning. Hence, in view of guided participation, spontaneous transfer, which is regarded as one of the highest cognitive capacities, is less likely to occur. However, it has to be beared in mind that Rogoff's research focused on infancy and early childhood. The comparisons drawn with other empirical studies, for which mostly adult subjects are employed, may be appropriate.

Implications for Teaching

Rogoff regards guided participation, in which an active learner participating in culturally organized activity with a more skilled partner, as an important means to enhance transfer. Moreover, she emphatically claims that both formal instructions and informal social interactions are essential for bridging the old and novel contexts. Other crucial features of guided participation include the importance of routine activities, tacit as well as explicit communication, supportive structuring of novices' efforts, and transfer of responsibility for handling skills to novices. Furthermore, she remarks that the apprenticeship system should involve a group of peers who serve as resources for one another in exploring the new domain and helping and challenging each other.

In sum, Rogoff's notion of apprenticeship in thinking with its emphasis on the supportive role played by an expert partner offers an inspiring perspective for interpreting transfer. Her meticulous integration of ethnographic and psychological evidence with her own theoretical claims results in a thought-provoking synthesis that deserves painstaking exploration and further advancement (Valsiner, 1991). Her theory stimulates the researchers concerned to reconsider the problem of "marriage" between theoretical and empirical lines of knowledge construction. Moreover, the need to build a novel methodology of developmental psychology is called forth.

Situated Cognition as Perceiving Affordances: Greeno's Theory

With the term "situativity theory", Greeno aims to promote situated cognition to a higher position in the hierarchy of concepts for studying the mind. Accordingly, situativity is assumed to be a general characteristic rather than a special kind of cognition. It refers to a point of view that cognitive activities should be understood primarily as interactions between agents and physical systems and other people (Greeno, 1992; Greeno & Moore, 1993). Greeno postulates his situativity theory mainly based on an ecological psychology perspective and applies Gibson's (1979/ 1986) notion of affordance to explain the mechanisms underlying situated cognition. He adapts the term affordance to refer to properties of things in the environment that are relevant to their contributions to interactions that people have with them. The issue of perceiving affordances is crucial in the theoretical view of situativity and such depends significantly on Gibson's pivotal concept of direct perception, which implies that environmental stimuli are simply picked up instead of being conceived with the mediated symbolic representations (e.g., a chair is perceived as "sit-on-able" and a path is perceived as "walk-on-able"). To advance one step further, Greeno attempts to expand the explanatory function of his theory by incorporating some ideas which are rooted in Barwise's (1989) situation theory in logic such as registered state of affairs, situation types and the temporal continuity of situation. Nevertheless, his postulations reflect to some extent his roots in information processing theory.

A Change in Epistemological Assumptions

Under the rubric of situated cognition, a radical change in epistemological assumptions is observed (Greeno, 1989). Rather than viewing knowledge as some form of "substance" residing in the minds of individuals, it can be understood as some kind of relations between an individual and a physical and/or social situation. Based on this relational view, knowing is the ability to interact with things and other people in a situation, and learning is the improvement in that ability, i.e., getting better in participating in a situated activity. The question of transfer, then, is to understand how learning to participate in an activity in one situation can influence (positively or negatively) one's ability to participate in another activity in a different situation. The answer must lie in the nature of the situation which depends on the goals activity, which are important as they direct individuals' attention to the features in a situation (i.e., perceiving affordance).

Mechanisms of Transfer: Affordance-Activity Coupling and the Role of Action Schemas

Greeno and his colleagues attempt to re-interpret the empirical findings of some traditional experiments on transfer of different natures under the framework of affordance (Greeno, Moore & Smith, 1993, pp. 110-140). They conclude that besides perceiving affordances, the construction of schemata contributes substantially to the success of transfer. It is claimed that whether the activity can be transferred successfully when the structuring of the activity changes in certain aspect depends on which affordance the action schema has incorporated in the initial learning, and how the subject applies the schema in transfer. The schemata so involved are processes rather than data structures. However, such a differentiation is vaguely explicated. In the affordance-activity view, transfer occurs because of general properties and relations of the person's interaction with features of a situation. If the affordance changes, then transfer depends on there being a corresponding transformation in the activity. Furthermore, symbolic representations can play an important role in transfer, but they are considered as only the instrumental parts of activities rather than being fundamental or ubiquitous. In fact, Greeno appears ambivalent towards the role of symbolic representations in understanding cognition. This can be vindicated by his ascribing an encompassing definition to representations (Greeno et al., 1993, p. 108). More to the point, Greeno et al. (1993) suggest that a hypothesis which includes symbolic cognitive representations can be adopted when there is evidence for such a representation. However, the argument then focuses on the very nature of evidence which depends critically on the problematic definition of representation.

Implications for Schooling and Instructional Methods

Based on his situated view of learning, Greeno (1989) comments that much of the knowledge that students acquire in school instruction is not relational in many situations in which generative relations would be valuable. With his epistemological assumption that learning involves construction of knowledge rather than its passive acquisition, Greeno (1991) suggests that learning environments should include collaborative settings where teachers act as partners, coaches as well as models, and where students can work together as well as engage in exploration of ideas. Furthermore, to enable transfer, Greeno et al. (1993) propose that instructions should influence the activity so that it includes attention to affordances that are invariant across changes in the situation and that will support successful interactions in situations that have been transformed.

In sum, Greeno has proposed an insightful alternative for understanding the problem of transfer under the novel perspective of his situativity theory. However, owing to the problematic characteristics inherent in the concept of affordance as illustrated by contrasting definitions (see e.g., Agre's, 1993, pp. 66-67, comments on Vera and Simon's, 1993a, explanations regarding the nature of affordances), the conjectures thus derived appear controversial and the variables involved are difficult to operationalize. Besides, his stance toward the uses of symbolic representations is somehow ambivalent. Nonetheless, as Greeno says "The shift of the level of analysis from hypothesized cognitive events to hypothesized interactive events appears to be a simple move. But the ways in which those interactive events are organized are open to empirical research" (Greeno, 1992, p. 1).

Situated Cognition as Socially Shared Cognition: Resnick's Theory

Based on the Vygotskian sociocultural approach, an evolving perspective with its principal postulation that social interactions act as constituents of cognition has been advocated by Resnick and some other theorists. The fact that human cognition is so varied and so sensitive to cultural context requires that mechanisms by which people actively shape each other's knowledge and reasoning processes are investigated (Resnick, 1991). Only by understanding the circumstances and the participants' subjective construction of the situation can a valid interpretation of the cognitive activity be established. The question "Can a person who contemplates lonely in a confined room be conceived as involving in socially shared cognition?" is aptly raised. The answer hinges on the claim that cognitive tools embody a culture's intellectual history. Not only theories, implicit or explicit, but even ways of reasoning themselves are socially determined. In the same vein, it can be argued that all mental activities, from perceptual recognition to memory to problem solving, involve either representations of other people or the use of artifacts and cultural forms that have a social history (Levine, Resnick & Higgins, 1993).

Evaluating Formal Schooling

Resnick has performed some insightful analyses on the missing links between practical intelligence and school knowledge with some intriguing evidence in the fields of arithmetic and literacy (Resnick, 1987, 1990, 1992). Some broad claims about the privileged status of school where knowledge so acquired bears on life after school are severely challenged. Some worrisome discontinuities between learning in school and the nature of cognitive activity outside school have been identified (Resnick, 1987, p. 16). Briefly said, the fact that traditional schooling focusses on individual, isolated activity, on unaided thought, on symbols correctly manipulated but divorced from experience, and on decontextualized skills, may be partly responsible for our school's difficulty of teaching processes of thinking and knowledge constructions, and for repeated failure to demonstrate transfer across situations (Resnick, 1989). In short, both the structure of the knowledge used and the social conditions of its use may be fundamentally mismatched.

Innovative Cognitive Strategies for Transfer

To explicate the problem of transfer, self-monitoring of cognitive processes is one of the novel conjectures proposed. Indeed, the habit of imposing meaning - the tendency to elaborate and seek relationships - has been considered as one of the major factors for generalizing knowledge and skills across contexts (Resnick, 1989). Taken together, this newly formulated mental discipline theory situates learning ability in a combination of skills and disposition for elaborative and generative mental work. This emergent orientation leads to the view that cognition must interact with motivational, emotional, and social aspects of a person's life. Moreover, Resnick attempts to unite situated cognition with a genetic account in which later developing competencies in some sense depend on earlier ones. Learning is a matter of passing through successive situations in which one becomes a competent actor. Through the process of adapting concepts or ways of acting borrowed from one's past to a particular situation, a new contextualized form of competence can be created.

Implications for Schooling

In view of the shortcomings identified in the venture of schooling currently practiced, a general need to redirect the focus of schooling to encompass more of the features of successful out-of-school functioning is well acknowledged. Accordingly, Resnick (1987) outlines the following implications. The foremost concern is that the treatment of the subject matter should be tailored to engage students in processes of meaningful construction and interpretation (e.g., Palinscar & Brown, 1984) that can block the symbol-detached-from-referent thinking. Alternatively, a special form of "bridging apprenticeship" that uses simulated work environments and specially designed social interactions may be more appropriate to meet the real-life need and can bridge the gap between theoretical learning and actual practice. Furthermore, schools should make their endeavor to prepare students to be good adaptive learners, so that they can perform effectively when facing transitions and breakdowns.

In sum, Resnick has put her efforts in revealing the discontinuity and mismatch between the knowledge outside and within school, which is the core factor that accounts for failure to transfer across contexts. She directs our attention to the important role played by social interactions in shaping cognition. For the improvement of the existing educational system, she proposes that a broad cultural shift in the direction of the socially shared cognition should be involved and that learning should be enhanced through apprenticeship training.

Situated Cognition as Coordinating Without Deliberation: Clancey's Theory

To rebut against the framing assumption that all behavior can be represented as symbolic models (Vera & Simon, 1993a), Clancey (1993) put forward his provocative contentions for the situated cognition approach. The skeleton of his theories, which incorporate some neuropsychological concepts and are inspired by Dewey's (1896/1981) as well as Bartlett's (1932) works (Clancey, 1992a), is the notion of ongoing coordinations between perception and action.

Neuropsychological Mechanisms: Perception-Action Coordinations

Based on his proposed "First-person and Third-person Representation" hypothesis, Clancey (1993) points out that one can interpret knowledge and its symbolic representations as the results of a sense-making process in which an observer (third-person) describes patterns of behavior of an intelligent agent. Conversely, first-person's interpretation of a representation (e.g., reading a map or plan) is inventive, not a process of retrieving definitions or mechanically reciting meaning. Human interpretation and hence use of symbols, plans, productions, etc. are not ontologically bound; understanding and comprehending (intending, believing, etc.) are not just manipulating symbolic categories, but are ongoing relations between perceiving and acting (Clancey, 1992a, 1993). More to the point, perception and action arise together automatically and are coordinated without involving any intermediate encoding-symbol manipulation- decoding sequence, thus avoiding combinatorical search. That is, coordination and learning are possible without deliberation, which is a classification observers impose on behavior.

Clancey (1993, p. 94) interprets situated cognition based on neuropsychological mechanisms. The essence of his propositions is a dynamic and adaptive cognitive architecture which consists of modular subsystems (including social and neural processes) whose organizations emerge dialectically (i.e., they are mutually constraining and separately coherent) and the overall problem is how coordination of these subsystems is possible. To substantiate his theoretical suppositions, Clancey cites some relevant observations inferred from neuropsychological research (Roschelle & Clancey, 1992). Additionally, he adopts Edelman's (1992) neural net model to illustrate situated action view of sensorimotor coordination (see Clancey, 1993, p. 97). Nevertheless, some critical comments against the neurology so stated have been made (see e.g., Vera & Simon, 1993b, di Sessa, 1993).

Interpretations of Transfer of Learning

On the basis of his situational stance, Clancey (1993) re-interprets various cognitive constructs. Particularly, the notion of externalization of knowledge and symbolic representation is controversial (see e.g. Sandberg & Wielinga, 1992) and has substantial impact on the problem of transfer. Accordingly, knowledge is a capacity to adaptively re-coordinate perceiving and acting and cannot be inventoried. It can therefore be postulated that knowledge cannot be simply transferred because it does not exist in transferable form (Clancey, 1992b). On the other hand, knowledge representations are not structures in the minds of people, but external, perceivable structures open to debate, negotiation and reinterpretation. He remarks that representing can occur within the brain, but always involves sensorimotor aspects and is interactive.

Furthermore, a situated theory of knowledge (Brown, Collins & Duguid, 1991a) challenges the widely held belief that the abstraction of knowledge from situations (i.e., representation) is the key of transferability. In the same vein, Clancey remarks that "Transfer is possible not because the student has memorized abstractions, but because these have become ways of seeing and coordinating activity" (1992b, p. 161). While disputing the "transfer of expertise" metaphor (i.e., pouring knowledge into the head of the student) for describing learning, Clancey claims that knowledge acquisition should be viewed as a process of creating representations, inventing language, and, in general, formulating models for the first time (Clancey, 1992a).

Implications for Design of Intelligent Machines and Tutoring Systems

In virtue of his expertise in AI, Clancey expresses his special interests in the impact of situated cognition theory on designs of intelligent tutoring systems. Arguing along the lines of Winograd and Flores (1986) and Suchman (1987) who suggest that situated cognition has strong design implications (e.g., human-machine interactions, handling of breakdowns), Clancey remarks that this emerging field of inquiry leads to "a different view of the observer-theoretician's relation to a machine's design and behavior" (Clancey, 1991, p. 362). In knowledge engineering as well as robot design ("situated automata"), the interactions of the agent with the world are accordingly much emphasized (Agre & Chapman, 1987; Clancey, 1991; Maes, 1990). Furthermore, Clancey (1992b) explicitly advocates that cognitive apprenticeship can enhance learning. He adds that, in effect, this instructional mode ties to new ideas of software design and new ways of developing tools in the context of practice. In fact, Clancey and his colleagues (Clancey & Joerger, 1990) have implemented apprenticeship learning through a rule-based expert system which include features of modelling, scaffolding, fading and sequencing. It also involves applying principles in the context of real-world (authentic) problems. They remark that advance of hardware technology can make delivery of complicated AI-based system commonplace, thereby further research efforts should be invested in exploiting the benefits of apprenticeship model.

In sum, Clancey's postulations are not easy to understand. The core concepts of his theory, for example, the issue of perception-action coupling (i.e., how perception is related to performance), are intricately defined in terms of neuropsychology. Nevertheless, his sharp criticism of symbolic processing system reminds us of the extent of the gap between neurobiology and cognitive science models, and offers a new perspective from which to re-conceptualize one of the most important as well as problematic theoretical constructs in psychology: representation.

Communalities and Differences in Situated Cognition Perspectives

Situated cognition, albeit with its origin being traced to Heideggerian and Dewey's philosophy (and to more recent Piagetian and Vygotskian sociocultural perspectives), still remains a "loosely coupled" school of thought. Undeniably, the radical concepts put forward by some situated cognition proponents require a major shift in world view and invoke significant epistemological changes. Being a new approach, situated cognition seems to offer a promising key to unlock the shackles bound to such an age-old problem as transfer. Roughly speaking, transfer involves certain kind of interaction, be it at cognitive, social or neuropsychological level, which enhances the performance of activity in a novel situation by repeating what has been experienced. Nonetheless, the terms employed in this oversimplified definition need to be qualified and elaborated for each of the aforementioned situated cognition perspectives.

As the views are so diversified, it is extremely difficult for these researchers to reach a consensus on the nature and significance of transfer. In spite of the diversifications so addressed, all of these situationists formulate their theories with the basic assumptions that there is indivisibility between cognition and culture, with the unit of analysis that is commonly grounded on the amalgamation of person, activity and setting, and with the core supposition that knowledge is actively constructed rather than passively absorbed by an intelligent agent.

The models reviewed in this section try to develop a new epistemology of knowledge and learning. We find also some instructional models in which the term of situatedness plays a major role. They will be discussed in the next section.

Situated Cognition and Instruction: Technology-Based Approaches

The Instructional Model of Cognitive Apprenticeship

As already described, the authors from the situated cognition camp favor apprenticeship arrangement for learning. The apprenticeship metaphor is taken from craft domains such as tailors or midwives (cf. Lave, 1991). Collins, Brown, and Newman (1989) have proposed an instructional approach for more cognitive domains. This cognitive apprenticeship model stresses the importance of the explication or reification of cognitive processes (e.g., strategies, heuristics) during learning. Thus, cognitive processes can be approximately as exposed - and thus open to feedback and reflection - as the more manual skill trained in traditional apprenticeship models.

With the cognitive apprenticeship model, it is intended to introduce the learner to an expert culture by authentic activities and social interaction, just as in craft apprenticeship. Ideally, the following process takes place: The learner starts out from the very beginning with authentic tasks, as far as he or she can accomplish them with his or her present knowledge state, which should be corrected and enlarged in the further learning process. The teacher or expert supports the learner by modelling, coaching, and scaffolding. The expert's scaffolding helps the student to successfully cope with problems that are somewhat beyond the scope of the learner if he or she works alone (cf. the Vygotskian concept of the "zone of proximal development"). The social-communicative exchange between expert and learner as well as among different learners is ascribed a central role. In this way, the cognitive concepts and processes are articulated and thereby explicated. Thus, they can be an object of reflection which fosters the induction of more general and abstract concepts or schemas. In addition, the communicative exchange provide the opportunity for the learner to get to know the concepts, strategies, beliefs of the expert and also of other learners that are in some respect more advanced. From this point of view, learning is a process of enculturation into an expert community. With growing competencies the learner can work more and more independently. The support by the expert is gradually withdrawn (fading). The setting keeps, however, its cooperative character. The fading of the support formerly provided by the expert ends up with the fostering of self-guided exploration. This means that the learner attacks novel problems and works primarily on his or her own.

Collins (1991) describes how central components of the cognitive apprenticeship approach, that is modelling, coaching, articulation, and reflection, can be and are implemented in computer-based learning environments. However, this discussion mainly focus on how single components can be implemented. The core of apprenticeship is the sequence from modelling to exploration as described above. Besides the computer-based apprenticeship system of Clancey and Joerger (1990), Lesgold and his colleagues (Gabrys, Weiner & Lesgold, 1993; Lajoie &

Lesgold, 1990) developed the system SHERLOCK, which includes all apprenticeship components. It is designed for the training of aviation electronics. SHERLOCK presents the learners with the problem of diagnosing failures in navigation components of complex aircrafts. Lesgold and his colleagues obtained some impressive results. Trainees in the field tests achieved the skill level in 20 to 25 hours working on SHERLOCK that normally takes four years of the job training (Gabrys et al., 1993).

Anchored Instruction

The Cognition and Technology Group at Vanderbilt (1991, 1992) developed the anchored instruction model to attack the inert knowledge problem. A basic feature of this approach is to present complex and near-to-reality problems as an anchor for learning. The primary means by which these problems are presented is the employment of interesting adventure stories. Several stories have been developed, primarily for learning mathematics. The problems to be solved are embedded in these stories that are presented by a video disk. Thus, using educational technology is central to the anchored instruction approach. The Cognition and Technology Group at Vanderbilt formulated seven design principles of the anchored instruction approach:

1. Video-based presentation format. This renders it easy to make the presentation of information motivating. In addition, the problems to be posed can be more complex and interconnected than in a written medium. Thus, even students with poor reading skills have the chance to construct rich mental models of the problem situation.

2. Narrative format. Well-formed stories provide a meaningful context for mathematical problem solving in at least two respects. First, the learner can see the purpose of the concepts to be learned. Second, mathematics is connected with familiar real-life contexts and not just with school-type learning tasks.

3. Generative learning format. The ending of the stories that presents the problem to be solved to the students is left open. The resolution must be provided by the students themselves. If the students generate the ending, this should increase the intrinsic motivation and gives the opportunity for active participation in the learning process.

4. Embedding data design. School problems are usually well-defined task with all necessary information given. Thus, the students have no opportunity to learn problem definition skills which are essential for solving real-world problems that are typically ill-defined. The mathematical problems are not explicitly defined and the needed numerical information is incidentally presented in the story. The students learn to search and select information and to define problems.

5. Problem complexity. Students cannot learn how to solve complex real-life problems unless they have the opportunity to do so. Thus, the problems are intentionally designed as complex, but yet manageable.

6. Pairs of related adventures. Concept learned in one context usually are bound to that context and can hardly be transferred to other problem contexts (situatedness of knowledge). The employment of pairs of video stories that tap on similar contents allows students to learn what is specific to each context and what is generalizable. Furthermore, pairs of stories provide multiple perspectives on the concepts to be learned.

7. Links across the curriculum. The stories can not only be used to learn about mathematics, but also about geography or navigation. Employing the same anchor for learning different subject matters enable the students to detect links across the curriculum and avoid the knowledge compartmentalization (Mandl, Gruber, & Renkl, 1993).

In recent papers the Cognition and Technology Group at Vanderbilt (in press) also stresses the social aspect of learning, that is, cooperative learning and the building of learning communities, just as what the Cognitive Apprenticeship approach advocates. Preliminary empirical evaluations of the anchored instruction approach are encouraging, although traditional paper-pencil tests that are constructed to evaluate traditional instruction are employed. An open problem is, however, to find ways to design testing procedures that fit the learning goal of these new instructional models.

Spiro's Instructional Theory of Cognitive Flexibility

Situated learning approaches model learning as an active, constructive process. Taken this for granted, traditional concepts of the nature of knowledge are doubted, for instance modelling knowledge as collection of facts which are rather independent of the situations in which they occur. In contrast, situated learning theories propose that knowledge is always constructed in specific contexts (Mandl & Prenzel, 1992). To make knowledge applicable outside the learning situation, therefore, requires the acquisition of knowledge that can be applied in many different situations. One instructional means to reach this goal is to confront the learner with a variety of situations in which the respective knowledge occurs. To confront learners with problems from multiple perspectives can increase the probability that their knowledge can be applied in multiple contexts.

The cognitive flexibility theory stresses the importance of providing multiple perspectives in which the knowledge to be acquired is embedded (Spiro, Feltovich, Jacobson, & Coulson, 1991; Spiro, Vispoel, Schmitz, Samarapungavan, & Boerger, 1987). Cognitive flexibility theory mainly deals with advanced knowledge acquisition in ill-structured domains (e.g., diagnosis of heart diseases, literary interpretation). These domains can be described by two basic characteristics: complexity of concepts and cases, and irregularity of cases with large variability of relevant features across different cases. Instruction following the theory of cognitive flexibility aims to induce multiple and, as a consequence, flexible representations of the knowledge which can be applied for problem solving in a great many of contexts. An instructional means to induce flexible multiple representations is to elucidate the same concept at different times, in different contexts, with different problem solving goals, and from different perspectives. Only this allows the learner to create a rich collection of aspects on the same concept which helps him or her to apply the knowledge in many different situations. Furthermore, this kind of instruction renders it possible to identify multiple relations to other concepts as well as common misconceptions and oversimplifications. To sum up, transferability of knowledge increases through multiple perspectives on the problem rather than through abstract context-free learning.

Cognitive flexibility is then viewed as the ability to construct knowledge representations from different elements resulting in broad applicability of knowledge. In particular, cognitive flexibility is indispensable in ill-structured domains in which no distinguished schemas exist having enough complexity to deal with a variety of real life problems. Representations which consist of multiple relations and integrate multiple perspectives provide a basis for coherent representations of complex subject matters, so that they can be successfully applied.

For the purpose of learning through multiple perspectives, hypertext techniques are employed. By their multiple connections across knowledge components, they allow flexible access of information from different directions, at different times, with different goals, etc.

According to Spiro and his colleagues, learning in this kind of medium should be the same as that of "landscape criss-crossing".

Critics of the theory of cognitive flexibility mostly address - as with other theories considered in this section - the lack of empirical evidence. Only sparse evidence about the effectiveness of multi-perspective learning exists (Jacobson, 1992; Jacobson & Spiro, 1992). Some results indicate that aptitude treatment interactions are likely to occur (Jacobson & Spiro, in press). Presumably, the effects of multi-perspective learning positively correlate with increasing learner's preference for learning in complex situations. The lack of empirical research is plausible, in view of the fact that this kind of instructions makes heavy demands concerning the activity of teachers as well as learners. As will be discussed in the fourth section of this chapter, on additional problem arises: the assessment of specific effects of multi-perspective instruction (Feltovich, Coulson, Spiro, & Dawson-Saunders, 1992; Feltovich, Spiro, & Coulson, 1991).

The situated-learning-based instructional models discussed above heavily rely on educational technology. These tools are employed in order to present more complex and authentic learning materials than those offered by the traditional instructional methods. To what extent educational technology can actually foster the acquisition of transferable knowledge in situated learning environments will be discussed in the next section.

Potentials and Pitfalls of Educational Technology for Implementing Situated Learning

In this section discussion we present three arguments with regard to the status of computers in situated learning.

Computer programs for situated learning are not effective learning environments in themselves. All computer programs that are employed for situated learning have so many degrees of freedom that many things can be done with them, both effective and useless ones. In a hypertext system, as employed by Spiro and his co-workers, the learner easily gets "lost in hyperspace" if no instructional help or embedding is given. Similarly, employing interesting video material, as done by the Cognition and Technology Group at Vanderbilt, does not guarantee good instruction. The major point we want to make with these examples is that it is not sufficient to provide a computer-based learning environment that includes some features of the situated learning models such as near-to-reality learning tasks. Didactic embedding and instructional support is necessary for effective learning.

There is (almost) always a gap between computer-based learning environments and reality and, therefore, a lack of authenticity. To overcome the gap between the school world and the real world outside is a primary goal of situated learning approaches. The employment of computer-based learning environments alone cannot, however, be a solution for this problem. It is not realistic to believe that the gap between these two worlds can be fully closed (Böhm, 1993). As long as there are schools, they will constitute a special setting for learning and they do not and should not fully correspond to out-of-school settings such as workplaces. Probably the only case in which computer-based learning fits perfectly the claim of situated learning models for authenticity is, when students learn in order to acquire computer related skills such as programming, working with user applications, and so on. In any other case, there is necessarily a gap between working on a computer and real world activity. One prominent German author who criticizes the over-stated expectation of the employment of computers for learning is von Hentig (1984). Somewhat provocatively he claims that an over-emphasis on technology in education leads to a steady disappearance of reality. There are some striking aspects in his argument, because there is surely a certain distance between a math problem on a video disk, especially designed for didactic purposes, and real-world mathematics problems. This gap is inherent in any type of educational technology. Learning with computers should, therefore, be seen as a connecting link between school-type learning and real practice. This link is a necessary one, however, as ample evidence shows the fact that the knowledge learned in school-like settings can rarely be directly used for practical problem solving. Learning with computers is, thus, best regarded as a preparation for later on-the-job learning and real acting as, for example, manager or physician.

The problem of adequate evaluation of computer-based learning environments with respect to situated learning is still unresolved. Although there are many claims that the employment of situated learning environments allows the student to construct applicable knowledge that can be used in practical problem solving, convincing empirical evidence is rare. A major problem is that the traditional tests do not fit the goals of situated learning. Therefore, it is difficult to evaluate whether situated learning environments have the expected effects. So why not construct tests that fit the objectives of situated learning? But what are the objectives? One important objective is that the students should construct applicable knowledge. Sure, but what does this mean? Can it theoretically be conceptualized as production systems, where there are, at least as the ultimate goal, procedures that fire automatically according to the principles of strength and specificity? Probably not! Flexible problem solving and knowledge application in complex domains needs more than automatized routines, it needs reflective evaluation of different actions and action sequences. Is this kind of reflective knowledge some type of metacognition? If the answer was yes, we would have the well-known problems that go with the concept of metacognition: What is cognition, what is metacognition, and is there any meta-metacognition? We could continue to consider other possible theoretical conceptions of applicable knowledge. However, to date, we have not found a satisfying answer. Our research group is currently working with the concept of conditionalized knowledge. This is knowledge about operators which are indexed by application conditions, goals, and side effects. But how can this knowledge be assessed? Asking students about operators, the goal to be achieved by them, about their application conditions and their side effects may be too much a "declarative" way of assessment. What is assessed might be relatively uncorrelated to what the students actually do. On the other side, inferring some implicit conditionalized knowledge from actions performed by the students in a specific problem solving task bears many uncertainties.

In sum, we claim that the employment of computer programs for situated learning needs evaluation and that this evaluation cannot be performed until a satisfying theoretical conceptualization of applicable knowledge is found.

Nevertheless, we do not want to discredit the computer as learning tool. It surely provides useful support for learning. However, the goal of a scientific analysis of the potential of computer-based learning with respect to situated learning is to identify the boundary conditions for its effective employment rather than its propagation just on the basis that new technology opens some appealing possibilities concerning what one can do with the computer.

Questions for Further Research

The situated cognition approach and its view on transfer is rather new. Thus, there are many open questions that further research has to tackle. We discuss three important issues that merit attention in the near future: Are the models of situated cognition precise enough? Do the situated cognition concepts provide predictions that depart from the traditional cognitive paradigm and that withstand empirical falsification trials? Can the theoretical and the instructional concepts of situated cognition and learning be more closely integrated?

The Lack Of Precision

One of the major problems inherent in the situated cognition approaches is its seemingly inconsistency which makes is susceptible to confusing interpretations. However, considering the different backgrounds of individual theorists, such divergence in views is to be expected. Being a new discipline, situated cognition approach inevitably has some drawbacks. There is a lack of a precisely defined and testable set of concepts and mechanisms that might account for a situated cognition system's behavior. Notions such as person-acting (Lave) and affordance (Greeno) do not fit common sense thinking and depart from traditional scientific concepts in significant ways. This may be an advantage to the extent that they bear a fresh perspective on unresolved problems such as the question of transfer. The disadvantage of such new, ill-defined, and contraintuitive concepts is that they are fuzzy and imprecise. This deficit is also related to the next issue, the missing empirical findings with respect to situated cognition.

Lacking Empirical Evidence

A very pressing problem is the empirical verifiability of the situated cognition approaches. The hypothesized concepts and processes are far too loosely defined to be subjectable to confirmation or falsification through observation and experiment. Furthermore, as situated cognition theories stress the importance of contexts, experiments in the laboratory, which try to control for the context, do not seem to be the ideal way of investigation anymore. From the perspective of situated cognition, context should not be controlled or ruled out, but integrated into the theoretical framework and the respective empirical studies. Thus, new research designs have to be developed that fit the situated cognition models. In order to see whether it is reasonable to claim that situated cognition theories can best explain the problem of transfer, empirical studies are required to prove the fruitfulness of this new perspective. Further research efforts to conduct systematic empirical research and to refine theoretical framework are to be called forth.

Coherence between Theoretical and Instructional Concepts

Up to date, the theoretical-conceptual models and the instructional approaches that are subsumed under the label of situated cognition are only loosely related. Authors from the theoretical-conceptual camp draw some instructional conclusions out of their assumptions and, vice versa, educationally oriented researchers refer to theoretical concepts of situated cognition. However, it can neither be stated that the instructional models are straightforward deductions from some basic models on situated cognition nor that the theoretical concepts of situated cognition can serve as valid basis of the educational models. On the contrary, there seems to be a contradiction between the theoretical and the instructional use of the term situated cognition or situated learning. On the one hand, the term situated is used in a descriptive way in order to characterize the nature of cognition and learning (e.g., Clancey, Greeno, Lave). This means that cognition and learning are always and under any circumstance situated. The second meaning of situatedness is a prescriptive one and it is primarily used within instructional research. It refers to learning processes in which the learner is actively involved in authentic problem solving. These two meanings of situatedness contradict each other. From the radical situated cognition point of view, there are no situated and non-situated learning environments, because cognition and learning are always anchored in situated activity. On the other hand, the claim of educational researchers that there is something that can be called non-situated learning challenges the basic assumption that learning is always situated. Unfortunately, these contradictions are often unrecognized and the term situated is used in a mindless way.

To sum up, the situated cognition perspective provides a fresh and new look upon cognitive phenomena. However, at the present stage, the theoretical conceptualizations are rather vague. Future research will show whether the situated cognition model can provide a more appropriate account of cognitive phenomena such as transfer.

References

Agre, p. E. (1993). The symbolic worldview: Reply to Vera and Simon. *Cognitive Science, 17*, 61-69.

Agre, p. E., & Chapman, D. (1987). Pengi: An implementation of a theory of activity. Proceedings of the *Sixth National Conference on Artificial Intelligence.*

Bartlett, F.C. (1932). *Remembering - A study in experimental and social psychology.* Cambridge: Cambridge University Press.

Barwise, J. (1989). *The situation in logic.* Stanford, CA: Centre for the Study of Language and Information, Stanford University.

Bassok, M. (1990). Transfer of domain-specific problem-solving procedures. *Journal of Experimental Psychology: Learning, Memory, and Cognition, 16*, 522-533.

Bassok, M., & Holyoak, K.J. (1989). Interdomain transfer between isomorphic topics in algebra and physics. *Journal of Experimental Psychology: Learning, Memory, and Cognition, 15*, 153-166.

Bassok, M., & Holyoak, K.J. (1990). *Conceptual structure and transfer between quantitative domains.* Boston: Paper presented at the annual meeting of the AERA.

Böhm, W. (1993). Ü ber das "Praktische" am Praktischen Lernen. In W Böhm, W. Hardt-Peter, K. Rydl, G. Weigand, & M. Winkler (Hrsg.), *Schnee vom vergangenen Jahrhundert. Neue Aspekte der Reformpädagogik.* Würzburg: Ergon.

Brown, J.S., Collins, A., & Duguid, p. (1991a). Situated cognition and the culture of learning. In M. Yazdani & R.W. Lawler (Eds.), *Artificial Intelligence and Education (Vol. 2).* Norwood, NJ: Ablex.

Brown, J.S., Collins, A., Duguid, p. (1991b). Debating the situation: Rejoinder to Palinscar and Wineburg. In M. Yazdani & R.W. Lawler (Eds.), *Artificial Intelligence and Education (Vol. 2).* Norwood, NJ: Ablex.

Catrambone, R., & Holyoak, K.J. (1989). Overcoming contextual limitations on problem-solving transfer. *Journal of Experimental Psychology: Learning, Memory, and Cognition, 15*, 1147-1156.

Chi, M.T.H., Feltovich, p. J., & Glaser, R. (1981). Categorization and representation of physics problems by experts and novices. *Cognitive Science, 5*, 121-152.

Chi, M.T.H., Glaser, R., & Rees, E. (1982). Expertise in problem solving. In R.J. Sternberg (Ed.), *Adavances in the psychology of human intelligence (Vol. 1).* Hillsdale, NJ: Erlbaum.

Clancey, W.J. (1991). The frame of reference problem in the design of intelligent machines. In K. VanLehn (Ed.), *Architectures for intelligence: The twenty-second Carnegie Mellon Symposium on Cognition.* Hillsdale, NJ: Erlbaum.

Clancey, W.J. (1992a). *"Situated" means coordinating without deliberation.* Paper presented at the McDonnell Foundation Conference "The Science of Cognition", Santa Fe, New Mexico.

Clancey, W.J. (1992b). Representations of knowing: In defense of cognitive apprenticeship. *Journal of Artificial Intelligence, 3*, 139-168.

Clancey, W.J. (1993). Situated action: A neuropsychological interpretation response to Vera and Simon. *Cognitive Science, 17*, 87-116.

Clancey, W.J., & Joerger, K. (1990). A practical authoring shell for apprenticeship learning. In M. Gardner, J.G. Greeno, F. Reif, A.H. Schoenfeld, A. diSessa, & E. Stage (Eds.), *Toward a scientific practice of science education*. Hillsdale, NJ: Erlbaum.

Cognition and Technology Group at Vanderbilt (1991). Technology and the design of generative learning environments. *Educational Technology, 31(5)*, 34-40.

Cognition and Technology Group at Vanderbilt (1992). The Jasper series as an example of anchored instruction: Theory, program, description, and assessment data. *Educational Psychologist, 27*, 291-315.

Cognition and Technology Group at Vanderbilt (in press). From visual word problems to learning communities: Changing conceptions of cognitive research. In K. McGilly (Ed.), *Classroom lessons: Integrating cognitive theory and classroom practice*. Cambridge, MA: MIT Press/Bradford Books.

Collins, A. (1991). Cognitive apprenticeship and instructional technology. In L. Idol & B.F. Jones (Eds.), *Educational values and cognitive instruction: Implications for reform*. Hillsdale, NJ: Erlbaum.

Collins, A., Brown, J.S., & Newman, S.E. (1989). Cognitive apprenticeship: Teaching the craft of reading, writing and mathematics. In L.B. Resnick (Ed.), *Knowing, learning and instruction: Essays in honour of Robert Glaser*. Hillsdale, NJ: Erlbaum.

D'Andrade, R.G. (1981). The cultural part of cognition. *Cognitive Science, 5*, 179-195.

Dewey, J. (1896/1981). The reflex arc concept in psychology. *Psychological Review*, III: 357-370, July. Reprinted in J.J. McDermott (Ed.), *The philosophy of John Dewey*. Chicago: University of Chicago Press.

diSessa, A.A. (1993). Responses. *Cognition and Instruction, 10(2&3)*, 261-280.

Edelman, G.M. (1992). *Bright air, brilliant fire: On the matter of the mind*. New York: Basic Books.

Falkenhainer, B., Forbus, K.D., & Gentner, D. (1989). The structure-mapping engine: Algorithm and examples. *Artificial Intelligence, 41*, 1-63.

Feltovich, p. J., Coulson, R.L., Spiro, R.J., & Dawson-Saunders, B.K. (1992). Knowledge application and transfer for complex tasks in ill-structured domains: Implications for instruction and testing in biomedicine. In D. Evans & V. Patel (Eds.), *Advanced models of cognition for medical training and practice*. Berlin: Springer.

Feltovich, p. J., Spiro, R.J., & Coulson, R.L. (1991). Learning, teaching, and testing for complex conceptual understanding (Conceptual Knowledge Research Project, Tech. Rep. No. 6). Southern Illinois University, School of Medicin, Springfield, Il.

Gabrys, G., Weiner, A., & Lesgold, A. (1993). Learning by problem solving in a coached apprenticeship system. In M. Rabinowitz (Hrsg.), *Cognitive science foundations of instruction*. Hillsdale, NJ: Erlbaum.

Gardner, W., & Rogoff, B. (1990). Children's adjustment of deliberateness of planning according to task circumstances. *Developmental Psychology, 26*, 480-487.

Gauvain, M., & Rogoff, B. (1989). Collaborative problem solving and children's planning skills. *Developmental Psychology, 25*, 139-151.

Gibson, J.J. (1979/1986). The theory of affordances. In J.J. Gibson, *The ecological approach to visual perception*. Hillsdale, NJ: Erlbaum. (Original work published in 1979).

Gick, M.L. (1985). The effect of a diagram retrieval cue on spontaneous analogical transfer. *Canadian Journal of Psychology, 39*, 460-466.

Gick, M.L., & Holyoak, K.J. (1980). Analogical problem solving. *Cognitive Psychology, 12*, 306-355.

Gick, M.L., & Holyoak, K.J. (1983). Schema induction and analogical transfer. *Cognitive Psychology*, *15*, 1-38.

Gick, M.L., & Holyoak, K.J. (1987). The cognitive basis of knowledge transfer. In S.M. Cormier & J.D. Hagman (Eds.), *Transfer of learning*. San Diego: Academic Press.

Greeno, J.G. (1989). Situations, mental models and generative knowledge. In D. Klahr & K. Kotovsky (Eds.), *Complex information processing: The impact of H.A. Simon* (21st Carnegie-Mellon Symposium on Cognition). Hillsdale, NJ: Erlbaum.

Greeno, J.G. (1992). The situation in cognitive theory: Some methodological implications of situativity. Presented at the *American Psychological Society*, San Diego, CA.

Greeno, J.G. (1991). Mathematical cognition: Accomplishments and challenges in research. In R.R. Hoffman & D.S. Palermo (Eds.), *Cognition and the symbolic processes: Applied and ecological perspectives*. Hillsdale, NJ: Erlbaum.

Greeno, J.G., & Moore, J.L. (1993). Situativity and symbols: Response to Vera and Simon. *Cognitive Science*, *17*, 49-59.

Greeno, J.G., Smith, D.R., & Moore, J.L. (1993). Transfer of situated learning. In D.K. Detterman & R.J. Sternberg (Eds.), *Transfer on trial: Intelligence, cognition, and instruction*. Norwood, NJ: Ablex.

Holland, J.H., Holyoak, K.J., Nisbett, R.E., & Thagard, P. (1986). *Induction: Processes of inference, learning, and discovery*. Cambridge, MA: MIT Press.

Holyoak, K.J. (1985). The pragmatics of analogical transfer. In G.H. Bower (Ed.), *The psychology of learning and motivation (Vol. 19)*. New York: Academic Press.

Holyoak, K.J., & Koh, K. (1987). Surface and structural similarity in analogical transfer. *Memory & Cognition*, *15*, 332-340.

Holyoak, K.J., Koh, K., & Nisbett, R.E. (1989). A theory of conditioning: Inductive learning within rule-based default hierarchies. *Psychological Review*, *96*, 315-340.

Holyoak, K.J., & Thagard, p. R. (1989). Analogical mapping by constraint satisfaction. *Cognitive Science*, *13*, 295-355.

Jacobson, M.J. (1992). Hypertext learning environments, cognitive flexibility, and the transfer of complex knowledge: An empirical investigation. Paper presented at the *NATO Advanced Study Institute on Psychological and Educational Foundations of Technology-Based Learning Environments*. Kolymbari/Crete.

Jacobson, M.J., & Spiro, R.J. (1992). Hypertext learning environments and cognitive flexibility: Characteristics promoting the transfer of complex knowledge. In L. Birnbaum (Hrsg.), *The International Conference on the Learning Sciences*. Proceedings of the 1991 Conference. Charlottesville: Association for the Advancement of Computing in Education.

Jacobson, M.J., & Spiro, R.J. (in press). Hypertext learning environments, epistemic beliefs, and transfer of knowledge. In S. Vosniadou, E. DeCorte, & H. Mandl (Eds.), *The psychological and educational foundations of technology-based learning environments*. Berlin: Springer.

Kintsch, W., & van Dijk, T.A. (1978). Toward a model of text comprehension and production. *Psychological Review*, *85*, 363-394.

Lajoie, S., & Lesgold, A. (1990). Apprenticeship training in the workplace: Computer coached practice environment as a new form of apprenticeship. *Machine-Mediated Learning*, *3*, 7-28.

Lave, J. (1988). *Cognition in practice: Mind, mathematics and culture in everyday life*. Cambridge: Cambridge University Press.

Lave, J. (1990a). The culture of acquisition and the practice of understanding. In J.W. Stigler, R.A. Shweder, & G. Herdt (Eds.), *Cultural psychology: Essays on comparative human development*. Cambridge: Cambridge University Press.

Lave, J. (1990b). Views of classroom: Implications for math and science learning research. In M. Gardner, J.G. Greeno, F. Reif, A.H. Schoenfeld, A. diSessa, & E. Stage (Eds.), *Toward a scientific practice of science education*. Hillsdale, NJ: Erlbaum.

Lave, J. (1991). Situating learning in communities of practice. In L.B. Resnick, J.M. Levine, & S.D. Teasley (Eds.), *Perspectives on socially shared cognition*. Washington DC: American Psychological Association.

Lave, J., & Wenger, E. (1991). Situated learning: Legitimate peripheral participation. Cambridge: Cambridge University Press.

Levine, J.M., Resnick, L.B., & Higgins, E.T. (1993). Social foundations of cognition. *Annual Review of Psychology, 44*, 585-612.

Maes, P. (Ed.) (1990). *Designing autonomous agents*. Cambridge, MA: MIT Press.

Mandl, H., Gruber, H., & Renkl, A. (1993). Misconceptions and knowledge compartmentalization. In G. Strube & F. Wender (Hrsg.), *The cognitive psychology of knowledge: The German Wissenspsychologie project*. Amsterdam: Elsevier.

Mandl, H., & Prenzel, M. (1992). Designing powerful learning environments. In J. Lowyck, P. de Potter, & J. Elen (Hrsg.), *Instructional design: Implementation issues*. La Huelpe: Proceedings of the I.B.M./K.U. Leuven Conference.

Novick, L.R. (1988). Analogical transfer, problem similarity, and expertise. *Journal of Experimental Psychology: Learning, Memory, and Cognition, 14*, 510-520.

Palinscar, A.S. (1989). Less charted waters. *Educational Researcher, 18(4)*, 5-7.

Palinscar, A.S., & Brown, A.L. (1984). Reciprocal teaching of comprehension-fostering and comprehension-monitoring activities. *Cognition and Instruction, 1*, 117-175.

Pea, R.D. (1990). Inspecting everyday mathematics: Reexamining culture-cognition relations. *Educational Researcher, 19(4)*, 28-31.

Resnick, L.B. (1987). Learning in school and out. Educational Researcher, 16(9), 13-20.

Resnick, L.B. (1989). Introduction. In L.B. Resnick (Ed.), *Knowing, learning and instruction: Essays in honour of Robert Glaser*. Hillsdale, NJ: Erlbaum.

Resnick, L.B. (1990). Literacy in school and out. *Daedalus, Spring*, 169-185.

Resnick, L.B. (1991). Shared cognition: Thinking as social practice. In L.B. Resnick, J.M. Levine, & S.D. Teasley (Ed.), *Perspectives on socially shared cognition*. Washington, DC: American Psychological Association.

Resnick, L.B. (1992). From protoquantities to operators: Building mathematical competence on a foundation of everyday knowledge. In G. Leinhardt, R. Putnam, & R.A. Hattrup (Eds.), *Analysis of arithmetic for mathematics teaching*. Hillsdale, NJ: Erlbaum.

Rogoff, B. (1984). Introduction: Thinking and learning in social context. In B. Rogoff & J. Lave (Eds.), *Everyday cognition: Its development in social context*. Cambridge, MA: Harvard University Press.

Rogoff, B. (1990). *Apprenticeship in thinking: Cognitive development in social context*. New York: Oxford University Press.

Rogoff, B. (1991). The joint socialization of development by young children and adults. In p. Light, S. Sheldon, & M. Woodhead (Eds.), *Learning to think: Child development in social context 2*. London: Routledge.

Rogoff, B., Gauvain, M., & Ellis, S. (1991). Development viewed in its cultural context. In p. Light, S. Sheldon, & M. Woodhead (Eds.), *Learning to think: Child development in social context 2*. London: Routledge.

Rogoff, B., & Wertsch, J.V. (1984) (Eds.). Children's learning in the "Zone of Proximal Development". *New Directions for Child Development, no. 23*. San Franciso: Jossey- Bass.

Roschelle, J., & Clancey, W.J. (1992). Learning as social and neural. Paper presented at the *AERA Symposium: Implications of cognitive theories of how the nervous system functions for research and practice in education*, Chicago.

Ross, B.H. (1989). Distinguishing types of superficial similarities: Different effect on the access and use of earlier problems. *Journal of Experimental Psychology: Learning, Memory, and Cognition, 15*, 456-468.

Rumelhart, D.E. (1975). Notes on a schema for stories. In D.G. Bobrow & A. Collins (Eds.), *Representations and understanding: Studies in cognitive science*. New York: Academic Press.

Sandberg, J., & Wielinga, B. (1992). Situated cognition: A paradigm shift? *Journal of Artificial Intelligence in Education, 3*, 129-138.

Singley, M.K., & Anderson, J.R. (1989). *The transfer of cognitive skill*. Cambridge, MA: Harvard University Press.

Spencer, R.M., & Weisberg, R.W. (1986). Context-dependent effects on analogical transfer. *Memory and Cognition, 14*, 442-449.

Sternberg, R.J. (1977). *Intelligence, information processing and analogical reasoning: The componential analysis of human abilities*. Hillsdale, NJ: Erlbaum.

Spiro, R.J., Feltovich, p. J., Jacobson, M.J., & Coulson, R.L. (1991). Cognitive flexibility, constructivism, and hypertext: Random access instruction for advanced knowledge acquisition in ill-structured domains. *Educational Technology, 31(5)*, 24-33.

Spiro, R.J., Vispoel, W.p. , Schmitz, J.G., Samarapungavan, A., & Boerger, A.E. (1987). Knowledge acquisition for application. In B.K. Britton & S.M. Glynn (Hrsg.), *Executive control processes in reading*. Hillsdale, NJ: Erlbaum.

Suchman, L. (1987). *Plans and situated actions: The problem of human-machine communication*. Cambridge: Cambridge University Press.

Valsiner, J. (1991). Building theoretical bridges over a lagoon of everyday events: A Review of Apprenticeship in thinking: Cognitive development in social context by Barbara Rogoff. *Human Development, 34(5)*, 307-315.

Vera, A.H., & Simon, H.A. (1993a). Situated action: A symbolic interpretation. *Cognitive Science, 17*, 77-86.

Vera, A.H., & Simon, H.A. (1993b). Situated action: Reply to reviewers. *Cognitive Science, 17*, 77-86.

von Hentig, H. (1984). *Das allmähliche Verschwinden der Wirklichkeit. Ein Pädagoge ermuntert zum Nachdenken über die Neuen Medien* [The continuous disappearance of reality. A educationalist provokes about thinking about new media]. München: Hanser.

Wineburg, S.S. (1991). Remembrance of theories past. In M. Yazdani & R.W. Lawler (Eds.), *Artificial Intelligence and Education (Vol. 2)*. Norwood, NJ: Ablex.

Winograd, T., & Flores, F. (1986). *Understanding computers and cognition: A new foundation for design*. Norwood, NJ: Ablex.

The Evolution of Research on Collaborative Learning

Pierre Dillenbourg, Michael Baker, Agnes Blaye, and Claire O'Malley

For many years, theories of collaborative learning tended to focus on how individuals function in a group. More recently, the focus has shifted so that the group itself has become the unit of analysis. In terms of empirical research, the initial goal was to establish whether and under what circumstances collaborative learning was more effective than learning alone. Researchers controlled several independent variables (size of the group, composition of the group, nature of the task, communication media, and so on). However, these variables interacted with one another in a way that made it almost impossible to establish causal links between the conditions and the effects of collaboration. Hence, empirical studies have more recently started to focus less on establishing parameters for effective collaboration and more on trying to understand the role which such variables play in mediating interaction. In this chapter, we argue that this shift to a more process-oriented account requires new tools for analyzing and modelling interactions.

Introduction

For many years, theories of collaborative learning tended to focus on how individuals function in a group. This reflected a position which was dominant both in cognitive psychology and in artificial intelligence in the 1970s and early 1980s, where cognition was seen as a product of individual information processors, and where the context of social interaction was seen more as a background for individual activity than as a focus of research in itself. More recently, the group itself has become the unit of analysis and the focus has shifted to more emergent, socially constructed, properties of the interaction. In terms of empirical research, the initial goal was to establish whether and under what circumstances collaborative learning was more effective than learning alone. Researchers controlled several independent variables (size of the group, composition of the group, nature of the task, communication media, and so on). However, these variables interacted with one another in a way that made it almost impossible to establish causal links between the conditions and the effects of collaboration. Hence, empirical studies have more recently started to focus less on establishing parameters for effective collaboration and more on trying to understand the role which such variables play in mediating interaction.

This shift to a more process-oriented account requires new tools for analyzing and modelling interactions. This chapter presents some of the major developments over recent years in this field, in both theoretical and empirical terms, and then considers the implications of such changes for tools and methods with which to observe and analyses interactions between learners. In so doing, we have tried to address both the work done in psychology and in distributed artificial intelligence (DAI). However, we have to acknowledge that this chapter has a bias towards psychology - not only because it reflects the interests of the authors to a large extent, but also because DAI has focused more on cooperative problem solving than on collaborative learning.

At this point we need to make a brief comment on this distinction: learning versus problem solving and collaboration versus cooperation. While psychologists consider that learning and problem solving are similar processes, computer scientists still address them separately. Different research communities (DAI versus machine learning, for example) have developed different techniques, some for learning and some for problem solving. The ,collaboration' versus ,cooperation' debate is more complex. Some people use these terms interchangeably. (Indeed, there is some disagreement amongst the authors themselves.) For the purposes of this chapter, in acknowledgment of distinctions that others in the field have made, we stick to a restricted definition of the terms. 'Collaboration' is distinguished from 'cooperation' in that cooperative work "... is accomplished by the division of labor among participants, as an activity where each person is responsible for a portion of the problem solving...", whereas collaboration involves the "... mutual engagement of participants in a coordinated effort to solve the problem together." (Roschelle & Teasley, in press).

Defining collaboration by the non-distribution of labor does not avoid ambiguities. Miyake has shown that some spontaneous division of labor may occur in collaboration: "The person who has more to say about the current topic takes the task-doer's role, while the other becomes an observer, monitoring the situation. The observer can contribute by criticizing and giving topic-divergent motions, which are not the primary roles of the task-doer." (Miyake, 1986; p. 174). O'Malley (1987) reported similar results with pairs attempting to understand the UNIX C-shell command interpreter. This distribution of roles depends on the nature of the task and may change frequently. For example, in computer-supported tasks, the participant who controls the mouse tends to be "executor", while the other is likely to be the "reflector" (Blaye, Light, Joiner, & Sheldon, 1991). Cooperation and collaboration do not differ in terms of whether or not the task is distributed, but by virtue of the way in which it is divided: in cooperation, the task is split (hierarchically) into independent subtasks; in collaboration, cognitive processes may be (heterarchically) divided into intertwined layers. In cooperation, coordination in only required when assembling partial results, while collaboration is "... a coordinated, synchronous activity that is the result of a continued attempt to construct and maintain a shared conception of a problem" (Roschelle & Teasley, in press).

Theoretical Issues: The Individual or the Group as the Unit

What is the nature of the dyad in collaborative learning? It can be viewed as comprising two relatively independent cognitive systems which exchange messages. It can also be viewed as a single cognitive system with is own properties. These two different answers to the question serve to anchor the two ends of the theoretical axis. At one end, the unit of analysis is the individual. The goal for research is to understand how one cognitive system is transformed by messages received from another. At the other end of the axis, the unit of analysis is the group. The challenge is to understand how these cognitive systems merge to produce a shared understanding of the problem. Along this axis, between the 'individual' and the 'group', we can find three different theoretical positions: socio-constructivist, socio-cultural and shared (or distributed) cognition approaches.

In this chapter we talk about an "evolution" along this axis because the social end has recently received more attention - maybe because it has been previously neglected. We do not mean to imply than one viewpoint is better than another: scientists need both pictures from microscopes and pictures from satellites. Moreover, for the sake of exposition, the approaches will be presented as more different than they actually are. Both Piaget and Vygotsky acknowledge the intertwined social and individual aspects of development (Butterworth, 1982).

The Socio-Constructivist Approach

Although Piaget's theory focused mainly on individual aspects in cognitive development, it inspired a group of psychologists (the so-called *Genevan School*) who in the 1970s undertook a systematic empirical investigation of how social interaction affects individual cognitive development (cf. Doise & Mugny, 1984). These researchers borrowed from the Piagetian perspective its structural framework and the major concepts which were used to account for development:

conflict and the coordination of points of view (centrations). This new approach described itself as a socio-constructivist approach: it enhanced the role of inter-actions with others rather than actions themselves. The main thesis of this approach is that "...it is above all through interacting with others, coordinating his/her approaches to reality with those of others, that the individual masters new approaches" (Doise, 1990, p.46). Individual cognitive development is seen as the result of a spiral of causality: a given level of individual development allows participation in certain social interactions which produce new individual states which, in turn, make possible more sophisticated social interaction, and so on.

Despite this theoretical claim, which suggests a complex intertwining between the social and the individual plane, the experimental paradigm used by its proponents involved two supposedly "individual" phases (pre- and post-test), separated by an intervention session in which subjects worked either alone (control condition) or in pairs. Evidence showed that, under certain conditions, peer interaction produced superior performances on individual post-test than individual training (for reviews, see Doise & Mugny, 1984; Blaye, 1988). The studies which established this tradition of research involved children in the age- range 5-7 years, and relied essentially on Piagetian conservation tasks. Where working in pairs facilitated subsequent individual performance, the mediating process was characterized as "socio-cognitive conflict", i.e. conflict between different answers based on different centrations, embodied socially in the differing perspectives of the two subjects. The social dimension of the situation was seen as providing the impetus towards or catalyst for resolving the conflict. Such resolution could be achieved by transcending the different centrations to arrive at a more advanced "decentred" solution. From this perspective, the question was asked: under which conditions might socio-cognitive conflict be induced? One answer was to pair children who were, from a Piagetian perspective, at different stages of cognitive development. However, it was emphasized that subsequent individual progress cannot be explained by one child simply modelling the other, more advanced, child. It has been repeatedly demonstrated that "two wrongs can make a right" (Glachan & Light, 1981). What is at stake here, then, is not imitation but a co-ordination of answers. Subjects at the same level of cognitive development but who enter the situation with different perspectives (due to spatial organization, for instance) can also benefit from conflictual interactions (Mugny, Levy & Doise, 1978; Glachan & Light, 1981).

Researchers in DAI report similar empirical results. Durfee et al (1989) showed that the performance of a network of problem solving agents is better when there is some inconsistency among the knowledge of each agent. Gasser (1991) pointed out the role of multiple representations and the need for mechanisms for reasoning among multiple representations (see Van Someren & Reimann, this volume). These findings concern the heterogeneity of a multi-agent system. Bird (1993) discriminates various forms of heterogeneity: when agents have different knowledge, use various knowledge representation schemes or use different reasoning mechanisms (induction, deduction, analogy, etc.). For Bird, heterogeneity is one of the three dimensions that define the design space for multi-agent systems. The other dimensions, distribution and autonomy, will be discussed later.

The success of the concept of conflict in computer systems is not surprising. This logical concept can be modelled in terms of knowledge or beliefs and integrated in truth maintenance systems or dialogue models. However, the main proponents of socio-cultural theory now admit that their view has probably been too mechanistic (Perret-Clermont et al., 1991). Blaye's empirical studies (Blaye, 1988) have highlighted the limits of "socio-cognitive conflict" as "the" underlying causal mechanism of social facilitation of cognitive development. Disagreement in itself seems to be less important than the fact that it generates communication between peer members (Blaye, 1988; Gilly, 1989). The role of verbalization may be to make explicit mutual regulation processes and thereby contribute to the internalization of these regulation mechanisms by each partner (Blaye, 1988). This interpretation leads us to the socio-cultural theory discussed in the next section.

The Socio-Cultural Approach

The second major theoretical influence comes from Vygotsky (1962, 1978) and researchers from the socio-cultural perspective (Wertsch, 1979, 1985, 1991; Rogoff, 1990). While the socio-cognitive approach focused on individual development in the context of social interaction, the socio-cultural approach focuses on the causal relationship between social interaction and individual cognitive change. The basic unit of analysis is social activity, from which individual mental functioning develops. Whereas a Piagetian approach sees social interaction as providing a catalyst for individual change, often dependent upon individual development, from a Vygotskian perspective, inter-psychological processes are themselves internalized by the individuals involved. Vygotsky argued that development appears on two planes: first on the inter-psychological, then on the intra-psychological. This is his 'genetic law of cultural development'.

Internalization refers to the genetic link between the social and the inner planes. Social speech is used for interacting with others, inner speech is used to talk to ourselves, to reflect, to think. Inner speech serves the function of self-regulation. A simple computational model of internalization has been developed by Dillenbourg and Self (1992). The system includes two agents able to argue with each other. The agent's reasoning is implemented as an argumentation with itself (inner speech). Each learner stores the conversations conducted during collaborative problem solving and re-instantiates elements from the dialogue for its own reasoning. The learner may for instance discard an argument that has been previously refuted by its partner in a similar context. The psychological reality is of course more complex, what takes place at the inter-psychological level is not merely copied to the intra-psychological, but involves an active transformation by the individual.

The mechanism through which participation in joint problem solving may change the understanding of a problem is referred to as "appropriation" (Rogoff, 1991). Appropriation is the socially-oriented version of Piaget's biologically-originated concept of assimilation (Newman, Griffin and Cole, 1989). It is a mutual process: each partner gives meaning to the other's actions according to his or her own conceptual framework. Let us consider two persons, A and B, who solve a problem jointly. A performs the first action. B does the next one. B's action indicates to A how B interpreted A's first action. Fox (1987) reported that humans modify the meaning of their action retrospectively, according to the actions of others that follow it. From a computational viewpoint, this mechanism of appropriation requires a high level of opportunism from agent-B, which must integrate agent-A's contribution, even if this action was not part of his plans. Like the previous approach, this theory also attaches significance to the degree of difference among co-learners.

Vygotsky (1978) defined the "zone of proximal development" as "...the distance between the actual developmental level as determined by independent problem solving and the level of potential development as determined through problem solving under adult guidance or in collaboration with more capable peers." We will see that this concept is important to understand some empirical results. Research in DAI does not directly refer to Vygotskian positions. This is somewhat surprising since the issue of regulation, which is central to the socio-cultural theory, is also a major issue in DAI. In computational terms, regulation is more often referred to as an issue of ,control' or ,autonomy'. For Bird (1993), it constitutes the second dimension of the design space for multi-agent systems. As in political structures, there exist centralized systems where control is achieved by a super-agent or a central data structure (e.g. blackboard architectures) and decentralized systems in which each agent has more autonomy. An agent is more autonomous if it executes local functions without interference with external operations (execution autonomy), if it chooses when and with whom it communicates (communication autonomy) and whether it self-organizes into hierarchical, serial or parallel sub-processes (structural autonomy) (Bird, 1993).

The Shared Cognition Approach

The concept of shared cognition is deeply intertwined with the situated cognition' theory (Suchman, 1987; Lave, 1988 - see also Säljö, this volume; Gruber et al., this volume). For those researchers, the environment is an integral part of cognitive activity, and not merely a set of circumstances in which context-independent cognitive processes are performed. The environment includes a physical context and a social context. Under the influence of sociologists and anthropologists, the focus is placed largely on the social context, i.e. not only the temporary group of collaborators, but the social communities in which these collaborators participate. This approach offers a new perspective on the socio-cognitive and the socio-cultural approaches, and has recently led to certain revisions by former proponents of the earlier theories.

Perret-Clermont et al. (1991), for example, question the experimental settings they had previously used for developing the socio-constructivist approach. They noticed that their subjects tried to converge toward the experimenter's expectations. The subjects' answers were influenced by the meaning they had inferred from their social relationship with the experimenter. Wertsch (1991) makes similar criticisms against work in the socio-cultural tradition: social interactions are studied as if they occur outside a social structure. Through language, we acquire a culture which is specific to a community. For instance, we switch grammar and vocabulary rapidly between an academic seminar room and the changing rooms of a sports centre. But overall, beyond a vocabulary and a grammar, we acquire a structure of social meanings and relationships (Resnick, 1991) that are fundamental for future social interactions. This approach challenges the methodology used in many experiments where the subjects perform post-tests individually, often in a laboratory setting. More fundamentally, this approach questions the theoretical bases on which the previous ones rely: "... research paradigms built on supposedly clear distinctions between what is social and what is cognitive will have an inherent weakness, because the causality of social and cognitive processes is, at the very least, circular and is perhaps even more complex" (Perret-Clermont, Perret and Bell, 1991, p. 50).

Collaboration is viewed as the process of building and maintaining a shared conception of a problem (Roschelle & Teasley, in press). While the previous approaches were concerned with the inter-individual plane, the shared cognition approach focuses on the social plane, where emergent conceptions are analyses as a group product. For instance, it has been observed that providing explanations leads to improved knowledge (Webb 1991). From the ‚individualist‘ perspective, this can be explained through the self- explanation effect (Chi, Bassok, Lewis, Reimann & Glaser, 1989). From a ‚group‘ perspective, explanation is not something delivered by the explainer to the explainee. As we will see in section 5, it is instead constructed jointly by both partners trying to understand each other (Baker, 1991).

The idea that a group forms a single cognitive system may appear too metaphorical to a psychologist. It does not surprise a computer scientist. While the natural scale for a psychological agent is a human being, the scale of a computational agent is purely arbitrary. The (vague) concept of agent is used to represent sometimes a single neurone, a functional unit (e.g., the ‚edge detector‘ agent), an individual or even the world. The granularity of a distributed system, i.e., the size of each agent, is a designer's choice. It is a variable that the designer can tune to grasp phenomena that are invisible at another scale. It supports systems with different layers of agents with various scales, wherein one may compare communication among agents at level N and communication among agents at level N+1. Dillenbourg and Self (1992) built a system in which the same procedures are used for dialogue among agents and for each agent's individual reasoning. Hutchins (1991) reports a two-layer system wherein he can tune communication patterns among the units of an agent (modelled as a network) and the communications among agents. According to the respective strengths of intra-network and inter-network links, he observes an increase or a decrease of the group confirmation bias which cannot be reduced to individuals' contributions. Gasser (1991) insists on properties of multi-agent systems which "will not be derivable or representable solely on the basis of properties of their component agents" (p. 112).

Empirical Issues: Effects, Conditions and Interactions

Not surprisingly, the different theoretical orientations we have just outlined have tended to employ rather different research paradigms. Generally, socio-cognitive experiments concerned two subjects of approximately the same age (or the same developmental level) while the Vygotskian setting involved adult-child pairs. Moreover, the Piagetian and Vygotskian paradigms used different collaborative tasks. We come back to these differences later. Other paradigms have been used independently of a particular theoretical framework, for instance the ‚reciprocal teaching' paradigm (Palinscar & Brown, 1984; Palincsar, 1987; Riggio et al., 1991) in which one learner plays the teacher's role for some of the time and then shift roles with the other learner. We can also distinguish empirical work according to the size of the groups involved (dyads versus larger groups) or ways in which mediating technologies are employed, as in computer-supported collaboration. There are also differences between the various approaches in terms of the research methods employed. In the socio-cognitive perspective, the methodology was to set up conditions hypothesized to facilitate learning and to compare the outcomes of this intervention with some control group. With such methods, collaboration is treated as a black box; the focus is on outcomes. In contrast, research from a socio-cultural point of view tends to employ micro genetic analyses of the social interaction. The focus is on the processes involved in social interaction. This is partly because of the importance attached to the concept of mediation in socio-cultural theory. Evidence is sought from dialogue for symbols and concepts which mediate social activity and which can in turn be subsequently found to mediate individual activity. The shared cognition approach obviously also favors the second methodology. Despite their intertwining, we have attempted to disentangle the different research paradigms and theoretical approaches. In what follows we describe the "evolution" of empirical research within three paradigms that differ with respect to the number and the type of variables that are taken into account.

The "Effect" Paradigm

Experiments conducted to answer the question 'Is collaborative learning more efficient than learning alone?' were fairly straightforward. The independent variable was ‚collaborative work' versus ‚work alone'. The choice of the dependent measures varied according to what the investigators meant by ‚more efficient'. The most frequent measure was the subject's performance when solving alone the task they previously solved with somebody else. Some researchers decomposed this dependent variable into several other measures of performance, such as the improvement of monitoring and regulation skills (Brown & Palinscar, 1989; Blaye & Chambres, 1991) or a decrease in the confirmation bias. Within this paradigm, the precise analysis of effects is the only way to understand the mechanisms that make collaborative learning efficient. This kind of research let to a body of contradictory results, within which the positive outcomes largely dominate (Slavin, 1983; Webb, 1991). Nevertheless, negative results cannot always be discarded as the result of experimental errors or noise. Some negative effects are stable and well documented, for instance the fact that low achievers progressively become passive when collaborating with high achievers (Salomon and Globerson,1989; Mulryan, 1992). There is a simple way to understand the controversial effects observed with the first paradigm: collaboration is in itself neither efficient nor inefficient. Collaboration works under some conditions, and it is the aim of research to determine the conditions under which collaborative learning is efficient. This brings us to the second paradigm

The "Conditions" Paradigm

To determine the conditions under which collaborative learning is efficient, one has to vary these conditions systematically. While the first experimental approach (in very general terms) varies only in terms of the dependent measures, the second experimental approach varies along two dimensions, both dependent and independent variables. Numerous independent variables have been studied. They concern the composition of the group, the features of the task, the context of collaboration and the medium available for communication. The composition of the group covers several other independent variables such as the number of members, their gender and the differences between participants. It is not possible here to give a complete overview of the findings concerning each of these variables. We will illustrate the work with three examples.

Group Heterogeneity

Group heterogeneity is probably the most studied variable. Scholars have considered differences with respect to general intellectual development, social status or domain expertise. They have considered objective and subjective differences in expertise (whether the subjects are actually different or just believe themselves to be so). We restrict ourselves here to objective differences between the task knowledge of each subject, a parameter which is relevant for DAI. For the socio-constructivist, this difference provides the conditions for generating socio-cognitive conflict. For the socio-cultural approach, it provides conditions for internalization. However, the nature of differences differs within each theoretical approach. Socio-cognitive theory refers to symmetrical pairs (i.e., symmetrical with respect to general intellectual or developmental level) where members have different viewpoints, whilst socio-cultural theory is concerned with asymmetric pairs where members have different levels of skill. Piaget (1965) argued that interaction with adults leads to asymmetrical power relations or social status, and that in such interactions adults or more capable children are likely to dominate. The pressure to conform in the presence of someone with higher perceived status is not likely, in this view, to lead to genuine cognitive change. Nonetheless, Rogoff (1990) notes that many studies from a Piagetian perspective have involved pairing, for example, conservers with non-conservers. This is hardly pairing children of equal intellectual ability and is more consistent with the Vygotskian position. The point of difference between the two approaches then is not one of 'equal' versus 'unequal' pairs, but exactly what this equivalence entails.

Researchers have attempted to determine the optimal degree of differences. If it is too small, it may fail to trigger interactions. If the difference is too large, there may be not interaction at all. For instance, in a classification task, Kuhn (1972) shown children solutions reflecting a difference of -1, 0, +1 or +2 levels compared to their own solutions. He only observed significant improvement in the +1 condition. This notion of optimal difference also emerges in DAI where Gasser (1991) notes that agents need a common semantics even to decide that conflict exists! The ‚zone of proximal development‘ defines an optimal difference in an indirect way, i.e. not as a difference between subjects A and B, but as a difference between how A performs alone and how A performs with B‘s assistance.

Heterogeneity is also function of the size of the group. Empirical studies showed that pairs are more effective than larger groups, but heterogeneity is not the only factor that intervenes. Groups of three are less effective because they tend to be competitive, whilst pairs tend to be more cooperative (Trowbridge, 1987). However, differences between group sizes seem to disappear when children are given the opportunity to interact with other in the class (Colbourn & Light, 1987)

Individual Prerequisites

A second set of conditions defines some prerequisites for efficient collaboration. It seems that collaboration does not benefit an individual if he or she is below a certain developmental level. We consider here the absolute level of the individual, not his or her level relative to the other group members. According Piaget, for a conflictual interaction to give rise to progress, it must prompt individual cognitive restructuring. This implies that a resolution of conflict which would be exclusively based on social regulations (compliance from one partner for instance) would prevent interaction from being efficient. Piaget's theory predicts that pre-operational children lack the ability to de-center from their own perspective and therefore benefit from collaborative work. Indeed, as others have noted (Tudge & Rogoff, 1989), Piagetian theory in this respect leads to something of a paradox. It is not clear whether social interaction leads to the decentration necessary to benefit from collaboration, or that decentration has to happen before genuine collaboration can take place.

Other research suggests that developmental factors need to be taken into account in resolving this issue. Azmitia (1988) looked at pairs of 5 year old with equivalent general abilities and found that when novices (with respect to the domain) were paired with experts on a model building task they improved significantly, whilst equal ability pairs did not. Azmitia argues that pre-schoolers may lack the skill to sustain discussions of alternative hypotheses. Vygotskian theory does not place the same sort of explicit developmental constraints on the ability to benefit from collaboration, but recent researchers (e.g., Wood et al., in press; Tomasello et al., 1993) have argued that certain skills in understanding other people's mental states are required for this which may set developmental constraints on collaborative learning. With a simple task this may be achievable at around 4 years of age, since children at this age can understand that another may lack the knowledge necessary to perform an action (or misrepresent the situation) and they can predict the state of the other's knowledge. However, with more complex tasks, which demand reasoning using that knowledge to predict the partner's actions on the basis of their belief and intentions may not be achievable until about 6 years. In order to achieve shared understanding in a collaborative activity, the child must also be able to coordinate all these representations and have sufficient skills to communicate with respect to them.

Research on peer tutoring has identified some conditions which are also relevant to collaborative learning. The first condition is that the child-tutor must be skilled at the task. Radziszewska and Rogoff (reported in Rogoff, 1990) found that training a 9 year old peer to the same level of performance as an adult on a planning task led to peer dyads performing as well as adult-child dyads and better than peer dyads in which neither partner had been trained. A second pre-requisite is the ability of the child to reflect upon his or her own performance with respect to the task. Thirdly, in order to tutor contingently (i.e., to monitor the effects of previous help on subsequent actions by the learner), the child has to be able to assess whether the learner's action was wrong with respect to the instructions or wrong with respect to the task, and then be able to produce the next tutorial action on the basis of both a representation of the previous instruction and an evaluation of the learner's response to that instruction. Ellis and Rogoff (1982) found that 6 year old children were relatively unskilled at contingent instruction compared with adult tutors. Wood et al. (in press) found that 5 year old peer tutors were similarly unskilled relative to

7 year old tutors, and that 5 year olds tended to have difficulty inhibiting their own actions sufficiently to allow their tutee' to learn the task. However, children at this age were better 'collaborators' than 3 year old comparison dyads.

Task Features

Tasks that have been typically used in collaborative learning from a Vygotskian perspective include skill acquisition, joint planning, categorization and memory tasks. In contrast, the implication from socio-cognitive theory is that tasks should promote differences in perspectives or solutions. Typically, conservation and coordination tasks involve perspective-taking, planning and problem solving. There is thus little overlap in the nature of tasks investigated from the Piagetian and Vygotskian perspective. It is also clear that the nature of the task influences the results: one cannot observe conceptual change if the task is purely procedural and does not involve much understanding; reciprocally one cannot observe an improvement of regulation skills if the task requires no planning. Some tasks are less "shareable" than others. For instance, solving anagrams can hardly be done collaboratively because it involves perceptual processes which are not easy to verbalize (if they are open to introspection at all). In contrast, some tasks are inherently distributed, either geographically (e.g., two radar-agents, receiving different data about the same aeroplane), functionally (e.g., the pilot and the air traffic controller) or temporally (e.g., the take-off agent and the landing-agent) (Durfee et al., 1989).

Interactions Between Variables

Researchers rapidly discovered that the independent variables we have described so far do not have simple effects on learning outcomes but interact with each other in a complex way. Let us for instance examine the interaction between the composition of the pair and the task features. Studies that have compared the relative benefits of interacting with adults versus interacting with peers suggest that they vary according to the nature of the task, with peers being more useful than adults in tasks which require discussion of issues. Adult-child interaction may be more controlled by the adult rather than being a reciprocal relationship. Children are more likely to justify their assertions with peers than with adults. Rogoff (1990) notes that the differences between socio-cognitive and socio-cultural approaches with respect to composition of dyads are reconcilable. As she points out, whilst Vygotsky focused on acquiring understanding and skills, Piaget emphasized changes in perspectives or restructuring of concepts. Tutoring or guidance may be necessary for the former, whilst collaboration between peers of equivalent intellectual ability may be better in fostering the latter (Damon, 1984).

So, how dyads or groups should be composed with respect to skills and abilities may depend upon what learning outcomes one is interested in (e.g., skill acquisition vs. conceptual change) and what tasks are involved (e.g., acquiring new knowledge versus restructuring existing knowledge). Although few studies have involved a direct comparison of peer collaboration and peer tutoring with the same task, the type of task may interact with the developmental level of the learner and the nature of the dyad. For example, Rogoff (1990) argues that planning tasks may be difficult for very young children because they require reference to things which are not in th 'here-and- now'. However, adults may be able to carry out such metacognitive or metamnemonic roles that are beyond children, whilst demonstrating to the child how such processing could be accomplished. So, certain types of task may have inherent processing constraints which in turn place constraints on how the interaction should be supported.

The "Interactions" Paradigm

The complexity of the findings collected in the second paradigm led to the emergence of a third one. This introduces intermediate variables that describe the interactions that occur during collaboration. The question Under which conditions is collaborative learning efficient? is split into two (hopefully simpler) sub-questions: Which interactions occur under which conditions and what effects do these interactions have? The key is to find relevant intermediate variables, i.e., variables that describe the interactions and that can be empirically and theoretically related to the conditions of learning and to learning outcomes. This methodology however raises interpretation difficulties: if some types of interactions are positively correlated with task achievement, it may be that such interactions influence achievement or, conversely that high achievers are the only subjects able to engage these type of interaction (Webb, 1991). Nevertheless, underlying this approach is a fundamental shift: it may be time to stop looking for general effects of collaboration (e.g., in global developmental terms) and focus instead on more specific effects, paying attention to the more microgenetic features of the interaction. We will illustrate this viewpoint by two examples that are important both in psychology and in DAI: explanation and control.

Explanation

One way of describing interactions is to assess how elaborated the help provided by one learner to the other is. This level of elaboration can be considered as a continuum which goes from just giving the right answer to providing a detailed explanation. Webb (1991) performed a meta-analysis of the research conducted on this issue. This synthesis lead to two interesting results: elaborated explanations are not related to the explainee's performance, but they are positively correlated with the explainer's performance. Webb explains the first result by the fact that learning from receiving explanations is submitted to several conditions which may not be watched by the explainer, e.g., the fact the information must be delivered when the peer needs it, that the peer must understand it and must have the opportunity to us to solve the problem. The second result, the explainer's benefit, has been observed by other scholars (Bargh and Schul, 1980). Similar effects (called the self-explanation effect) have been observed when a learner is forced to explain an example to himself (Chi, Bassok, Lewis, Reimann & Glaser, 1989). A computational model of the self-explanation process have been proposed by VanLehn & Jones (1993). The main principle is that the instantiation of general knowledge with particular instances creates more specific knowledge, a mechanism that has also been studied in machine learning under the label ‚explanation-based learning‘ (Mitchell et al., 1986).

It would nevertheless be a mistake to consider self-explanation and explanation to somebody else as identical mechanisms. This would dramatically underestimate the role that the receiver plays in the elaboration of the explanation. As we will see in section 5, an explanation is not a message simply delivered by one peer to the other, but the result of joint attempts to understand each other. Webb (1991) found that non-elaborated help (e.g., providing the answer) is not correlated with the explainer's performance and is negatively correlated with the explainee's performance in the case where the explainee actually asked for a more elaborated explanation. Webb explains these results by the fact that providing the answer while the student is expecting an explanation does not help him or her to understand the strategy, and may lead the explainee to infer an incorrect strategy or to lose his or her motivation to understand the strategy.

These findings partially answer the second sub-question of this paradigm, the relationship between categories of interaction and learning outcomes. The first sub-question concerns the conditions in which each category of interaction is more likely to occur. Webb (1991) reviewed several independent variables concerning group composition, namely, the gender of group members, their degree of introversion or extraversion and their absolute or relative expertise.

With respect to the latter, explanations are more frequent when the group is moderately heterogeneous (high ability and medium ability students or medium ability and low ability students) and when the group is homogeneously composed of medium ability students. Some other group compositions are detrimental to the quality of explanations: homogeneous high ability students (because they assume they all know how to solve the problem), homogeneous low ability groups (because nobody can help) and heterogeneous groups comprising high, medium and low ability (because medium ability students seem to be almost excluded from interactions). Verba and Winnykamen (1992) studied the relationship between categories of interactions and two independent variables: the general level of ability and the specific level of expertise. In pairs where the high ability child was the domain expert and the low ability child the novice, the interaction was characterized by tutoring or guidance from the high ability child. In pairs where the high ability child was the novice and the low ability child the expert, the interaction involved more collaboration and joint construction.

Control

Rogoff (1990, 1991) conducted various experiments in which children solved a spatial planning task with adults or with more skilled peers. She measured the performance of children in a post-test performed without help. Overall she found better results with adult-child than with child-child pairs but, more interestingly, she identified an intermediate variable which explains these variations. Effective adults involved the child in an explicit decision making process, while skilled peers tended to dominate the decision making. This was confirmed by the children who collaborated with an adult; those who scored better in the post-test were those for which the adults made the problem solving strategy explicit. These results are slightly biased by the fact that the proposed task (planning) is typically a task in which metaknowledge plays the central role. A socio-cultural interpretation would be that the explication of the problem solving strategy provides the opportunity to observe and potentially internalize the partner's strategy. From a socially shared cognition viewpoint, one could say that making the strategy explicit is the only way to participate in each other's strategy and progressively establish a joint strategy.

Tools for Observing Interactions

When collaboration is mediated via a computer system, the design of this system impacts on the collaborative process. This mediation has methodological advantages: the experimenter may have explicit control over some aspects of collaboration (e.g., setting rules for turn taking, determining the division of labor or distribution of activities). The effects of the computer as medium also has pedagogical aspects: to support the type of interactions that are expected to promote learning. We describe three settings in which the computer influences collaboration.

Two Human Users Collaborate on a Computer-Based Task

Until relatively recently, one of the main advantages associated with computer use in schools was seen in terms of the potential for individualized learning. However, since schools generally have more students than computers, children often work in groups at the computer. Several empirical results suggest that group work - at least dyadic work - at the computer may enhance the benefit derived from the collaborative learning situation (for a review, see Blaye et al, 1990). The specific questions to be addressed here deal with the extent to which learner(s)-computer interaction and human-human interaction can reciprocally enhance one another. For instance, interfaces which induce a specific distribution of roles between learning partners help to foster social interaction (O'Malley, 1992; Blaye et al., 1991). Such interfaces can serve to scaffold the executive and regulative aspects of the collaborative task. Another interesting example concerns the principle of immediate feedback which was seen as a critical feature in the first generation of educational software. It seems that immediate feedback may prevent fruitful exchanges between human co-learners because they then rely on the system to test their hypotheses instead of developing arguments to convince one another (Fraisse, 1987). In other words, aspects of the software can modify the socio-cognitive dynamics between the learning partners. In particular, the computerised learning environment constitutes in itself a mediational resource which can contribute to create a shared referent between the social partners (Roschelle & Teasley, in press). This research does not aim to build a 'theory' of human-human collaboration at the computer. The fact that the medium (i.e., the computer) is similar is by no means a sufficient reason to unify this field of research. Different interfaces, different computer-based tasks and activities may yield very different interactions and learning outcomes. However, for the sake of simplicity, we refer generically to computer-based activities in order to discuss the other general parameters which exert an influence (e.g., frequency of feedback, representations induced by the interface, role distribution, etc.).

Computer-Mediated Collaboration

While the previous setting was influenced by research in educational technology, the setting considered here has developed in parallel with work on ,computer-supported cooperative work' (CSCW). This discipline covers communication systems from simple electronic mail to more advanced 'groupware' (Schrage, 1991). There are various ways in which computers can support communication. In the past, this technology has been restricted to textual communication, but developments in broad bandwidth technology allow for more exciting possibilities such as synchronous shared workspaces and two-way audio-visual communication. Generally speaking, broad bandwidth is expected to afford greater opportunities for collaboration. This does mean that older technologies should be superseded. For instance, asynchronous text-based communication provides time for reflection on messages and allows students lacking in confidence to learn nevertheless by 'eavesdropping' on conversations. In addition, low bandwidth communication may have some advantage in that, if it takes time and costs money in terms of connect time and if displays are restricted to a screen at a time, students may be forced to consider their responses more carefully.

Computer-mediated communication settings enables the experimenter to consider the communication bandwidth as factor. For instance, Smith et al. (1991) observed that task distribution was easier with a larger bandwidth (i.e., when seeing each other via video instead of audio-only communication) and when the setting gave users the feeling of being side-by-side, through having a shared workspace. They also observed that establishing face-to-face contact seems to be important during reflection stages, e.g., when partners discuss their observations, hypotheses or strategies. This fits in with research on mediated communication which, in general, suggests that face-to-face communication is more effective than audio-only communication for tasks which involve elements of negotiation.

Human-Computer Collaborative Learning

Human-computer collaboration refers to situations where the system and the human user share roughly the same set of actions. We don't include systems which support an asymmetric task distribution, as between a user and a word processor, for instance. We describe two types of system where some learning is supposed to result from collaborative activities: apprenticeship systems and learning environments. Most of these systems do not actually fully satisfy the symmetry criterion. An apprenticeship system is an expert system that refines its knowledge base by watching a human expert solving problems. The human expert is actually more teaching the system than collaborating with him or her, but the techniques developed are relevant to collaborative learning. The expert's behavior is recorded as an example and the system applies explanation-based learning (EBL) techniques to learn from this example.

In ODYSSEUS (Wilkins, 1988), the system attempts to explain each human action in order to improve the HERACLES-NEOMYCIN knowledge base. An explanation is a sequence of metarules that relate the observed action to the problem-solving goal. If ODYSSEUS fails to produce the explanation, it tries to "repair" its knowledge base by relaxing the constraints on the explanation process. LEAP (Mitchell et al., 1990) applies a similar approach to the design of VLSI circuits. The user can reject the proposed solution and refine the circuit him or herself. In this case, LEAP attempts to create rules that relate a given problem description to the circuit specified by the expert-user. LEAP explains why the circuit works for the given input signal and then generalizes the explanation to create the rule premises.

The interesting aspect is that these systems attempt to acquire the metaknowledge used by an expert, a central issue in the Vygotskian approach. However these systems rely on EBL techniques which requires a complete theory of the domain. Human learners theories are rarely complete and consistent. Some research has been carried out to by-pass this problem by integrating EBL with analogical and inductive learning (Tecuci and Kodratoff, 1990).

Not surprisingly, the idea of human-computer collaborative learning has also been applied to educational software. It has firstly been suggested as an alternative technique for student modelling (Self, 1986), then as an attempt to break the computer omniscience that dominates educational computing (Dillenbourg, 1992). An interesting issue here concerns the necessity to have a plausible co-learner. Along the continuum of design choices, we can discriminate levels of 'sensitivity'. At the first level, we could imagine an ELIZA-like system which randomly asks questions in order to involve the learner in plausible collaborative activities. Second level systems include a co-worker, i.e., an agent which solves problems during the interaction but which is not learning. For instance, the Integration Kid (Chan & Baskin, 1988) does not learn, but jumps (an the tutor's request) to the next pre-specified knowledge level. At the third level, we have a real co-learner, i.e., a learning algorithm whose outputs are determined by its activities with the world, including its interactions with the human learner (Dillenbourg & Self, 1992). This research has not yet produced enough empirical data to determine whether more sensitive systems are more efficient than less sensitive one.

Another interesting issue to be addressed here is that the phenomena observed in human-human collaboration are repeated in human-computer collaboration. Salomon (1990) raises an important point in terms of knowing whether human-computer interaction has potential for internalization similar to human-human conversations. He suggests (Salomon, 1988) that some graphic representations could have this potential. We observed (Dillenbourg, in press) that learners were not very 'tolerant' with the computer: firstly, they had difficulties in accepting that the computerised partner makes silly mistakes, then, when the computer was repeatedly wrong, they stopped making suggestions altogether. The advantage of human-computer collaborative systems for the study of collaboration is that the experimenter can tune several parameters regarding to the pair composition (for instance, the initial knowledge of the co-partner).

Tools for Analyzing Interactions

At the present state of research, it is not clear which theoretical perspective is most fruitful for analyzing interactions, although incidence of socio-cognitive conflict appears to be limited and restricted largely to Piagetian tasks (Blaye, 1988). A number of researchers (e.g., Webb, Ender & Lewis 1986; Blaye, Light, Joiner & Sheldon 1991; Behrend & Resnick 1989) have shown that various interactive measures other than "conflict" have a positive correlation with learning outcomes. It may be, as Mandl & Renkl (1992) suggest, that this uncertainty in the field is due to the fact that the Piagetian and Vygotskian perspectives as they stand are simply too global to allow proper explanation of the different results. These authors thus argue that "more local", domain/task-specific theories should be developed. As Barbieri & Light (1992) point out, "[s]tudies in collaborative learning at the computer usually do not go into a detailed analysis of interaction ..." (p. 200), despite the fact that it is "... important to analyze the quality of the interaction more closely." (p. 200).

Analysis Categories

Most researchers have generally used quite global categories of analysis grouped according to (at least) the following ‚oppositions' : (1) social / cognitive, (2) cognitive / metacognitive, and (3) task / communicative. We briefly discuss each in turn. With respect to the social/cognitive distinction, for example, Nastasi & Clements (1992) distinguish "social conflict" (i.e., not related to the problem, such as "name calling", "criticism", etc.) from "cognitive conflict" (which concerns the task conceptualization or solution). Only the latter was expected to (and did in fact) have a positive correlation with individual improvement. In terms of the cognitive/metacognitive distinction, Artzt and Armour-Thomas (1992) coded "episodes" such as reading, as cognitive, and understanding, planning and analyzing as metacognitive. Several types of episodes such as "exploring" and "verifying" solutions were categorized as cognitive and metacognitive. The working hypothesis was that "the most successful groups, in terms of both solving the problem and getting active involvement of all the group members, should be those with the highest percentages of metacognitive behaviors" (Artzt & Armour-Thomas, 1992, p. 165). The third discrimination is between task and communicative levels. The communicative level is reached when the students are trying to achieve a shared understanding by establishing common referents, by giving "commentaries" whilst performing actions, for example (Barbieri & Light, 1992). Task-level analysis categories include "negotiation" (Barbieri & Light, op. cit.), or more generally "task construction". As with the cognitive/metacognitive distinction, many analysis categories combine both communicative and (extra-communicative) task aspects, which is not surprising since the objective is to study their interrelation. For example, Webb, Ender and Lewis (1986) used analysis categories that combined simple speech act types (e.g., question, inform) with parts of the task decomposition (e.g., knowledge of commands, syntax, etc. in computer programming). In fact, whilst there may exist utterances in dialogue that are purely concerned with managing the interaction (such as managing turn-taking, requesting an utterance to be repeated, etc.), in task-oriented dialogues, most utterances concerning the task also have a communicative dimension.

To summarize, researchers distinguish management of communicational and social relations from performance of cognitive and metacognitive aspects of the extra-communicative task. Within these two broad categories, different forms of conflict are identified. There is, however, a more fundamental analytical problem to be solved: if individual cognitive progress is associated with cooperation or collaboration in the interaction, then we need to identify when students are in fact cooperating or collaborating, and when they are not really addressing each other (such as "problem-solving in parallel"). This brings us back to the issue raised in the introduction concerning the theoretical distinction between cooperation and collaboration. But, the question now is: how do we know when students are truly collaborating? Which kind of interactions can be identified as collaborative?

In order to address this question, Roschelle and colleagues introduced the notion of a "Joint Problem Space", consisting of jointly agreed goals, methods and solutions. At the level of social interaction, in order to determine what is in fact "shared" or "mutually accepted", it was necessary to determine when a "Yes" signalled ‚genuine' agreement and when it merely indicated "turn taking" ("I can hear you, go on", etc.). This latter problem has been extensively studied in linguistics within a general model for linguistic feedback (Allwood, Nivre & Ahlsn 1991; Bunt 1989). Thus, the meaning of "yes" in a given dialogue context depends on the preceding speech act (answering "yes" to a yes/no question is different from responding "yes" to a statement) and the polarity of the utterance (answering "yes" to "It is raining" may signal acceptance, whereas "yes" after "It isn't raining" can mean "oh yes it is !" or "yes, I agree that it isn't raining"). More generally, utterances like "yes", "no", "ok" and "mhm" give feedback at the level of perception ("I can hear you"), comprehension ("I can hear and understand you") and agreement/disagreement ("I hear you, understand, and agree"). (The first two of these are generally referred to as 'backchannel' responses which serve to facilitate turn-taking.) Deciding on the meaning of these expressions in a given dialogue context is thus quite complex, but necessary if we are to understand when students are really collaborating and co-constructing problem solutions. At present this line of research on the pragmatics of communication remains to be exploited in the field of collaborative learning.

Conversation Models

A promising possibility for collaborative learning research therefore is to exploit selective branches of linguistics research on models of conversation, discourse or dialogue to provide a more principled theoretical framework for analysis. Two types of interaction have been universally referred to in collaborative learning research: negotiation, often referred to within the Vygotskian "cooperation" approach as an indicator of joint involvement in task solutions, and argumentation, as a possible means for resolving socio-cognitive conflict. In the remainder of this section we review some research in language sciences and AI which may be relevant to analyzing these interactional phenomena in cooperative problem-solving dialogues.

Negotiation

In the context of joint problem-solving, we can view negotiation as a process by which students attempt (more or less overtly or consciously) to attain agreement on aspects of the task domain (how to represent the problem, what sub-problem to consider, what methods to use, common referents, etc.), and on certain aspects of the interaction itself (who will do and say what and when). In DAI, "communication protocols" based on negotiation between artificial agents have been developed for resolving resource allocation conflicts (Bond & Gasser, 1988; Rosenschien, 1992). Two main negotiation strategies may be used: (1) mutual adjustment, or refinement of the positions of each agent, and (2) competitive argumentation (Sycara 1988,1989), where one agent attempts to convince the other to adopt his proposition. This illustrates the fact that quite specific conditions are necessary in order for negotiation to be used as a strategy: the agents must be able and willing to relax their individual constraints, and the task must possess the required ‚latitude' (if the answer is as clear and determinate as "2+2=4", there is no space for negotiation) (Adler et al, 1988). Baker (forthcoming) describes the speech acts and strategies used in collaborative learning dialogues, where a third strategy (other than refinement and argumentation) is "stand pat" - one agent elicits a proposal from the other, using the second agent as a "resource". In other words, we can see at least three different types of negotiation behaviors, where each may be hypothesized to give different learning outcomes: (1) co-constructing problem solutions by mutual refinement, (2) exploring different opposed alternatives in argumentation, and (3) one student using the other as a resource.

There is, however, another type of negotiation that is common to any verbal interaction, and which takes place at the communicative, rather than the task, level: negotiation of meaning. The general idea is that the meaning of utterances in verbal interaction (or at least, the aspect of meaning that plays a determining role) is not something that is fixed by speakers and their utterances, but is rather something to be jointly constructed throughout the interaction by both speakers. This continuous process of adjustment of meaning will be a major determinant of what will be internalized at an individual level. Edmondson (1981) refers to this as "strategic indeterminacy", meaning that negotiation of meaning is not a ,defect' of interaction, but is rather constitutive of it to the extent that specific interactive mechanisms exist that allow mutual understanding to emerge. Thus Moeschler (1985) states that "Without negotiation the dialogue is transformed into monologue, the function of the interlocutor being reduced to that of a simple receptor of the message." (Moeschler, 1985, p. 176). For example, if one speaker (S1) makes the utterance "the mass is greater for the red ball", and another (S2) replies "No it isn't", S1 can reply with, "no, no, I wasn't saying it was, it was just wondering", thus negotiating the illocutionary value of the utterance to be a question, rather than an affirmation. We can observe this process of negotiation of meaning most clearly in so called "repair sequences" (misunderstanding becomes an explicit object of discourse), but it is important to note that from the point of view of most linguistics schools concerned with conversation, discourse or dialogue, "negotiation" is not a type of isolated sequence that may occur in a dialogue, it is a process operating throughout any dialogue (Roulet, 1992).

Attaining shared understanding of meanings of utterances is a necessary condition for collaborative activity (one cannot be said to be ,really' collaborating, or agreed, if one doesn't understand what one is collaborating or agreed about), and as such the collaborative activity determines the degree to which ,full' or ,complete' mutual understanding needs to be attained. From a cognitive perspective, Clark & Shaefer (1989) have expressed this fact in terms of the speakers' adherence to a criterion of "grounding": "The contributor and the partners mutually believe that the partners have understood what the contributor meant to a criterion sufficient for current purposes" (Clark & Schaefer, ibid., p. 262). Speakers do this by generating units of conversation called "contributions". "Contributions" have two phases: a presentation phase and an acceptance phase. They are recursive structures in that each acceptance is itself a new presentation, which the hearer is invited to consider. In acceptance phases, speakers provide evidence of continued understanding, to a greater or lesser degree. The recursion terminates when evidence has been provided of the weakest form sufficient for current purposes at a given level of embedding.

Types of evidence provided are conditional on the adjacency pair which constitutes a contribution. They include continued attention, initiation of the relevant next contribution, acknowledgment (feedback or backchannels such as nods, or utterances such as "uh-huh", "yeah", etc.), demonstration (hearer demonstrates all or part of what he has understood A to mean), and display (hearer displays verbatim all or part of speaker's presentation). Contributions may be generated in one of a number of contribution patterns, such as "contributions by turns", by "episodes" (corresponding to the "stand pat" negotiation strategy, described above), and by collaborative completion of utterances. The latter pattern is an indicator par excellence of collaboration in verbal interactions. Krauss and Fussell (1991) observed that, during social grounding, the expressions used to refer to objects tend to be progressively abbreviated (provided that the partner confirms his or her understanding in the abbreviation process). Interestingly, the same phenomena of abbreviation is observed during internalization (Kozulin, 1990; Wertsch, 1979, 1991), i.e., as the difference between social and inner speech. This difference is due to the fact that "inner speech is just the ultimate point in the continuum of communicative conditions judged by the degree of ,intimacy' between the addresser and addressee" (Kozulin, 1990, p. 178). These similarities between social grounding and internalization fit with the ,distributed cognition' view that questions the arbitrary boundary between the social and the individual. As thinking is described as a language with oneself (Piaget, 1928; Vygotsky, 1978), internalization may be the process of grounding symbols with oneself.

We can ask whether similar grounding mechanisms also occur in human-computer collaboration. Some experiments with MEMOLAB (Dillenbourg et al., 1993) revealed mechanisms of human-computer grounding: the learner perceives how the system understands him and reacts in order to correct eventual misdiagnosis. Even in DAI, authors start to emphasize the need for each agent to model each other (Bird, 1993) and exchange self-descriptions (Gasser, 1991).

Turning finally to argumentation, we noted above that it is one of the strategies which may be used in collaborative interactions. As such, the way in which conflict or disagreement may be resolved in an ensuing argumentation phase may be strongly influenced by the context of the higher level goal of achieving agreement. For example, students often take the "least line of resistance" in argumentation, shifting focus to some minor point on which they have agreed, and thus never "really" resolving the conflict (Baker 1991). This may be related to the following question posed by Mevarech and Light (1992, p. 276): "Is conflict itself sufficient as an "active ingredient", or is it the co-constructed resolution of such conflict which is effective?" It therefore seems clear that detailed analysis of argumentations in collaborative dialogues may help to give finer-grained indications for explaining some experimental results. At present, little research has been done on this (but see Trognon & Retornaz, 1990; Resnick et al, 1991), and a vast literature on argumentation in language sciences remains to be exploited (this is not the place to review such a literature, but see for example Toulmin, 1958; Barth & Krabbe, 1982; van Eemeren & Grootendorst, 1984; Voss et al., 1986; Miller, 1987).

Synthesis

Collaboration is not simply a treatment which has positive effects on participants. Collaboration is a social structure in which two or more people interact with each other and, in some circumstances, some types of interaction occur that have a positive effect. The conclusion of this chapter could therefore be that we should stop using the word ‚collaboration' in general and start referring only to precise categories of interactions. The work of Webb, reported above, showed that even categories such as ‚explanation' are too large to be related to learning outcomes. We have to study and understand the mechanisms of negotiation to a much greater depth than we have so far. We do not claim that conversational processes are exclusive candidates for explaining the effects observed. The ‚mere presence' of a partner can, in itself, be responsible for individual progress. Neither should we discard the role of non-verbal communication in collaboration. However, verbal interactions probably provide, at present, more tractable ways in which to tackle the development of computational models of collaborative learning.

In various areas of cognitive science psychologists and computer scientists have developed computational models together. This is not the case for collaborative learning. We hope that this chapter will help psychologists and researchers in machine learning to develop models of collaborative learning. Both in psychology and in computer science, individual learning and verbal interactions have been studied separately. The challenge is to build a model for how the two interrelate, for how dialogue is used as a means for carrying out joint problem- solving and how engaging in various interactions may change the beliefs of the agents involved.

References

Adler, M.R., Alvah, B.D., Weihmayer, R., & Worrest, W. (1988). Conflict-resolution strategies for nonhierarchical distributed agents. In *Distributed Artificial Intelligence : Volume II*. London: Pitman Publishing.

Allwood, J., Nivre, J., & Ahlsn, E. (1991). On the semantics and pragmatics of linguistic feedback. *Gothenburg Papers in Theoretical Linguistics, 64.*

Artzt, A.F., & Armour-Thomas, E. (1992). Development of a Cognitive- Metacognitive Framework for Protocol Analysis of Mathematical Problem Solving in Small Groups. *Cognition and Instruction, 9(2)*, 137-175.

Azmitia, M. (1988). Peer interaction and problem solving: When are two heads better than one? *Child Development, 59*, 87-96.

Baker, M.J. (1991). The Influence of Dialogue Processes on the Generation of Students' Collaborative Explanations for Simple Physical Phenomena. *Proceedings of the International Conference on the Learning Sciences* . Evanston Illinois, USA.

Baker, M.J. (to appear). A Model for Negotiation in Teaching-Learning Dialogues. To appear in *Journal of Artificial Intelligence in Education.*

Barbieri, M.S., & Light, P.H. (1992). Interaction, gender, and performance on a computer-based problem solving task. *Learning and Instruction, 2*, 199-213.

Bargh, J.A., & Schul, Y. (1980) On the cognitive benefits of teaching. *Journal of Educational Psychology, 72*, 593- 604.

Barth, E.M., & Krabbe, E.C.W. (1982). *From Axiom to Dialogue : A philosophical study of logics and argumentation*. Berlin: Walter de Gruyter.

Behrend, S., & Resnick, L.D. (1989). Peer collaboration in a causal reasoning computer task. *Golem 1 (12)*, 2-4.

Behrend, S., Singer, J., & Roschelle, J. (1988). A methodology for the analysis of collaborative learning in a physics microworld. *Proceedings of ITS-88*. Montreal, June 1-3.

Bird, S.D. (1993). Toward a taxonomy of multi-agents systems. *International Journal of Man-Machine Studies, 39*, 689-704.

Blaye, A. (1988). *Confrontation socio-cognitive et resolution de problemes*. Doctoral dissertation, Centre de Recherche en Psychologie Cognitive, Universite de Provence, 13261 Aix-en-Provence, France.

Blaye, A., & Light, P. (1990). Computer-based learning: The social dimensions. In H.C. Foot, M.J. Morgan, & R.H. Shute (Eds.), *Children helping children*. Chichester: J. Wiley & Sons.

Blaye, A., & Chambres, P. (1991). Hypercard as a psychological research tool-Experimental studies. In A. Oliveira (Ed.), *Hypermedia couseware: structures of communication and intelligent help*. Berlin: Springer-Verlag.

Blaye, A., Light, P.H., Joiner, R., & Sheldon, S. (1991). Joint planning and problem solving on a computer-based task. *British Journal of Developmental Psychology, 9*, 471-483.

Bond, A.H., & Gasser, L. (1988). *Readings in Distributed Artificial Intelligence*. San Mateo, Calif. : Morgan Kaufmann.

Brown, A.L., & Palincsar, A.S. (1989). Guided cooperative learning and individual knowledge acquisition. In L.B. Resnick (Ed), *Knowling, learning and instruction, essays in honor of Robert Glaser.* Hillsdale, NJ: Lawrence Erlbaum Publisher.

Bunt, H.C. (1989). Information dialogues as communicative action in relation to partner modelling and information processing. In N.M. Taylor, F. Nel, & D.G. Bouwhuis, *The Structure of Multimodal Dialogue*. North- Holland : Elsevier Sciences Publishers.

Butterworth, G. (1982). A brief account of the conflict between the individual & the social in models of cognitive growth. In G. Butterworth & P. Light (Eds.), *Social Cognition*. Brighton, Sussex: Harvester Press.

Chan, T.-W., & Baskin, A.B. (1988) . "Studying with the prince", The computer as a learning companion. Proceedings of the *International Conference on Intelligent Tutoring Systems.* Montreal, Canada.

Chi, M.T.H., Bassok, M., Lewis, M.W., Reimann, P., & Glaser, R. (1989). Self-explanations: how students study and use examples in learning to solve problems. *Cognitive Science, 13,* 145-182.

Clark, H.H., & Schaeffer, E.F. (1989). Contributing to Discourse. *Cognitive Science, 13,* 259-294.

Colbourn, C.J., & Light, P.H. (1987). Social interaction and learning using micro-PROLOG. *Journal of Computer-Assisted Learning, 3,* 130-140.

Damon, W. (1984). Peer education: The untapped potential. *Journal of Applied Developmental Psychology, 5,* 331-343.

Dillenbourg, P. (1992). *Human-Computer Collaborative Learning.* Doctoral dissertation. Department of Computing. University of Lancaster, Lancaster LA14YR, UK.

Dillenbourg P. (in press). Distributing cognition over brains and machines. In S. Vosniadou, E. De Corte, B. Glaser, & H. Mandl (Eds), *International Perspectives on the Psychological Foundations of Technology-Based Learning Environments.* Hamburg: Springer-Verlag.

Dillenbourg, P., & Self, J.A. (1992). A computational approach to socially distributed cognition. *European Journal of Psychology of Education, 3(4),* 353-372.

Dillenbourg, P., Hilario, M., Mendelsohn, P., Schneider, D., & Borcic, B. (1993). *The Memolab Project. Research Report.* TECFA Document. TECFA, University of Geneva.

Doise, W., & Mugny, W. (1984). *The Social Development of the Intellect.* Oxford: Pergamon Press.

Doise, W. (1990). The development of individual competencies through social interaction. In H.C. Foot, M.J. Morgan, & R.H. Shute (Eds.), *Children helping children.* Chichester: J. Wiley & Sons.

Durfee, E.H., Lesser, V.R., & Corkill, D.D. (1989). Cooperative Distributed Problem Solving. In A. Barr, P.R. Cohen, & E.A. Feigenbaum (Eds.), *The Handbook of Artificial Intelligence (Vol. IV).* Reading, Massachusetts: Addison-Wesley.

Edmondson, W. (1981). *Spoken Discourse : A model for analysis.* London: Longman.

Ellis, S., & Rogoff, B. (1982). The strategies and efficacy of child versus adult teachers. *Child Development, 43,* 730-735.

Fox, B. (1987). Interactional reconstruction in real-time language processing. *Cognitive Science, 11(3),* 365-387.

Fraisse, J. (1987). Etude du rle perturbateur du partenaire dans la dcouverte d'une stratgie cognitive chez des enfants de 11 ans en situation d'interaction sociale. *Bulletin de Psychologie, 382,* 943-952.

Gasser, L. (1991). Social conceptions of knowledge and action: DAI foundations and open systems semantics. *Artificial Intelligence, 47,* 107-138.

Gilly, M. (1989). A propos de la thorie du conflit socio-cognitif et des mcanismes psycho-sociaux des constructions: perpectives actuelles et modeles explicatifs. In N. Bednarz & C. Garnier (Eds.), *Constructions des savoirs: obstacles et conflits.* Montral: Agence d'ARC.

Glachan, M.D., & Light, P.H. (1981). Peer interaction and teaching: can two wrongs make a right? In G. Butterworth & P.H. Light (Eds.), *Social cognition: studies of the development of understanding.* Brighton: Harvester Press.

Howe, C., Tolmie, A., Anderson, A., & Mackenzie, M. (1992). Conceptual knowledge in physics: the role of group interaction in computer-supported teaching. *Learning and Instruction*, 2, 161-183.

Hutchins, E. (1991). The Social Organization of Distributed Cognition. In L. Resnick, J. Levine, & S. Teasley (Eds.), *Perspectives on Socially Shared Cognition*. Hyattsville, MD: American Psychological Association.

Kozulin, A. (1990). *Vygotsky's psychology. A biography of ideas*. Harvester, Hertfordshire.

Krauss, R.M., & Fussell, S.R. (1991). Constructing shared communicative environments. In L. Resnick, J. Levine, & S. Teasley (Eds.), *Perspectives on Socially Shared Cognition*. Hyattsville, MD: American Psychological Association.

Kuhn, D. (1972). Mechanisms of change in the development of cognitive structures. *Child development*, 43, 833-844.

Lave J. (1988). *Cognition in Practice*. Cambridge: Cambridge University Press.

Mandl, H., & Renkl, A. (1992). A plea for "more local" theories of cooperative learning. *Learning and Instruction*, 2, 281-285.

Mevarech, Z.R., & Light, P.H. (1992). Peer-based interaction at the computer: looking backward, looking forward. *Learning and Instruction*, 2, 275-280.

Miller, M. (1987). Argumentation and Cognition. In *Social and Functional Approaches to Language and Thought*. London: Academic Press.

Mitchell, T.M., Keller, R.M., & Kedar-Cabelli S.T. (1986). Explanation-Based Generalization: A Unifying View. *Machine Learning*, 1(1), 47-80.

Mitchell, T.M., Mabadevan, S.M., & Stienberg, L.I. (1990). LEAP: A learning apprentice for VLSI design. In Y. Kodratoff & R.S. Michalski (Eds), *Machine Learning* (Vol. III). Palo Alto, CA: Morgan Kaufmann.

Moeschler, J. (1985). *Argumentation et Conversation: Elments pour une analyse pragmatique du discours*. Paris: Crdif-Hatier.

Mugny, G., Levy, M., & Doise, W. (1978). Conflit socio-cognitif et dveloppement cognitif: l'effet de la prsentation par un adulte de modles "progressifs" etde modles "rgressifs" dans une preuve de reprsentation spatiale. *Revue Suisse de Psychologie*, 37, 22-43.

Mulryan, C.M. (1992). Student passivity during cooperative small group in mathematics. *Journal of Educational Research*, 85(5), 261-273.

Miyake, N. (1986). Constructive Interaction and the Iterative Process of Understanding. *Cognitive Science*, 10, 151-177.

Nastasi, B.K., & Clements, D.H. (1992). Social-cognitive behaviors and higher-order thinking in educational computer environments. *Learning and Instruction*, 2, 215-238.

Newman, D., Griffin P., & Cole M. (1989). *The construction zone: working for cognitive change in school*. Cambridge University Press: Cambridge.

O'Malley, C. (1987). Understanding Explanation. *Cognitive Science Research Report No. CSRP-88*, University of Sussex (GB).

O'Malley, C. (1992). Designing computer systems to support peer learning. *European Journal of Psychology of Education*, 7(4), 339-352.

Palincsar, A. (1987). Collaborating for collaborative learning of text comprehension. Paper presented at the *Annual Conference of the American Research Association*, April. Washington DC.

Palincsar, A.S., & Brown, A.L. (1984). Reciprocal Teaching of Comprehension-Fostering and Comprehension - Monitoring Activities. *Cognition and Instruction*, 1(2), 117-175.

Perret-Clermont, A.N., Perret F.-F., & Bell, N. (1991). The social construction of meaning and cognitive activity in elementary school children. In L. Resnick, J. Levine, & S. Teasley (Eds.), *Perspectives on Socially Shared Cognition*. Hyattsville, MD: American Psychological Association.

Piaget, J. (1928). *The language and thought of the child*. New York: Harcourt.

Piaget, J. (1965). *Les tudes sociologiques*. Genve: Droz.

Radziszewska, B., & Rogoff, B. (1988). Influence of adult and peer collaborators on children's planning skills. *Developmental Psychology, 24*, 840-848.

Resnick, L.B. (1991). Shared cognition: thinking as social practice. In L. Resnick, J. Levine, & S. Teasley (Eds.), *Perspectives on Socially Shared Cognition*. Hyattsville, MD: American Psychological Association.

Resnick, L.B., Salmon, M.H., & Zeitz, C.M. (1991). The Structure of Reasoning in Conversation. Proceedings of the *Thirteenth Annual Conference of the Cognitive Science Society*. Hillsdale, New Jersey : Lawrence Erlbaum Associates.

Riggio, R.E., Fantuzzo, J.W., Connelly, S.C., & Dimeff, L.A. (1991). Reciprocal peer tutoring: A classroom strategy for promoting academic and social integration in undergraduate students. *Journal of Social Behaviour and Personality, 6(2)*, 387-396.

Rogoff, B. (1990). *Apprenticeship in Thinking: Cognitive Development in Social Context*. Oxford: Oxford University Press.

Rogoff, B. (1991). Social interaction as apprenticeship in thinking: guided participation in spatial planning. In L. Resnick, J. Levine, & S. Teasley (Eds.), *Perspectives on Socially Shared Cognition*. Hyattsville, MD: American Psychological Association.

Roschelle, J. (1992). Learning by collaboration: Convergent conceptual change. *Journal of the Learning Sciences, 2*, 235-276.

Roschelle, J., & Teasley, S. (in press). The construction of shared knowledge in collabrative problem solving. In C.E. O'Malley (Ed.), *Computer-supported collaborative learning*. Heidelberg: Springer-Verlag.

Rosenschein, J.S. (1992). Consenting Agents: Negotiation Mechanisms for Multi-Agent Systems. Proceedings of the *Thirteenth International Joint Conference on Artificial Intelligence [IJCAI-93]*. San Mateo, CA: Morgan Kaufmann.

Roulet, E. (1992). On the Structure of Conversation as Negotiation. In H. Parret & J. Verschueren (Eds.), *(On) Searle on Conversation*. Amsterdam: John Benjamins.

Salomon, G., & Globerson, T. (1989). When teams do not function the way they ought to. *International journal of educational research, 13(1)*, 89-100.

Salomon, G. (1988). AI in reverse: computer tools that turn cognitive. *Journal of educational computing research, 4*, 12-140.

Salomon, G. (1990). Cognitive effects with and of computer technology. *Communication research, 17(1)*, 26-44.

Schrage, M. (1990). *Shared Minds. The new technologies of collaboration*. New York: Random House.

Self, J.A. (1986). The application of machine learning to student modelling. *Instructional Science, 14*, 327-338.

Slavin, R.E. (1983). *Cooperative learning*. New York: Longman.

Smith, R.B., O'shea, T., O'malley, C., Scanlon, E., & Taylor, J. (1989). *Preliminary experiments with a distributed, multi-media problem solving environment*. CITE Report 86. Institute of Educational Technology, Open University, Milton Keynes MK76AA, UK.

Suchman, L.A. (1987). *Plans and Situated Actions. The problem of human-machine communication.* Cambridge: Cambridge University Press.

Sycara, K. (1988). Resolving Goal Conflicts via Negotiation. Proceedings of the *AAAI-88 Conference*, St. Paul Minnesota (USA).

Sycara, K. (1989). Multiagent Compromise via Negotiation. In L. Gasser & M.N. Huhns (Eds.), *Distributed Artificial Intelligence: Volume II.* London: Pitman Publishing.

Tecuci, G., & Kodratoff, Y. (1990). Apprenticeship learning in imperfect domain theories. In Y. Kodratoff & R.S. Michalski (Eds.), *Machine Learning, Vol. III.* Palo Alto, CA: Morgan Kaufmann.

Tomasello, M., Kruger, A.C., & Ratner, H.H. (1993). Cultural learning. *Behavioral and Brain Sciences, 16,* 495-552.

Toulmin, S. (1958). *The Uses of Argument.* Cambridge: Cambridge University Press.

Trognon, A., & Retornaz, A. (1990). Opposition des points de vue et solution du problme des quatre cartes. *Verbum XIII (1-2)*, 39-55.

Trowbridge, D. (1987). An investigation of groups working at the computer. In K. Berge, K. Pezdec, & W. Banks (Eds.), *Applications of cognitive psychology: Problem solving, Education and Computing.* Hillsdale, NJ: Lawrence Erlbaum Associates.

Tudge, J., & Rogoff, B. (1989). Peer influences on cognitive development: Piagetian and Vygotskian perspectives. In M. Bornstein & J. Bruner (Eds.), *Interaction in Human Development.* Hillsdale, NJ: Lawrence Erlbaum Associates.

Van Eemeren, F.H., & Grootendorst, R. (1984). Speech Acts in Argumentative Discussions. Dordrecht-Holland: Foris Publications.

VanLehn K., & Jones R.M. (1993). Learning by explaining examples to onself: A computational model. In S. Chipman & A.L. Meyrowitz (Eds.), *Foundations of knowledge acquisition: cognitive model of complex learning.* Boston: Kluwer Academic Publishers.

Verba, M., & Winnykamen, F. (1992). Expert-novice interactions: Influence of power status. *European Journal of Psychology of Education, 6,* 61-71.

Voss, J.F., Blais, J., & Means, M.L. (1986). Informal reasoning and subject matter knowledge in the solving of economics problems by naive and novice individuals. *Cognition and Instruction, 3(4),* 269-302.

Vygotsky, L.S. (1962) .*Thought and Language.* Cambridge, MA: MIT Press.

Vygotsky, L.S. (1978). *Mind in Society: The Development of Higher Psychological Processes.* Cambridge, MA: Harvard University Press.

Webb, N.M. (1991). Task related verbal interaction and mathematics learning in small groups. *Journal for Research in Mathematics Education, 22(5),* 366-389.

Webb, N.M., Ender, P., & Lewis, S. (1986). Problem-Solving Strategies and Group Processes in Small Groups Learning Computer Programming. *American Educational Research Journal, 23(2),* 243-261.

Wertsch, J. V. (1979). The regulation of human action and the given-new organization of private speech. In G. Zivin (Ed.), *The development of self-regulation through private speech.* New York: John Wiley & Sons.

Wertsch, J.V. (1985). Adult-Child Interaction as a Source of Self-Regulation in Children. In S.R. Yussen (Ed.), *The growth of reflection in Children.* Madison, Wisconsin: Academic Press.

Wertsch, J.V. (1991). A socio-cultural approach to socially shared cognition. In L. Resnick, J. Levine, & S. Teasley (Eds.), *Perspectives on Socially Shared Cognition.* Hyattsville, MD: American Psychological Association.

Wilkins, D.C. (1988). *Apprenticeship learning techniques for Knowledge Based Systems*. Doctoral Dissertation. Report STAN-CS-88-142. Stanford University, CA.

Wood, D., Wood, H., Ainsworth, S., & O'Malley, C. (in press). On becoming a tutor: Towards an ontogenetic model. *Cognition & Instruction*.

A Developmental Case Study on Sequential Learning: The Day-Night Cycle

Katharina Morik and Stella Vosniadou

Investigations of sequencing effects in learning have a long tradition in psychology, education, and machine learning. The studies were, however, oriented towards a simple learning task, namely learning a target concept or concept hierarchy from examples. In this chapter, we first provide a brief overview of the research on sequencing effects from the perspective of machine learning (see also Langley, this volume). We conclude each section by stating the demand for investigating sequencing effects in complex learning tasks. We then motivate why we believe that this research should be interdisciplinary by presenting a case study. Although not yet completed, these case studies show more clearly what we aim at than a purely theoretical justification.

Previous Research on Sequencing Effects

Since the influential paper by Asch (1946) which showed that the impression of a person depends to quite a degree on the first traits recognized (primacy effect), in psychology it has been investigated how initial information affects the manner in which a learner incorporates subsequent knowledge into what he or she knows. In concept identification studies the importance of the order in which positive and negative examples are presented to the learner could be demonstrated (e.g., by Hovland and Weiss, 1953). More recently, variability and frequency of category members (positive examples) have been taken into account. Elio and Anderson found out that starting with a low-variance set of examples before presenting less representative category members led to a better learning performance than presenting consistently representative example sets (Elio and Anderson, 1984). The closeness of examples to the target concept was found crucial in an experimental investigation (Lee et al., 1988). The more relevant features are exhibited by examples early on, the faster learning approximates the target concept.

Work on sequencing effects referred to learning one, isolated concept from category members. This learning model does not take into account that learning is not performed solely on the basis of examples, but is also guided by instructions, that the learning goal is not an isolated concept but a complex concept structure, and that learning occurs even if there are no observable category members.

In machine learning, order effects have been recognized within the framework of hill-climbing algorithms (Winston, 1975). Effects of the order in which examples are presented to an incremental learning algorithm have been observed in conceptual clustering (Michalski and Stepp, 1983; Fisher 1987). If on the basis of first examples a good concept can be formed according to some evaluation criterion, then the target concept might be missed if the correct incorporation of subsequent examples requires to decrease the evaluation. This problem of a local maximum or foothill problem (being trapped in an imperfect solution because the perfect solution requires one to move away from the goal) is well-known in artificial intelligence. The modeling of scientific discovery has applied hill-climbing approaches to learning (Nordhausen and Langley, 1990). The conservative approach to keep with a hypothesis that perfectly covered the first observations made, although later on counter-examples are discovered, was considered to be analogical to scientific discovery processes (Langley et al., 1987).

Order effects have also been viewed as a chance to enhance learning by optimizing the order of examples (MacGregor, 1988). The learning task was to differentiate between two concepts where the concept and the examples are represented by binary feature vectors. Samples should start with minimal deviation from the target concept and increase the deviation over the sequence (fast-match heuristic). Alternatively, examples which are most similar to the two disjoint categories should be presented early in the sequence of presentation (close-call heuristic). By investigating heuristics that determine helpful sequences of examples, machine learning research meets educational research - in a simplified way, though. Again, the learning task was simply to learn classification rules from examples for one concept.

Within the probably approximately correct (PAC) learning paradigm of computational learning theory, the required number of examples has been investigated (sample complexity). First approaches to modeling teaching try to take into account more than only the cardinality and distribution of samples (Jackson and Tomkins, 1992). However, the PAC paradigm remains restricted to learning one isolated concept from examples.

The approaches to learning where sequencing effects have been studied are restricted in several ways:

- a concept is represented by attributes and their values - relations between attributes or concepts are not represented;

- only one concept or a hierarchy of subconcepts to one concept is learned - a complex concept structure that forms a theory has not been investigated with respect to effects of input order;

- the learner is informed about the target concept only by examples or observations - other input such as direct information or explanations of a teacher has not been taken into account.

There are, however, approaches in machine learning that go beyond this restricted setting:

- relational representations of concepts have been developed in the framework of inductive logic programming (ILP) (Muggleton, 1991);

- approaches to theory formation and revision - closely related to inductive logic programming since Shapiro's influential book (Shapiro, 1983) - model an evolving theory (Emde, 1987);

- where ILP takes as input background knowledge in addition to examples, explanation-based learning optimizes a given domain theory regarding an example of a good problem solution (Mitchell et al. 1986), and theory formation and revision enhances a set of rules by incorporating new facts (Rajamoney 1990; Wrobel, 1994).

The question of sequencing does not apply to some algorithms within these frameworks, as there is always a unique learning result for a set of examples (e.g., Kietz and Morik, 1994). To others the question does apply, but they have not yet been used for investigating effects of input order. The matter of sequencing effects is different for complex concept structures in a rich learning situation and single concept learning from examples or observations. In the classical learning problem, a feature is clearly distinguished from a concept. For instance, features may be color, size, and shape with the respective values:

{red, blue, yellow}, {big, small}, and {square, circle}.

Examples are described by a feature vector,

e.g., [red, big, square].

The concept is described in terms of features where some may be irrelevant, i.e. all values are allowed. For instance, [?, big, square] describes all big squares of any color. A hierarchy of feature values need be given in advance as a taxonomy. If this taxonomy is to be learned, this is done by preceding learning passes in which relations between features are represented as rules. These rules are then compiled into the taxonomy, which, in turn, is used for further learning. Alternatively, meta-rules, i.e. rules about rules, could be learned.

If we use a richer representation, the distinction between features and concepts disappears. A concept becomes another concept's feature. For instance, the class of object pairs where one object can be stacked on the other object can be defined by the following rules[1].

safe_to_stack (X,Y) :- lighter (X,Y).

lighter (X,Y) :- weight(X, V1), weight (Y, V2), less (V1, V2).

weight (X, Z) :- volume (X, V), density (X, D), product (V, D, Z).

The predicate *lighter* is a feature for *safe_to_stack* but is at the same time a concept that is defined in terms of the predicates *less* and *weight*, where the latter, in turn, is defined using *volume, density,* and *product.* Examples can be described at several levels, e.g.

safe_to_stack (block,endtable), weight(endtable, 5), volume(block, 1), density(block, 1).

safe_to_stack (book, box), lighter (book, box).

safe_to_stack (cup, endtable), lighter(cup, endtable), weight(cup, 1), less (1,5).

Learning the relational concept of *lighter* may be crucial for learning the concept *safe_to_stack.* We can imagine a sequence of learning tasks each with its particular example sets. A top-down approach would learn the rules from the top concept (*safe_to_stack*) to the bottom concept (*weight*). A bottom-up approach would first present examples for *weight*, then those for the relation *lighter*, and finally those for *safe_to_stack.*

This learning scenario allows to include direct information in the form of additional background knowledge. For instance, the rule for calculating weight could be input by a teacher. Or the definition of *safe-to_stack* could be directly given. It is of interest whether providing the basic rule or the top rule better supports the learning of the remaining target rules. Moreover, it is an open question whether first some examples should be shown before direct information is given - maybe depending on the learner's current hypothesis.

The examples can convey all information from all levels or a mixture of features (concepts) at several levels, or information only of one level. Moreover, the instance can be the same for learning tasks at different levels (as was the case in the examples above, where the endtable occurred twice), or not.

We may also think of a situation where the concept of weight is first learned in terms of volume:

weight (X, Z) :- volume (X,Z).

This rule is overly general but the order of examples may be such that they fit the rule in the beginning. A new example then contradicts the acquired rule. For instance:

volume(cube, 2), density (cube, 3).

applying the overly general rule would produce

weight (cube, 2), safe_to_stack (cube, endtable)

---

1. <conclusions: - <condition>, <condition>.

where, in fact, it is the case

weight (cube, 6), not(safe_to_stack (cube, endtable)).

Such a counter-example can refine the rule for *weight* in a revision step. It is of interest here that in the work of Wrobel (1994) it was advantageous to refine a rule set with respect to a set of counter-examples, instead of handling one contradiction at a time.

The small example should illustrate that for complex concept structures we have a sequence of learning tasks, a sequence of descriptors (basic features or concepts) in addition to the sequence of particular instances. Questions about sequencing effects in this framework are the following:

- Are there crucial concepts within a theory which have to be learned before the overall theory can be acquired? Or, at least, are there concepts that ease the learning of the overall theory?

- In which way should examples of and information about the complex concept structure (theory) be mixed in order to increase learning performance?

- Is there a rule of thumb that determines the appropriate order in which information should be presented?

- Should examples be presented such that first an overgeneralization is learned that is refined by further information or examples?

- Are there cases in which learning a wrong concept first is necessary for learning the correct theory? Or, alternatively, are there wrong concepts that prohibit to learn the correct theory in the way that hill-climbing approaches can be trapped at a local maximum?

It is an interesting question in its own right how to characterize the input to learning, as frequency or representativeness of examples are no longer the relevant characterizations of the input. Also the notion of a *crucial concept* needs to be made precise. Although one can build upon research in scientific discovery, theory formation and revision, and inductive logic programming, investigating the above problems remains a challenge.

Instead of continuing our analysis of former research on sequencing effects, we will now introduce an example of human learning for which sequencing questions are of importance and illustrate its analysis in terms of machine learning constructs.

The Development of Knowledge about the Day-Night Cycle: A Case Study

Psychological Observations

Developmental and cognitive psychologists usually think of „commonsense theories"[1] as „theories" which are based not on scientific information but on observation and information transmitted through language and the culture. For example, with respect to astronomy we often talk about „the sun setting", or „going behind the mountain", we say that „the night is coming", etc. This type of everyday talk is more consistent with the phenomenal observation that the sun goes down behind the mountain than with accepted scientific explanation of the day/night cycle. Similarly, in the case of concepts like force and heat, among others, the everyday usage is usually very different from the scientific meaning of these terms.

---

1. The term „theory" is used here to denote a relational framework which includes explanations of phenomena and not necessarily a well-formed scientific theory.

The interesting question from a sequencing point of view is not so much the commonsense theory itself but the process of *changing* the commonsense theory as one is exposed to scientific information. Here, a number of interesting questions involving possible sequencing effects arise, such as the following: Are some pieces of scientific information easier to be understood and incorporated in a commonsense theory than others? Are some pieces of information more likely to give rise to misconceptions than others? Is there an optimal sequence that one should follow in instruction for the purpose of changing a commonsense theory into a scientific one?

During the last years there has been a surge of research investigating how students acquire knowledge about the physical world, and, more particularly, how they come to understand some of the currently accepted scientific explanations of phenomena such as heating, moving, falling, etc. This research has produced agreement on at least one fundamental issue: Children are not „blank slates" when they are first exposed to the culturally accepted scientific views, but bring to this learning task initial knowledge about the physical world, which appears to be based on interpretations of everyday experience, and which exerts considerable influence on the way scientific information is understood.

The Vosniadou & Brewer (1994) developmental study on the day/night cycle is of particular interest because it provides a detailed description of the initial explanations of the phenomenon of the alternation of day and night that children have constructed, and of the way these explanations change during the elementary school years, as children are exposed to the currently accepted scientific information. The description of these explanations make it possible to formulate hypotheses regarding possible learning mechanisms and sequence effects in the learning process.

Vosniadou & Brewer (1994) investigated elementary school childrens' explanations of the day/night cycle by asking a series of questions regarding the disappearance and appearance of the sun and of the moon at night, the apparent movement of the sun and of the moon, the disappearance of the stars during the day, etc. They tried to understand the mental representations children constructed in the process of answering these questions and to determine whether these representations were used in a consistent fashion across a number of questions. Their results showed that the majority of the children used in a consistent fashion a small number of relatively well-defined mental models of the day/night cycle, which appear in Figure 1.

These mental models were grouped in three categories:

- *Initial Models* consistent with observations and cultural information coming from everyday experience;

- *Synthetic Models* that represent attempts to reconcile the scientific explanation of the day/night cycle with aspects of the initial model; and

- *Scientific Models* consistent with the currently accepted scientific view.

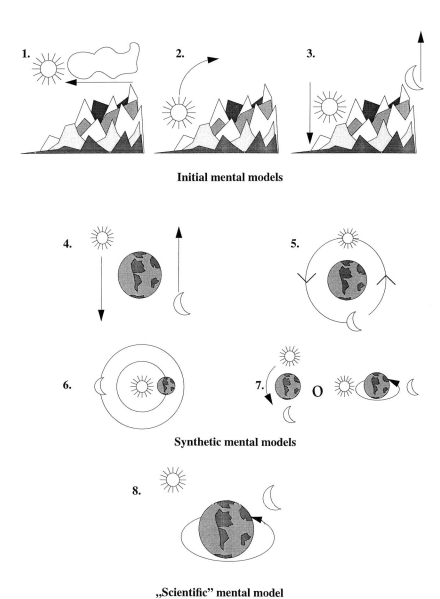

Initial mental models

Synthetic mental models

„Scientific" mental model

Figure 1: Overview of Models found in the Vosniadou & Brewer (1994) study

The results showed that the younger children formed Initial Mental Models of the day/night cycle, according to which night is caused because the sun goes down behind the mountains and the moon comes up, clouds or darkness cover the sun, or the sun moves far out in space (13 out of 20 first graders formed initial models of the day/night cycle, while only 2/20 third graders and 1/20 fifth grader). The older children constructed Synthetic Models of the day/night cycle (grade 1: 3/20; grade 3: 7/20; grade 5: 11/20). Synthetic Models differed from the scientific explanation along three dimensions: what moves (sun, moon or earth), how it moves (rotates or revolves), and whether the moon is causally implicated in the day/night cycle. A number of the younger children thought that the sun and the moon revolve around the earth. Some children mixed up the earth's rotational and revolutionary movements and thought that the earth revolves around the sun once every 24 hours. Many of the older children formed a model of an up/down rotating earth with the sun and moon fixed at opposite sides. According to this model, night happens as the earth rotates down, away from the sun and towards the moon which is located in some part of the sky where it is always night! Only one child constructed a mental model of the day/night cycle which seemed to be similar to the scientific one.

While the Vosniadou and Brewer developmental study is cross-sectional and not longitudinal, there are a number of interesting sequence effects that are suggested by the data. One such effect is the finding that all the children in our sample who were operating on the basis of a mental model of a flat and supported earth gave explanations of the day/night cycle based on Initial Models, that is explanations that did not depend on the rotational or revolutionary movement of the earth, or even explanations that required the sun or the moon to move „down to the other side of the earth". We interpreted this finding as indicating that the model of the earth poses constraints on how information regarding the explanation of the day/night cycle is interpreted. It is not possible to understand that the earth rotates around its axis if you have a model of a flat earth, supported by ground or resting on an ocean of water. Children must first understand that the earth is a sphere, then that this sphere rotates around its axis, and finally how the rotational movement of the earth accounts for the alternation of day and night.

Another interesting finding had to do with the interpretation of the direction of the earth's axis rotation by the children who had understood that the earth is a sphere. There were 23 children in our sample who had formed a mental model of a spherical earth and 13 of these children attributed the day/night cycle to the rotational movement of the earth. All of these 13 children, however, conceptualized the earth as rotating in an up/down direction (i.e., rotation around an axis through the equator).

One explanation for this preference may be found in the similarities that exist in the model of a rotating earth and a fixed sun and moon (model 7a, Figure 1) and the model of a stationary earth and an up/down moving sun and moon (model 4, Figure 1). These two models are identical with the exception that in one the day/night cycle is explained in terms of the up/down movement of the sun and the moon whereas in the other it is explained in terms of the up/down rotation of the earth. It may be the case that it is easy for children who have formed model number 4 to move to model number 7a when they are told that the reason for the disappearance of the sun is the movement of the earth around its axis.

Another possible explanation for such a preference may be found in childrens' belief that the sun is located above the top of the spherical earth, rather than in the plane of the earth's equator. Such a belief may be the remnant of an initial model of the day/night cycle, based on everyday experience, which children continue to hold even when they have understood that the shape of the earth is spherical. Given such a belief, the creation of a model of the day/night cycle with explanatory adequacy requires an up/down rotation of the earth, so that the person located on the top part of the earth, facing the sun, will be away from the sun when it is night.

Again, the above mentioned findings suggest that the mental model of the earth, the sun, and the moon that children have constructed imposes constraints on the way new information is interpreted with the result that some synthetic models or misconceptions are more likely to occur than others depending on the original state.

In general, Vosniadou & Brewer (1994) have explained the formation of synthetic models of the day/night cycle (and of the shape of the earth in an earlier study, see Vosniadou & Brewer, 1992), to result from the gradual lifting of certain constraints which operate on initial models of the earth under the influence of new information provided through instruction.

Layout of a Computational Model

Modeling complex explanations and the shift from one explanation to the next demands from a computer program to offer at least the following capabilities:

- representation of multiple concepts and relations;

- accepting examples and direct statements as input and inferring new facts from rules;

- knowledge revision of learned or told rules on the basis of contradictory new information;

- using background knowledge for learning.

The MOBAL system is one of the ILP systems that fulfills these demands (Morik et al., 1993). Therefore, we decided to use this system for modeling the empirical data of the developmental study by Vosniadou and Brewer (1994). The overall structure of the computational model consists of different types of knowledge and inferential relations between them:

- descriptions of observations (here: of day and night phenomena),

- assumptions about things that cannot be verified by observation alone (here: the shape of the earth, the movement of sun and earth),

- explanations of observations that use assumptions and predict new events to be observed (here: night in Australia when there is day in Europe, ability to move around the earth without reaching an end, ...),

- meaning postulates of spatial relations, states, events, and processes (here: the meaning of *in, between, above,* ...),

- descriptions of related observations (here: other cases of moving out of sight, e.g., *rotating, revolving, hiding, covering*).

The overall learning process is considered to be inductive as well as deductive. From cases of disappearance (e.g., the sister is behind a door, father cannot be seen any more when he is driving away, a coin is hidden in the sand, one cannot see what is in the back) general rules are inductively learned that explain why something cannot be seen any more. These general rules partially apply to the observations of day and night by simply instantiating a rule with the observer, the earth, and the sun. However, the rules cannot be completely instantiated because some features of earth, sun, and the universe cannot be observed but are preconditions for the application of a rule. The remaining instantiations must be filled by assumptions. For instance, one explanation for disappearance is that an object covers another object like the door covers the sister. The object that covers the other object must be larger and not transparent. Now, if this general rule is to be applied to the observations of day and night, the sun is instantiated as the covered object, but what is large and not transparent so that it can cover the sun for the observer? As the covering object must be between the observer and the covered object, it must be in the sky. As clouds are in the sky, the child may instantiate the covering object by clouds. This is an assumption. The general rule is instantiated by observations and assumptions. Together with meaning postulates, predictions can be deductively made. Hence, questions can be answered, such as, e.g., „Where are the clouds at day time?" or „Where is the sun at night?" or „Is the sun still shining at night?" The conceptual change concerning earth and sun in this model takes place at the assumed knowledge. It is triggered by a contradiction (e.g., clouds are transparent). Figure 2 gives an overview of the overall structure of the model.

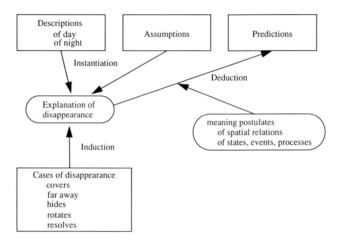

Figure 2: Structure of the knowledge types and their inferential relations

The operational model (i.e., the model implemented by the system) is then to be used for experiments. The questions to be tested are:

- Is there an optimal order of input statements to teach the scientific explanation for the day/night cycle?

- Is there a crucial concept to be acquired in order to learn the scientific explanation?

- Is there a natural order in which different explanations are tried?

- Can the order of different explanations for the day/night cycle be explained in computational terms?

The important question at the meta-level is:

- Do computational terms correspond to entities that are part of the psychological theory?

If, for instance, we find a measure for the distance of one explanation to the scientific target explanation in computational terms, does it make sense to psychologists? Can it be transferred to other domains?

The layout for modeling conceptual change computationally as presented here touches upon an open research question in Artificial Intelligence. Note that the explanations for the day/night cycle are proof trees for a prediction. Without given assumptions, these proofs do not succeed and deliver partial proofs. There are many possible assumptions for completing the proof, exponential in the number of known objects with the properties that are demanded by a rule. In ILP, the completion of a partial proof has been modeled by inverse resolution (Wirth, 1988). User interaction is needed in order to control the complexity of this inductive inference. Can we interpret this user interaction in educational terms as necessary teacher input? Another way to deal with the creation of assumptions is to view it as an abductive inference step. However, it is not yet known how to control abductive reasoning. The field of analogical reasoning is of importance here (e.g., Bell and Tausend, 1992; Wirth and O'Rorke, 1992).

A First Approach to Representing Different Explanations

In a first approach we have put apart the problem of having the system create the appropriate assumptions. We have prepared sets of assumptions beforehand, each corresponding to one of the explanation types found in children: Initial, Synthetic, and Scientific model. Setting the abduction problem aside, enough problems remain to be solved. First, the day/night cycle is intertwined with every-day experience. Hence, the domain to be modeled cannot easily be separated from events that need not be modelled. We have made some pragmatic decisions that were not psychologically verified. Hence, it could have happened that some background knowledge that is used by children is not present in the computational model. Second - and related - , the children use spatial reasoning in their explanations. The formal representation of spatial relations is a demanding area of Artificial Intelligence. As the case study should not become a research project on spatial reasoning, some appropriate „short-cuts" had to be found. Third, observations and theoretic statements could well have a different influence on handling contradictions. Possibly, what can be directly perceived is more reluctant to changes than what is being told. This difference could be modeled using MOBAL's inference engine (Emde, 1991). However, the complexity of the model would be drastically increased. Even without modeling this distinction, the model exploits all computational resources. Fourth, the natural language description of the children's explanations can be represented in infinitely many ways. Each representation makes explicit an interpretation of what the children meant and how the learning process works. These interpretations ask for empirical verification. As a first step, we used our own intuition.

Based on these simplifications, Mühlenbrock (1994) has designed and implemented a computational model of nine explanations of the day/night cycle. We summarize this model and experiments with it on the following pages.

Let us begin by explaining some important representational decisions. MOBAL's representation formalism is a restricted predicate logic with higher concepts (meta-level facts and rules)[1]. A concept can be represented by a predicate. A rule with this predicate in the conclusion then describes a necessary condition for the concept. Alternatively, a concept can be represented as a constant term which is an argument of a predicate. The concept is then described by the predicates that are true for the corresponding term. For instance, we might represent the concept *earth* in two ways:

earth(object1) or stationary (earth).

The impact of the decision becomes clear if we take into account that the learning tool of MOBAL learns about predicates and the instantiation refers to constant terms. We decided that

---

1. The MOBAL system consists of several modules, among them an inference engine, a learning component, a revision component, and structuring tools for terms and predicates. Since it would exceed this chapter, we rely on the reader's intuitive understanding of logical expressions. To those that are interested in the formal basis and technical details of MOBAL, the book is recommended (Morik et al., 1993).

with respect to the earth notion the instantiation is more important for the case study. Predicates are used to formalize spatial relations, processes, and properties. These are also concepts. As was mentioned above, in a complex concept structure, terms together with their descriptors are concepts, but predicates (relations) are also concepts. These relational concepts form a concept structure because of the inference rules linking them. For instance, the predicate

    covers (<object>, <object>, <object>, <event>)

models that something of the sort *object* covers something, again of the sort *object*, for something of the sort *object* in a particular event[1]. An instantiation is

    covers (cloud, sun, me, event0)

describing that the cloud covers the sun for the observer in the *event0*, which corresponds to sunset. The *covers* concept has sufficient and necessary conditions which determine its meaning:

- Sufficient condition:

    not(between (O1, O2, O3, S1)) & invisible (O2, O1, O3, S2) & state_seq (S1, E, S2) & not(stationary (O1, E)) --> covers (o1, o2, o3, e).

- Necessary condition:

    covers (o1, o2, o3, e) --> disappears (o2, o3, e).

The concept *disappears* is linked with the concept *covers* by the inference rule shown. The necessary condition for *covers* is a sufficient condition for *disappears*. These rules can be inductively learned from cases such as as[2]:

    not(between (door, sister, me, before)),
    invisible (sister, door, me, after),
    state_seq (before, close_door, after),
    not(stationary (door, close_door)),
    covers (door, sister, me, close_door),
    disappears (sister, me, close_door).

If the system is asked whether the sun disappears at sunset by the query

    :- disappears (sun, me, event0)

it can prove this proposition by proving

    covers (O1, sun, me, event0)

using the sufficient conditions for *covers*. In order for the proof to succeed, it has to be proven that all premises are true for the instantiation of *O2* by *sun*, *O3* by *me*, and *E* by *event0*. Note, that the instantiation of *o1*, *s1*, and *S2* need not be determined by the instantiation of *o2*, *o3*, and *E*. In all models, there are just two states, day and night, and two events, sunrise and sunset, but

---

1. Constant terms are sorted into a hierarchy of equivalence classes, the sort taxonomy. In the day-night cycle domain, the sorts *object, event,* area, and *state* are the basic ones. Other classes comprise subsets.

2. As usual, we use capital letters for variables.

O1 could be instantiated by several objects. Each instantiation leads to a different proof. In this case, *O1* can only be bound to *cloud*, as no other non-stationary objects that are big and opaque are known to the system[1].

The proofs use the definitions of the concepts *between, invisible, state_seq*, and *stationary*.

in (O1, A1, O2, S) & in (O3, A2, O2, S) & complementary(A1, A2) &
ne(O1, O2) & ne(O3, O2) --> between (O2, O1, O3, S).

between(O1, O2, O3, S) & opaque(O1) & bigger(O1, O3) --> invisible(O2, O1, O3, S).

next_event (S1, E) & next_state (E, S2) --> state_seq (S1, S2).

Facts about *in, complementary,* and *opaque* are given for each model of a particular type of explanations of the day/night cycle. Facts about *bigger, next_event,* and *next_state* are the same for all models of explanation. Also the definition of areas is defined once for all. Each object has areas in three dimensions around it. The neighborhood of areas is described by the *next_area* predicate. The proof terminates when it finds a true fact for a premise. Given the facts

opaque (cloud), not(stationary(cloud)), in (me, up, earth, S), in (earth, down, me, S), in (earth, left, earth, S), in (earth, right, earth, S), in (earth, down, earth, S)

and the corresponding *in* facts for the events E, *covers (cloud, sun, me, event0)* can be proven. The latter three facts express that everything below the observer is earth. The earth is infinite, has no back side. Hence, these facts express a particular notion of the earth and only this notion allows to use the *covers* rule for explaining that the sun disappears.

There are other ways to explain disappearance

hides (O1, O2, O3, E) --> disappears (O1, O3, E).

rotates (O1, O2, E) --> disappears (O1, O2, E).

revolves (O1, O2, E) --> disappears (O1, O2, E).

The predicates *hides, rotates,* and *revolves* again have their sufficient conditions that explicate their meaning. The revolving model states that the sun moves around the earth. The rotation model states that the sun is stationary and the earth is rotating below the sun.

in (sun, up, earth, state0), in (sun, right, earth, event0),

in (sun, down, earth, state1), in (sun, left, earth, event1).

This model is closest to the scientific one. It only disregards the annual cycle.

In addition to the disappearance rules, there are appearance rules that correspond to them. There are rules for hiding, rotating and revolving around to become perceivable again. Similar to the examples above, one can prove or predict the sun to become visible and shining down on the observer after sunrise.

In summary, Mühlenbrock (1994) has represented:

---

1. This illustrates what was said about the self-containedness of a computational model. Where a child knows many objects from many domains of knowledge, the system is restricted to one domain.

- a set of rules defining various ways of appearance, disappearance, and cyclic dis/reappearance,

- a set of basic rules describing spatial relations, events, states, and their sequencing,

- sets of facts, each describing a particular understanding of the main objects of the day-night cycle, namely, the earth, the sun, and objects in the earth - these correspond to the   assumptions in our overall structure,

- a set of basic facts defining relations between areas and the like - these are common to all explanation types,

- a set of integrity constraints that make explicit contradictions, e.g., two different objects cannot be at the same place.

The computational model is partly validated in that questions that children were asked in the empirical study were also used as queries to the computational model:

Where is the sun at night? :- in (sun, X, Y, state1).

Does the earth move? :- stationary (earth).

Does the sun move? :- stationary (sun).

The finding in the empirical study, that 23 of 60 children answered „up" to the question: „Which way do you look to see the earth?" (Vosniadou and Brewer, 1992) is in conflict with our computational model of spatial relations.

Experiments With the First Modeling Approach

MOBAL detects contradictions in a knowledge base. The basic facts, integrity constraints[1], rules, and one of the fact sets describing assumptions constitute a consistent model of the day/night cycle. When adding to this model the correct assumptions of the scientific model, contradictions occur. They show the difference between the particular naive explanation of the day/night cycle and the explanation to be learned. In teaching, the correct assumptions are not offered at once. At each state of the teaching process, the adequate information has to be selected.

One way of teaching is to present one true statement that contradicts an assumptions and thus lets the proof in the computational model fail. In the example above, stating that clouds are not opaque lets the *covers* rule fail. The modified set of assumptions lets the *hides* rule succeed: hills are opaque and the sun now moves behind the hills at sunset. A teacher could now either state that the sun is stationary or that the sun is on the other side of the earth at night. The first option does not allow any rule to apply. The *revolves* as well as the *rotates* rule both presuppose that the earth is round. The change from the *covers* explanation to that of hiding keeps the assumption that the earth is filling all areas except the one above the earth. Therefore, the teacher should state that the sun is on the other side of the earth at night. The naive statements about the earth are then withdrawn and the *revolves* rule becomes successful which states that the sun is moving up and down. Now, the teacher can contradict the assumption that the sun is

---

1. Integrity constraints explicitly represent what counts as a contradiction. Instead of writing
in(O1, A1, O2, T) & ne(O1, O2) & ne(A1, A2) --> not(in(O1, A2, O2, T)) which derives negated facts so that their corresponding positive ones lead to a contradiction, one can express that the same object cannot be at different places at the same time using an integrity constraint:
in(O1, A1, O2, T) & in(O1, A2, O2, T) & ne(O1, O2) & ne (A1, A2) -->.

stationary. As the earth is already viewed as being entirely surrounded by space, the *rotates* rule, i.e. the almost scientific explanation, succeeds. This sequence of information leads to the development of explanations as they are observed in children. It is a computational simulation of the developmental order of different conceptualizations of the day/night cycle. The computational model shows that stating too early that the sun is stationary blocks all rules to be applied. It makes explicit the following guideline for teaching:

> Present the smallest set of statements that contradict necessary assumptions of the current wrong conceptualization and make other explanations possible!

The first approach to modeling the empirical findings of the day/night cycle study offers a test-bed for hypotheses about appropriate sequences of input. Further experiments with the computational model are needed to find information sequences that lead to the target explanations and those that lead to a dead end where no rule is applicable. These sequences are then examples for good and wrong teaching from which characterizations of good sequences could be learned. The exploration is needed in order to show whether the sequence described above is the optimal one or whether there exists a better one. It is also needed in order to verify whether the earth being surrounded by space or the sun being stationary are crucial concepts.

Why an Interdisciplinary Approach?

Interdisciplinary research is of particular interest for the investigation of sequencing effects. Trying to computationally model some of the aspects psychologists have formulated about human learning of common-sense knowledge is a challenging goal for computer scientists. Even if the goal is never met, the efforts to approximate it result in more sophisticated algorithms and computer systems. A computational model offers to psychologists a tool for making experiments where the „subject" of learning can be directly inspected and the impact of a change in the model can be observed in the system's behavior.[1] In the course of building up a computational model, statements that seemed to be self-understood need to be made explicit and questions arise as to whether a factor that influences the system behavior has a corresponding factor in the psychologists's model of human behavior. These questions can lead to further psychological research (Strube et al., 1993).

Formalizing everyday knowledge has fascinated artificial intelligence from its very beginning on. Of course, one has to separate a relatively small and self-containing theory within everyday knowledge in order to be capable of representing the knowledge and running experiments. The explanation for the day/night cycle is such a theory. It fits most of our requirements for the investigation of sequencing effects: The scientific explanation is taught at school and has to be integrated into explanations that were created in response to the observations that the sun goes up in the morning, gives us light during daytime, and sets down in the evening, so that during night-time it is almost dark. The scientific explanation uses concepts that are different from what can be individually perceived: the earth is round and rotating around the sun. The history of science shows the states of the process that led to today's scientific explanation. One way to model the acquisition of the scientific theory would be to have a learning system go through these known states. This is the approach pursued in the machine learning subfield *scientific discovery*. Another approach is to model the steps that children take in their learning of the culturally accepted theory. This *developmental approach* has the advantage that experiments can be

---

1. As computer models are very complex, it would be naive to consider their inspection a straightforward task. Moreover, one has to distinguish between those features of the system that are relevant for the simulation from those that are artifacts of the machine.

made with children in order to find answers to questions that come up when computationally modeling the learning process. The historical process cannot be run again in a modified way. Moreover, the input to this process is only partially known.

References

Asch, S.E. (1946). Forming Impressions of Personality. *Journal of Abnormal and Social Psychology, 41*, 258-290.

Bell, S., & Tausend, B. (1992). Analogical Reasoning for Logic Programming. In Muggleton (ed.), *Inductive Logic Programming*. London: Academic Press.

Elio, R., &Anderson, J.R. (1984). The Effects of Information order and Learning Mode on Schema Abstraction. *Memory and Cognition, 12*, 20-30.

Emde, W. (1987). Non-Cumulative Learning in METAXA.3. In Proceedings *IJCAI-87*. Los Altos: Morgan Kaufmann.

Emde, W. (1991). *Modellbildung, Wissensrevision und Wissensrepräsentation im Maschinellen Lernen*. Berlin, Heidelberg, New York: Springer.

Fisher, D. (1987). Knowledge Acquisition Via Incremental Conceptual Clustering. *Machine Learning Journal, 2*, 130-172.

Hovland, C.L., & Weiss, W. (1953). Transmission of Information Concerning Concepts Through Positive and Negative Information. *Journal of Experimental Psychology, 45*, 175-182.

Jackson, J., & Tomkins, A. (1992). A Computational Model of Teaching. In Proceedings *Computational Learning Theory*. ACM Press.

Kietz, J.-U., & Morik, K.J. (1994). A Polynomial Approach to the Constructive Induction of Structural Knowledge, *Machine Learning Journal, 14*, 193-217.

Langley, P., Simon, H.A., Bradshaw, G.L., & Zytkow, J.M. (1987). *Scientific Discovery - Computational Explorations of the Creative Processes*. Cambridge, MA: MIT Press.

Lee, E.S., Mac Gregor, J.N., Bavelas, A., Lam, N., Mirlin, L., & Morrison, I. (1988). The Effects of Error Transformations on Classification Performance. *Journal of Experimental Psychological Learning*.

Michalski, R.S., & Stepp, R.E. (1983). Learning From Observation - Conceptual Clustering. In Michalski, Carbonell, Mitchell (eds), *Machine Learning - An Artificial Intelligence Approach*. San Mateo: Morgan Kaufmann.

Mitchell, T. M., Keller, R.M., & Kedar-Cabelli, S.T. (1986). Explanation-Based Generalization - A Unifying View. *Machine Learning Journal, 1*, 47-80.

Morik, K., Wrobel, S., Kietz, J.-U., & Emde, W. (1993). *Knowledge acquisition and machine learning*. London: Academic Press.

Mühlenbrock, M. (1994). *Computational Models of Learning in Astronomy*, Research Report of the unit VIII of the Computer Science Dept. of the Univ. Dortmund No. 11.

Muggleton, S. (ed.) (1991). *Inductive Logic Programming*. London: Academic Press.

Nordhausen, B., & Langley, P. (1990). An Integrated Approach to Empirical Discovery. In Shrager, Langley (eds.), *Computational Models of Scientific Discovery and Theory Formation*. San Mateo: Morgan Kaufmann.

Nussbaum, J. (1985). The Earth as a Cosmic Body. In Driver, Guesne, Tiberghien (eds.), *Children's Ideas in Science*. Milton Keynes: Open University Press.

Rajamoney, S. (1990). A Computational Approach to Theory Revision. In Shrager, Langley (eds.), *Computational Models of Scientific Discovery and Theory Formation.* San Mateo: Morgan Kaufmann.

Shapiro, E.Y. (1983). *Algorithmic Program Debugging.* Cambridge, MA: MIT Press.

Sneider, C., & Pulos, S. (1983). Children's Cosmographies - Understanding the Earth's Shape and Gravity. *Science Education, 66,* 211-227.

Strube, G., Habel, C., Hemforth, B., Konieczny, L., & Becker, B. (1993). Kognition. In Görz (ed), *Künstliche Intelligenz.* Bonn: Addison Wesley.

Vosniadou, S., & Brewer, W.F. (1992). Mental Models of the Earth - A Study of Conceptual Change in Childhood. *Cognitive Psychology, 24,* 535-585.

Vosniadou, S., & Brewer, W.F. (1994). Mental Models of the Day/Night Cycle. *Cognitive Science, 18,* 123-183.

Winston, P.H. (1975). Learning Structural Descriptions from Examples. In Winston (Ed.), *The Psychology of Computer Vision.* New York: McGraw-Hill.

Wirth, R. (1988). Learning By Failure to Prove. In Sleeman (ed.), Proceedings of the third European Working Session on Learning. London: Pitman.

Wirth, R., & O'Rorke, P. (1992). Constraints for Predicate Invention. In Muggleton (ed.), *Inductive Logic Programming.* London: Academic Press.

Wrobel, S. (1994). *Concept Formation and Knowledge Revision - A Demand-Driven Approach to Representation-Change,* Ph. D. Thesis Univ. Dortmund, to appear at Kluwer, Dordrecht.

Subject Index

A

abductive reasoning 144
abstract data types 119
abstract knowledge 38, 48, 50, 51, 55
abstraction 110, 116, 118, 133, 139
accretion 27, 161
accuracy increase 26
acquisition of mental models 29
acquisition of search-control knowledge 163
acquisition of symbol systems 33
ACT 2
action control 142
action replacement 46
action schemas 173
ACT-R 130
adaptation of learning behavior 139
adaptive agents 43
adaptive systems 146
adult-child interactions 172
affective components of learning 98
affordance 102, 173, 174
affordance-activity coupling 173
alternation method 162
analogical reasoning 25, 45, 168
anchored instruction 179
apprenticeship learning 171, 175
appropriation 192
APT 117
aptitudes 97
AQ17.HCI 117
argumentation 51, 203, 205
articulation 178
artifacts 88, 91
assimilation 192
attribute order 157
attribute-value representation 66
authenticity 181
autodidactic learning 141

B

backpropagation 160, 161
backward reasoning 113
BACON 3, 117
Bayesian classifier 158
behaviorism 23, 30, 40, 97
belief revision 53
bias. See language bias

bidirectional learning operators 159
blame assignment 43, 140

C

candidate elimination algorithm 155
CARAMEL 117
case-based reasoning 75
case-based representation 133, 136, 138
categorization 111
CIGOL 117
CITRE 117
CLINT 117
close-call heuristic 213
clustering systems 159
coaching 178
COBWEB 75, 78, 159
cognitive anthropology 170
cognitive apprenticeship 177, 178
cognitive conflict 202
cognitive consistency 53
cognitive flexibility 180
cognitive restructuring 196
cognitive science 4
cognitive socialization 84
cognitivist perspective 83
collaboration 189, 193, 202
collaboration and computers 199
collaborative learning 15, 100, 189
collaborative learning algorithms 66
COLT 110
commonsense knowledge 225
commonsense theories 215
communities of practice 171, 178
competence 39
comprehensibility 63, 65, 110
comprehension monitoring 145
computational complexity 79
computational learning theory 76
computational models 63, 77, 113, 120, 169, 205, 219, 225
computational models of commonsense knowledge 225
computer metaphor 30
computer technology 89
computer-based apprenticeship systems 178
computer-based learning 104
computer-mediated collaboration 200

Author Index